The Hands' Measure

Published by Nunavut Arctic College Media
www.nacmedia.ca
Box 600, Iqaluit, NU, X0A 0H0

Publishing services provided by Inhabit Education

ISBN: 978-1-897568-41-5

Printed in Canada.

Library and Archives Canada Cataloguing in Publication

The hands' measure: essays honouring Leah Aksaajuq Otak's contribution to Arctic science / edited by John MacDonald and Nancy Wachowich.

Includes bibliographical references and index.
ISBN 9781897568415 (softcover)

1. Otak, Leah. 2. Oral history—Nunavut—Igloolik. 3. Inuit—Nunavut—Igloolik—Social life and customs. 4. Social sciences—Research—Nunavut—Igloolik. 5. Igloolik (Nunavut)—History. 6. Igloolik (Nunavut)—Biography. 7. Festschriften. I. Otak, Leah, honouree II. MacDonald, John, 1940–, editor III. Wachowich, Nancy, 1966–, editor

E99.E7H36 2018   971.9004'9712   C20189038810

The Hands' Measure

Essays Honouring Leah Aksaajuq Otak's
Contribution to Arctic Science

EDITED BY
John MacDonald and
Nancy Wachowich

For Makpa and Inuralaaq
And in memory of Qajaaq

CONTENTS

A Stitch in Time

Inuktut, Sewing, and Self-Discovery

Eva Aariak

W HEN I WAS INVITED TO CONTRIBUTE to this volume honouring Leah Otak, it immediately occurred to me how similar our
life experiences had been. Although Leah was a few years older than
I, the parallels in our lives were many. We had both been born "on
the land," as they say—Leah in Iglurjuat, north of Igloolik, and I in
Qikiqtaukat, across Adams Sound, southeast from Arctic Bay. Our
early years were spent living on the land with our families, leading
what we now nostalgically look back on as the traditional Inuit way of
life, by today's standards incredibly uncomplicated and independent.
It was during this period that our very earliest memories and attachments were formed. This way of life, which we now think of as idyllic,
ended suddenly in the early 1960s, with the Canadian government's
decision to establish settlements across the Arctic, eventually drawing us all from the spacious lands of our childhoods into crowded,
government-administered settlements.

A pattern familiar to many of our generation quickly took shape. We were enrolled in our respective federal day schools in Arctic Bay and Igloolik, and a few years later we were sent away for further education. Leah was sent first to Inuvik and then to Fort Smith, while I was sent to the Churchill Vocational Centre in Churchill, Manitoba, followed by high school in Ottawa.

Looking back, our formal schooling away from home was to have profound consequences for the ways in which our lives unfolded, in what we gained, lost, and eventually recovered. Learning English and becoming immersed in southern culture certainly equipped us to understand, negotiate, and even confront the rapid changes taking place in our homeland. But being away at school also deprived us of the kinds of traditional teachings our mothers and aunts would have received when they were our age, and which they would have given us in turn had we been home with them during those years.

After school, when I was back in Arctic Bay, I soon realized that my command of Inuktut had suffered. I was no longer using words that I had learned as a child from my grandfather, Amarualik. As well, I felt strongly that something was missing in my life. Later, I sensed this was a desire to have the knowledge and skills my mother possessed and practised, the ones to do with being a real Inuk. Achieving this desire came to me quite easily through my natural inclination to be with elders, to talk with them, and to hear their stories. The quality of their language humbled and absorbed me—they spoke the Inuktut equivalent of the "Queen's English"! My aunt, Arnakallak, had an endless supply of wonderful stories and information about the old days. It was through my conversations with elders that I began to develop a deep appreciation of the richness of my language and how traditional Inuktut words are so succinct in their meaning. This realization inspired me to learn more, and so began my lifelong habit of noting down Inuktut terms and expressions little used nowadays but nevertheless essential for preserving the richness of Inuktut. Even now, rarely do I have a conversation with an elder without collecting an additional two or three words. I was not at all surprised to discover that Leah, out of the same motivations, had developed a similar obsession for collecting Inuktut vocabularies. She jotted down words whenever and wherever she heard them, which were later added to the archives of the Igloolik Oral History Project.

Being away from our culture, in a sense, forced us to fully appreciate its significance in our lives—and so, in addition to language, we also shared a deep commitment to mastering the traditional skin-sewing practices of our ancestors. We learned these skills primarily from our mothers, aunts, and mothers-in-law—of course, at a much later age than normal, trying to make up for lost time. Our teachers were patient and thorough, and it was through them that we came to fully appreciate the inseparable links between language and cultural activities. Acquiring traditional sewing skills goes far beyond learning to be a competent seamstress. Taught in its proper way, the wide range of Inuit sewing practices incorporates trusted, age-old knowledge of the environment, of the seasons, and of the life cycles and anatomy of the animals on which we depend. Beyond this, the whole idea of traditional sewing also gives us an understanding of Inuit regional and individual identity, of cultural symbolism, and even of the role of certain taboos connected with sewing in the old days. The complexities of sewing, skin preparation, and pattern-making can be fully understood only through the unique words describing the various techniques and processes used. Leah makes this point strongly in her 2005 paper, "Iniqsimajuq," which lists and describes the many complex stages of preparing caribou skin for sewing.

More than anything else, the connections we made to our heritage through our efforts to become proficient in skin sewing, while striving to learn, or relearn, the intricacies of our first language, made us feel centred and more grounded as Inuit. Our deliberate reclaiming and use of these essential parts of our traditions amazingly gave us the confidence to bridge the cultural gap between the two worlds in which we lived. It was through this empowerment we were able to make the best of both worlds without feeling at all threatened or intimidated in either one.

My fondest memory of Leah is from my visit with her at the Igloolik Research Centre in 1999, shortly after my appointment as the Languages Commissioner of Nunavut. Here, she was obviously very much in her element and happy with her work. Despite her usual calm demeanour, Leah couldn't hold back her excitement as she took me on a tour of her offices, showing me how she managed the Igloolik Oral History Project, which by this time was well known throughout Nunavut and beyond. She explained how the project was started as a method of preserving the expressive richness and depth of Inuktut by Igloolik elders who were concerned about the changes in culture and weakening of the language as a result of settlement life. The way Leah and her colleagues at the Research Centre went about this work was fascinating, the aim being to interview and record as many elders as possible on as many topics as possible. In this way, unique words and expressions were gathered not as isolated terms, but always as part of a unique story which could only be told properly in Inuktut.

In conversations with Leah, I learned how deeply inspired she was by her involvement with the Oral History Project. She emphasized how her work had helped her to build on the cultural traditions she had learned as a child, as well as to recover some of what she had lost while away at school. She played a major part in shaping the project's development and emphasis during her long association with its work over the last twenty years of her life. Leah's intense interest in the role of women in traditional culture was reflected in many of the project's interviews about traditional medicine, childbirth, and child raising—and, of course, about sewing, skin preparation, and clothing, which she was particularly passionate about. Her wide understanding of these subjects meant that during the interviews with elders, she could ask knowledgeable questions and, just as importantly, understand their complex answers.

Leah's work in oral history and language is a remarkable achievement based on her early recognition of the essential place of Inuit values, traditional skills, and, above all, Inuktut in today's Nunavut. For her, these things were of primary concern. Of course, talking about the importance of Inuit culture is easy; doing something positive about it, especially over the long term, takes a huge amount of determination and commitment. In this, Leah was her own best example. Year after year, through her family life, her community involvement, and her professional work, she strived hard to put her beliefs into practice. She was convinced that Inuit youth, struggling with the confusions of the modern world, would benefit enormously—as she herself had (and, indeed, as I have, too)—from a conscious reclaiming of our culture, language, and history. Without being sentimental or boastful, she understood better than most the feeling of confidence, balance, and genuine identity we get from an active, ongoing engagement with the culture and language of our grandparents. Leah's lifelong example of this engagement is her enduring legacy.

INTRODUCTION

Leah Aksaajuq Otak

The Measure of a Stitch and the Art of Translation

Nancy Wachowich

You can get the measure of a woman by the neatness of her stitches. It was Leah Aksaajuq Otak who first dictated and explained the old adage to me. That was back in February 1997, in the midst of Igloolik's "Language Week," an event she was organizing. In the months and years that followed, a deeper meaning in this statement was made clear in my conversations with Leah and the research questions that she inspired. Leah was an Inuk educator, cultural activist, and community leader. When she took an interest in a visiting scholar's work, she quite literally opened a world to them: a world in which human insight was generated through the friction and synergies existing between cultures, and where the scholarly provinces of the arts, humanities, social sciences, and natural sciences could be enriched by cross-cultural exchanges of knowledge, on equal grounds. In the honing of perceptiveness, in the attention she offered, and in the trust she awarded, Leah gifted the many contributors to this collection a valued sense of what it is to be an Arctic specialist and scholar. Since that first meeting, now more than twenty years distant, for me the exercise of writing has always, in some measure, been about writing for, and being accountable to, Leah and her community of Inuit intellectuals. Leah was the figure looking over my shoulder as I wrote. My scholarly, literary, and moral conscience. And, in spite of her death in March 2014, aged sixty-four, so she remains today.

There is little mystery as to why Leah Aksaajuq Otak was so acclaimed and respected in her community of Igloolik, in Nunavut, and among Arctic scholars internationally. She cared deeply about how her people were represented by academic researchers, curators, journalists, educators, and artists, and she showed this concern by being intellectually engaged and painstakingly exacting, and also by carefully fostering and holding a careful middle ground. As a woman raised in one cultural setting—on the land in camps around Igloolik—and then compelled to be trained in another, Leah well understood that Inuit must struggle for their place in contemporary society against two equally great dangers. The first is the derogatory Western view of Indigenous hunting cultures that disparaged its practitioners as less evolved, or not quite wholly modern. The second is the contention, equally pervasive and destructive, that Inuit culture is in its death throes. Leah was ever ready to insist on the sophistication of Inuit culture, its vibrancy and adaptiveness, and the insights gained from bringing Inuit epistemologies and wisdom to bear on contemporary political issues and social problems, both in her home settlement and further afield. The need she recognized was one of establishing even ground. She also recognized the value of academic research to Inuit communities, but only *if* collaborations were on equal footing. She showed how courtesy and care are crucial to a shared enterprise, and when it was not evident, Leah was the figure slipping away quietly, surreptitiously, so as not to cause direct offence, but making feelings plain nonetheless.

OF TALES TOLD

This book is a collection of research stories inspired by Leah Aksaajuq Otak, told by eighteen scholars who hold her in the highest regard. Narratives and tales such as these—of journeys taken, of people encountered, of observations made—were, as Leah often explained, used by her forebears to share knowledge and information about their worlds of experience. Stories were integral to everyday life. Inuit hunters from her childhood, and for centuries before that, returned home to tell of routes travelled, landscapes observed, weather experienced, and animals and other beings encountered. Wives and families recounted their own stories in kind. In Chapter 8 of this volume, Claudio Aporta reflects upon the interconnections between storytelling and wayfinding, drawing on the teachings of Inuit travelling companions and elders' testimonies from the Igloolik Oral History Project archives as sources to transmit environmental, ancestral, and spiritual knowledge.[1]

The confidence and mastery with which Inuit elders stitch a tale can be a source of inspiration and wonder to visitors raised in a writing tradition where orality is a less valued, practised, and nuanced art form. This awe is reflected in many contributions to this volume, and perhaps expressed most intensely in Hugh Brody's meditation on the resourceful commandeering by Mittimatalingmiut (Pond Inlet) elders of a 1974 documentary film project (Chapter 6). These were individuals, he recalls, "for whom oral culture was their culture, for whom to be able to set out thoughts and tell stories was central to being an effective adult" (161). Storytelling can be a well-practised performative event that brings speakers and listeners together, merging subjective experiences and communal interpretations. Leah Otak would often describe how as children she and her siblings fell asleep listening to elders' tales and then, upon waking, would join other family members in recounting the vivid detail of dreamworlds visited during the night's passing. Noah Richler's and Sylvie LeBlanc's stories in this collection (Afterword and Chapter 16) convey, respectively, Leah's efforts to keep this tradition alive with younger generations and the warmth and intimacy such narrative routines inspired. Storytelling brought families together to share ancestral memories, contemporary experiences, and future visions. Likewise, it integrated the lives of animals and humans, aligned past and present, and fused dreamscapes with waking worlds, providing new forms of consciousness and insight. Jack Hicks (Chapter 9) describes how elders like Noah Piugaattuk made strategic use of oral histories to directly counteract cultural misunderstandings and redress contemporary social problems associated with suicide. Stories can be told with tactical intent, sometimes pointedly so. Kenn Harper (Chapter 5) throws into question the reliability of court testimony by engaging in a close reading of the archival oral histories relating to an infamous 1922 murder investigation in Mittimatalik. Oral history does more than just relay information about the past. Testimonies, the likes of those told by historic witnesses and court translators, and which Harper scrutinizes, are interpretive. They are tools to bring the past into correspondence with the present, providing scope for imagining new futures.[2] This edited collection takes stock of how Arctic research can contribute to this narrative synergy. Among its contributors—each a storyteller in his or her own right —narrative is a means to establish grounds for a new research terrain, and a principled and sustained engagement inspired by Leah Aksaajuq Otak's storied lifeworld.

OF LIVES LIVED

Among the celebrations of Leah Aksaajuq Otak in the pages that follow, several show her as an extraordinary individual. This is wholly true, but she was also representative of a generation. In many ways, Leah was a woman of her age. She was born in 1950, at the start of a period that would be marked by extreme social change in the Arctic. A childhood spent travelling between ancestral hunting and fishing camps around Igloolik (a time remembered as tranquil) was altered immeasurably by enrolment in federal day school in Igloolik. Excelling in studies, she was identified for a select group judged especially receptive to assimilation through intensive education programs. She boarded at residential schools in Ottawa, Fort Smith, and later Inuvik, thousands of miles distant from family. Leah's reflections on this early phase in life often pointed to feelings of loss and separation, experiences that find their echo in Eva Aariak's and George Qulaut's contributions to this volume (Foreword and Chapter 1). For Leah's mid-20th century generation of Inuit, the impacts of assimilation and schooling policies in Arctic Canada were profound. While some of their parents spoke of the imposition of mandatory school laws as a necessary, if still unpalatable, means of adaptation to modernity, far more expressed feelings of powerlessness and anguish when surrendering children to the school officials who arrived by airplane or boat at family camps each autumn.

Inuit testimonials, commissioned reports, and scholarship appearing subsequently have tracked, in various ways, the often devastating effects that residential and federal day school programs had on individuals and families.[3] Sheena Kennedy Dalseg (Chapter 11) describes inquiries into the history and consequences of southern-derived education policies on schooling in Igloolik from the perspective of public policy research. By the late 1950s and early 1960s, increased pressure on Inuit to move in from their camps, and an anxious need to be located closer to their school-age children and to nursing stations, drew in most families across the Canadian Arctic to live year-round in newly established settlements. Stories of small resistances to more dominant policies of assimilation endure, such as that of Leah's maternal grandfather, Qulittalik, and his stubborn refusal to settle in town, or those of Inuit families who quickly returned to outpost camps just a few years after moving into settlements.[4] For the most part, the difficulties experienced during this transition were deeply etched into individual lives. Hugh Brody's ethnography *The People's Land*, produced from fieldwork undertaken in early 1970s Mittimatalik, documents these struggles and the authoritative, sometimes overbearing, relationships he witnessed, pitching federal government, church, and school officials up against Inuit. Settlements were designed to operate, he observed, very much like microcosms of southern Canadian society, and were administered according to Western notions of time, space, and etiquette. Many Inuit adults were left feeling hemmed in and claustrophobic at the new strictures and controls. As time passed, efforts by Inuit and incomer-residents originating from the south helped bridge the cultural divide, and new cultural practices began appearing that syncretized Inuit and Western traditions. Louis-Jacques Dorais (Chapter 10) documents one such cultural incorporation, recalling his own experience attending a Quaqtamiut wedding in 2015, where established elements of Christian wedding rituals were adapted to fit with Inuit social conventions. While examples of cultural pastiche might be more and more common in churches, offices, medical clinics, and schools in the North, in other settings Brody's early characterization of boundaries formed by colonial practices of admittance and segregation still rings true. Colonialism is imagined and reimagined in the North in a multitude of ways.

Nearly fifty years have passed between the publishing of this volume commemorating Leah Aksaajuq Otak's life and work, and that lost period of her youth, when Canadian government assimilation policies were at their height. Later in life, Leah reflected on the experience of southern schooling, and her quiet and determined efforts to push back against the excesses of such programs. These stories covered vast distances, crisscrossing sites north and south—touching on landscapes travelled, places lived, people she came to know—and yet more often than not they came to rest on an intimacy of experience, alighting on efforts to relearn Inuit land-based skills, return to a language, and reclaim an apprenticeship denied to her in adolescence.[5] A compassionate person, Leah also undoubtedly felt quite viscerally the effects of colonial policy on the autonomy and authority of her parents' generation. Scholars who worked closely with Leah could not help but be moved by the dedication shown and reverence paid to her father and mother, older relatives, and other elders of the settlement, who returned her attentions with clear adoration and an appreciation for the role she took on as valued intern. She, in turn, worked tirelessly to pass on that cultural legacy to her children.

OF CULTURES TRANSLATED

Reconciliation was most certainly a powerful driving force for Leah Aksaajuq Otak, one located across different trajectories: intellectual, political, linguistic, moral, psychological, intimately familial. To this end, she worked as a translator and research administrator, sponsoring

Leah Aksaajuq Otak and Nancy Wachowich with their babies, Makpa and Hector. Igloolik, May 2005. Photo by John MacDonald

and supporting visiting scholars with skill and poise, collaborating on, co-authoring, or authoring academic works.[6] She was a member of the Canadian Polar Commission (2002–04); she spearheaded language and cultural revitalization programs in her community. Later in her life, she fostered children born to her extended family who, having spent their early years in the south, were then in need of guidance in the Inuit way. Leah's dedicated call was in addressing the reverberating effects of Arctic colonial policies: this she undertook through alliance, by creating partnerships that bridged cultural divides and finding ways in which to use research for collaborations to the benefit of her people. Yet, despite these efforts to generate understanding, Leah was also ready to acknowledge that there will always be Inuit concepts and understandings that do not do not find kinship or harmony with western knowledge systems.

In his contribution to this volume (Chapter 13), anthropologist Willem Rasing reflects upon frictions that exist between systems of belief and knowledge making, describing research as a shared process of exploration and self-exploration mutually embarked upon by visiting researchers and Inuit interlocutors. In my conversations with Leah over the years, we often came to focus on, and delight in, such moments and occasions where our knowledge systems diverged, finding reward in teasing these moments apart to reflect upon our differing subjectivities so as to interrogate further the arrival and effects of Western knowledge traditions to the North.[7] Leah approached any apparent disjuncture between Inuit and non-Inuit frameworks not necessarily as a point of discord, but instead one of philosophical potential or creative insight.

Leah's kind of generous sensibility springing to mind is one that critical theorist Walter Benjamin considered when writing on "the task of the translator." The translator approaches a text, Benjamin observed, not to produce a literal rendering, but instead to find moments of convergence between language systems, to search out inherent meanings lending themselves to comparison ([1922] 2002). The process is not reductive, but productive and resourceful. Sometimes what is most meaningfully translatable is an intimately small point, a fractional element in a larger cultural framework of meaning. In Edith Grossman's book reflecting on her life's work, *Why Translation Matters*, the Nobel laureate Spanish-English translator of fiction and poetry describes translation as "deep reading," an exercise in which

> we endeavor to hear the first version of the work as profoundly and completely as possible, struggling to discover the linguistic charge, the structural rhythms, the subtle implications, the complexity of meaning and suggestion in vocabulary and phrasing, and the ambient cultural inferences and conclusions these tonalities allow us to extrapolate. (Grossman 2010, 8–9)

The practice of translation, Grossman suggests, is thus akin to artistic discovery: "It expands and deepens our world, our consciousness, in countless, indescribable ways" (2010, 140).

Those who undertake this exacting and creative work—translators like Leah Aksaajuq Otak—are understood to occupy in-between

spaces in society. They are often the bilingual or multilingual philos-
ophers and poets, those with an informed curiosity, an appreciation of
cultural differences and sameness, and a telling feel for the intensities,
rhythms, and complexities of meaning and the subtle shadings of language and culture. Those who knew Leah might reasonably suspect
that in her understatedness she would struggle to allow any formal
comparison with the philosopher-poet, but her work with elders
documenting Inuit Qaujimajatuqangit and working with fellow Inuit
and cultural outsiders interpreting Inuit understandings and creative practices had her operating informally in precisely these terms.
In later years, she came to further prominence as a trusted authority
on matters of Inuit cultural history, material culture, creative arts,
and Inuktitut lexicon and grammar. She found ways to translate Inuit
and Western knowledge traditions, working across both sides of the
cultural divide. And working at this cultural interface, as many will
know, is no easy task.

Working tirelessly alongside Leah and her peer group in efforts
at cultural translation and revitalization were her parents, older relatives, and elders, all eager to rebuild and document what they feared
had been lost to federal schooling. Among these activists, cultural
documentation and cultural translation mattered. George Qulaut
(Chapter 1) describes how, in 1969, his grandfather Itikuttuq gifted
him a tape recorder along with the following instruction: "I want you
to record legends and *aja-ja* songs when I have visitors" (35). This was
the initial impetus, Qulaut recalls, for his later founding of the Igloolik
Oral History Project. Itikuttuq's wishes were shared by others. Qulaut
also describes renowned oral historian Noah Piugaattuk expressing
a desire to have his own recordings translated into English "so that
researchers could better understand Inuit ways, Inuit opinions" (40).[8]
Willem Rasing also recalls Piugaattuk thanking him and his Inuit
co-investigators, whom he considered co-authors in his work, "for
the questions that made him reflect upon his own (past) life" (272).
Subsequent younger generations also now recognize themselves as
having a stake in these processes of cultural and linguistic translation.
Children and young adults are coming to appreciate how training

in Inuit land skills, epistemologies, and perceptual orientations can serve as a way to deal with the social disruption and crises in contemporary settlement life. Consequently, the translation dictated by scholarly research, though never complete or literal, can come to be understood as an act of reclamation, a highly generative process that, through analogies and comparison, holds elements of Inuit culture up as exemplary. As Walter Benjamin wrote in his 1921 essay: "A real translation is transparent; it does not cover the original, does not block its light but instead allows the source to shine all the more fully by expanding it and opening it up to artistic discovery and fruitful exchange" (Benjamin [1922] 2002, 260). Noah Piugaattuk, who was eight years Benjamin's junior, had similar insight. Translation matters because it opens texts up and inspires new connections and stories, and through this becomes integral to processes of human understanding and shared histories.

OF CROSS-CULTURAL COLLABORATIONS

Leah was not alone in making efforts to stimulate intellectual exchange and reflection. Rather, she was a participant in a well-established and longstanding historical tradition of Inuit collaboration with cultural outsiders in processes of ethnographic knowledge production. Such relationships are not unique to the Arctic. Existing commentaries focus on the enduring impacts of collaborative research undertaken side-by-side with Indigenous peoples in publicly engaged scholarship over a long history (see, for example, Lassiter 2005). Whether read with or against the grain of Arctic ethnographic, autobiographical, historical, and archival texts, one finds ample evidence of this collaborative tradition. Story upon story from the North reveals the countless ways in which Inuit cultural interlocutors have, for a century and more, been pivotal to the successes of Arctic research. Their interventions have been life-saving—for travellers vulnerable to and unfamiliar with weather extremes and environmental conditions— and also life-shaping, as judicious agents determining the kinds of knowledge that can be translated across cultural boundaries. The role of Inuit collaborators in cross-cultural knowledge production is credited to more or less a degree in the historical ethnographic texts, depending on the period and the individual author, as John MacDonald rightly points out in his chapter on Amitturmiut research relationships (Chapter 2). What was sparse mention of Inuit contributions has moved into a more open understanding of Inuit research agendas and more purposefully collaborative research.

Other contributors to this volume, Eva Aariak and George Qulaut most notably, describe lifelong efforts to capacity-build with scholars, public figures, and elders, as well as pointing to challenges faced in the search for productive common ground. Birgit Paukzsat (Chapter 7) shows how, in Greenland, shared interests in traditional marine technology, cross-cultural alliance building, and sport led to the establishment of the Kayak Club Nuuk. Rowley (Chapter 14) and LeBlanc (Chapter 16) recall a united appreciation for geomorphological features and historic landscapes, Kennedy Dalseg (Chapter 11) and Rasing (Chapter 13) a joint commitment to education and legal policy, and Engelstad (Chapter 3) an alliance in the cultural heritage of skin clothing.

J. C. H. King (Chapter 4) backdates the earliest evidence of what is now referred to as "knowledge exchange" to the 1822–23 overwintering of Parry and Lyon's icebound ships, *Fury* and *Hecla*, near Igloolik island, when Inuit and explorers exchanged goods and information. John MacDonald draws these originating relationships towards the cultural conditions and concerns of the 20th century. Such observations and analyses are themselves informed by research relationships spanning decades, informed by cross-cultural conversations, shared scholarly interests, moral commitments, and time spent travelling and living in Inuit camps and settlements. The lesson is clear: long-term engagements enable research that is respectful in purpose, leading to shared, co-produced outcomes, such as the compilation of community archives (Rasing), the co-authorship of texts (Rowley), and a better understanding of Arctic collections held in metropolitan museum collections (Engelstad and King). They also inspire efforts on the part of Inuit community members and community organizations, such as the Igloolik Hamlet Council, to harness the labour and craft of research for locally defined purpose (see Qulaut, Chapter 1; MacDonald, Chapter 2; and Kennedy Dalseg, Chapter 11).

Collaboration can easily be depicted as a relatively new phenomenon in Arctic social science, born of the convergence of Inuit sovereignty movements and growing ethical standards and policies in the academy. These contemporary procedures are not flawless, though nor were historical precedents. Evidence of fractious or subjugating research relationships surface in Inuit oral history, as well as ethnographic, historical, and scientific records across the periods. MacDonald (Chapter 2) recounts in rich detail the history of textual representation (and misrepresentation) that emerged out of encounters in the Amitturmiut region. This complex record of engagement can provide resource for contrasting arguments and caricature, characterizing the Arctic professional research community and Inuit as hostile to one another, or opposing in relation. The connections between social science research and colonial or imperial rule are fully evidenced, and this exposure has been critical to the reconceptualization of scholarship as accountable to research subjects.[9] Nonetheless, a singular or generalized reading of research relationships cannot ever do full or proper justice to the multivalent and fractured nature of colonialism, with all its subtle nuances, ambivalences, and contradictions.[10] It is important to acknowledge the careful, deliberate, and strategic Amitturmiut efforts to harness scholarly interest through collaboration (see MacDonald, Chapter 2) and other instances of parties seeking to re-centre meaning-making along equal and dialogical lines. Stories of cross-cultural misunderstanding, miscommunication, disrespectful treatment of Inuit subjects, and objectification join with those more sincere, equal, and recognized collaborative efforts at cultural translation and those moments at camps and geological sites (LeBlanc, Rowley), on the sea ice (Aporta), in kitchens (Rasing, Brody), at weddings (Dorais), while building a kayak (Paukzstat), closely examining a museum artefact (Engelstad, King), and sifting through historical and archival texts (MacDonald, King, Harper, Hicks) where likeness rather than difference, and a sense of shared enterprise, come to the fore.

OF FAMILY TRADITIONS

Operating in the role of cultural translator, Leah Aksaajuq Otak followed in a family tradition. Zipporah Piungittuq, her mother, was a gifted seamstress whose collaborations with the British Museum (1986 and 1996) and the Smithsonian Institution's National Museum of the American Indian (2004) on skin sewing exhibitions were well known (see Engelstad, Chapter 3). Leah escorted her mother to Washington in 2004 to open the Smithsonian exhibit. Together they spoke to American museum audiences on the artistry and vitality of Inuit skin garment making.

Aipilik Inuksuk, Leah's beloved father, had a deep interest in archaeology, nurtured through an enduring friendship with Arctic archaeologist/administrator Graham Rowley, and later his extended family. Graham's daughter Susan Rowley helped carry this relationship into the next generation, collaborating with Leah in an archaeological field school and documenting artefactual and geological data (Chapter 14). The alliance struck between Aipilik Inuksuk and Graham Rowley was part of the decision taken by the Canadian government to situate a new research facility in Igloolik—the Igloolik Research Centre, where Leah was professionally based for the last twenty years of her career. Aipilik was also a first-rate sculptor, well known for his miniature polar bear carvings crafted from walrus teeth, some of which are held in the Vatican Museum.

Leah's uncle, Noah Nasuk, was one of the first ordained Inuit Anglican priests. Mark Evaloarjuk, another uncle, acted as a long-time Member of the Legislative Assembly for the Northwest Territories, an advocate for the Inuit Cooperative movement in the NWT, and a board member of Canadian Arctic Producers (the Inuit art marketing organization). Caleb Apak, a third uncle, was a founder of the Baffin Regional Health Board and active in education policy development. Rhoda Akittiq Innuksuk, Leah's older sister, served as president of the national representational organization for Inuit in Canada (the Inuit Tapirisat of Canada, now Inuit Tapiriit Kanatami) and of Pauktuutit (Inuit Women's Association of Canada). Rhoda was also co-author (with Susan Cowan) of the book *We Don't Live in Snow Houses Now*, an oral history of culture change in the High Arctic told through the experiences of Inuit artists in and around Arctic Bay (Innuksuk and Cowan 1976). Actor Pakak Innuksuk, Leah's younger brother, has been instrumental in promoting Inuit theatre and film in northern and southern venues, and with arts companies such as Igloolik Isuma Productions. Pakak is recognized and respected locally for his commitment to mentoring young actors in Nunavut and offering training in media skills; he has also worked on Arctic cruise vessels as cultural interpreter, artist, and drum dance performer. Michael Inuksuk, Leah's oldest son, is an accomplished air pilot on northern flight routes, and Toby, her daughter, travelled internationally as a cultural ambassador with the Inuit performance collective Artcirq and currently works as an intern CBC Inuktitut announcer, translating news stories into Inuktitut while training through Nunavut Arctic College as an interpreter/translator.

Leah Aksaajuq Otak interviewing her mother, Piungittuq, for the Igloolik Oral History Project. 2006. Photo by John MacDonald

OF WORKING WORLDS

Drawing inspiration from her forebears and with an eye to future generations, Leah Aksaajuq Otak identified and fostered new spaces of cross-cultural convergence and reconciliation. This work began in the mid-1970s, at the interface of Inuit and Western healing traditions, when she worked as a medical interpreter at the Igloolik health centre. A career shift into broadcasting media was another means for critical reflection: in 1979 she worked for the CBC Northern Service Broadcaster in Montreal, translating English news items to Inuktitut. Next followed a social work position at the Nanisivik mines outside Arctic Bay, and a job as housing manager. A move back to Igloolik followed, and a new role managing the day-to-day work of the Igloolik Research Centre and administering both the Igloolik Oral History Project and the Inullariit Elders Society. Here she facilitated research bringing Inuit elders together with scholars from geographical, earth, and social sciences and across the arts, humanities, and education in the documentation, promotion, and advancement of Inuit knowledge. With the institution of the Government of Nunavut's Department of Culture, Language, Elders and Youth in Igloolik, Leah then turned to promoting Inuit culture at a governmental level. Leah Aksaajuq Otak's successes operating as cultural advocate demonstrate her commitment to issues of cultural representation. However, to truly understand how Leah went about this work, it is important to locate her efforts within the context of the greater cultural movements in Igloolik dating back to her youth.

The late 1960s and early 1970s witnessed the emergence of new social politics in the Canadian North as the effects of post–Second World War government policies of Northern development were implemented and Inuit were incorporated into Canadian welfare and education systems. Historical and anthropological paradigms from the turn of the century characterizing Iglulingmiut as a "remote people" led to a uniquely active research environment developing in Igloolik, with "tradition" constructed and institutionalized as a domain of special value. John MacDonald (Chapter 2) describes in detail a still longer historical provenance for such narratives. The prevailing characterization of

Igloolik as a traditional place had rather more to do with the imposition of Western modernist categories of remoteness and modernity
than it did with actual barriers on travel to this eastern High Arctic
locale. Nonetheless, it did contribute to Igloolik taking primacy over
other settlements as a hub for research. This characterization grew
considerable in the period between 1968 and 1972, when government
officials and scientists working as part of the International Biological
Programme Human Adaptability Project (IBPHAP) identified Igloolik
as its Canadian Arctic field site, bringing dozens of interdisciplinary
academics and graduate students northward to collect social science
and biometric data from the local population. With the advent of
this project, Igloolik was rendered a laboratory, and local Inuit found
themselves the subject of a range of what some considered invasive
medical testing (blood sampling, skin grafts, and water immersion
tests were conducted), as well as social science surveying. Researchers
became known locally as *qaujisartiit* (those trying to know), a designa-
tion that could be read either positively or negatively, depending on
the meeting. It is clear the program left some in the local population
uneasy and uncomfortable, as subjects of research tactics quite rightly
felt to be colonial, coercive, and disempowering.[11] Yet, stories of these
resident researchers also exist that did not make it into the scientific
reports: those of mutual respect between scientists and elders, and
of friendship and camaraderie developing, notably between visiting
student researchers and young Inuit students recently returned from
residential school of similar ages and conversant in the same 1960s
music and trends in popular culture.

The departure of the IBPHAP scientists from Igloolik coincided
with a cultural revitalization movement in Igloolik. The institution
of Inuit cultural and political organizations by a residential schooled
generation led to an Inuit cultural renaissance of sorts, detailed by
MacDonald (Chapter 15). It gained obvious momentum in Igloolik,
by then a self-designated centre of sorts for Inuit tradition, home to
many of the students who had been sent away to residential school,
some eager to relearn their culture and advance local land claim and
sovereignty issues.[12] Leah was a member of this cohort, choosing to

engage with researchers and scholars personally, making efforts to redress legacies of assmiliation in her town. Work undertaken in the last two decades of her life significantly shifted the type and nature of Arctic research emerging from Igloolik. Carefully and deliberately, she fostered research relationships she deemed beneficial to her people, engaging many who are contributors to this volume in shared processes of knowledge making, always with an eye to causes beneficial to a common good.

Of Enduring Legacies

In light of her recent death, it is perhaps my earliest conversations with Leah that I now recall as the most intense and illuminating, taking place in the severe cold of winter 1997, while I was billeted in the research bunkhouse located near her mother's house. At the time, Leah was busy running various Inullariit Elders Society programs, as well as tending daily to her widowed mother and caring for many relatives,

Leah Aksaajuq Otak measuring a woman's caribou legging boot (c. 1822) with her forearm. British Museum, London, 2000. Photo by John MacDonald

and her two children, Toby and Qajaaq, then aged ten and eight. I would catch sight of Leah and her kids each morning, in the winter light, treading single file past my window, then heading through the snow to the weather monitoring station in front of the house to take the daily temperature readings. We spoke as officemates, as anthropologist and interlocutor, but most often as newfound friends. Caribou-skin sewing was Leah's passion, and later a topic for publication.[13] She organized caribou-skin processing and sewing workshops each Wednesday evening. Here I joined elders from the Inullariit Society and young women apprentices keen to learn traditional skills. The deep cultural significance of skin sewing gained more and more meaning to me in these months—something returned to by Aariak, Engelstad, and King in contributions to this volume. Skin sewing draws together the stuff and sinews of life: husband and wife, mother and daughter, animal and human, existences on the land and in the settlement. As months turned to years, our companionship matured, and discussions of skin sewing would refract many other concerns and enable differing comparisons. Leah had an expert's habit of calling on sewing metaphors and analogies to speak to contemporary issues, combining the practical and the theoretical in a language I could understand. A great seamstress, she explained, must master all trades, being at once artist, designer, biochemist, zoologist, climatologist, as well as always a grandmother, aunt, sister, mother, daughter. And seams will not hold by themselves. They require reinforcing stitches.

Before the chapters following that pay full homage to the life and work of Leah Aksaajuq Otak, a final image comes to mind, one drawn upon by other contributors to this volume. It is of Leah, during a visit paid to the stores of the British Museum, London, inspecting a 180-year-old parka collected from her ancestors, turning it inside out (to the obvious alarm of the curator-conservators present) to see if the stitches in the garment still held. They did. As will the seams Leah sewed in her life. And so the measure of a woman was properly taken.

BIBLIOGRAPHY

Asad, Talal. 1974. *Anthropology and the Colonial Encounter.* London: Ithaca Press.

Benjamin, Walter. [1922] 2002. "The Task of the Translator." In *Walter Benjamin: Selected Writings, Volume 1: 1913–1926 [1922]*, edited by Marcus Bullock and MIchael W. Jennings, 253–263. Cambridge, MA: Harvard University Press.

Brody, H. 1975. *The People's Land.* Vancouver: Douglas and MacIntyre.

Cruikshank, Julie. 1998. *The Social Life of Stories: Narrative and Knowledge in the Yukon Territory.* Lincoln and London: University of Nebraska Press.

Driscoll, B. 1987. "Pretending to be Caribou: The Inuit Parka as an Artistic Tradition." In *The Spirit Sings: Artistic Traditions of Canada's First Nations*, 169–180. Calgary: Glenbow Museum Press.

Gough, K. 1968. "Anthropology and Imperialism." *Monthly Review* 19: 12–27.

Grossman, Edith. 2010. *Why Translation Matters.* New Haven and London: Yale University Press.

Idlout, Lori, and Leah Otak. 1995. "Welcome to Igloolik." In *Our Wonderful World, Level 4*, edited by Norma Kennedy and Anne McInnes, 9–24. Scarborough, Ontario: Ginn Publishing.

Ingold, T. 2000. *The Perception of the Environment: Essays on Livelihood, Dwelling and Skill.* London: Routledge.

Innuksuk, Rhoda, and Susan Cowan. 1976. *We Don't Live in Snow Houses Now: Reflections of Arctic Bay.* Edmonton: Hurtig.

Jackson, Michael. 2002. *The Politics of Storytelling: Violence, Transgression, and Intersubjectivity.* Copenhagen: Museum Tusculanum Press.

Kwon, H. 1998. "The Saddle and the Sledge: Hunting as Comparative Narrative in Siberia and Beyond." *The Journal of the Royal Anthropological Institute* 4(4): 115–127.

Lassiter, Luke. 2005. "Collaborative Ethnography and Public Anthropology." *Current Anthropology* 46(1): 83–106.

Law, J., and Wen-yuan Lin. 2010. "Cultivating disconcertment." *The Sociological Review* 58(s2): 135–153.

McGregor, Heather. 2010. *Inuit Education and Schools in the Eastern Arctic.* Vancouver: UBC Press.

Capturing Souls
Beginnings of Oral History Work in Igloolik[1]

George Quviq Qulaut

In a way, it all started with my grandfather, Itikuttuq. Around the time of my birth, Robert Petersen, the Greenlander who was with Jørgen Meldgaard around Igloolik in 1954, wanted to interview my grandfather with a tape recorder.[2] My grandfather, thinking that the tape recorder would capture his soul, refused to be interviewed. Later he seems to have regretted that decision because, shortly after my father died in 1968, my grandfather gave me a tape recorder in the summer of 1969—it was a small Sony reel-to-reel model. He said, "I know what this is—it's a good thing there is no music in it—so, I want you to record legends and *aja-ja* songs when I have visitors." By this time, my grandfather had noticed that our stories and songs were being lost. He saw the tape recorder as a way of preserving them. Tapes were hard to get then, but I managed to make about eight recordings and I looked after them carefully before I went off to school in Ottawa in 1974. To my disappointment, when I came back to Igloolik the following summer, the tape recorder and all the tapes had been taken away. Years later, in 1990, the individual who had taken the tapes announced on the community radio that he wanted to sell them. I immediately went over to his house and asked that he return them to me, but he refused. This experience, the result of my grandfather's request many years before, I believe made me open to the importance of recording oral history.

I first started to think about collecting the elders' stories in 1983. At the time I was working at the Eastern Arctic Scientific Resource Centre, as the Igloolik Research Centre was called in those days. The scientist-in-charge at the time was Andy Rode.[3] I was working at the centre as a technician, running the seismograph and the weather stations and interpreting for scientists coming from the south to do fieldwork in Igloolik.

In the fall of 1983, Andy was going to be away from Igloolik for a period of three or four months to work in Ottawa and the Yukon. Before his departure in October he told me I should start a project of my own, something that would occupy my mind. The work should be of my choice, whatever I thought would be best for me. Initially, we never thought to do oral history—we never thought of that—but mainly of doing other projects that Andy could help me with while he was away.

So I thought about it. Aipilik Inuksuk, Leah Otak's father, was the janitor at the centre. He used to tell lots of stories about the past, good stories. He was also concerned about the failure of the Inummariit Society and its museum, which had been run by Igloolik's priest, Father Fournier.[4] I thought about it very, very seriously. And then one day I said to Aipilik, "How do you feel about anthropologists taking away a lot of your knowledge, interviewing you so they write their theses and publish their papers but none of it ever coming back to Igloolik?" I said I thought this was the wrong way. It would be better if we talked to people who would keep our traditions alive because it is so important to have this knowledge in our community—and besides, many of the elders, the old people, have nothing else to do, and they want to talk and pass on their knowledge. Aipilik agreed. But Thomas Kublu, who was at that time the maintenance person at the Research

Centre, disagreed. He was completely against it because our culture was changing quickly. He said, "Leave the past alone—the past is the past."[5] But with Aipilik's encouragement I decided we should try to get a tape recorder and start recording the elders. We would work with the elders over the winter months. So that's exactly how the project got started.

In December, I arranged a meeting with all the elders who would be involved in the project—there were about a dozen of them—including Kupaak, Iqallijuq, Kappianaq, Nutarkittuq (who felt his wife was too young to participate), François Quassa and his wife, Noah Piugaattuk, Aipilik and his wife, Piungittuq, and also Irngaut and his wife. I also had Ukalik come in—he, too, felt his wife was too young. Iyerak did not want to be involved because he was so close to my father, so he declined out of respect. These elders had lived most of their lives on the land, with very little southern contact, and they were the proper people we should talk to. I explained to them what I had in mind, and I told them this project is quite important because of what I, and Aipilik, had learned working at the Research Centre. I told them about researchers and scientists, especially the anthropologists who do a lot of interviews with Inuit, how they are doing it for themselves, to write a thesis or for some publication, and that none of this is coming back to the community. I know, of course, that my grandchildren will be able to read the anthropologists' writings, but these writings will be from a Qallunaat point of view.

At this meeting I used myself as an example to explain why the project was so important. I had been taught English at a very early age, while away in hospital or at residential school. I had almost forgotten my own culture, especially my own language. If it wasn't for the elders who helped me to recover my lost language and culture, I would not be where I am today. It was hard for the elders to understand this because they had not lived this loss as I had. I was speaking from the heart. To show them how much our ways were changing I mentioned to them that their children—the elders' children—had now become their parents' teachers, teaching them how best to live in a wooden house with four corners! I urged them to take steps to preserve as much of their knowledge as possible before it was lost, and to do it in the Igloolik dialect, so that my grandchildren's grandchildren would be able to hear and understand the interviews in our own language. This was necessary because through the influences of CBC Radio, along with video and television, we end up using—without even knowing it—words that are not our own. In this way, a lot of our Igloolik dialect is dying off.

I knew that many of the elders were reluctant, even ashamed, to talk about their traditional ways because of religion—especially the Anglicans. But I explained how important it is for the younger generation to know about things in the past, the things we have to know about in order to understand our history and culture. By the end of the meeting, the elders understood what I was getting at and accepted my ideas. In fact, they became very excited about what we planned to do.

We needed equipment, of course, to carry out the project. I called Walter Slipchenko, who at that time worked with the Circumpolar Division at the Department of Indian and Northern Affairs in Ottawa.[6] He, too, was enthusiastic about my plan and was willing to provide a tape recorder—a reel-to-reel tape recorder—and some tapes, but I would have to buy more tapes later. So, within a month Walter had sent a brand-new tape recorder. I showed it to the elders and said that this is a tool that you will be talking to. Irngaut really got excited over that—he wanted to do it. But he was ashamed of the way he spoke, ashamed that people would not understand him. Aipilik, too, wanted very much to be involved, along with George Kappianaq. Piugaattuk came in later; at first he was just observing and listening. He was not saying much.[7]

During that first meeting, we discussed various ways of gathering knowledge. Three types of interviews were planned. The first would involve people like me doing the interviewing, people who had very little knowledge of the past, but could speak the language. The second kind of interview would have people like Emile Imaruittuq asking the questions.[8] It was his generation that saw the coming of Christianity and grew up experiencing the changes in our society. Lastly, the third form of interview would involve an elder interviewing an elder, talking about the past, and ensuring that words and expressions we normally don't hear would be recorded and preserved. The *Inummariit* style of conversation—the real Inuit way—is no longer in existence. Indeed, as soon as a young person walks in on elders conversing, their language changes immediately. It switches. It was all in the process of changing, and that really started the Oral History Project.

I told the elders I was sorry that I had no money to pay them, just to say thank you. That's when Noah Piugaattuk started expressing himself. He immediately banged on the table and said, "Quviq, you're turning into a white man! What you have said is very powerful and we want to do it. We are very much for it. My payment will be the time when your grandchildren's grandchildren can hear and understand every word I say in Inuktitut." And everyone said, "*Iittiaq, taimainni-artuq*": "Indeed, that's the way it will be, that's our payment."

Noah Piugaattuk (c. 1900–1995) was the principal inspiration for the Igloolik Oral History Project and one of its main contributors. Photo © B. Alexander/ Arcticphoto

The elders really wanted to be involved in the project, so I attempted a few interviews, but for various reasons this initial phase to the work was not very successful, and some of the religious elders started to question the project. Only a few interviews were completed and I'm not sure where these are now. But, importantly, the idea of an oral history project had been formed and the importance of recording traditional knowledge was generally accepted. It would just take time to get things going.

Shortly after John MacDonald took over the Research Centre from Andy Rode in March of 1985, we had a second meeting about the Oral History Project with the elders. We agreed that the project should be approached differently. For instance, they said there were some things that would be hurtful to talk about, that the children should not hear, certain beliefs like shamanism. I agreed with them, saying they could talk about anything they wanted, anything they thought would be appropriate. I also encouraged them to talk about traditional life to their children and grandchildren. It was around this time that the project started to take off. We began to get funding from the Department of Indian and Northern Affairs, and from the Science Institute of the Northwest Territories. The oral history work now became an official project of the Igloolik Research Centre, and soon people like Paul Irngaut, Leah Otak, and Louis Tapardjuk were hired to help with the interviewing and translation work. At this time, in keeping with my original idea, we now encouraged all visiting researchers to leave copies of their elders' interviews at the Research Centre—most researchers cooperated, but some didn't. In 1985, the many interviews deposited by Paqulluk—that's the name we gave Willem Rasing— became the start of the Igloolik Oral History archives.[9]

Piugaattuk wanted the interviews to be translated into English so that researchers could better understand Inuit ways, Inuit opinions. Also, because he could see our dialect was changing so rapidly by people picking up different words and expressions from other areas in Nunavut.

I mentioned earlier that Piugaattuk sort of stayed behind, not saying too much, until the project started to become a reality and he now understood what we were really trying to do. At first, he did a few interviews—but he did many more after his wife died. In a way he was using the interviews to help himself heal, to manage his sorrow. He said to me, "*Aipaqarruunnirłuni aijaqattaqarunnirłuni puigurpallianirman,*" meaning now that his spouse is dead, he is very quiet, doesn't talk much, and is forgetting a lot of things that should be passed on. But with the tape recorder and interviews his memories started to come back and he got very excited. So, I encouraged him—and all the other elders as well—to take little cassette recorders, to have their grandchildren interview them.

There were some elders who were not involved in the project. I encouraged them to come over to the Research Centre to be interviewed, but they never showed up. Shortly before they died some of them regretted that they had not been interviewed. Joe Tasiuq and his wife were among these. Tasiuq openly said that he thought there would be a lot of religious objection to him talking about shamanism, which he knew about, and which was a bit hush-hush. His wife really regretted not being interviewed, because she, too, knew lots about shamanism from the Kivalliq region. She had wanted to be involved, but there were stories that she was asked not to repeat. There were others as well who wanted to be involved—like Annulik, with whom I share the name Kuttiq, but she couldn't say a word out of respect for our namesake connections, our *tuqłurausiit*.[10] I respected that, but I also regretted it.

Through the Oral History Project, I felt that we had accomplished something unique, very different from other communities in Nunavut. Even though latterly I was not involved in the project, I am pleased I was involved right from the beginning, and worked hard to get it started, and that I was able to pass it on knowing that people like Leah Otak and Louis Tapardjuk would be able to continue the work. This is something so good that will go on for a long time. People will use it. That was the purpose, to have it used for the future. All recognition for the project should be given to the elders, not to the people who assisted them. It's the elders who should be recognized and respected for their work.

Numerous times I shed tears because I was so happy about my involvement in the project. Once was when the Igloolik Elders' Society—the Inullariit Society—was presented with the Northern Science Award in 1998.[11] And again a few years ago, when Nunavut Arctic College took over responsibility for the project. At that time, Michael Shouldice was president of the college and he made a presentation to the full Nunavut Caucus explaining how the college would be using the Igloolik interviews for educational purposes because they're the best-documented, richest, and strongest source of oral history in Nunavut. As Speaker of the Legislative Assembly, I thanked Michael Shouldice very much, telling him that this is exactly what the elders would have wanted—this was their goal when they started the Oral History Project, not for themselves, but something that would be used in the future. In my mind's eye, I can see these elders smiling, even though they are no longer with us. This is the payment that they were waiting for—that's all they were asking, that their interviews would be used. To me that's a great accomplishment, and I'm very proud that at the beginning, I was part of it all.

I came to understand very well the part I had in starting the Oral History Project when, one day, Piugaattuk asked me to come over to his house. He said that because he would not live much longer he just wanted to thank me for my work on the project. Words, he said, were not enough, and to show his appreciation he had made me a small hunter's *qulliq*—a soapstone lamp—just to say *qujannamiik*, "thank you." I treasure this gift. Every now and then on special occasions such as Christmas and New Year's, I light Piugaattuk's *qulliq*.

CHAPTER 2

Stories and Representation

Two Centuries of Narrating Amitturmiut History

John MacDonald

When I was a child no one talked about ways to preserve customs.
That was all Inuit knew, and we couldn't foresee a time when
it would be necessary to record them.
Leah Otak, 2014

ARGUABLY, NO INUIT GROUP in Canada has been narrated so extensively, so variously, or for so long as the Amitturmiut of the
northeastern Foxe Basin in Nunavut, Canada. The area, locally known
as Amittuq, is home to the present-day communities of Igloolik and
Hall Beach.[1]

This essay outlines the nature of these narratives over almost two
centuries, beginning with the first European contact in 1822 through
to the present day.[2] The latter part of this lengthy span saw at least partial

control of the narrative evolve from the almost exclusive prerogative of outsiders—the Qallunaat—to the Amitturmiut themselves.

The Amitturmiut story, of course, did not begin with their coincidental "discovery" by Europeans in the 19th century. Long before this portentous event, Amitturmiut history was passed down unfailingly from generation to generation, carried forward in the language of legends telling of creation, of society's values, and of the complexities of negotiating the animal and spirit worlds on which they depended. Family history was carried forward in the names given to individuals at birth, and a sense of enduring, shared belonging to the land was validated through the long-remembered stories attached to the intimate network of geographical place-names defining their territory. While the Amitturmiut shared a basic cosmology, worldview, language, and economy with other Inuit groups, they nevertheless saw and represented themselves as distinct. They told their own story.

All this was to change with the arrival of Europeans, a seemingly chance encounter, but one that would alter forever the way in which the Amitturmiut related to themselves, to their universe, and to the

Interior of an Amitturmiut snowhouse in 1822. A walrus scapula in the snowhouse wall to the right of the woman's head serves as a shelf to hold a mirror, beads, and a pair of scissors obtained from Parry's expedition. Illustration by G.F. Lyon, engraved by E. Finden (Parry 1824, 160)

world beyond. They were gradually to lose control of their own story, becoming first objects of confused curiosity and, by the early 20th century, perennial grist for the mills of anthropological enterprise. Unwittingly, the Amitturmiut became actors in other people's narratives.[3]

Amitturmiut historical representations can be divided into three distinct phases of Qallunaat incursions into the Amittuq area, each in turn producing its own characteristic time-bound narrative. By far the longest phase, the "expedition era"—lasting from 1822 until 1939—was characterized by an assortment of sporadic, irregularly spaced, and temporary visits from Qallunaat expeditions largely intent on geographic and scientific discovery. By the end of this period, less transient visitors, in the form of missionaries and traders, began arriving in the area. The next stage—occurring between the end of the Second World War and the early 1960s—saw the presence of Qallunaat increase rapidly, finally reaching their permanent settlement in Igloolik around 1962, when the Canadian government established a settlement on the island (see Crowe 1969, 89–103). Over the next several years, responding to the government's coercive blandishments, most of the area's Inuit had moved from the land into the settlement. Driven by rapid social and cultural disintegration following this move, the third phase—still evolving—began in 1969 with the first tentative steps taken by Amitturmiut themselves to formally document their stories, history, and traditional knowledge. This measure—entailing the intrusion of pencil, paper, and tape recorder, not to mention the limitations of the interview—signalled a major departure from the natural, unobtrusive processes of social and cultural continuity fostered by oral traditions, which until then had sustained Amitturmiut society for generations.

WILLIAM EDWARD PARRY, 1821–23

Recording Amitturmiut "life and customs" began with the visit of a Royal Navy expedition (1821–23) sent from Britain to the northern reaches of the Foxe Basin.[4] The expedition was led by William Edward Parry, then on his second attempt to find a Northwest Passage from the Atlantic to the Pacific along the Arctic coast of North America.

Parry and his crews overwintered twice in the region, coming into close and extended contact with Amitturmiut families—particularly those living around Igloolik Island at that time—between July 1822 and August 1823.[5] Shortly after the expedition's return to England, Parry and his second-in-command, George Francis Lyon, each published lengthy, well-illustrated accounts of the voyage. The books were well received by the British reading public, hungry for accounts of imperial voyages to far-off places and new geographical discoveries, and excited by the prospects of finding a Northwest Passage. In addition, an emerging Romantic-era fascination with the sublime and exotic imparted an extraordinary cachet to Arctic voyages, which British publishers, particularly John Murray, were quick to exploit.[6]

What distinguished Parry's and Lyon's narratives from those of earlier Arctic voyages was the impressive amount of space their journals, especially Lyon's, devoted to observations and descriptions of Inuit life. This was made possible for two reasons: the unprecedented length of the expedition's visit among the Amitturmiut, and, more importantly, the exceptional interest paid to their Inuit hosts by Parry, Lyon, and a number of their officers, particularly William Hooper, who documented all aspects of their Inuit hosts' social conditions, means of livelihood, language, and culture.[7] Read together, the journals of Parry and his officers anticipate many aspects of classical ethnography and, as such, constitute the earliest writings in this genre touching on the Inuit of Foxe Basin and, more generally, of northern Baffin Island. Parry's and Lyon's books were illustrated by engravings, based on Lyon's accurate sketches, depicting Amitturmiut individuals, their activities, and their material culture.[8] In the years immediately following their publication, the expedition's journals, and especially the sections about Inuit, were abridged, paraphrased, and serialized in the British popular press, even finding their way into children's stories and poetry illustrated with adaptations of Lyon's drawings.[9] For the remainder of the 19th century, this wide, popular coverage of the Amitturmiut established them, par excellence, as the archetypical "Esquimaux" (Brody 1987, 19).[10]

Inuit women of Igloolik in winter dress, 1823. Illustration by G.F. Lyon, engraved by E. Finden (Parry 1824, 160)

CHARLES FRANCIS HALL, 1867 AND 1868

Forty-five years after Parry left, the Amitturmiut were again visited by an outsider, the American adventurer Charles Francis Hall, who made two brief visits to the Igloolik area in the mid-1860s.[11] Hall purchased dogs from the Amitturmiut to aid in his futile search for survivors of the lost Franklin expedition, some of whom were rumoured to have sought refuge in Igloolik. Despite his brief visits, Hall's field notes—partially written up, paraphrased, and published by J.E. Nourse—expand upon Parry's observations of Amitturmiut life.[12] Hall usefully records some of the material changes that had occurred in Inuit society since their first European contact and gives details of Inuit encampments on Tern Island and the Oogliit Islands near Igloolik. Hall is careful to record (albeit in his awkward, idiosyncratic orthography) the names of the principal Inuit he met. He made a special point to closely interview Amitturmiut about Parry's visit to Igloolik forty-five years earlier, gathering contrasting accounts of various events reported earlier, including the punishment Parry gave to an Inuit shaman accused of theft (Nourse 1879, 350).[13]

ALFRED TREMBLAY, 1913

The Amitturmiut were left alone for another forty-five years until March of 1913, when Alfred Tremblay, a French-Canadian pros-pector, reached Igloolik overland from Arctic Bay with the help of Inuit guides and dog teams. He was the first Qallunaaq to travel this route. Tremblay, a member of Joseph Bernier's fruitless "gold rush" expedition (1912–13) to northern Baffin Island, had journeyed to the Amittuq area hoping to trap white foxes and search for mineral depos-its.[14] Blissfully unaware of Hall's earlier visit, in his autobiographical account he proudly casts himself as the first white man to reach Igloolik since Parry. Tremblay published a memoir in 1921 under the title *Cruise of the Minnie Maud.* In stark contrast to Parry's restrained style, Tremblay's writing is a disordered mixture of material drawn indiscriminately from other sources (often Parry) interspersed with self-regarding, cavalier passages recounting his own adventures. From this hodgepodge, we can still extract useful information about travel routes between Arctic Bay and Igloolik, seasonal distribution of Inuit camps in the area, Inuit place-names, and the accessibility of wildlife during his travels. Importantly, like Hall, many of his Inuit travelling companions are mentioned by name, which—again, despite their idiosyncratic spellings—means they can be linked to present-day Igloolik and Pond Inlet families. Tremblay makes the first published mention of the Ataguttaaluk starvations, one of Amittuq's defining events. This occurred around 1904, when an Inuit family travelling by dog team between Pond Inlet and Igloolik became stranded due to adverse snow conditions. Starvation ensued, and the entire party died except for one woman, Ataguttaaluk, who survived by eating the remains of her dead relatives.[15]

Tremblay also shows that, by the time of his visit, the Amitturmiut were already participants in the fur-trapping economy, journeying either north to Pond Inlet or south to the Aivilik area to trade their catch.

FIFTH THULE EXPEDITION, 1922–23

A decade after Tremblay's brief sojourn, the Amitturmiut again received visitors, but this time of quite a different order: members of the "Fifth Thule Expedition," led by the Dane Knud Rasmussen. Unlike his predecessors, Rasmussen had not come in search of the Northwest Passage, nor was he looking for the lost Franklin expedition, or prospecting for elusive gold deposits. He had come first and foremost to meet the Inuit and hear their stories. Born in Greenland, and of part-Inuit ancestry, he possessed a passion for dog-team travel, summed up in his maxim "give me winter, give me dogs, and you can keep the rest." This passion, combined with his indomitable curiosity about Inuit origins, life, and culture, fuelled his determination to visit all the Arctic's Inuit groups from Greenland to Siberia. The high point of this goal was the Fifth Thule Expedition, in which Rasmussen and his companions travelled across Arctic America contacting virtually every Inuit group on the continent straddling the Arctic Circle.[16] The expedition's reports included scientific monographs on Arctic geology, geography, botany, zoology, archaeology, and ethnography, which together established a broad basis for subsequent Arctic research. The enduring legacy of the Fifth Thule Expedition, however, rests mainly on Rasmussen's extensive writings about Inuit and on the ethnographic reports of Therkel Mathiassen and Kaj Birket Smith. Of poetic bent, and fluent in Greenlandic, Rasmussen had unparalleled linguistic access to the Inuit he visited, an advantage made clear in the richness and depth of his observations found in his seminal study *Intellectual Culture of the Iglulik Eskimos*, published in 1929.

BRITISH CANADIAN ARCTIC EXPEDITION, 1936–39

The last of the "expedition era" visits to the Amitturmiut occurred in the years immediately prior to the Second World War. Under T.H. Manning, the British Canadian Arctic Expedition (1936–39)—centred on the northern Foxe Basin—undertook scientific fieldwork in geography, geology, ornithology, and archaeology, the latter crucially important from the perspective of Inuit prehistory. Excavations made by the expedition's archaeologist, Graham Rowley, on Avvajja Island (near Igloolik) demonstrated conclusively the presence of an earlier Arctic culture, the "Dorset," a semi-mythical people long known to the Amitturmiut as Tuniit. At the time of Rowley's visit, Étienne Bazin, a Roman Catholic priest, had already established a mission at Igloolik. Bazin's journals and letters offer a missionary's view of the introduction of Catholicism to the area in the face of opposition from Inuit shamans and competition from Anglican missionaries (Rasing 2010, 167–170).[17] Interested in archaeology himself, Bazin gave Rowley numerous artifacts, obtained over several years, from local Inuit. These objects, combined with finds from Rowley's own excavations, added significantly to understanding the island's prehistory (King 2014, 46–55). Rowley published his memoirs of the expedition in 2007, giving a respectful and detailed account of Amitturmiut conditions just prior to the disruption their society was about to undergo in the years following the war.[18]

FRAMING THE NARRATIVE

Clearly, the production of narrative was a natural consequence of exploration. Once home, travellers were compelled—either by sponsors or their own inclinations—to share their experiences with the world. Accordingly, journals, reports, scientific papers, and books of various sorts, sometimes copiously illustrated, were disseminated to a southern readership eager to partake vicariously in Arctic journeys.[19] Apart from works dealing with specialized topics such as geology or entomology, the Amitturmiut inevitably played a part in these narratives, ranging from their principal role in Rasmussen's *Intellectual Culture of the Iglulik Eskimos* to their relatively minor part in Tremblay's *Minnie Maud*.

Always subjective, these accounts were inevitably coloured by the time's prevailing attitudes towards Indigenous peoples at each period: biases that could be, and sometimes were, moderated by the narrator's own interests, empathy, powers of observation, education, and linguistic ability. Parry and Lyon, for instance—whose accounts on balance offer a genuinely sympathetic picture of Inuit life in the higher regions of the Arctic, a culture hitherto largely unchanged by direct contact with the outside world—frequently lapse into 19th-century European prejudices, rarely losing sight of their presumed British superiority.[20] But regardless of the narrator's sympathies, the Amitturmiut were unavoidably represented to the world through a European perspective.[21] Moreover the narratives are crafted or "framed" to meet the perceived interests of a specific audience.[22] In this vein, Rasmussen, intent on presenting a pristine view of Inuit life in his *Intellectual Culture of the Iglulik Eskimos*, virtually ignores the intrusion of modernity into Amitturmiut society evident everywhere at the time of his visit (see

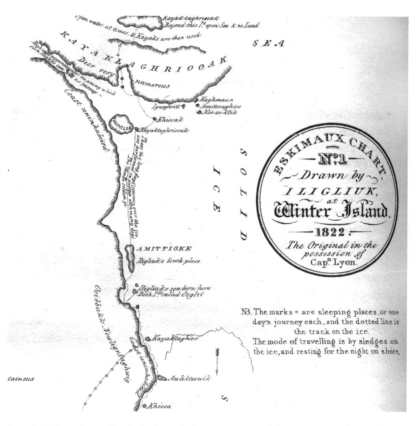

Detail of chart drawn by Iligliuk, including a portion of the east coast of Melville Peninsula from Ammituq to Igloolik Island. Following the publication of Parry's 1821–24 journal, Iligliuk was celebrated for her "astonishing precision" in map-making. Drawn by Iligliuk, 1822, lithographed by C. Hullmandel (Parry 1824, 225)

Wachowich 2006, 125). He avoids important questions about the implications of Christianity then sweeping the area; the spread of the syllabic writing system; the introduction of firearms and steel traps, and the concomitant rise of the trapping and trading economy.[23] Seeking the opinions of his Inuit interlocutors on questions of incipient modernity and its reception among the Amitturmiut would have added a valuable dimension to his narrative.[24] With the notable exception of much of Rasmussen's material—including in particular his *Iglulik and Caribou Eskimo Texts*, where the narrator's Inuktitut appears alongside the English translation (Rasmussen 1976)—the published accounts of these early expeditions to the Amittuq region contain few of the voices of individual Inuit.[25] That said, and the aforementioned limitations acknowledged, most of the Qallunaat narratives conserve, in varying degrees, information crucial in reconstructing aspects of Amitturmiut social history, particularly when used in concert with oral histories gathered from Igloolik Inuit elders over the past thirty years.[26]

THE OBSERVERS OBSERVED

A point often missed in the lopsided narratives of encounters between Europeans and Indigenous peoples everywhere is that representation ran in both directions: the observers were themselves observed.[27] Thus, most of the "pantheon" of early Qallunaat visitors, from Parry to Rowley, found their way into local lore. And they were not always remembered in as heroic a manner as they might have liked.

In Amitturmiut oral tradition, Parry and his men had come to Igloolik explicitly to find the bones of their ancestral mother, Uinigumasuittuq, who, through her union with a dog, had become the progenitor of the Qallunaat race in ages past. From the Inuit perspective, what other explanation could account for Parry's long-predicted appearance on Igloolik's shore?[28] Parry, of course, was unaware of this mythical glossing of his bold Northwest Passage quest. Another local account tells that when Parry left Igloolik Island in August 1823, a shaman, Quliiqaujaq, resentful of Parry's dalliance with his wife, caused a barrier of ice to form around the island to thwart the approach of other Qallunaat ships (Paniaq 1990).

Parry's reputation among the Amitturmiut evolved and changed over time. Both Hall and John Rae gathered stories from Inuit portraying him as a healer and provider (Rae 1850, 40, 42, 147; Nourse 1879, 129, 296, 301). Yet today in Igloolik, Parry is remembered mainly as a brutal punisher for ordering the lashing of an Inuk suspected of theft (MacDonald 2012). The ice-borne curse said to have been conjured by the resentful shaman on Parry's departure was broken only in 1913 when, according to Rosie Iqallijuq, Alfred Tremblay, on his arrival overland from Arctic Bay, fired his pistol onto Igloolik's shore and declared the island "captured" (as one would a wild animal), adding that from now on, Qallunaat ships would again be able to reach the island.[29] Piugaattuk records that Taamali—Tremblay—was known as a "mentally unstable" man and feared for his tendency to violence.[30]

Suzanne Niviattian, a child at the time of Rasmussen's visit to the Amittuq area, vividly recalled surrendering her treasured little wooden dolls, *inuujait*, to one of the expedition's white men, probably Therkel Mathiassen, called Tikili in Inuktitut:

> I started to cry for I did not wish to part with them. My mother told me to give them to him, so she put them away in a bag in which we were playing with them. She handed the bag over to him and he left. I was left with nothing, including all the lemming skins and other small things that were part of the *inuujait*. In return I got a few pages of plain paper, that was not much of a trade, but my mother did not seem to mind, I guess there was no paper available anywhere. (Niviattian 1990, IE-130)[31]

Graham Rowley, or Makkuktunnaaq (the little young man), and his travelling companion Reynold Bray, Umiligaarjuk (the little bearded one), are remembered fondly in the oral history records of the region, albeit with some wonderment. Their arrival at Igloolik in midwinter 1937, having travelled by dog team from Repulse Bay, was greeted with bemused astonishment. Of note was their pitiful inability to wear caribou-skin clothing properly and, in Bray's case, an infestation of body lice the likes of which Inuit had never seen before

(MacDonald 2004, 223–224). Rowley left Igloolik to return south in September 1939, just as the Hudson's Bay Company was setting up a permanent trading post on the island, joining the already established Roman Catholic mission.[32] These two agencies, representatives of trade and Christianity—typically the forerunners of Arctic colonialism—formed the nucleus of what would become the present-day town of Igloolik.

TRANSITIONS 1940–65

Until the early 1960s the majority of the Amitturmiut lived more or less independently in hunting camps dispersed along the shores of Melville Peninsula and nearby Baffin Island, coexisting interdependently with, but at a distance from, the Hudson's Bay Company and competing Roman Catholic and Anglican missionaries. Their dealings with traders revolved mainly around white fox trapping, an activity that had already altered their traditional subsistence patterns as their reliance on European goods such as firearms, traps, metal tools, and fabrics escalated. Christianity, which first reached Igloolik in the 1920s through Inuit agency, had by the 1940s—on the surface at least—displaced traditional shamanistic beliefs and practices.[33] The occasional official exchanges between Amitturmiut and the remote Canadian government were mediated indirectly and erratically through the traders, through missionaries, and by itinerant members of the Royal Canadian Mounted Police (RCMP) during their annual patrols from the detachment in Pond Inlet. Over the years these agencies and their idiosyncrasies became known, predictable quantities, and were slowly incorporated into the Amitturmiut worldview.

Written records from this period naturally emphasize the various preoccupations—commercial, religious, or administrative—of the agencies with which the Amitturmiut interacted. Records held in the archives of the Hudson's Bay Company, the Roman Catholic and Anglican missions, and the RCMP offer valuable, matter-of-fact information on the day-to-day social conditions, economy, population distribution, and movement of the area's Inuit prior to the establishment of the settlements.[34] In this genre, a genealogy extracted from the *Liber Animorum* (Book of Souls) of St. Étienne's Mission, Igloolik, provides a good example. Compiled by Fr. Jean-Marie Trébaol, the genealogy lists Inuit families, whether Catholic parishioners or not, resident in the Igloolik area in the late 1950s. Families' antecedents and interrelationships are methodically recorded and cross-referenced. In Trébaol's quaint, sometimes moralistic idiom, the genealogy also includes terse remarks on "custom adoption," "concubinage," "abduction," murder, and accidental death.[35]

A noteworthy exception to the agency reports was *Eskimo* magazine, published by the Oblate Fathers of the Diocese of Churchill-Hudson Bay. Launched in 1944, the magazine eventually (in 1953) came under

Portraits of Amitturmiut, sketched by G.F. Lyon in 1822–23. Over forty years later, Charles Francis Hall showed some of Lyon's drawings to Inuit he met at Igloolik, who judged the likenesses movingly accurate. Iligliuk, the map-maker, is depicted centre left. G.F. Lyon, engraved by E. Finden (Lyon 1825, 128)

the editorship of Fr. Guy Mary-Rousselière—known to the Amitturmiut as Ataata Mari (Father Mary). For the next four decades, the magazine reflected Mary-Rousselière's interest in archaeology and ethnography by publishing numerous articles on Inuit culture, many of them with Amitturmiut relevance (Rankin 2011, 78).[36] These articles—some based on early tape-recorded interviews made in Nunavut by Mary-Rousselière, and often illustrated with his own photographs and sketches—in many ways anticipated more formal localized attempts, introduced between the late 1960s and mid-1980s, to record and document Amitturmiut traditions.[37]

During this transitory stage three significant monographs relating to the Amitturmiut were published: David Damas's *Iglulingmiut Kinship* (1963); Gerard Anders's *Northern Foxe Basin: An Area Economic Survey* (1965); and Keith Crowe's *A Cultural Geography of Northern Foxe Basin* (1969).[38] These three works, each from a different perspective, provide a picture of Amitturmiut society on the cusp of great change. Graham Rowley's pre-war archaeological investigations were furthered in the 1950s by Jørgen Meldgaard of the National Museum of Denmark and his team.[39] Photographic documentation also took place during this period through the work of Richard Harrington (1952–53) and Jean Malaurie (1960–61), a French anthropologist whose powerful images, not published until 2001, greatly add to the written descriptions of the time.[40] Photography by outsiders was later to become problematic for Inuit of the region, particularly with the rise of animal-rights activists who used images of dead animals, killed by Inuit, to further their cause. By the mid-1980s the Igloolik Hamlet Council was vetting professional photographers and in some cases barring them from joining walrus hunts. One reader of Malaurie's book demonstrates that Igloolik's concerns were not without foundation:

> I wasn't pleased at all with this book. It had terrible pictures of slaughtered animals. I don't know what the author was thinking when he posted those pictures in the book. They were totally gross! I would not recommend this book to anyone![41]

Until the early 1960s most Amitturmiut continued to live on the land, moving between camps in response to the migrations of the animals on which they depended, mainly seals and walrus, supplemented seasonally by caribou, fish, and migratory birds. Specialized knowledge of the local environment and its ecology, along with the skills necessary to utilize the land's resources, remained essentially intact and were passed down seamlessly to succeeding generations. Importantly, the language, Inuktitut, remained resilient, as did many aspects of Amitturmiut intellectual, spiritual, and artistic life embodied in song, drum dance, and storytelling. Amitturmiut elders today look back on this period of their history with an understandable nostalgia, an idealized time when relations with the Qallunaat world were mediated at arm's length in manageable equilibrium. During this hiatus, life's cadences were still largely determined by events in nature: the weather, the turning of the seasons, and the inevitable imperatives of the hunt.

This equilibrium was suddenly disrupted in the mid-1960s following a series of events originating in the distant south. In 1954 construction began on the Distant Early Warning Line (DEW Line), a string of defensive Cold War radar stations operated jointly by the American and Canadian Air Forces across the Arctic. The DEW Line, in addition to imposing alien structures on the landscape, brought previously unimagined access to the region in terms of transportation and communications.[42] In 1958, Prime Minister John Diefenbaker declared his "Northern Vision," a call to action aimed mainly at exploiting the Arctic's rich mineral resources. Popular books by the author Farley Mowat, depicting poverty and starvation among Inuit living on the barren grounds west of Hudson Bay in the 1950s, captured the imagination of the Canadian public.[43] The need to intervene intensified with alarming reports during that period of epidemic levels of tuberculosis among Inuit generally. Political expediency spurred the government to implement a range of measures aimed at delivering health, housing, and education programs to the North. Hastily contrived, and with little or no consultation with those directly involved, the government moved quickly to implement these programs, all of them predicated on the requirement that Inuit move off the land into designated settlements where social programs could be more efficiently administered. This was the justification for the so-called in-gathering policy which, to no avail, was vigorously opposed by the churches and the Hudson's Bay Company.[44] Because of this policy, by 1965, all but a few of the Amitturmiut had moved from the land into the settlements of Igloolik or Hall Beach.[45] In actual distance the move was relatively insignificant, but it was immeasurable in terms of its social and cultural displacement and eventual consequences.[46]

As the settlement of Igloolik grew, so did the proliferation of government agencies whose administrators, often with little knowledge of the Arctic and scant understanding of Inuit society, usurped Inuit leadership roles. The demands of settlement life, including formal schooling in English, interfered relentlessly with oral transmission

Aerial photograph of Igloolik in 1954, showing the Hudson's Bay buildings (centre) and the Roman Catholic Mission (bottom right). John MacDonald collection

processes. The complex attributes of traditional culture and language were no longer being passed down to the younger generations.[47] Increasingly sedentary, the Amitturmiut became less inclined to hunt. Within a generation or so, semi-urban life had begun to isolate Inuit from the nourishing environment just beyond the fringes of the settlement. In an interview, Nathan Qamaniq, an Amitturmiut elder, categorically expresses his opinion that Inuit culture cannot thrive in a semi-urban environment:

> You need to be outside the settlement to learn these things. You need to be away from this place. You have to endure hardship every now and then … it is a good way to learn. You need to travel over thin ice and face other dangers. (Qamaniq 2002)

Qamaniq, along with others of his generation who witnessed their people's withdrawal—coerced or otherwise—from the land, marks the move to the settlement as the beginning of an irreversible decline in Amitturmiut autonomy, culture, language, and traditions.

RECORDING AMITTURMIUT ORAL HISTORY—THE BEGINNINGS

The impulse to record and document oral history is often motivated by an awareness that a way of life is under threat from some form of social dislocation or change, whether embraced or imposed. Loss is evident everywhere: loss of knowledge, skills, values, language, and—most poignantly—of personal and collective histories. For Inuit, whose cultural continuity relied entirely on oral transmission now threatened by increasing urbanization and Western-style schooling, there was the added awareness that much of their knowledge and history resided, precariously, in the memories of a fast-diminishing number of elders. These circumstances brought Amitturmiut to participate in formal efforts to record and preserve their traditions—first through the creation of Igloolik's Inummariit Association in 1969, and later, in the mid-1980s, through the Igloolik Oral History Project.

Between these dates an endeavour of great political significance took place across the Northwest Territories, namely the Inuit Land Use and Occupancy Project (ILUOP), which established the basis for the Inuit Land Claim Agreement, leading eventually to the establishment of Nunavut in 1999. Using innovative techniques, the ILUOP conducted extensive interviews with Inuit across the territory, including the Amitturmiut. Information recorded during the ILUOP, duly analyzed by the project's researchers, was issued in a three-volume report edited by Milton Freeman (Aporta 2016). Using testimony given by Inuit, detailed maps were meticulously drawn—probably among the first examples of Indigenous "cultural mapping" in the world—demonstrating conclusively the indelible bond between the Inuit, their land (including the sea ice), and its life-sustaining resources. Hugh Brody, who wrote the report's section covering northern Baffin Island and the northern Foxe Basin, points out that project as a whole was remarkable "for the extent to which [it] set out Inuit intellectual culture on the basis of listening to what Inuit say."[48]

INUMMARIIT ASSOCIATION, 1969

An ethos of collective, self-conscious cultural preservation has no precedent in Inuit society, nor was it deemed necessary until rapid, externally driven change began to pervade their lives.[49] As Leah Otak writes in the introduction to her book on Inuit kinship and naming customs: "When I was a child no one talked about ways to preserve customs" (Otak and Pitsiulak-Stevens 2014, 12).

An often overlooked feature of the early, formal projects aimed at Amitturmiut cultural preservation is that they were rarely "homegrown." Such endeavours typically originated through initiatives proposed by interested—though seldom by disinterested—transitory Qallunaat, be they priests, government administrators, or researchers, whose suggestions ideally resonated with community aspirations at large, but more often, and crucially, with a small number of motivated Inuit individuals personally committed to preserving aspects of their cultural heritage. Necessarily, such "institutionalized" projects were collaborative. The Qallunaat "cultural brokers" sought funding through various granting agencies and provided the required technical and administrative support, while Inuit elders and other participants enthusiastically contributed their knowledge, skills, and expertise. This symbiotic arrangement, while often productive, was inherently precarious in that such projects were liable to diminish or, in some cases, cease completely on the withdrawal or departure of the so-called cultural brokers.[50]

In Igloolik, the first collaborative Oral History Project paradoxically had its genesis in a priest's desire for atonement and reparation. Father Louis Fournier, Igloolik's resident priest at the time, had long urged his parishioners to send their children to the residential school at Chesterfield Inlet; most parents complied with the priest's wishes.[51] In time it became painfully evident that the children returning from residential school were fast losing their ability to speak nuanced Inuktitut, along with many of the aptitudes and attitudes needed for life on the land. As Louis Tapardjuk recalls, "A lot of parents were complaining; they were saying to the priest 'what have you done to our children?' Father Fournier gave [these complaints] a lot of thought and his response was to start the Inummariit Association."[52]

It was through the Inummariit Association that the Amitturmiut took the first tentative steps to record and document their traditional knowledge. Elizabeth Qulaut, who at the time was working as a clerk for the local co-operative store in Igloolik, recalls being approached by Fournier in 1969:

> He was thinking of starting an association which would be called the Inummariit Association. He explained that he was going to gather some stories, either through tapes or through written papers; he also mentioned that he was going to build a museum in Igloolik. They would ask women to make traditional clothing—and anything that has something to do with Inuit culture. He asked me if I would be interested in gathering up the stories, and then I would transcribe them and translate them into English. At that time I was working very closely with Therese Taqqaugaq. She knew a lot of traditional words that I didn't know or understand at all. So I worked [with the Inummariit]

from, I think, 1969 to 1976. This is when the Inummariit publications [the "Inummariit Series"] were produced. People just brought over papers on which their stories were written in Inuktitut syllabics. [The stories were about] anything at all—*aja-ja* songs, games—how to make clothing … anything. Some used tape recorders; they taped themselves. I did transcribing of tapes. Because Father Fournier was running the whole thing he had someone, I think, in Québec [print the publications]—these were the same publishers who published the Catholic prayer books. When I stopped in 1976 it was still going on. At that time Father Fournier had already created a retreat in Ikpik Bay [on the west coast of Foxe Basin].[53]

Not long after Fournier's departure for Ikpik Bay, publication of the Inummariit Series ended, along with its associated storytelling and knowledge collection.[54]

Through the Inummariit Association, Father Fournier also initiated and oversaw the construction of a large, concrete, igloo-shaped building with an interior circular gallery, intended to function both as a meeting place for Inummariit members and as a museum to house representative items of Amitturmiut material culture. Completed in 1972, the Igloolik Cultural Centre, as it was then known, was plagued with heating and condensation problems from the start.[55] Only a decade after its opening the building was forced to close and fell into disrepair due to financial difficulties compounded with community indifference. By the mid-1990s the structure had become derelict and was a safety hazard. In consequence, the Igloolik Hamlet Council ordered it torn down. Demolition was completed in a single day; however, before all the debris could be removed, a child playing on the site was crushed and killed by a shifting piece of concrete rubble. A tragic end to Father Fournier's efforts at atonement.

THE MIDNIGHT SUN—NIPISUILA (1969–74)

The creation of the Inummariit Association coincided with the appearance of Igloolik's first and only newspaper, *The Midnight Sun—Nipisuila*.[56] The paper, printed on a Gestetner machine, carried articles

in Inuktitut syllabics and English covering local news, public an-
nouncements, opinion pieces from readers, and occasionally items
of particular cultural significance.[57] In this category, the paper is best
known for publishing, in English translation, the verses of a drum
song composed and performed by Igloolik's François Tamnaruluk to
commemorate the visit of "Their Excellences Governor General and
Mrs. Mitchener to Igloolik" in May 1969.[58] Typical of such impromptu compositions, parts of the song are self-deprecating—the singer
doubts his skills: "The song is not too good ... Ai, Ai, Ai; The song is
sometimes mixed up ... Ai, Ai, Ai. The end is coming; we are running
out of words, Ai, Ai, Ai."

In 1980 Robin Gedalof included Tamnaruluk's song in her anthology
of Inuit writing, thereby saving it from total obscurity. She comments
that, in the old days, such songs were composed to celebrate a "special event," adding that "the visit of Queen Elizabeth's representative
to an Arctic community ... was sufficiently important to revive the
tradition" (Gedalof 1980, 48). A decade later, Tamnaruluk's song was
repurposed by an academic to make an astonishing point about re-
sistance in "post-colonial" Indigenous writing. In this recasting, the
song, far from being a vice-regal welcome, was glossed as a subtle
repudiation of the monarchy:

> What makes this a potent political statement is the refusal, built into
> the diminishing and self-parodying text, to play the part and pay the
> expected homage to the crown but instead to choose to take the stage
> and turn the occasion into a play within a play—with the power to
> expose and shock. (Arthur 1990, 32–33)

This wholly incorrect interpretation of Tamnaruluk's impromptu
song, taken out of context to serve a speculative literary point, provides an extreme example of how Inuit oral texts, when translated
and published, can easily lead to misrepresentation. The challenges
of appropriately mediating and "repurposing" translated oral history
texts frequently requires close consideration of many factors and circumstances not evident in the text itself.[59]

IGLOOLIK ORAL HISTORY PROJECT

In 1985 George Qulaut, then operations manager at the Igloolik Research Centre, convened several meetings with Igloolik elders to consider renewed approaches to oral history collection. The meetings resulted in a strong consensus on the necessity of recording and documenting Amitturmiut traditional knowledge. Subsequent discussions with elders in 1986 led to the formal start of the Igloolik Oral History Project under the auspices of the Research Centre.[60]

Work on the project began with the selection of the participants. A set of elders—men and women—were chosen by their peers for the initial interviews. Those selected had spent their formative years "on the land," were recognized as having a thorough knowledge of Amitturmiut traditions and language, and were willing and able to communicate their knowledge. The overarching aim of the project, driven by the elders' concern over the rapid erosion of Inuktitut among the younger generations, was to record the interviews in accurate

Igloolik c. 2005. The Igloolik Research Centre is the round building in the centre left of the photograph. Photo by John MacDonald

Inuktitut, with all its richness and intricate vocabulary.[61] Of all aspects of their heritage now under threat, elders took language to be the most vulnerable, pointing out that only through the proper use of Inuktitut could their culture and traditions be adequately communicated. Other major goals included recording personal and family histories as well as compiling a record of local traditional knowledge and land-based life skills. Relational naming practices (*tuqłurausiit*) and geographic place-names were singled out for special attention (Otak and Pilsiulak-Stevens 2014).

Employees of the Igloolik Research Centre (then a federal government agency) coordinated the project on behalf of the elders, assisting with a range of tasks, including fundraising and financial management.[62] They participated in many of the interview sessions, suggesting topics and structuring interview questions, providing interpretation and translation, and, after the sessions, undertaking transcription, documentation, and archiving of the interview materials. They also introduced innovative ways of eliciting in-depth knowledge from the interview process. High levels of discourse, for instance, were achieved by recording two knowledgeable elders talking or reminiscing about a specific topic. This technique often produced a rich overview of the topic under discussion, rendered in well-nuanced Inuktitut, enhanced by specialized terms and phrases no longer in general use. Over a period of some twenty-five years, Leah Otak and Louis Tapardjuk were the mainstays of this effort, bringing consistency and continuity to all aspects of the work, particularly the translation.[63] Both Leah and Louis derived deep personal satisfaction from their work with the project, reclaiming knowledge denied to them in their childhoods. "I was learning all the things I never learned," recalls Louis.

> Learning new words, and trying to understand what they really meant … I was finally able to get all the information and knowledge that was denied to us because we were sent to [residential school]. Rather than crying over spilled milk, I did something about it.[64]

AMITTURMIUT ORAL HISTORY, RESEARCHERS, AND SCIENCE

The Amitturmiut have a long history of interaction with the emissaries of Western science, dating back to their first contact with Europeans during Parry's visit in 1822. This association continued in the following century, notably with visits from Rasmussen's Fifth Thule Expedition in 1921, the British Canadian Arctic Expedition in the late 1930s, and from Meldgaard and his archaeological team in the 1950s. From the late 1960s onwards, with the community's participation in the International Biological Programme Human Adaptability Project (c. 1968–72), followed by the opening of the Igloolik Research Centre in 1975, the Amitturmiut have had practically daily interactions with visiting southern scientists.[65] Locally, the researcher could be known by various names, such as *paqulluk*, "nosy one"—or, more benignly, *qaujisarti*, "one trying to know" (Wachowich 2014, 129).

Some researchers would be given nicknames reflecting their particular interests. Thus, Tom Manning, an ornithologist and leader of the British Canadian Arctic Expedition (1936–39) became known to the Amitturmiut as Qupannuaq—"the snow bunting." Likewise, Bernard Saladin d'Anglure's irrepressible enthusiasm for shamanism earned him among some Amitturmiut the gently ironic name Angakkuunasugijuq—"he who thinks himself a shaman."

From the beginning, researchers often relied on a principal Inuit associate. Personable, locally influential, with an intuitive gift for eliciting and communicating the knowledge sought by the researcher, such associate facilitators were also essential for their liaison skills. Parry, Hall, and Rasmussen would have been far less successful without the assistance of Iligliuk, Hannah, and Awa, respectively. Notable associates in the past fifty years, for instance, have included Pacome Qulaut, Noah Piugaattuk, Rosie Iqallijuq, Inuki Kunuk, Aipilik Inuksuk, Emile Imaruittuq, Maurice Arnatsiaq, George Qulaut, Louis Tapardjuk, Paul Irngaut, Theresa Iyerak, and Leah Otak.[66]

While usually amicable on a personal level, the generalized relationship in Igloolik between the community and visiting scientists was, and remains, ambivalent. Aside from issues surrounding the relevance

Paapaq Maliki, Victor Aqatsiaq, and George Qulaut, consultants for the British Museum's *Living Arctic* exhibition (London 1987), demonstrate aspects of Inuit traditional life. Photo by *Times of London*

of their work, researchers are seen by some as exploitative, taking knowledge and information from the community without returning it. As early as 1961, Jean Malaurie was told that "scientists are building their careers on us."[67] This notion persists and was instrumental in George Qulaut's proposal, made a few years prior to the start of the Igloolik Oral History Project, to "keep the elders' stories" in the community.[68]

Such misgivings about researchers were amplified by a perceived denigration of Inuit knowledge in the face of Western science.[69] Discounted as quaint and anecdotal, Inuit views of the world were seemingly given credence only when restated through the perspectives of southern researchers. This issue was a factor in the decision to translate the project's interviews into English—the elders decided that the wider world should be made aware of first-hand accounts of Inuit traditions. The decision reflected concerns that researchers, particularly biologists, were especially dismissive of Inuit knowledge of ecology, the environment, and animal migration. From the elders' stance, professional biologists relied solely on Western science to inform their research which, in turn, often shaped—adversely, from the Inuit point of view—the government's policies and regulations on wildlife management.[70]

On one important level, the close collaboration between the community's elders and visiting researchers has been particularly fortuitous. Through the interview process, researchers, with their specific expertise, are usually able to elicit a greater breadth and depth of information on the topic at hand than might otherwise be obtained. That elders instinctively warm to the knowledgeable researcher is often evident in the richness of material gathered during the interview. In this way, notable discourses, revealing valuable aspects of contrasting knowledge systems, were recorded on an array of topics under the general rubric of oral history, including, for example, kinship, customary law, belief systems, music, European contact history, skin sewing, toolmaking, navigation, climate change, cosmology, astronomy, archaeology, and ecology.[71]

Noah Piugaattuk being interviewed for the Igloolik Oral History Project by Louis Tapardjuk, c. 1990. Photo © B. Alexander/Arcticphoto

Over the past four decades, the gradual inclusion of Inuit oral history, and by extension the participation—direct or indirect—of Inuit knowledge holders in Arctic research, is a welcome, long-overdue development. Recently, however, there's a growing concern among some in academia that the indiscriminate use of oral history and its apparent predominance over other sources of knowledge is counterproductive. Kenneth Pratt, encouraged by the use of native Alaskan oral history in historical research, nevertheless surmises that this development "has moved the research pendulum to a renewed fixation on quasi-romantic interpretations of the Indigenous past [to the detriment] of thorough historical scholarship" (Pratt 2016, 308). For her part, Béatrice Collignon (2016), while highly valuing participatory research projects, suggests that they "have become the norm, in such a way that in many North American universities and in some Inuit regions they are now considered the only acceptable form of research" (414). She characterizes the emergence of a "new type of social scientist whose work is now more that of a facilitator than a scholar or academic." Though gratified that Inuit knowledge is now "at the centre of Inuit studies," she also argues that this knowledge itself needs to be researched so that it can be better understood from an epistemological perspective (Collignon 2016, 414).[72]

A related topic is the nature of cooperation between southern researchers and Inuit knowledge holders in the production of scholarly material. Dubbed "multiple-voice accounts" by Yvon Csonka, he submits that such "hybrid" collaborations may, "to a degree that is difficult to identify, be controlled essentially by the White professional" (Csonka 2004, 17). A point well taken. He also touches on issues of authorship and cultural appropriation, which are increasingly entering the debate around the use and application of oral history.[73]

Concepts used to discuss current dynamics in Inuit society are also open to debate. The construct of "cultural loss" provides one example. Frédéric Laugrand and Jarich Oosten (2010) have pointed out that perceptions of Inuit cultural loss are often conflated with the notion that Inuit society, once in contact with Western civilization, is inevitably doomed, apt to "disappear or be absorbed" (372–373). They argue that social change is more appropriately discussed in terms of transition, adaptation, and transformation, which emphasize Inuit cultural resilience and continuity in the face of modernity.[74] Pointing to Inuit embracing Christianity, syllabic writing, and Scottish square dancing, Laugrand and Oosten (2010) see development in Inuit society over the past two hundred years as a "continuous process of enrichment, [where] Western traditions [become] part and parcel of Inuit culture" (373).[75] The particular "enrichments" cited, however, were those slowly absorbed during that lengthy, relatively stable period in Amitturmiut history occurring between initial European contact and the move into settlements. By contrast, the rapid, Rubicon-like transition from land to settlement marked, for the Amitturmiut, an immediate loss of autonomy, quickly followed by an irreversible diminishment of the authority their culture and language would have within the settlement milieu. Amitturmiut elders emphatically believe these losses are the source of the widespread social malaise experienced in their communities today.[76] When they acknowledge enrichment—and they do—it is in the material rather than in the cultural realms.

Hugh Brody and Leah Otak at the British Museum's storage rooms in Shoreditch, London, selecting items of traditional Inuit clothing for display in the museum's *Annuraaq: Arctic Clothing from Igloolik* exhibition, 2001. Photo by John MacDonald

Valid as these considerations are in the academic sphere, they have little direct bearing on the reception and use of oral history resources at the community level. Rarely removed from its original matrix, oral history here is framed more immediately and intimately with its multi-faceted connections to family, community, and the past. Inevitably, some of the interviews can invoke nostalgia or a sentimental glossing of the past, sharpened, no doubt, by "then and now" comparisons with the stresses and strains of current settlement life. Hugh Brody (2007) cautions against dismissing the "mythic representation" in such narratives:

> When Inuit speak of the power and meaning of the land or "culture," they are not slipping into some form of romantic self-deception but recognizing, rather, that "the rediscovery of knowledge about lands and heritage can be a powerful and valuable resource ... for it has to do with sense of self and place in the world." (19–20)

AMITTURMIUT ORAL HISTORY AS A RESOURCE

The oral history collection, brought together by the project and now standing at some six hundred interviews, is widely used. Highly valued by educators as a major resource for culturally relevant curricula, multimedia materials deriving from the interviews have been published and circulated throughout Nunavut and beyond.[77] Researchers, particularly those engaged in the social, biological, and environmental sciences, consult the interviews regularly. Over the past three decades, the quantity of scientific literature—in the form of journal articles, conference papers, academic theses, and monographs, much of this stemming directly or indirectly from the project's oral history archive—is unmatched in any other Nunavut community. As a direct result of their collaboration with the project and its contributors, museums, including the British Museum in London and the National Museum of the American Indian in Washington, D.C., have fundamentally reshaped the ways in which they represent and interpret Inuit culture.[78]

For all this, the project remains first and foremost a community resource for the Amitturmiut. Through the interviews, for example,

Inuit personal names and the complexity of the relationships they embody are rediscovered, as are the place-names and the linked histories of their traditional lands surrounding the settlement. Using the project's materials in the classroom, children explore with wonder and pride how their grandparents lived; young, aspiring hunters learn something about sea ice conditions, wayfinding, and survival on the land; and Inuit teachers inform themselves about language use and local history. The audiotaped interviews are cherished by family members, and elders' recordings, many of them made almost two generations ago, are played weekly over the community's FM radio station. Amitturmiut legends preserved in the project's archives have been dramatized for radio, television, and film productions.[79] Another important outcome of the project, not foreseen at the beginning, is the community's re-enacting of long-abandoned or vanishing traditions and skills, including festivities observed on the sun's return after winter darkness. The reappearance of the sun on Igloolik's horizon in mid-January marks the start of an annual celebration promoting traditional games, dress, drum dancing, throat singing, storytelling, and igloo building. In these ways, the project and its outreach programs help to reaffirm Amitturmiut identity and community solidarity.

In keeping with the intentions of the elders who first gave life to this work, the project is more about preservation than revival. Though no substitute exists for the natural processes of oral transmission which had safeguarded Amitturmiut cultural continuity prior to the move from the land, the project nevertheless leaves an accessible record, voiced in rich, flawless Inuktitut, of collective and individual family histories, of lives lived autonomously on, and through, the land, and of the knowledge and skills needed to live these lives. Such records are necessarily incomplete. Nevertheless, over many years, the project has documented sufficient information to construct a vivid and coherent account of a way of life irrevocably past.

The narratives gathered through the project invite reassessment of Amitturmiut history and traditions as represented in explorers' tomes, in traders' and missionaries' journals, in government administrative reports, and in the publications of researchers. In this way, the

Inuit games held in the Ataguttaaluk School gym during the Sun's Return festivities in 2002. Leah Otak, one of the event's principal organizers, is seen in the centre of the photograph. Photo by John MacDonald

project's cumulative interviews stand as an essential, often corrective complement to the filtered narratives of outsiders, ultimately giving the Amitturmiut a familiar voice in their own history.

In his contribution to this volume, George Qulaut relates how in the mid-1950s his grandfather, Itikuttuq, fearing a tape recorder would capture his soul, refused to be interviewed by a visiting researcher. Some fifteen years later, in 1969, Itikuttuq, by then acutely aware of the challenges confronting his community in the face of modernity, came to regret his decision. With astonishing prescience, he gave George a gift—a tape recorder—and asked him to collect the old stories and songs of his people. Itikuttuq's equating of the spoken word with the soul touched on the essential significance of heritage carried uniquely in language and storytelling. It was this apt notion—the vital role of language in sustaining culture—which motivated the Igloolik Oral History Project to capture, in Itikuttuq's axiom, at least something of the Amitturmiut soul.

BIBLIOGRAPHY

Alexander, B., and C. Alexander. 1996. *The Vanishing Arctic*. London: Blandford.

———. 2011. *Forty Below: Traditional Life in the Arctic*. Dorset: Arctic Publishing.

Anand-Wheeler, Ingrid. 2002. *Terrestrial Mammals of Nunavut*. Iqaluit: Department of Sustainable Development.

Anders, G. 1965. *Northern Foxe Basin: An Area Economic Survey*. Ottawa: Department of Northern Affairs and National Resources.

Aporta, Claudio. 2004. "Routes, Trails and Tracks: Trail Breaking among the Inuit of Igloolik." *Études/Inuit/Studies* 28, no. 2: 9–38.

———. 2016. "The Power of Maps: Inuit Land Use and Occupancy Project." In *Early Inuit Studies: Themes and Transitions, 1850s–1980s*, edited by Igor Krupnik, 354–373. Washington, D.C.: Smithsonian Institution Scholarly Press.

Appelt, Martin, Bjarne Grønnow, and Hans Christian Gulløv. 2007. "Jøgen Meldgaard 1927–2007." *Arctic* 60, no. 2: 215–216. www.jstor.org/stable /40513126.

Arthur, Kateryna Olijnyk. 1990. "Beyond Orality: Canada and Australia." *ARIEL: A Review of International English Literature* 21, no. 3: 23–38.

Bennett, John, and Susan Rowley. 2004. *Uqalurait: An Oral History of Nunavut*. Montreal and Kingston: McGill-Queen's University Press.

Boas, Franz. 1888. "The Central Eskimo." In *Bureau of American Ethnology Sixth Annual Report*, 409–669. Washington, D.C.: Bureau of American Ethnology.

Brody, Hugh. 1975. *The People's Land: Eskimos and Whites in the Eastern Arctic*. London: Penguin Books.

———. 1987. *Living Arctic: Hunters of the Canadian North*. London: Faber and Faber.

Carpenter, Edmund. 1997. "19th Century Aivilik Iglulik Drawings." In *Fifty Years of Arctic Research: Anthropological Studies from Greenland to Siberia*, edited by R. Gilberg and H.C. Gulløv, 71–92. Copenhagen: National Museum of Denmark.

Cavell, Janice. 2008. *Tracing the Connected Narrative: Arctic Exploration in British Print Culture, 1818–1860*. Toronto: University of Toronto Press.

Choque, Charles, O.M.I. 1998. *Guy Mary-Rousselière 1913–1994*. Churchill, Manitoba: R.C. Episcopal Corporation.

Collignon, Béatrice. 2016. "A Reminiscence of Transition 1992–2012." In *Early Inuit Studies: Themes and Transitions, 1850s–1980s*, edited by Igor Krupnik, 410–416. Washington, D.C.: Smithsonian Institution Scholarly Press.

Colombo, John Robert. 1981. *Poems of the Inuit*. Ottawa: Oberon Press.

Cooke, Alan, and Clive Holland. 1978. *The Exploration of Northern Canada, 500 to 1920. A Chronology*. Toronto: The Arctic History Press.

Copeland, A. Dudley. 1985. *Coplalook: Chief Trader, Hudson's Bay Company 1923–1939*. Winnipeg: Watson and Dwyer Publishing.

Crowe, Keith. 1969. *A Cultural Geography of Northern Foxe Basin, NWT*. Ottawa: Department of Indian Affairs and Northern Development. open .library.ubc.ca/cIRcle/collections/ubctheses/831/items/1.0102285.

Cruikshank, Julie. 1994. "Oral Tradition and Oral History: Reviewing Some Issues." *Canadian Historical Review* LXXV, no. 3: 403–418.

Csonka, Yvon. 2004. "New Debates and New Orientations in Inuit Ethnohistory." *Société suisse des Américanistes / Schweizerische Amerikanisten-Gesellschaft Bulletin* 68: 15–21.

Damas, David. 1963. *Iglulingmiut Kinship and Local Groupings: A Structural Approach*. Ottawa: Department of Northern Affairs and National Resources.

———. 2004. *Arctic Migrants/Arctic Villagers: The Transformation of Inuit Settlement in the Central Arctic*. Montreal and Kingston: McGill-Queen's University Press.

Eber, Dorothy. 2008. *Encounters on the Passage: Inuit Meet the Explorers*. Toronto: University of Toronto Press.

Gedalof, Robin, ed. 1980. "Ipellie, Alootook (illustrator)." In *Paper Stays Put: A Collection of Inuit Writing*. Edmonton: Hurtig.

Gilberg, Rolf, and Hans Christian Gulløv, eds. 1997. *Fifty Years of Arctic Research: Anthropological Studies from Greenland to Siberia*. Ethnographical Series, Vol. 18. Copenhagen: Department of Ethnography, National Museum of Denmark.

Gordon, Bryan C. 1994. "Father Guy Mary-Rousselière (1913–1994)." *Arctic* 47, no. 3 (September): 318.

Harper, Kenn. 2006. "Taissumani." *Nunatsiaq News Online*, August 18. www
.nunatsiaq.ca/stories/article/Taissumani_August_18_1956_Greenland
_Leaders_Visit_Baffin_Island.

———. 2013. *In Those Days: Collected Writings on Arctic History*. Inuit Lives
Book 1. Iqaluit: Inhabit Media.

Hastrup, Kirsten. 2016. "Knud Rasmussen: Explorer, Ethnographer, and
Narrator." In *Early Inuit Studies: Themes and Transitions, 1850s–1980s*,
edited by Igor Krupnik, 111–135. Washington, D.C.: Smithsonian Institution Scholarly Press.

Imaruittuq, Emile, ed. 1985. *Iliniarruminaqtuiit (Illngaruminaqtuiit)*. Igloolik:
The Igloolik Adult Education Centre.

Iqallijuq, Rosie. 1991. Interview IE-204. Igloolik Oral History Project. Igloolik.

King, J.C.H. 2014. "Masterpieces of the Mind: Dorset Miniatures from Igloolik, Nunavut." *American Indian Art Magazine* 40, no. 1: 46–55.

King, J.C.H., and Henrietta Lidchi, eds. 1998. *Imaging the Arctic*. London:
The British Museum Press.

King, J.C.H., Birgit Pauksztat, and Robert Storrie, eds. 2005. *Arctic Clothing*.
London: The British Museum Press.

Laugrand, Frédéric B., and Jarich G. Oosten, eds. 2009. *Ethnographic Recordings of Inuit Oral Traditions by Father Guy Mary-Rousselière (OMI)*.
Iqaluit: Nunavut Arctic College.

———. 2010. *Inuit Shamanism and Christianity: Transitions and Transformations in the Twentieth Century*. Montreal and Kingston: McGill-Queen's
University Press.

MacDonald, John. 2000. *The Arctic Sky: Inuit Astronomy, Star Lore, and Legend*. Toronto: Royal Ontario Museum/Nunavut Research Institute.

———. 2001. "Igloolik Clothing on Display at New British Museum Exhibit."
Nunatsiaq News Online, March 2. www.nunatsiaqonline.ca/stories/article
_print/18213.

———. 2004. "Graham Westbrook Rowley (1912–2003)." *Arctic* 57, no. 2
(June): 223–224.

———. 2012. "Iglulingmiut and the Royal Navy: Narratives and their After-
math." In *Linguistic and Cultural Encounters in the Arctic: Essays in Memory
of Susan Sammons*, edited by Louis-Jacques Dorais and Frédéric Laugrand,

143–151. *Les Cahiers du CIÉRA* (supplementary issue October 2012). Laval: Centre interuniversitaire d'études et de recherches autochtones.

Malaurie, Jean. 1982. *The Last Kings of Thule*. New York: E.P. Dutton.

———. 2001. *Call of the North: An Explorer's Journey to the North Pole*. New York: Harry N. Abrams.

Mallory, Carolyn, and Susan Aiken. 2004. *Common Plants of Nunavut*. Iqaluit: Nunavut Department of Education.

Mary-Rousselière, Guy. 1955. "The Tunit According to Igloolik Traditions." *Eskimo* 35: 14 19.

———. 1984. "Iglulik." In *Handbook of North American Indians*, Vol. 5: *The Arctic*, 431–446.

Mathiassen, T. 1928. *Material Culture of the Iglulik Eskimos. Report of the Fifth Thule Expedition*, Vol. 6, no. 1. Copenhagen: Gyldendalske Boghandel, Nordisk Forlag.

Meldgaard, Jørgen. 1960. *Eskimo Sculpture*. London: Methuen.

Morice, A.G. 1943. *Thawing Out the Eskimo*. Boston: The Society for the Propagation of the Faith.

Niviatttian, Susanne Akatsiaq. 1990. Interview IE-130. Igloolik Oral History Project. Igloolik.

Nourse, J.E. 1879. *Narration of the Second Arctic Expedition made by Charles F. Hall [1864–69]*. Washington, D.C.: U.S. Naval Observatory.

Nunavut Department of Education. 2016. *Nunavut Approved Curriculum and Teaching Resources (2015–2016)*. Iqaluit: Nunavut Department of Education. www.gov.nu.ca/sites/default/files/nu_cur_guide_2015-2016_final.pdf.

Otak, Leah Aksaajuq. 2005. "Iniqsimajuq." In *Arctic Clothing*, edited by J.C.H. King, Birgit Pauksztat, and Robert Storrie, 74–79. London: The British Museum Press.

Otak, Leah Aksaajuq, and Peesee Pitsiulak-Stevens, eds. 2014. *Inuit Kinship and Naming Customs (Baffin Region)*. Iqaluit: Nunavut Arctic College.

Paniaq, Hervé. 1990. Interview IE-141. Igloolik Oral History Project. Igloolik.

Parry, William Edward. 1824. *Journal of a Voyage for the Discovery of a North-west Passage from the Atlantic to the Pacific: Performed in the Years 1821-22-23, in His Majesty's Ships Fury and Hecla, under the Orders of Captain William Edward Parry, R.N., F.R.S., and Commander to the Expedition*. London: John Murray.

Pharand, Sylvie. 2012. *Caribou Skin Clothing of the Igloolik Inuit.* Iqaluit: Inhabit Media.

Picco, Ed. 1993. "Hall Beach (Sanijraajaq)." In *The Baffin Handbook*, edited by W. Richard Hamilton, 248–253. Iqaluit: Nortext.

Piugaattuk, Noah. 1986. Interview IE-064. Igloolik Oral History Project. Igloolik.

———. 1993. Interview IE-248. Igloolik Oral History Project. Igloolik.

Pratt, Kenneth, L. 2016. "A Retrospective on the Development and Practice of Alaskan Eskimo Ethnohistory, 1940–1985." In *Early Inuit Studies: Themes and Transitions, 1850s–1980s*, edited by Igor Krupnik, 289–321. Washington, D.C.: Smithsonian Institution Scholarly Press.

Qamaniq, Nathan. 2002. Interview IE-496. Igloolik Oral History Archive. Igloolik.

Qikiqtani Truth Commission. 2014. *Community Histories 1950–1975.* Iqaluit: Qikiqtani Inuit Association. See also: www.qtcommission.ca/en/reports /communities

Qulaut, George. 1997. "A Birthday Tribute." In *Fifty Years of Arctic Research: Anthropological Studies from Greenland to Siberia*, edited by Rolf Gilberg and Hans Christian Gulløv, 9. Ethnographical Series, vol. 18. Copenhagen: Department of Ethnography, National Museum of Denmark.

Rae, John. 1850. *Narrative of an Expedition to the Shores of the Arctic Sea, in 1864 and 1847.* London: T. and W. Boone.

Rankin, Sharon. 2011. *A Bibliography of Canadian Inuit Periodicals.* Quebec City: Presses Université du Québec.

Rasing, Willem, C.E. 2010. "Review of Étienne Bazin, Oblat de Marie Immaculée: Pionnier des Missions en Pays Inuit by Bazin, Eric, Charles, Gabriel, Hervé, and Jean-Francois. Editions Clea, 89. Dijon, 2008." *Études/Inuit/Studies* 34, no. 1: 167–170.

———. 2017. *Too Many People: Order and Nonconformity in Iglulingmiut Social Processes.* Iqaluit: Nunavut Arctic College Media.

Rasmussen, Knud. 1927. *Across Arctic America. Narrative of the Fifth Thule Expedition.* New York: G.P. Putnam's Sons.

———. 1929. *Intellectual Culture of the Iglulik Eskimos. Report of the Fifth Thule Expedition 1921–24*, Vol. VII, no. 2. Copenhagen: Nordisk Forlag.

————. 1976. *Iglulik and Caribou Eskimo Texts*. New York: AMS Press.

Richard, Pierre. 2001. *Marine Mammals of Nunavut*. Iqaluit: Qikiqtani School Operations.

Rowley, Graham W. 1940. "The Dorset Culture of the Eastern Arctic." *American Anthropologist* XLII (January–March): 490–499.

————. 2007. *Cold Comfort: My Love Affair with the Arctic*. McGill-Queen's Native and Northern Series. Montreal and Kingston: McGill-Queen's University Press.

Rowley, Graham, and Susan Rowley. 1997. "Igloolik Island Before and After Jørgen Meldgaard." In *Fifty Years of Arctic Research: Anthropological Studies from Greenland to Siberia*, edited by R. Gilberg and H.C. Gulløv, 269–276. Copenhagen: Department of Ethnography, National Museum of Denmark.

Saint-Pierre, Marjolaine. 2009. *Joseph-Elzéar Bernier: Champion of Canadian Arctic Sovereignty*. Translated by William Barr. Montreal: Baraka Books.

Saladin d'Anglure, Bernard. 1990. "Frère-lune (Taqqiq), soeur-soleil (Siqiniq) et l'intelligence du Monde (Sila). Cosmologie inuit, cosmographie arctique et espace-temps chamanique." *Études/Inuit/Studies* 14, no 1-2: 75–139.

Schultz-Lorentzen, Finn. 1976. *Arctic*. Toronto: McClelland and Stewart.

Semeniuk, Robert. 2007. *Among the Inuit*. Vancouver: Raincoast Books.

Stern, Pamela R., and Lisa Stevenson, eds. 2006. *Critical Inuit Studies: An Anthology of Contemporary Arctic Ethnography*. Lincoln, Nebraska: University of Nebraska Press.

Thisted, Kirsten. 2010. "Voicing the Arctic: Knud Rasmussen and the Ambivalence of Cultural Translation." In *Arctic Discourses*, edited by Anka Ryall, Johan Schimanski, and Henning Howlid Wærp, 59–81. Cambridge: Cambridge Scholars Publishing.

Trébaol, Jean-Pierre (compiler). 1958. *Liber Animorum* of St. Étienne Mission, Igloolik. [English translation 1985].

Tremblay, Alfred. 1921. *Cruise of the Minnie Maud: Arctic Seas and Hudson Bay, 1910–11 and 1912–13*. Quebec City: The Arctic Exchange and Publishing Limited.

Ukkumaaluk, William. 2009. "Ataguttaaluk." In *The Ethnographic Recordings of Inuit Oral Traditions by Father Guy Mary-Rousselière (OMI)*, edited by F. Laugrand and J.G. Oosten, 110–111. Iqaluit: Nunavut Arctic College.

Usher, Peter. 1970. *Fur Trade Posts of the Northwest Territories 1870–1970.* Ottawa: Department of Indian Affairs and Northern Development.

———. 1971. *Fur Trade Posts of the Northwest Territories, 1870–1970.* Ottawa: Department of Indian Affairs and Northern Development.

Wachowich, Nancy. 2001. *Saqiyuq: Stories from the Lives of Three Inuit Women.* Montreal and Kingston: McGill-Queen's University Press.

———. 2006. "Cultural Survival and the Trade in Igloolik Traditions." In *Critical Inuit Studies: An Anthology of Contemporary Arctic Ethnography*, edited by Pamela R. Stern and Lisa Stevenson, 119–138. Lincoln, Nebraska: University of Nebraska Press.

———. 2014. "Stitching Lives: A Family History of Making Caribou Skin Clothing in the Canadian Arctic." In *Making and Growing: Anthropological Studies of Organisms and Artefacts*, edited by E. Hallam and T. Ingold, 206–228. Farnham: Ashgate (Anthropological Studies of Creativity and Perception).

CHAPTER 3

Restoring an Ancestral Legacy

Museum Collections, Inuit Clothing,
and Communities

Bernadette Driscoll Engelstad

By the early 20th century, museums in Europe and North America had gained prominence as important research institutions and centres for public education. From London, Berlin, and Copenhagen to Washington, New York, and Ottawa, museum collections reflected an era of global exploration with a focus on natural history and the rich diversity of human cultures. For many museums, the Arctic had become an area of special interest. Through the collecting efforts of explorers, traders, whalers, and missionaries—as well as scientific expeditions—institutions acquired extensive collections of Inuit material culture, including animal fur and skin clothing worn by Inuit across the Arctic. As a result, caribou fur, sealskin, gutskin, and bird-skin clothing—the work of ancestral hands—was on prominent display and preserved in museum storerooms throughout Europe and North America.

Until recently, detailed information on these collections was confined mainly to museum records, expedition reports, and ethnographic publications. Over the past thirty years, however, major museum exhibitions, often accompanied by well-documented catalogues, and research projects (many initiated in the North) have focused greater attention on the design, production, and cultural significance of Arctic fur clothing. Furthermore, research involving fieldwork with Inuit elders and seamstresses has radically reshaped the utilitarian perspective that once described Arctic fur clothing, providing deeper insight into the metaphoric, symbolic, and cosmological features incorporated in its ancestral design.[1]

In 2001, the British Museum presented the exhibition *Annuraaq: Arctic Clothing from Igloolik.* During a research visit to Igloolik, Leah Aksaajuq Otak worked closely with British Museum curator Jonathan King to prepare for the exhibit. In May 2001, the British Museum hosted a seminal conference on Arctic clothing, bringing together Inuit and Yup'ik seamstresses, clothing designers, and representatives of native cultural organizations from Alaska, the Canadian Arctic, and Greenland, along with museum curators, independent scholars, and students from design schools across the United Kingdom. The keynote address, "Our Clothing, Our Culture, Our Identity," by Veronica Dewar, then president of the Pauktuutit Inuit Women's Association, focused on women's cultural production, emphasizing the need to protect Inuit clothing traditions, particularly the *amautik,* from misappropriation by Western commercial interests (Dewar 2005). Together with Leah Otak's paper, "Iniqsimajuq: Caribou-skin Preparation in Igloolik, Nunavut," Inuit, Yup'ik, and Greenlandic speakers—Rhoda Akpaliapik Karetak, Elena Charles, Chuna McIntyre, and Dixie Masak Dayo, among others—discussed regional variations in clothing traditions and the cultural ideology richly embedded in Arctic clothing design. Directly and indirectly, presenters described the emotional investment and personal satisfaction found in producing clothing for oneself and for family members.[2] Their published essays

complement the historic ethnographies of the 19th and early 20th cen-
turies, as well as more recent exhibitions and monographs—notably
Caribou Skin Clothing of the Igloolik Inuit (Pharand 2012, 1975a,b);
The Inuit Amautik: I Like My Hood to Be Full (Driscoll 1980); *Copper
and Caribou Inuit Skin Clothing Production* (Oakes 1991); *Sanutujut:
Pride in Women's Work: Copper and Caribou Inuit Clothing Traditions*
(Hall, Oakes, and Webster 1994); *Our Boots: An Inuit Woman's Art*
(Oakes and Riewe 1995); and *Sinews of Survival: The Living Legacy of
Inuit Clothing* (Issenman 1997)—which have renewed scholarly and
community interest in Arctic clothing design.[3]

Building on the foundation of the *Annuraaq* conference, this chapter describes museum collections of historical Inuit fur clothing and
curatorial practices that facilitate access to these collections through
exhibitions, publications, collection visits, and online access to digital
databases for community research. In the publication *Yup'ik Elders
at the Ethnologisches Museum Berlin: Fieldwork Turned on Its Head*,
Ann Fienup-Riordan recounts the September 1997 visit of a Yup'ik
research team to study historical artifacts brought from Alaska to Berlin by Johan Adrian Jacobsen in the 1880s (Figure 1). Describing their
visit as a form of visual repatriation, Fienup-Riordan (2005, 280–289)
recalls that the physical handling of objects—"Things of our Ancestors"—evoked a visceral response from team members, generating a
wellspring of personal experiences, songs, stories, and long-forgotten
memories associated with these historic objects. As a complement to
on-site visits, digital technology enables researchers across the North
to access distant museum collections. In the fifteen years since the
Annuraaq conference, digital technology—along with institutional
efforts to enhance this technology—has transformed access to museum collections, extending the research and educational function
of the museum beyond its physical location, and thereby restoring
community knowledge of these historic collections.[4]

INUIT FUR CLOTHING IN MUSEUM COLLECTIONS

Throughout the early period of Arctic exploration, sealskin, caribou
fur, and gutskin clothing collected by European explorers served as

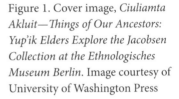

Figure 1. Cover image, *Ciuliamta Akluit—Things of Our Ancestors: Yup'ik Elders Explore the Jacobsen Collection at the Ethnologisches Museum Berlin*. Image courtesy of University of Washington Press

proof of an expedition's contact with native peoples. Objects made by Inuit found their way into private collections belonging to European nobility, Admiralty officers, wealthy merchants, whalers, and missionaries. Many of these collections, directly or through family descendants, eventually came into museum collections. Founded in 1753, the British Museum is regarded as the first national public museum, open free to "all studious and curious Persons."[5] The nucleus of the museum's Arctic collection, presented by John Barrow of the British Admiralty, features objects procured by officers of the Royal Navy while in search of the Northwest Passage. This collection was later augmented by items acquired during the search for survivors of the Franklin expedition (c. 1848–59). An important acquisition from this period includes the Inuinnait (Copper Inuit) woman's caribou fur ensemble collected by Captain Richard Collinson in the 1850s (Figure 2). Two of the drawings by Edward Adams, assistant surgeon on Collinson's ship, the H.M.S. *Enterprise*, preserved at the Scott Polar Research Institute, Cambridge University, provide "the first visual record of the Copper Inuit of northwestern Victoria Island" (Condon

1996, 24). Almost fifty years later, British adventurer David Hanbury (c. 1900) presented the British Museum with an exquisite dance cap crowned with a loon's beak, worn exclusively in the Inuinnait region. Fur trader Joseph F. Bernard acquired an extensive collection of Inuinnait clothing and cultural objects (c. 1910–16). Initially donated to Loyola College of Montreal (and later destroyed by fire), a portion of this collection was presented to the Museum of Archaeology and Anthropology at Cambridge University (see Hall 2005), while a smaller collection acquired by Bernard was purchased by the University of Pennsylvania Museum of Archaeology and Anthropology. In addition to Inuit cultural objects preserved in other British museums (see King, this volume), the National Museum of Scotland also benefited from the early collecting of Captain William Edward Parry (1820s) and Hudson Bay Company (HBC) staff, including Dr. John Rae (1850s) and Roderick MacFarlane (1860s), many of whom originated from the Shetland and Orkney Islands (Lindsay 1993).

Figure 2. Exhibition announcement, John Barrow Collection at the Royal Polytechnic Institute. The original caption identifies the figure on the left as female and the figure on the right as male. *London Illustrated News*, July 14, 1855. Image courtesy of Russell Potter

The museum movement in Great Britain spurred its development in North America through the unexpected bequest of British geologist James Smithson. In the absence of a family heir, Smithson (of noble, if unacknowledged, lineage) entrusted his fortune to the United States of America with the purpose of establishing an institute for the "increase and diffusion of knowledge" (Ewing 2007). Established in 1846 by an Act of the U.S. Congress, the Smithsonian Institution today encompasses nineteen museums, research centres, and the National Zoo in Washington, D.C. Declaring the Arctic to be "of no ordinary importance," the Smithsonian's first Secretary, Joseph Henry, supported the collecting efforts of Robert Kennicott (1859–62; 1865–66) and William J. Fisher in Alaska, as well as the HBC factor Roderick R. MacFarlane in the Canadian Arctic (Fitzhugh 2009). Brought together in the 1860s, the MacFarlane collection preserves the cultural legacy of Inuvialuit families from the Mackenzie Delta region, many of whose descendants perished in devastating epidemics during the late 19th and early 20th centuries (Alunik, Kolausok, and Morrison 2003; Lyons 2010; Métayer 1966).

Following the U.S. acquisition of the Alaska territory in 1867, the Smithsonian's Arctic holdings grew rapidly through the fieldwork of William H. Dall (1865–85) in western Alaska and the Aleutians; Lucien M. Turner (1871–77) in St. Michael, Alaska, as well as in the Aleutians (1877–78); Edward W. Nelson (1877–81) in the Yukon, Kuskokwim, and Bering Strait regions; and Lt. Patrick Henry Ray, John Murdoch, and E.P. Herendeen in northern Alaska (for a detailed history, see Fitzhugh 2009). In addition to fieldwork in Alaska, Lucien Turner collected extensively among Inuit and Innu families in the Ungava region of northern Labrador, expanding the depth and geographic scope of the Smithsonian's Arctic collections (Turner [1894] 2001).

The historic collections of Inuit fur clothing at the American Museum of Natural History (AMNH) in New York City form a vital counterpart to the Smithsonian collections from Alaska, Labrador, and the central Canadian Arctic. Established in 1869, the Museum's Arctic collections were brought together primarily by Lt. Robert Peary (north Greenland); James Mutch (east Baffin Island); Captain George Comer (west coast of Hudson Bay, Southampton Island, Greenland); and Vilhjalmur Stefansson (northern Alaska and western Canadian Arctic). Appointed Assistant Curator in the Museum's Ethnology

Division in 1896, Franz Boas had carried out his own doctoral fieldwork on Baffin Island in 1883–84 (Freed 2012). Often referred to as the "Father of American Anthropology," Boas continued his ethnographic interest in the Arctic by recruiting James Mutch, manager of the Scottish whaling station at Cumberland Sound, and the New England whaling captain George Comer to serve as surrogate fieldworkers, collecting material culture and recording oral traditions and cultural practices. Captain Comer collected over three thousand Inuit ethnographic artifacts as well as archaeological specimens for the museum during his voyages to the Canadian Arctic and Greenland. An avid photographer, Comer also produced over three hundred photographs and sixty sound recordings of Inuit songs, as well as creating a remarkable collection of plaster facial casts—portrait casts of more than two hundred Inuit who gathered to work or travelled to trade at the American whaling station at Cape Fullerton/Qatiktalik (Calabretta 1984, 2008a, b; Engelstad and Calabretta 2014; Harper 2008, 2016; Ross 1975, 1984a, b; Saladin d'Anglure 1984).

With financial support from the National Endowment for the Humanities, the AMNH has produced a remarkable database of its North American Native collections, which provides access to artifact images and ethnographic data by region, culture, object type, catalogue number, material, and collector/donor. In addition, researchers can assemble personal portfolios of images for comparative study. Software functions provide multiple views of numerous artifacts and allow the viewer to examine details of material, construction, and decoration with enlargement, zoom, and rollover features. Almost twenty-three hundred artifacts from the Comer collection appear on the museum's online database, including caribou fur garments, domestic tools, and hunting equipment from Inuit groups along the west coast of Hudson Bay, as well as sealskin garments and cultural objects from Inuit collected on Baffin Island and Southampton Island.[6] In 1908, AMNH sponsored the Stefansson-Anderson Arctic Expedition under the direction of Vilhjalmur Stefansson and zoologist Dr. Rudolph M. Anderson. Their four-year journey (1908–12) among Inuit groups in northern Alaska, the Mackenzie Delta, and coastal regions of the central

Canadian Arctic, including Victoria Island—an isolated region that had had only sparse, intermittent contact with Europeans—made a significant contribution to the museum's expanding Arctic collections (Stefansson 1914).

Brought together primarily by Peary, Comer, and Mutch in the eastern Arctic and Stefansson in the Mackenzie Delta and central Canadian Arctic, the Arctic collections of the AMNH provide a meaningful extension of the museum's Jesup North Pacific Expedition (1897–1902), a monumental endeavour directed by Franz Boas to compare the languages, social customs, and ethnography of Siberian and Alaskan peoples in an effort to understand the prehistoric migration of Arctic peoples from Asia to North America. Boas's oversight of the ethnographic work of George Comer and James Mutch in the eastern Arctic—as well as the museum's role in supporting the Peary and Stefansson-Anderson expeditions—extends the circumpolar reach of the Jesup North Pacific Expedition across the expanse of the North American Arctic.[7]

Capitalizing on its supporting role in the Stefansson-Anderson Arctic Expedition, the Geological Survey of Canada organized the Canadian Arctic Expedition (1913–18), to be carried out under the joint leadership of Stefansson and R.M. Anderson, with the purpose of undertaking a more extensive program of geographic exploration and scientific research in the more remote area of the central Canadian Arctic. With the loss of the expedition's flagship, the *Karluk,* resulting in the tragic deaths of several crew members and scientists, personal differences between Anderson and Stefansson intensified. Consequently, the expedition split into separate northern and southern parties, with Stefansson undertaking geographic exploration and Anderson supervising the scientific research of the southern party. With the death of French ethnographer Henri Beuchat—a colleague of Marcel Mauss—during the loss of the *Karluk,* the young Oxford-trained anthropologist Diamond Jenness became responsible for carrying out the ethnographic work of the expedition (Jenness 1921, 1928, 1946; S. Jenness 2011; Morrison and Germain 1995).

From the station base of the southern party at Bernard Harbour, Jenness spent several months in the company of an Inuinnait couple, Ikpakhuak and Higilak, on Victoria Island. Although only a small number of clothing items are illustrated in his published report (1946), Jenness amassed a remarkably extensive collection of Inuinnait men's, women's, and children's parkas, trousers, and kamiks, including dance garments and shamanistic clothing, preserved in the collection of the Canadian Museum of History. The catalogue of the 1994 exhibition *Sanutujut: Pride in Women's Work*, organized by curator Judy Hall, provides an in-depth survey of historical Inuit clothing from the Kitikmeot and Kivalliq regions of Nunavut in Canada's central Arctic (Hall et al. 1994). In preparation for the exhibition, Hall worked closely with Inuit seamstress Lizzie Ittinuar (Arviat, Nunavut) and the Inuinnait research team of Elsie Nilgak, Alice Omingmak, and Julia Ogina of Ulukhaktok, Northwest Territories, during study visits to Ottawa—an early initiative in reconnecting Inuit researchers and communities with the ancestral artifacts in the collection of the Canadian Museum of History (Figure 3).

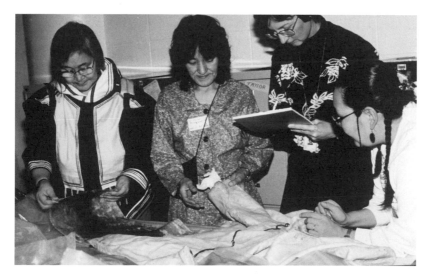

Figure 3. Inuinnait Research Team from Ulukhaktok, NWT. From left to right: Elsie Nilgak, Alice Omingmak, Judy Hall (curator), and Julia Ogina at the Canadian Museum of Civilization (now Canadian Museum of History). Fall 1992. Photo by B.D. Engelstad

The Netsilingmiut clothing collection at the University of Oslo's Museum of Cultural History extends knowledge of Inuit clothing design across the central Canadian Arctic. Brought together by the Roald Amundsen expedition (1903–05) while overwintering at Gjoa Haven on King William Island, the collection is well described in the 1974 monograph by J. Garth Taylor (unfortunately, out of print). Through a recent collaboration with the community of Gjoa Haven, the Oslo Museum arranged to transfer sixteen artifacts from the Amundsen collection for display in the newly opened Nattilik Heritage Centre. As curator emeritus Tom G. Svensson writes,

> The intention of this symbolic act is mainly to contribute to the cultural history of the Netsilik as reflected in their material expressions … 16 artifacts may not appear as an impressive number, on the other hand, the entire collection is now about to be accessible on our data-base, which means new channels for exchange of information regarding the total Amundsen collection will hereby be created. This can be viewed as an extension of the repatriation as such, and, we believe, will be advantageous for both parties. (Svensson 2014)

Figure 4. Netsilingmiut man's parka, caribou fur, UEM 15779, Amundsen Expedition, 1903–1905. Gjoa Haven/ Uqsuqtuuq, Nunavut, 1903–05. © Museum of Cultural History, University of Oslo, Norway. Photo by Adnan Icagic, courtesy of the Museum of Cultural History, University of Oslo

The museum's database, now accessible in Norwegian, Inuktitut, English, and French, features well-sized photographs and detailed documentation for over nine hundred artifacts from the Netsilingmiut collection (Figure 4).[8]

The Danish Fifth Thule Expedition (1921–24), undertaken by Knud Rasmussen, Kaj Birket-Smith, Therkel Mathiassen, and Greenland Inuit Arnalulunguak and Qavigarssuaq (Miteq), brought together an exceptional collection of Inuit songs, social customs, fur clothing, domestic tools, and hunting equipment, as well as the first systematically excavated archaeological collection of the Thule culture in the Canadian Arctic. Richly illustrated in the expedition's published reports, the ethnographic collection of the Fifth Thule Expedition is preserved in the National Museum of Denmark (Birket-Smith 1945; Mathiassen 1927; Rasmussen [1929] 1976, [1930] 1976, [1931] 1976, [1932] 1976). The museum collection in Copenhagen provides an outstanding survey of Arctic fur clothing, material heritage, and spiritual culture from Arctic Canada and Greenland (Figure 5). In

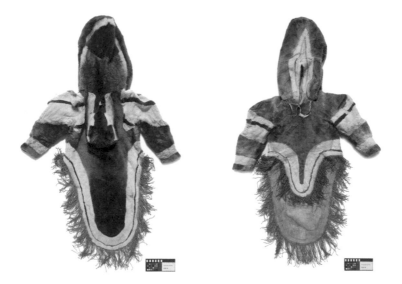

Figure 5. Netsilingmiut woman's parka (front and back), caribou fur, P29.10, Fifth Thule Expedition, 1921–24. National Museum of Denmark. Photograph by Roberto Fortuna, courtesy of the National Museum of Denmark

addition, a sophisticated online database provides high-resolution images of Arctic clothing that can be viewed in the round, along with a close-up function that provides excellent detail of material and production techniques.[9]

The ratification of the Greenland Home Rule Act in 1979 initiated a series of discussions regarding the return of Greenlandic cultural material from Denmark (Jakobsen 2010; Thorleifsen 2010), resulting in the decision to divide the Gustav Holm collection, acquired in East Greenland in the 1880s, between the National Museum of Denmark and the National Museum of Greenland in Nuuk.[10] Following a comprehensive exhibit of the Holm collection in Copenhagen in 1985, 235 of the 464 objects were transferred to the National Museum in Nuuk (Nuttall 2004, 871). To date, more than 28,000 archaeological artifacts and 1,158 ethnographic artifacts have been returned to Greenland. As Daniel Thorleifsen (2010, 87), former director of the Greenland National Museum and Archives, writes, "Repatriation is inextricably bound with the restoration of cultural pride and identity." Furthermore, as curator Aviaja Rosing Jakobsen (2010, 76) notes,

> In many ways foreign researchers and early scientists overlooked or misunderstood the Indigenous concepts of *Inua* and *Sila*, the Inuit holistic point of view. The tangible part of the cultural heritage is mostly described, however there is a gap in information relating to the immaterial part of the cultural heritage. Since the Inuit Institute, now Ilismatusarfik (University of Greenland) was founded in the early 1980s, new Greenlandic scientists have been educated. It is now their responsibility to develop new theories and methods for the study of the spiritual culture and immaterial cultural heritage of Greenland.

BEYOND THE MUSEUM STOREROOM: RESEARCH, EXHIBITS, AND PUBLICATIONS

Throughout the 1980s and 1990s, academic research, museum exhibits, illustrated catalogues, and publications began to focus more fully on Inuit clothing design. The exhibition *The Inuit Amautik: I Like My Hood to Be Full,* presented at the Winnipeg Art Gallery in 1980, linked the maternal design of the woman's parka (*amautik*) with the portrayal of maternal themes in sculpture and graphic art by contemporary Inuit artists (Figure 6). Inuit clothing specialists Annie Napayok (Whale Cove, Nunavut) and Charlotte St. John (Arviat, Nunavut) directed sewing workshops in conjunction with the exhibition. Each took part in subsequent projects associated with the *Amautik* exhibit,[11] including an overseas exhibition in 1985 and collection visits to the Manitoba Museum of Man and Nature, the Royal Ontario Museum, and the National Museum of Man (now the Canadian Museum of History) in 1987. Sharing photographs from this research with delegates at the Annual General Meeting of the Pauktuutit Inuit Women's Association in Taloyoak, Annie Napayok reported that delegates were surprised to discover that historical Inuit fur clothing was preserved in museum storerooms across Canada and beyond (Engelstad 2010).

Figure 6. Exhibition installation, *The Inuit Amautik: I Like My Hood to Be Full*, Winnipeg Art Gallery, August 9–October 26, 1980. Photo by Ernest Mayer, courtesy of the Winnipeg Art Gallery

In 1983, the Glenbow Museum began to organize the exhibition *The Spirit Sings: Artistic Traditions of Canada's First Peoples* as the cultural centrepiece of the 1988 Winter Olympics in Calgary, Alberta. At a time when most museum artifacts were only accessible via ethnographic reports and handwritten ledgers, the curatorial committee researched museum collections across North America, Europe, and the former Soviet Union, selecting over 650 cultural objects that had been long removed from First Nation and Inuit communities.[12] The two-volume, fully illustrated catalogue for *The Spirit Sings* exhibition provided a significant resource for community research as well as early academic courses in Native Studies in university curricula. The protest by the Lubicon Lake Cree First Nation against Shell Oil, the exhibit's corporate sponsor, called for museums to refuse loans to the exhibition, bringing international attention to the exploitation of energy reserves on Indigenous lands (Phillips 2011). Simultaneously, the exhibit *Living Arctic* at the Museum of Mankind in London, sponsored by Indigenous Survival International, focused attention on the economic distress experienced by Inuit hunters across the North due to the import ban on sealskin products by the European Union (Brody 1987). In response to the call for a stronger Indigenous voice in national and international affairs, the conference "Preserving Our Heritage," organized by the Canadian Museums Association and the Canadian Museum of Civilization in association with the Assembly of First Nations, was convened in November 1988.[13] As a result of this conference, the Task Force on Museums and First Peoples was formed to examine a range of issues regarding the relationship between First Nations and the museum community. The final report of the Task Force, released in 1992, transformed museum policy across Canada.[14] Similarly, the passage of the Native American Graves Protection and Repatriation Act (NAGPRA) by the U.S. Congress in 1990 established legislative guidelines governing the return of human remains, burial goods, and spiritual objects to Indigenous communities across the United States from museums and institutions receiving federal funding. In particular, NAGPRA legislation has led to important collaborations between native groups in Alaska and the Smithsonian Institution, developing innovative programs in educational outreach and collection-based research.

Beginning in the 1980s, the Smithsonian Institution launched an exceptional program of Arctic exhibitions, publications, and projects. In 1982, *Inua: Spirit World of the Bering Sea Eskimo*, organized by William Fitzhugh and Susan Kaplan (now director of the Peary-Macmillan Arctic Museum), highlighted the Alaskan collection of Edward Nelson, in storage at the Smithsonian for over one hundred years. As well, in 1984, the *Handbook of North American Indians* released the Arctic volume, edited by David Damas, featuring an encyclopedic collection of archaeological and ethnographic essays by noted Arctic anthropologists. In a historic collaboration with the Museum of Anthropology and Ethnography in Saint Petersburg (then Leningrad), the Smithsonian Institution, along with the American Museum of Natural History and the Canadian Museum of Civilization (now the Canadian Museum of History), organized the 1988 exhibition *Crossroads of Continents: Cultures of Siberia and Alaska*. Co-authored by William Fitzhugh and Aron Crowell, the exhibit catalogue features over four hundred artifacts, maps, and historic illustrations documenting the cultural heritage of Yup'ik, Inupiat, Athapaskan, and Tlingit communities in Alaska, and of Koryak, Chukchi, Even, Evenk, and Yakut peoples in northeastern Siberia. An insightful essay by Valérie Chaussonnet, "Needles and Amulets: Women's Magic," describes patterns and design features of caribou fur and animal skin clothing across the region, emphasizing the symbolic aspects of pan-Arctic clothing design. In the tradition of circulating the *Inua* exhibit (Rowley 1988), smaller versions of the *Crossroads of Continents* exhibit were presented in communities in Alaska (Chaussonnet 1995) and Siberia (Krupnik 1996). In 1988, the Smithsonian's Arctic interests culminated in the creation of the Arctic Studies Center (ASC) under the direction of archaeologist William Fitzhugh. In addition to research, exhibits, and publications, the ASC maintains a prominent web presence with digital access to virtual exhibitions, research summaries, and publications.[15] The online database for the Arctic collections is regularly updated with catalogue documentation and photographs of individual artifacts.[16]

In a landmark effort to make the Smithsonian's Alaskan collections accessible to native communities, educators, students, and residents in Alaska, the ASC partnered with the Anchorage Museum of History and Art, opening a regional curatorial office under the direction of anthropologist Dr. Aron Crowell in 1994. The inaugural exhibition, *Living Our Culture/Sharing Our Heritage: The First Peoples of Alaska*, featuring over six hundred objects of Yup'ik, Inupiat, Athapaskan, Unangax, and Tlingit origin from the Smithsonian's National Museum of Natural History and National Museum of the American Indian collections, opened in 2010. Online access to digital images of artifacts, along with updated catalogue documentation, often with Indigenous terminology and commentary by native specialists discussing the material, production, use, history, and cultural significance of individual artifacts, enrich the exhibition.[17] Video recordings documenting production workshops on a variety of topics, including the production of bentwood hats as well as preparing and sewing gutskin and creating decorative quillwork, are accessible on the ASC website.[18]

The Smithsonian's National Museum of the American Indian (NMAI) holds a broad mandate that encompasses the cultural legacy of Indigenous peoples throughout the western hemisphere. The NMAI has presented several Arctic exhibitions, including the work of contemporary Inuit artists Abraham Anghik Ruben and Annie Pootoogook with solo exhibitions at the Museum's main building in Washington, D.C., and the George Gustav Heye Center in New York City. The NMAI, as well as the Smithsonian's Arctic Studies Center in Washington, D.C., and Anchorage, also offer opportunities for community research, internships, and educational outreach. The NMAI exhibition *Infinity of Nations: Art and History in the Collections of the National Museum of the American Indian*, at the Heye Center in New York City, presents a broad selection of historic fur clothing by Inuit and Yup'ik seamstresses, including a beautifully decorated beaded parka from Nunavut. In an accompanying video program, Bernadette

Miqqusaaq Dean (2010b; Rankin Inlet, Nunavut) discusses the art of Inuit beadwork and challenges faced by Inuit during the whaling period. In the exhibit catalogue, Dean (2010a , 259) writes, "I have looked at different beadwork on *tuillis* and have concluded that each piece of work is about creative self-expression; it's about making something that is different and unique, a desire to be different, unique, and beautiful."

Working with the Calista Elders Council in Bethel, Alaska, and with Yup'ik colleagues Marie Meade and Alice Rearden, Alaskan anthropologist Ann Fienup-Riordan has guided a series of exhibitions and publications on Yup'ik cultural heritage, establishing a meaningful channel for the voices of Yup'ik elders and community researchers. The 1996 exhibit of Yup'ik dance masks, entitled *Agayuliyararput/Our Way of Making Prayer*, opened to Yup'ik viewers in the community of Toksook Bay, Alaska, before embarking on a more traditional museum tour.[19] A bilingual publication, *Ciuliamta Akluit: Things of Our Ancestors* (Meade and Fienup-Riordan 2005), documents the animated discussions of the Yup'ik research team in the storeroom of the Ethnologisches Museum in Berlin in 1997. In addition, this project laid a solid foundation for the 2007 exhibition *Yuungnaqpiallerput: The Way We Genuinely Live: Masterworks of Yup'ik Science and Survival*, involving the participation of over fifty Yup'ik elders and cultural specialists.[20]

The increased ability of Arctic researchers to visit and study museum collections opens up new opportunities for independent research as well as potential partnerships between museums and Northern communities. In collaboration with the Arctic Studies Center in Washington, D.C., a team of Inuvialuit elders, researchers, and university-based colleagues working with Smithsonian curator Stephen Loring completed an in-depth study of the Inuvialuit collection brought together by Roderick MacFarlane in the 1860s. In storage for over 150 years, the MacFarlane collection provides a rich repository of historic fur clothing, domestic tools, and hunting equipment from the Mackenzie Delta region. This research presents an impressive program of historical study, workshops, articles, and community and conference presentations, including the re-creation of an Inuvialuit woman's caribou fur parka from the 1860s. Project results are accessible through a multi-layered website incorporating interactive maps, artifact records, photographic images, community media, lesson plans, teachers' guides, and discussion transcripts.[21]

In 2008, the Mystic Seaport Museum in Mystic, Connecticut, presented the exhibition *Frozen In: Captain George Comer and Hudson Bay Inuit*, the first to explore Captain Comer's contribution to Inuit cultural history. Organized by curator Fred Calabretta, the exhibit included the exquisite beaded parka created by Nivisanaaq (Shoofly), as well as historical photographs and whaling journals from the Mystic Seaport Museum collection, personal items from the Comer family collection, and a replica of the deckhouse on Comer's whaling schooner, the *Era*—the studio setting for many photographs taken by Comer (Calabretta 2008a, b). In conjunction with the exhibit, the Museum's online database features almost three hundred photographs from the Comer collection.

Two exceptional artifacts collected by Captain George Comer for the American Museum of Natural History—the beaded *tuilli* of Nivisanaaq (Shoofly) and the shamanic vestments of the Igloolik *angakkuq* Qingailisaq—have each stimulated innovative and rewarding projects of cultural revitalization. In 1999, Bernadette Miqqusaaq Dean and Rhoda Karetak visited New York to study the beaded parka created by their ancestor, Nivisanaaq (Shoofly). This visit seeded an impressive research initiative with the visit of Inuit elders, teachers, and cultural specialists to six North American museums with significant collections of Inuit cultural heritage. Organized by Bernadette Miqqusaaq Dean and documented by filmmaker Zacharias Kunuk, the research team examined historical collections of Inuit fur clothing, domestic tools, and hunting equipment at the American Museum of Natural History (New York), the University of Pennsylvania Museum of Archaeology and Anthropology (Philadelphia), Smithsonian's National Museum of Natural History, the National Museum of the American Indian (Washington, D.C.), the Royal Ontario Museum (Toronto), and the Canadian Museum of Civilization (now the Canadian Museum of

History) (Ottawa). A forty-nine-minute documentary recording the project, entitled *Inuit Piqutingit (What Belongs to Inuit)*, is available via the IsumaTV website.[22]

Through a project directed by anthropologist Bernard Saladin d'Anglure (1983, 67–83), Inuit seamstresses replicated the extraordinary shaman's outfit, consisting of a caribou fur tunic, hat, and gloves belonging to the Igloolik *angakkuq* Qingailisaq. Collected by Captain George Comer in 1902, design motifs on the tunic recall a vision the shaman recounted to Comer, initially published by Boas (1907, 509–510). A subsequent account, provided by the shaman's son, Ava, was also published by Knud Rasmussen ([1929] 1976, 205–206). Working from photographs of the original outfit in the collection of the American Museum of Natural History, seamstresses in Igloolik made replicas of the shaman's vestments for the Canadian Museum of History, Université Laval, and the Prince of Wales Northern Heritage Centre in Yellowknife. Two additional replicas, created by Igloolik seamstress Rachel Uyarasuk, are in the collection of the British Museum, London, and in a private collection. Prominently featured in the film *Journals of Knud Rasmussen*, by Zacharias Kunuk, the shaman's outfit is also the subject of a series of limited-edition prints by Germaine Arnaktauyok, including *The Shaman's Apprentice, At the Height of His Power, Kindred Spirits,* and *Shaman's Coat.*[23]

In stark contrast to the historical benefit of preserving Inuit material heritage, one must also question the cultural impact of removing objects from their ancestral home. As a case in point, the successive visits of traders and scientific expeditions to the remote Inuinnait (Copper Inuit) region of the central Canadian Arctic in the early 1900s resulted in the acquisition of the most comprehensive collection of Inuit regional culture to be preserved in distant museum collections. This abrupt removal of the material possessions of Inuit families over a remarkably short period of time (c. 1905–24) hastened the adoption of imported goods, including European and Inuvialuit clothing styles, culminating in a profound loss of traditional cultural knowledge and material heritage. By the 1930s, Inuinnait caribou fur clothing had disappeared from use, although the memory of its ancestral design was retained in the drawings and prints of Ulukhaktok elders Helen Kalvak and Mark Emerak (Driscoll 1987c).

The effort to revive the Inuinnait clothing tradition took place in Ulukhaktok in the 1990s through the initiative of Julia Ogina (Figure 7), who created a young girl's parka in contemporary material modelled from a black-and-white photograph, and elder Elsie Nilgak (a daughter of Helen Kalvak), who supervised the creation of Inuinnait/Kangiryuarmiut clothing for the Central Arctic dance group (Engelstad 2005). In 2004, a research project on literacy brought Inuinnait elders and cultural specialists, including Emily Kudlak and Alice Kaodloak from Ulukhaktok, together with Helen Balanoff (NWT Literacy Council) and Cynthia Chambers (University of Lethbridge). Documented in the exhibition *Pihuaqtiuyugut: We Are the Long Distance Walkers*, hosted by the Prince of Wales Northern Heritage Centre in 2008, this project explores the complex meaning of "literacy" in Inuit oral society. It demonstrates that ancestral knowledge is encoded not only in stories and songs but also in messages communicated through ancient tent rings and *inuksuit*, as well as the design of tools, hunting equipment, and clothing, including design elements often regarded simply as "decoration." Following a visit by Inuinnait researchers to the British Museum in 2012, cultural workshops in Ulukhaktok and other communities in the Kitikmeot region have supported a major effort to revive and restore Inuinnait ancestral heritage. In 2015, Inuinnait representatives from the Kitikmeot Heritage Society (Cambridge Bay, Nunavut) visited the historic collections from the Inuinnait region at the National Museum of Denmark, laying the groundwork for collaborative projects, including a research visit of elders in November 2017.

Museum-based projects, community workshops, and museum exhibits continue to build a strong foundation of traditional knowledge for future generations, and much remains to be learned from these initiatives. The partnership between the National Museum of Denmark and the National Museum of Greenland in sharing the ethnographic collection brought together by Holm, as well as the recent collaboration between the Museum of Cultural History in Oslo

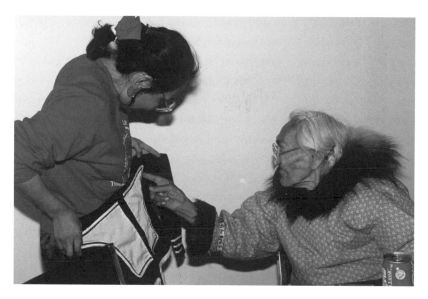

Figure 7. Elder Agnes Nigiyok and Julia Ogina discuss design features of an
Inuinnait parka for a young girl. Ulukhaktok, NT, 1992. Photo by B.D. Engelstad

and the Nattilik Heritage Centre in Gjoa Haven, Nunavut, provide
two exceptional models for future endeavours. In addition, the bold
initiative of the Smithsonian's Arctic Studies Center in establishing a
Northern base in Anchorage with a curatorial office, exhibit program,
workshops, research opportunities, and an extensive web-based
presence, provides an outstanding model for collaboration between
major institutions and Northern communities. Similar museum-com-
munity partnerships across the Arctic would serve local and regional
audiences, promoting educational programs and cultural projects
involving students, teachers, and families. A focus on student internships and collection visits would further develop the interest of youth
in the museum profession as well as in the broader realm of education,
the arts, and tourism. The skilful replication of museum artifacts for
exhibition in the North would support traditional skills in clothing
design and production while providing employment opportunities
for experienced seamstresses and training for youth. Exhibits organized by community-based curators would complement the school
curriculum at all levels while providing a deeper understanding of

Inuit cultural knowledge for transient workers and support for the developing tourism sector across the North.

In closing, there continues to be an urgent need to increase the knowledge and understanding of Inuit cultural history beyond the North. Only by strengthening the knowledge base of students and decision-makers within the public domain across North America and beyond will a respectful and culturally relevant understanding of the Arctic—its people, its history, its imposing strength and inherent vulnerability—become a global reality. The continued exhibition, study, and sharing of Arctic ethnographic and archaeological collections— the legacy of ancestors—represents a meaningful and purposeful step in this direction.

BIBLIOGRAPHY

Alunik, Ishmael, Eddie D. Kolausok and David Morrison. 2003. *Across Time and Tundra: The Inuvialuit of the Western Arctic.* Gatineau, Quebec: Canadian Museum of Civilization.

Birket-Smith, Kaj. 1945. *Ethnographical Collections from the Northwest Passage.* Translated by W.E. Calvert. Report of the Fifth Thule Expedition, 1921–1924, vol. 6, pt. 2. Copenhagen: Gyldendal.

Boas, Franz. [1888] 1964. *The Central Eskimo.* Lincoln: University of Nebraska.

———. 1901. "The Eskimo of Baffin Land and Hudson Bay, from Notes Collected by Capt. George Comer, Capt. James Mutch, and Rev. E.J. Peck." *Bulletin of the American Museum of Natural History* 15, Part 1. New York: American Museum of Natural History.

———. 1907. "Second Report on the Eskimo of Baffin Land and Hudson Bay, from Notes Collected by Captain George Comer, Captain James S. Mutch and Rev. E.J. Peck." *Bulletin of the American Museum of Natural History* 15, Part 2. New York: American Museum of Natural History.

Bogoras, Waldemar. [1904–09] 1975. *The Chukchee.* The Jesup North Pacific Expedition, 7. Memoirs of the American Museum of Natural History. Leiden/New York: G.E. Stechert. Reprint, New York: AMS Press.

———. [1913] 1975. *The Eskimos of Siberia.* The Jesup North Pacific Expedition, 8(3). Memoirs of the American Museum of Natural History, Vol.

12. Leiden: E.J. Brill; New York: G.E. Stechert. Reprint, New York: AMS Press.

Brody, Hugh. 1987. *The Living Arctic*. London: Faber.

Buijs, Cunera. 2004. *Furs and Fabrics: Transformations, Clothing and Identity in East Greenland*. Mededelingen van het Rijksmuseum voor Volkenkunde Leiden, no. 32. Leiden: CNWS Publications, Leiden University.

Buijs, Cunera, and Jarich Oosten, eds. 1997. *Braving the Cold: Continuity and Change in Arctic Clothing*. Leiden: CNWS Publications, Leiden University.

Calabretta, Fred. 1984. "Captain George Comer in the Arctic." *Log of Mystic Seaport* 35, no. 4 (Winter): 118–131.

———. 2008a. "Rediscovering a Discoverer: The Fascinating Research Behind Explorer Captain George Comer." *Mystic Seaport Magazine* (Spring 2008): 20–25.

———. 2008b. "The Work of Captain George Comer: Whaling and Anthropology in the Arctic." *Sea History Magazine* (Summer 2008): 18–22.

Charles, Elena. 2005. "My Recollections—*Nengqerralria*, Yupiaq Elder Elena Charles." In *Arctic Clothing*, edited by J.C.H. King, Birgit Pauksztat, and Robert Storrie, 31–33. Montreal and Kingston: McGill-Queen's University Press.

Chaussonnet, Valérie. 1988. "Needles and Amulets: Woman's Magic." In *Crossroads of Continents: Cultures of Siberia and Alaska*, edited by W.W. Fitzhugh and A. Crowell, 209–226. Washington, DC: Smithsonian Institution Scholarly Press.

———. 1995. *Crossroads Alaska: Native Cultures of Alaska and Siberia*. Washington, D.C.: Arctic Studies Center, National Museum of Natural History, Smithsonian Institution.

Chaussonnet, Valérie, and Bernadette Driscoll. 1994. "The Bleeding Coat: The Art of North Pacific Clothing." In *Anthropology of the North Pacific Rim*, edited by W.W. Fitzhugh and Valerie Chaussonnet, 109–131. Washington, D.C.: Smithsonian Institution Scholarly Press.

Condon, Richard G., with Julia Ogina and the Holman Elders. 1996. *The Northern Copper Inuit: A History*. Norman: University of Oklahoma Press.

Crowell, Aron, Rosita Worl, Paul C. Ongtoogak, and Dawn D. Biddison, eds. 2010. *Living Our Cultures, Sharing Our Heritage: The First Peoples of Alaska*. Washington, D.C.: Smithsonian Books.

Dayo, Dixie Masak. 2005. "How Do We Heal?" In *Arctic Clothing*, edited by J.C.H. King, Birgit Pauksztat, and Robert Storrie, 34–36. Montreal and Kingston: McGill-Queen's University Press.

Dean, Bernadette Miqqusaaq. 2010a. "Inuit Amauti or Tuilli (Woman's Parka)." In *Infinity of Nations: Art and History in the Collections of the National Museum of the American Indian*, edited by Cecile Ganteaume, 258–259. New York: HarperCollins Publishers in association with the National Museum of the American Indian, Smithsonian Institution.

———. 2010b. "Video Program: Commentary on Inuit Women's Beaded Parkas, Clothing Production, and the Historic Whaling Era in Nunavut." *Infinity of Nations* exhibition, Smithsonian Institution, National Museum of the American Indian, New York, 2010–present.

Dewar, Veronica. 2005. "Our Culture, Our Clothing, Our Identity." In *Arctic Clothing*, edited by J.C.H. King, Birket Pauksztat, and Robert Storrie, 23–26. Montreal and Kingston: McGill-Queen's University Press.

Driscoll, Bernadette. 1980. *The Inuit Amautik: I Like My Hood to Be Full*. Winnipeg: The Winnipeg Art Gallery.

———. 1983. "The Inuit Caribou Parka: A Preliminary Study." MA thesis, Carleton University, Ottawa.

———. 1984. "Sapangat: Inuit Beadwork in the Canadian Arctic." *Expedition* 26, no. 2: 40–47.

———. 1987a. "Pretending to be Caribou: The Inuit Parka as an Artistic Tradition." In *The Spirit Sings: Artistic Traditions of Canada's First Peoples*, edited by J. Harrison, 169–200. Toronto: McClelland and Stewart in association with the Glenbow Museum.

———. 1987b. "Arctic." In *The Spirit Sings: Artistic Traditions of Canada's First Peoples, A Catalogue of the Exhibition*, 109–131. Toronto: McClelland and Stewart in association with the Glenbow Museum.

———. 1987c. "Helen Kalvak and Mark Emerak Memorial Portfolio." Catalogue and limited edition prints by the artists. Ulukhaktok, NWT: Holman Art Shop.

Eber, Dorothy Harley. 1989. *When the Whalers Were Up North: Inuit Memories from the Eastern Arctic*. Montreal and Kingston: McGill-Queen's University Press.

Engelstad, Bernadette Driscoll. 2005. "Dance of the Loon: Symbolism and Continuity in Copper Inuit Ceremonial Clothing." *Arctic Anthropology* 42, no. 1: 33–47.

———. 2010. "Curators, Collections, and Inuit Communities: Case Studies from the Arctic." In *Sharing Knowledge & Cultural Heritage: First Nations of the Americas: Studies in Collaboration with Indigenous Peoples from Greenland, North and South America*, edited by Laura van Broekhoven, Cunera Buijs, and Pieter Hovens, 39–52. Leiden: Sidestone Press.

Engelstad, Bernadette Driscoll, and Fred Calabretta. 2014. "Inuit Facial Casts: Capt. George Comer Collection, American Museum of Natural History." Illustrated guide, unpublished, in the possession of the authors and on file at the Archives of the American Museum of Natural History.

Ewing, Heather. 2007. *The Lost World of James Smithson: Science, Revolution and the Birth of the Smithsonian*. New York: Bloomsbury.

Fienup-Riordan, Ann. 1996. *The Living Tradition of Yup'ik Masks: Agayuliyararput (Our Way of Making Prayer)*. Translations by Marie Meade. Seattle and London: University of Washington Press in association with the Anchorage Museum of History and Art and the Anchorage Museum Association.

———. 1997 *Yuungnaqpiallerput (The Way We Genuinely Live): Masterworks of Science and Survival*. Seattle and London: University of Washington Press in association with Anchorage Museum Association and Calista Elders Council.

———. 2005. *Yup'ik Elders at the Ethnologisches Museum Berlin: Fieldwork Turned on its Head*. Seattle and London: University of Washington Press in association with Calista Elders Council.

Fitzhugh, W.W. 2009. "'Of No Ordinary Importance': Reversing Polarities in Smithsonian Arctic Studies." In *Smithsonian at the Poles: Contributions to International Polar Year Science*, edited by I. Krupnik, M.A. Lang, and S.E. Miller, 61–77. Washington, D.C.: Smithsonian Institution Scholarly Press.

Fitzhugh, William W., and Aron Crowell, eds. 1988. *Crossroads of Continents: Cultures of Siberia and Alaska*. Washington, D.C.: Smithsonian Institution Scholarly Press.

Fitzhugh, William W., and Susan A. Kaplan. 1982. *Inua: Spirit World of the Bering Sea Eskimo.* Washington, D.C.: Smithsonian Institution Scholarly Press.

Freed, Stanley A. 2012. *Anthropology Unmasked: Museums, Science, and Politics in New York City*, Vols. 1–2. Wilmington, Ohio: Orange Frazer Press.

Ganteaume, Cécile, ed. 2010. *Infinity of Nations: Art and History in the Collections of the National Museum of the American Indian.* New York: HarperCollins Publishers in association with the National Museum of the American Indian, Smithsonian Institution.

Hall, Judy. 2005. "'The Greatest Individual Hunter of Material in the North': Collecting in Alaska, Canada and Chukotka with Captain Joseph-Fidele Bernard." *American Indian Art Magazine* 30, no. 4 (Autumn): 68–77.

Hall, Judy, Jill Oakes, and Sally Qimmiu'naaq Webster. 1994. *Sanatujut: Pride in Women's Work (Copper and Caribou Inuit Clothing Traditions).* Hull, Quebec: Canadian Museum of Civilization.

Harachak, Jana. 2005. "Seams of Time." In *Arctic Clothing*, edited by J.C.H. King, B. Pauksztat, and R Storrie, 28–30. London: The British Museum.

Harper, Kenn. 2008. "The Collaboration of James Mutch and Franz Boas. 1883–1922." *Etudes/Inuit /Studies* 32, no. 2: 53–71.

———. 2016. "Collecting at a Distance: The Boas-Mutch-Comer Collaboration." In *Early Inuit Studies: Themes and Transitions, 1850s–1980s*, edited by Igor Krupnik, 89–110. Washington, D.C.: Smithsonian Institution Scholarly Press.

Issenman, Betty Kobayashi. 1997. *Sinews of Survival. The Living Legacy of Inuit Clothing.* Vancouver: UBC Press.

Jacobsen, Johan Adrian. [1884] 1977. *Alaskan Voyage 1881–1883: An Expedition to the Northwest Coast of America.* Translated by Erna Gunther. Chicago: University of Chicago Press.

Jakobsen, Aviaja Rosing. 2010. "The Repatriation of Greenland's Cultural Heritage from Denmark to Greenland." In *Sharing Knowledge & Cultural Heritage: First Nations of the Americas: Studies in Collaboration with Indigenous Peoples from Greenland, North and South America*, edited by Laura van Broekhoven, Cunera Buijs, and Pieter Hovens, 75–82. Leiden: Sidestone Press.

Jenness, Diamond. 1921. *The Life of the Copper Eskimos. Report of the Canadian Arctic Expedition, 1913–18*, Vol. 12A. Ottawa: F.A. Acland Printer to the King's Most Excellent Majesty.

———. 1928. *The People of the Twilight*. New York: Macmillan Publishing Co. Reprint, Chicago: University of Chicago Press.

———. 1946. *Material Culture of the Copper Eskimo. Report of the Canadian Arctic Expedition, 1913–1918*, Vol. 16. Ottawa: King's Printer.

Jenness, Stuart E. 2011. *Stefansson, Dr. Anderson and the Canadian Arctic Expeditions, 1913–1918: A Story of Exploration, Science and Sovereignty*. Mercury Series. History Paper 56. Ottawa: Canadian Museum of Civilization.

Jochelson, Waldemar. [1908] 1975. *The Koryak*. The Jesup North Pacific Expedition 6. Memoirs of the American Museum of Natural History. Leiden and New York: G.E. Stechert. Reprint, New York: AMS Press.

Karetak, Rhoda Akpaliapik. 2005. "Amautiit." In *Arctic Clothing*, edited by J.C.H. King, Birket Pauksztat, and Robert Storrie, 80–83. Montreal and Kingston: McGill-Queen's University Press.

Kendall, Laurel, and Igor Krupnik, eds. 2003. *Constructing Cultures Then and Now: Celebrating Franz Boas and the Jesup North Pacific Expedition*. Contributions to Circumpolar Anthropology 4. Washington, D.C.: Arctic Studies Center, National Museum of Natural History, Smithsonian Institution.

King, J.C.H., Birgit Pauksztat, and Richard Storrie, eds. 2005. *Arctic Clothing*. Montreal and Kingston: McGill-Queen's University Press.

Kleinschmidt, Gertrud. 2005. "Formal Clothing: The Greenlandic National Costume." In *Arctic Clothing*, edited by J.C.H. King, Birgit Pauksztat, and Robert Storrie, 104–107. Montreal and Kingston: McGill-Queen's University Press.

Krupnik, Igor. 1996. *Perekrestki kontinentov. Kul'tury korennykh narodov Dal'nego Vostoka I Aliaski*. Russian version of the exhibit catalog: V. Chaussonnet, ed., *Crossroads Alaska: Native Cultures of Alaska and Siberia*. Washington, D.C.: Arctic Studies Center.

Krupnik, Igor, and William W. Fitzhugh. 2001. Gateways. Exploring the Legacy of the Jesup North Pacific Expedition, 1897–1902. Contributions to Circumpolar Anthropology 1. Washington, D.C.: Arctic Studies Center, National Museum of Natural History, Smithsonian Institution.

Kudlak, Emily, Alice Kaodloak, Ulukhaktok Elders, with Cynthia Chambers and Helen Balanoff. 2008. *Pihuaqtiuyugut: We are the Long Distance Walkers*. Ulukhaktok Literacy Research Project. NWT Literacy Council. https://www.nwtliteracy.ca/sites/default/files/research/935-long%20 walkers-proof.pdf.

Kunuk, Zacharias, and Bernadette Miqqusaaq Dean, dirs. 2006. *Inuit Piqutingit: What Belongs to Inuit*. 49 min. www.isuma.tv/isuma-productions/inuit -piqutingit.

Lindsay, Debra. 1993. *Science in the Subarctic: Trappers, Traders, and the Smithsonian Institution*. Washington, D.C.: Smithsonian Institution Scholarly Press.

Loring, Stephen. [1894] 2001a. "Introduction." In *Ethnology of the Ungava District: Hudson Bay Territory*, edited by Lucien M. Turner, vii–xxxii. Washington, D.C.: Smithsonian Institution Scholarly Press.

Lyons, Natasha. 2010. "The Wisdom of Elders: Inuvialuit Social Memories of Continuity and Change in the Twentieth Century." *Arctic Anthropology* 47, no. 1: 22–38.

Mathiassen, Therkel. 1927. *Archaeology of the Central Eskimo*. 2 vols. Report of the Fifth Thule Expedition 1921–24, Vol. 4, no. 1–2. Copenhagen: Glydendal.

Maulding, Glenna C. Kiana. 2005. "Kiana Creations: Inupiaq Parkaks as Wearable Art." In *Arctic Clothing*, edited by J.C.H. King, Birgit Pauksztat, and Robert Storrie, 148–152. Montreal and Kingston: McGill-Queen's University Press.

McIntyre, Chuna. 2005. "Quiet and Reserved Splendor: Central Yup'ik Eskimo Fancy Garments of Kuskokwim Bay, Bering Sea." In *Arctic Clothing*, edited by J.C.H. King, Birgit Pauksztat, and Robert Storrie, 37–40. Montreal and Kingston: McGill-Queen's University Press.

Meade, Marie. 1990. "Sewing to Maintain the Past, Present and Future." *Etudes/Inuit/Studies* 14, no. 1–2: 229–239.

Meade, Marie, trans., and Ann Fienup-Riordan, ed. 1996. *Agayuliyararput, Kegginaqut, Kangiit-llu: Our Way of Making Prayers, Yup'ik Masks and the Stories They Tell*. Seattle: University of Washington Press.

———. 2005. *Ciuliamta Akliut: Things of Our Ancestors: Yup'ik Elders Explore the Jacobsen Collection at the Ethnologisches Museum Berlin*. Seattle: University of Washington Press.

Métayer, Maurice, ed. 1966. *I, Nuligak*. Translated by M. Métayer. Ontario: Peter Martin Associates Ltd.

Morrison, David and Georges-Herbert Germain. 1995. *Inuit: Glimpses of an Arctic Past*. Gatineau: Canadian Museum of Civilization.

Murdoch, John. [1892] 1988. *Ethnological Results of the Point Barrow Expedition*. Washington, D.C.: Smithsonian Institution Scholarly Press.

Nelson, Edward W. [1899] 1983. *The Eskimo about Bering Strait*. Washington, D.C.: Smithsonian Institution Scholarly Press.

Nuttall, Mark. 2004. *Encyclopedia of the Arctic*, Vols 1–3. London: Taylor and Francis Publishers.

Oakes, Jillian E. 1991. *Copper and Caribou Inuit Skin Clothing Production*. Canadian Ethnology Service, Mercury Series, Paper 118. Ottawa: Canadian Museum of Civilization.

Oakes, Jill, and Rick Riewe. 1995. *Our Boots: An Inuit Woman's Art*. Vancouver and Toronto: Douglas & McIntyre.

———. 1998. *Spirit of Siberia: Traditional Native Life, Clothing, and Footwear*. Washington, D.C.: Smithsonian Institution Scholarly Press.

Oosten, Jarich. 1997. "Amulets, Shamanic clothes and Paraphernalia in Inuit Culture." In *Braving the Cold: Continuity and Change in Arctic Clothing*, edited by Cunera Buijs and Jarich Oosten, 105–130. Leiden: CNWS Publications, Vol. 49, Leiden University.

Otak, Leah Aksaajuq. 2005. "Iniqsimajuq: Caribou-skin Preparation in Igloolik, Nunavut." In *Arctic Clothing*, edited by J.C.H. King, Birgit Pauksztat, and Robert Storrie, 74–79. Montreal and Kingston: McGill-Queen's University Press.

Petrussen, Frederikke. 2005. "Arctic Clothing from Greenland." In *Arctic Clothing*, edited by J.C.H. King, Birgit Pauksztat, and Robert Storrie, 45–47. Montreal and Kingston: McGill-Queen's University Press.

Pharand, Sylvie. 1975a. "Clothing of the Iglulik Inuit." Unpublished manuscript. Canadian Ethnology Service, National Museum of Man, National Museums of Canada.

———. 1975b. "Les vetements des Inuit Iglulik." MA thesis, Laval University, Quebec.

———. 2012. *Caribou Skin Clothing of the Igloolik Inuit*. Iqaluit and Toronto: Inhabit Media.

Phillips, Ruth B. 2011. *Museum Pieces: Toward the Indigenization of Canadian Museums*. Montreal and Kingston: McGill-Queen's University Press.

Rasmussen, Knud. [1929] 1976. *Intellectual Culture of the Iglulik Eskimos*. Copenhagen: Gyldendal. Reprint, New York: AMS Press.

———. [1930] 1976. *Intellectual Culture of the Caribou Eskimos: Iglulik and Caribou Eskimo Texts*. Copenhagen: Gyldendal. Reprint, New York: AMS Press.

———. [1931] 1976. *The Netsilik Eskimos: Social Life and Spiritual Culture*. Copenhagen: Gyldendal. Reprint, New York: AMS Press.

———. [1932] 1976. *Intellectual Culture of the Copper Eskimos*. Copenhagen: Gyldendal. Reprint, New York: AMS Press.

Ross, W. Gillies. 1975. *Whaling and Eskimos: Hudson Bay 1860–1915*. Publications in Ethnology, no. 10. Ottawa: National Museum of Man.

———. 1984a. *An Arctic Whaling Diary: The Journal of Captain George Comer in Hudson Bay 1903–1905*. Toronto: University of Toronto Press.

———. 1984b. "George Comer, Franz Boas, and the American Museum of Natural History." *Etudes/Inuit/Studies* 8, no. 1: 145–164.

Rowley, Susan. 1998. *Inua: Spirit World of the Bering Sea Eskimo*. Washington, D.C.: Department of Anthropology, National Museum of Natural History, Smithsonian Institution.

Saladin d'Anglure. 1983. "Ijiqqat: voyage au pays de l'invisible inuit." *Etudes/Inuit/Studies* 7, no. 1: 67–83.

———. 1984. "Les masques de Boas: Franz Boas et l'ethnographie des Inuit." *Etudes/Inuit/Studies* 8, no. 1: 165–179.

Stefansson, Viljhalmur. [1913] 1971. *My Life with the Eskimo*. New York: Collier.

———. 1914. *The Stefansson-Anderson Arctic Expedition: Preliminary Ethnographic Results*. Anthropological Papers of the American Museum of Natural History 14 (1).

Svensson, Tom. 2014. "Culture and Politics: A Comment on Two Recent Cases of Repatriation in the Arctic." *Arctic Studies Newsletter*, April 2014, no. 21: 27–29. www.mnh.si.edu/arctic.

Taylor, J. Garth. 1974. *Netsilik Eskimo Material Culture: The Roald Amundsen Collection from King William Island*. Oslo: Universitetsforlaget.

Thorleifsen, Daniel. 2010. "The Greenland Collections: Repatriation as a Starting Point for New Partnerships." In *Sharing Knowledge & Cultural Heritage: First Nations of the Americas: Studies in Collaboration with Indigenous Peoples from Greenland, North and South America*, edited by Laura van Broekhoven, Cunera Buijs, and Pieter Hovens, 83–89. Leiden: Sidestone Press.

Turner, Lucien M. [1894] 2001. *Ethnology of the Ungava District: Hudson Bay Territory.* Washington, D.C.: Smithsonian Institution Scholarly Press.

Van Brockhaven, Laura, Cunera Buijs, and Pieter Hovens. 2010. *Sharing Knowledge & Cultural Heritage: First Nations of the Americas: Studies in Collaboration with Indigenous Peoples from Greenland, North and South America.* Leiden: Sidestone Press.

Zerehi, Sima Sahar. 2015. "Inuit Shaman Parka 'Copied' by KTZ Design Well-Studied by Anthropologists." *CBC News*, December 2. www.cbc.ca /news/canada/north/inuit-shaman-parka-design-history-1.3345968.

CHAPTER 4

Inuit Lives and Arctic Legacies

Leah Otak, Edward Parry, and Igloolik[1]

J. C. H. King

One of Leah Otak's Inuktitut names was Ivalu, meaning thread or sinew. This usually refers to the back sinew of the caribou, and it neatly encapsulates and symbolizes Leah in the way in which I knew her over a period of twenty years. Sinew is traditionally used as a strong, durable twine, employed in making skin clothes and footwear from waterproof sealskin and warming caribou fur, ensuring the comfort and survival of hunters on the land. When Leah was young, making and creating skin clothing was part of everyday life. In 1967 Leah, already at school, and her family moved permanently off the land from Iglurjuat, on Baffin Island, and into the settlement of Igloolik. This was the moment, if you like, when independent living on the land ended.[2] That moment of rapid change can be contrasted with another one, the first recorded contact between outsiders and Igloolik. On this occasion, the earliest surviving Inuit clothing collected in

Nunavut was obtained by William Edward Parry, during his second expedition in search of the Northwest Passage between 1821 and 1823.

I last met Leah in Igloolik in September 2013, when embarking on a project to understand the Dorset collections (now at the University of Cambridge) made by Graham Rowley in Foxe Basin in the 1930s. She, already unwell, kindly set up a visit to nearby Avvajja, simply and without fuss, where Rowley had excavated intricately carved ivories. Whenever I asked for her help, from the first time I met her, she would look me in the eyes, open her face very wide, and sigh—and respond to my question, however simple or silly it may have been, with a helpful reply. That was her way, and that is why her leadership was important.

My first visit to Igloolik had been made in 1986, to research the Museum of Mankind's exhibition *Living Arctic* (1987), organized with Hugh Brody, Georges Erasmus, Cindy Gilday, and Dave Monture, in cooperation with the Igloolik Research Centre.[3] George Qulaut guided me in Igloolik. There I met Leah's sister Rhoda Innuksuk, at that time the president of the then Inuit Tapirisat of Canada, an important phase of her extraordinary career in public service. I also met Leah's parents. Her mother, Zipporah, made a caribou-skin outfit for the exhibition, and later an eider duck foot–skin bag and other articles were acquired for the collection.[4] That winter Graham Rowley took me to Winterlude, the winter festival in Ottawa, where Pakak Innuksuk, later to star in the celebrated film *Atanarjuat* (2001), was performing. So I encountered Leah's family before getting to know Leah during the 1990s.

At that time the Museum of Mankind, where I worked, was in the process of closing and moving to the main British Museum building. Within this period of change and development, leading to the opening of the North American Gallery in 2000, funding was available at the British Museum for conferences and publications. Tapping into this funding, the first of these conferences was about photography, "Imaging the Arctic." The meeting was organized with George Qulaut, who spoke of his grandmother's portrait photograph in the British Museum, and run by Henrietta Lidchi.[5] The next Arctic project was an exhibition and conference about Inuit clothing, *Annuraaq: Arctic Clothing from Igloolik*. In connection with the *Annuraaq* exhibition I visited Igloolik in November 2000 and consulted again with the Inulla-riit Elders Society and with Leah, then with the Nunavut government's Director of Culture and Heritage; on that visit I also went out to the fish camp of George Qulaut and made a small collection for the British Museum.

Shortly after my visit to Igloolik, Leah came to London in December 2000 to examine the early Inuit collections. She visited Franks House, the storehouse where the collections were then preserved, and examined the earliest Inuit clothing obtained by Edward Parry. Included in the collection is a caribou parka and a pair of trousers, and also a sample of bleached sealskin, to which her comment is attached. Leah wished especially to examine the inside of the clothing, to see what stitches were used, and I remember, viscerally, the moment of concern when she turned the 180-year-old pants inside out, wondering whether the stitches and skin would hold—which they did. While in London Leah ran a workshop to discuss traditional techniques of production and preservation of clothing. Interviewed by *Nunatsiaq News* on her return to Nunavut, she said, "I was amazed how well-preserved most of the clothing was, especially the older pieces, which had been collected over 100 years ago … The skin was still soft, and the sinew stitches almost as tight as when they were first made." She added that it was thrilling to actually handle caribou-skin clothing made in Igloolik almost 200 years ago.

Annuraaq was set up at the heart of the British Museum: in the grand saloon, at the head of the main stairs overlooking the newly opened Great Court at the centre of the building. The exhibition, which ran for three months between February and May 2001, was small, contained in half a dozen cases, but with an important web presence accessible until a few years ago. *Annuraaq* and its conference (March 29–31) was reported on by Betty Issenman (2002) in *Études/Inuit/Studies*, in an article entitled "Erudition and Emotion at the British Museum."

The conference proceedings were turned into a book by Birgit Pauksztat and Robert Storrie, which was published in 2005: *Arctic Clothing of North America: Alaska, Canada, and Greenland.* That year the book won the R.L. Shep Ethnic Textiles Book Award.[6] This award was presented by the Textile Society of America. What was remarkable was that the volume contained only one article about textiles, on clothing from the Norse settlement of Greenland! Leah herself contributed an important article explaining the importance of the initial work which takes place before tailoring and sewing begins, "Iniqsimajuq: Caribou-Skin Preparation in Igloolik, Nunavut." Two years later I visited Igloolik, where I distributed copies of the book and met with the Elders Society and with Leah.[7]

This straightforward account is intended to provide a narrative understanding of the way in which Leah, with her numerous other duties and commitments, helped in a project that made known clothing traditions from across the North American Arctic. In an important sense the most significant moment in the project was that when Leah examined and assessed the collections made by Parry in the Igloolik area 180 years earlier. When I was asked to contribute to this volume, it seemed fitting that the memorial and summary essay below should provide something additional to this. So what follows is an initial account of the principal surviving evidence for collections made by William Edward Parry, both at the British Museum and elsewhere in Britain.

THE FIRST COLLECTIONS FROM FOXE BASIN

William Edward Parry (1790–1855),[8] usually known as Edward Parry, was perhaps the foremost Arctic explorer of the generation educated at sea during the Napoleonic wars. Like John Franklin (1786–1847) and Frederick William Beechey (1796–1856) he undertook significant voyages, but unlike the other two, Parry had a successful colonial career away from the navy, turning the Australian Agricultural Company (1839–44) into a profitable corporation. Staunchly Christian, Parry was an effective leader, minimizing deaths from scurvy and other causes. Born into a Welsh family—ascending each generation on the social scale—in the spa city of Bath, Parry was much admired by friends and colleagues. Very experienced before accompanying John Ross on his inconclusive voyage of 1818, when Ross mistook clouds for impassable mountains and returned prematurely from Baffin Bay, Parry was straightforward, and a good scientist. Most importantly, he was a fluent writer who left behind a huge correspondence that well details all of his activities, of the heart and mind as well as of naval matters.

Parry's first and most successful expedition was that of 1819–20, when he reached far west through the Arctic Archipelago. This expedition included the first Royal Navy overwintering, at Winter Harbour, Melville Island. There, building on knowledge from whalers as well as from the navy, Parry systematized practical methods for ensuring the health and safety of the crew. These relate particularly to diet and to the need and use of anti-scorbutics, the intelligent use of alcohol, and measures taken to ensure both a dry, warm environment and the prevention of fires. His letters and journals detail his scientific interests, mostly in the collection of intangible data, especially meteorology, and—particularly on his second voyage—his relationship with Inuit and appreciation of their qualities and knowledge.

Parry's second voyage, directed to travel south of Baffin Island, was in its immediate outcomes less successful. Sailing north of Southampton Island, he mapped, with Inuit assistance, much of the coast from Repulse Bay north to Fury and Hecla Strait. There Parry was stopped by pack ice in two seasons from travelling west through the strait. He overwintered at Winter Island, off the Melville Peninsula, in 1821–22, and then at Igloolik in 1822–23. In February 1822 the expedition was joined by Inuit for six months, and Parry was again in close contact with Inuit the following year. This period of approximately eighteen months gave the expedition an unprecedented opportunity for hearing and speaking Inuktitut, for describing Inuit life, and for learning about and collecting Inuit artifacts. Parry was particularly fortunate to be accompanied by George Francis Lyon (1795–1833) as his second in command. Lyon was already a traveller in Africa, spoke Arabic, and, less conventionally, was interested in other peoples. He was also an excellent watercolourist whose drawings, published as copper engravings, conveyed to a European public for the first time images of Inuit life in what is now Nunavut. Three volumes appeared in 1824.[9] Parry (1824) published an official account of the voyage, *Journal of a Second Voyage for the Discovery of a North-West Passage from the Atlantic to the Pacific, Performed in the Years 1821–22-23, in His Majesty's ships Fury and Hecla...* This was then followed by further details, *A Supplement to the Appendix of Captain Parry's Voyage for the Discovery of a North-West Passage, in the Years 1819-20: Containing an Account of the Subjects of Natural History.* Lyon (1824), having turned over his private journal to the Admiralty, was encouraged to publish this seemingly more lighthearted account of the voyage, *The Private Journal of Captain G.F. Lyon, of H.M.S. Hecla, during the Recent Voyage of Discovery under Captain Parry...*

As mentioned, Parry recognized and employed Inuit as mapmakers and guides. Conventionally, the collection of information, ethnographic observation, and the acquisition of artifacts are treated as slightly separate phenomena. In the case of the Iglulingmiut of Foxe Basin, however, it is clear that Parry and Lyon regarded maps, the drawings made by Inuit, and the clothing and equipment supplied to the expedition as part of a whole as a system of knowledge made available by Inuit through trade, in the context of a degree of mutual respect. The artifacts which were collected therefore reflect a rather different relationship between Indigenous and incomer than that in, for instance, the Pacific, whether Polynesia or Australia. The clothing, hunting gear, and kayaks, full-size and models, are not oddities in themselves but rather curiosities in the original meaning: objects worthy of study, understanding, and use. The articles collected represent artifact types rather than, say, specific regalia from a hierarchical society or ancestor figures from shrines—regalia with whose use the collectors were familiar, and of which Parry and his men had firsthand experience. When distributed to collections and museums, these survivals from the voyage, while representing the exotic and the other, embody a system of knowledge—appreciated, and employed, by naval officers and sailors.

The surviving collections of Inuit material culture from the second voyage must be placed in this much wider context of the natural sciences, and of the development of proto-ethnography, the descriptive engagement of Europeans with other people. Earlier accounts of exotic people are contained in travel accounts extending back into and before the 16th century. Frobisher's publications include details of Inuit, and this is reflected in titles that speak of accounts of countries and people; all of this comes from reinvigorated classical traditions in the Renaissance. In the 17th century divines published accounts of the manners and customs of heathens and of the Holy Land. A century later Cook's voyages, with accompanying scientists such as Joseph Banks, one of Parry's mentors, made available long accounts of previously uncontacted native nations in the Pacific. Importantly, these expeditionary accounts are most detailed at first contact. This is to some extent reflected in the difference between the narratives of the Vancouver Expedition of 1791–95, where relatively few peoples new to Europeans were encountered, in comparison to those of Cook in Pacific North America in 1778–79. Ross's voyage of 1818 encountered for the first time the Inughuit, or Arctic Highlanders of Northern Greenland, and this is reflected in the official account, both in the description and in the publication of engravings of sled, harpoon, and knife, and in the description of that first encounter with its depiction of Ross. It is notable for introducing to the world the metal from the Cape York fall of meteorites. The essential, obvious difference in the relationship between Parry and Inuit at Winter Island is that Parry could not, unlike Cook or Vancouver, have simply sailed away should his relationship with Inuit have turned sour or awkward. In being enforced by the ice to overwinter, the dynamics of the relationship had to be respectful, and the opportunities for observation and recording were almost ideal. One has to consider how things might have been different if a choleric, ill-tempered commander such as Vancouver, who fought with his scientist Archibald Menzies and was violent towards his officers and men, had been in charge at Winter Island. While anthropology as a discipline was not to be fully instituted until the middle of the 19th century, the ancient trope of monographs publishing the "manners and customs" of different nations continued, and in a sense it was to underwrite anthropology and its cognate disciplines of ethnology and ethnography. So one of the most important of such works written from fieldwork, Lane's *Manners and Customs of the Modern Egyptians*, appeared in 1836, a year before the first founding of what would become the Royal Anthropological Institute.

What follows is an account of the material culture from Winter Island and Igloolik in 1822–23. Descriptive analysis of voyage collections began in the 1970s with the work of Erna Gunther on the Pacific Northwest Coast and that of Peter Whitehead and Adrienne Kaeppler about materials from Cook's voyages. Those accounts began with the objects themselves. In contrast, this account begins with the illustrations of artifacts. This is because of limitations of space. The most immediate source is that provided by the two engravings published by Parry. Related drawings by Lyon of artifacts are included. This is followed by an appendix describing the accession into the British Museum in 1824 of an official collection, followed by other articles, and a century later a second collection, which had been retained by the Parry family. Other collections which are or may be associated with Parry's second voyage are then listed.

PARRY'S ENGRAVINGS

The two copper engravings published by Parry of Inuit material culture are entirely conventional in character. Both prints are titled and acknowledged in the same way: "Eskimaux Implements, Weapons &c. Drawn by Captn. Lyon R.N. Engraved By Edwrd. Finden." Edward Francis Finden (1791–1857) came from a family of prolific artists and engravers. A notebook of watercolours by Lyon executed for the engravings is in the Anthropology Library, British Museum. The format of the engravings, of juxtaposed heterogeneous materials with varied scales and degrees of artistic licence, was derived from herbals and adapted to scientific publications in the 18th century. Those appearing in 18th-century voyages usually stress the curious and exceptional; Parry instead stresses the usefulness and intelligence of objects. The engravings are important because they provide immediate links between artifacts and the contemporary narrative and available text. Surviving objects in collections (briefly summarized in an appendix), which were collected by the expedition, can in the future be brought into the centre of the discussion.

The largest group of artifacts brought back on the ships is that used to illustrate Parry's account of Inuit life. These are keyed into his essay "Some Further Account of the Esquimaux of the Melville Peninsula and the Adjoining Islands; More Particularly Winter Island and Igloolik." This includes information additional to that brought into the expedition narrative. The essay (Parry 1824, 492–553) is illustrated with two engravings, the first illustrating twelve numbered items and the second illustrating fifteen. These twenty-seven items are sequentially numbered and (mostly) mentioned in the text to elucidate Parry's detailed explanation of Inuit technology and material culture. In these descriptions Parry uses, in a familiar manner, the Inuktitut names. This chapter, towards the end of the account of the voyage, is exceptional in the interest and care with which Parry deals with artifacts, treating the subject with respect in the manner of a scientist. Many Inuit artifacts are also described but not illustrated with examples. This includes a fish spear or leister (*kakivak*; Parry 1824, 509) included in the Lyon watercolours. While this grouping in the engravings is the largest gathering together of Inuit artifacts, it was not kept together and unfortunately not deposited in a single institution. Indeed, many of the items seem to have been retained or disposed of at will by Parry and Lyon. Many may be located in museum collections, although it is likely that the more fragile items, particularly the artifacts of skin, have not survived. At least two are likely to represent items in the British Museum, those being the large cooking pot and the muskox-horn drinking cup; others may be in the National Museum of Scotland. Parry's (1824) essay, which includes an account of Inuit health by Edwards (543–549), is a very general ethnography with an account of belief systems, language, appearance, and population statistics. The essay is followed by an Inuktitut vocabulary (Parry 1824, 554–571). It is important to note, obviously and essentially, that illustrations vary between those that represent a generic artifact, type of scene, or article, and those that were drawn from life and represent an actual object. The Parry engravings of Inuit artifacts include those drawn from life as well as those which are likely to be idealized and reduced, and reproduced from memory or a field sketch. They are closely related to a small sketchbook by Lyon with watercolours of Inuit articles, some of which were used in the engraved prints.[10]

1/1. Soapstone cooking pot, *ukkusik*. The pot is described with the seal-oil lamp jointly in a couple of paragraphs (502–503)[11]; later this is augmented with a description of cooking, food preferences, the snow as a source of drinking water, and the temperature (near freezing) preferred (505–506). The rectilinear shape of the pot is given, and the all-important same-size relationship to the lamp is mentioned. Parry calls the pot the second most important domestic article after the lamp. He is particularly interested in the way that these fragile vessels were repaired with bindings and pegs and caulked with grease. The generic, thumbnail-sized illustration is likely to represent the extremely large, and well-repaired, example in the British Museum.

1/2. Soapstone lamp, *qulliq*. Parry describes in satisfying detail the lamp in a snowhouse, its automatic fuelling, with blubber hung above to drip down, the moss wick, and the beautiful light created (502–503). He records the temperature, just above freezing near the lamp, becoming cooler (of course) the farther away one goes. He notes that each family will have its own lamp. Most remarkable, apparently, is that he describes the rack above the lamp required for drying clothes—but of course one of the central duties of naval officers was to ensure proper domesticity, that ships remained dry, and that dry clothes were available to sailors at all times. Again, Parry's empathy with Inuit is made explicit. He discusses where the soapstone is sourced, how Inuit close to the source specialize in making lamps, and where the asbestos wick trimmer was found. The detailed illustration of a lamp with wick trimmer and blubber does not seem to represent the large example in the British Museum, and may derive from one of Lyon's field sketches.

1/3. Adze fitted with an axe blade, an unlocated article probably illustrated from life (536), included in the Lyon watercolour sketchbook. Parry says that he came across two or three axes bounded transversely to form adzes. He comments on Inuit woodworking abilities and the likely use of steaming and bending wood for the making of kayak frames. He believed that non-Europeans preferred adzes to axes for woodworking.

1/4. Snow goggles (547). The pair engraved from the Lyon water-colour sketchbook—and decorated with geometric designs that relate to those on combs and used in tattoos—has not been located. Parry's narrative alludes to the importance of snow goggles for Inuit and for his expedition on numerous occasions. Edwards (547) used this pair to discuss snow blindness and the method of construction, including the hollowing out of the interior to allow for the movement of eyelashes. He says they are made of wood, as is the pair accessioned into the British Museum in the 1920s and said to have been made by the expedition rather than by Inuit. Another pair of Parry goggles, of antler and undecorated, was accessioned into the British Museum in 1824.

1/5. Snow shovel (499). The description of the construction of an *igluvigaq* or snowhouse is detailed (499–501) and, like most of the rest of the descriptions, is derived if not from participant observation, then at least from detailed scrutiny and a recording of the process. It is accompanied by a floor plan of a snowhouse, and the language used is highly respectful: the tunnel entrance is, unusually, described as being Gothic—that is, it is given a religious aspect. In describing the construction Parry accurately talks of the cutting of the snow blocks; he does not, however, say that metre-long snow blocks, while looking light, are actually rather heavy and require strength and agility to manipulate. This suggests that he did not himself try to build a snowhouse. He talks of piling up snow with the shovel on the outside for insulation, but does not mention the necessity of storing shovels vertically to avoid their disappearing under the drift of snow. For the interior he mentions the mattress or insulator between deerskins and snow, made of baleen or birch, having already passed to the British Museum the baleen example. The engraving of the shovel, with detailed figuring of the wood and bindings, seems to have been executed after an actual, as-yet-unlocated example.

1/6. Dog whip. Parry wrote extensively about dogs, as well as the manufacture and use of sleds, and compared the European treatment of dogs with that of the Inuit. He accurately accounts for the breeding, training, and deployment of dogs and of sleds (514–521). The only dog-related item illustrated in the engravings is the whip, probably an actual unlocated example, mentioned on page 517. His familiarity with sled travel enables Parry to describe not simply the physical aspects of the whip but also its effectiveness in use. He emphasizes the importance of not striking the dogs when travelling since this would disturb the smooth running of the team. In this account Parry describes how sometimes sleds were made from bowhead whale jawbones, and he also refers to the use of wood and of frozen, non-rigid materials to construct runners. The sled in Exeter at the Royal Albert Memorial Museum & Art Gallery, which has single piece bone runners, may have been acquired and collected by Parry because it was atypical, and represented, in its use of whale material, an ideal, highly exotic type in the creation of this everyday object.

1/7. Man's fringed checkerboard skin headband, of bleached and unbleached skin (498). Parry provides a detailed description of clothing, with Inuktitut terms, and of ornamentation (494–498)—as well he might, since he and his crew used Inuit clothing for their own comfort and protection. The description of the headband comes at the end of this more general account. His occasional illustrations of Inuit clothing include both eccentric and sometimes standard items, and sometimes, as here, a rare, unusual, and beautiful article. The headband was probably worn during a drum dance on a winter occasion and is unlocated.

1/8. Muskox drinking cup (504). This item is briefly described, with the upturned bent handle with notches meant to ensure a good grip when eating greasy food. This engraving may refer to the example in the British Museum.

1/9. Muskox drinking cup (505). This, probably an unlocated actual example, is different from the previous cup: its handle is left straight but roughened to enable secure handling.

1/10. Fishing line (509). This is constructed with an ivory sinker to the hook, metal (which Parry says is made from a bent nail), a leader probably made of plaited sinew, and a line of sealskin wound around the two ends of a bent length of antler or bone, which acts as a fishing rod. The engraving probably represents an unlocated example.

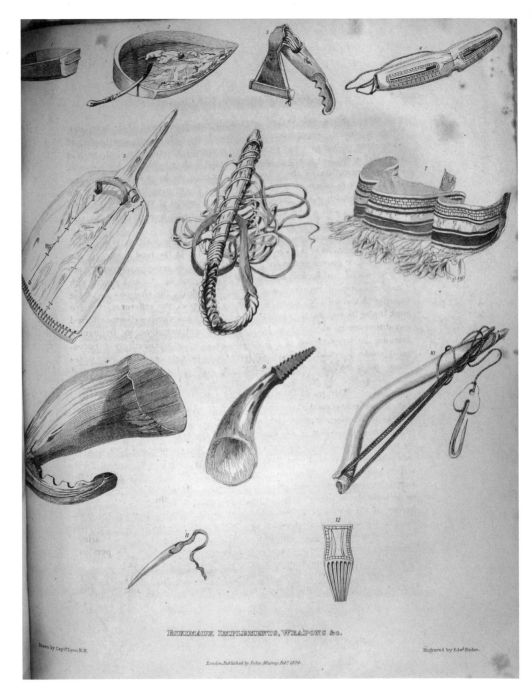

ESKIMAUX IMPLEMENTS, WEAPONS &c.

Drawn by Capt.ⁿ Lyon R.N.

Engraved by Edw.ᵈ Finden.

London, Published by John Murray, Feb.ʸ 1824.

Engraved plate from Parry 1824, 550

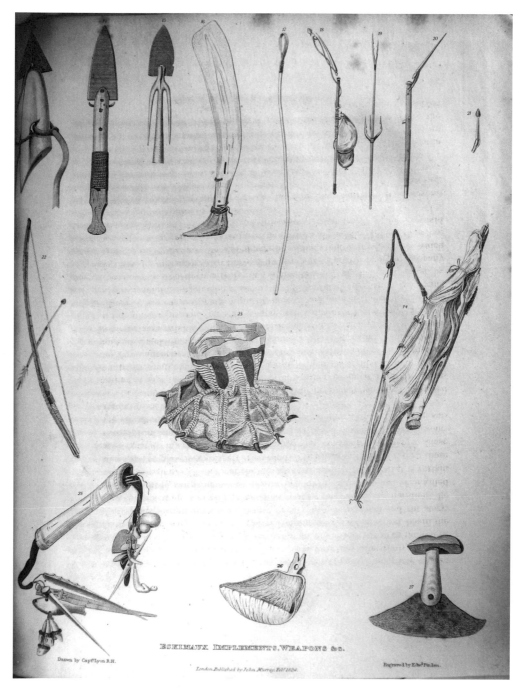

ESKIMAUX IMPLEMENTS, WEAPONS &c.

Drawn by Capt.ⁿ Lyon R.N.

London. Published by John Murray. Feb.ʸ 1824.

Engraved by E.ⁿ Finden.

Engraved plate from Parry 1824, 550

1/11. A threaded needle, rather generic in depiction, is illustrated on a separate page to the needle case (item 2/25). It is however engraved from the sketch in the Lyon notebook. Parry (537) describes the neatness of the work of Inuit women, with a long account of clothing, and is (rightly) especially fulsome in his description of the sewing required to make waterproof boots, and particularly on the need to draw the needle only partially through the skin which would otherwise let in water:

> the water-tight boots and shoes are "stitched." The latter is performed in a very adroit and efficacious manner, by putting the needle only half through the substance of one part of the seal-skin, so as to leave no hole for admitting the water.

However, Parry describes bone needles as clumsy and says that Inuit already had three-sided faceted iron needles. He describes how they were stored: drawn into pieces of skin, they were then pulled into a bone needle case; Parry also describes the skin thimble cases. Again it may seem unusual for a naval officer to describe and illustrate the seemingly humble needle, but of course sailors were responsible for making and repairing their own clothes and for the continual upkeep and repair of sails.

1/12. Comb (493–494). Parry includes a long description of the importance of hair and appearance for both men and women among the Inuit; he explains how much lustrous long hair was appreciated and how well it was looked after by women, with elaborate bindings in the best instance—and in plaits for those less careful. He also talks about lice and about grooming. He did not often observe, however, the use of the ivory comb, and, counterintuitively, was of the opinion that they were more of ornamental than practical use. However, surviving 19th-century Canadian combs are generally well worn, and it would be strange if they were not used in preparing hair before binding and in eliminating lice. The engraving is apparently a representation of an actual unlocated example. The comb in the Lyon notebook does not relate closely to the engraved example.

1/13. Harpoon head, with a unilateral barbed shank of antler or ivory, and a blade of iron (507). This is included in the Lyon water-colour sketchbook. While Parry is rather dismissive of the harpoon itself, he describes the way it works and detaches itself from the har-poon head in detail. The harpoon head, on the other hand, he says, requires art and ingenuity. He describes the bearded-sealskin line attached to the harpoon, carried by the hunter on his back, and adds that its important characteristic is that it does not freeze rigid. The complete harpoon is illustrated separately (item 1/18).

1/14. Parry illustrates both the ivory snow knife, *panna*, and here the iron flensing knife, which he also refers to as *panna* (503–504), mentioning that the illustration was provided by Lyon. More specif-ically, the flensing knife in Inuktitut is called *pilaut*. The iron blade example illustrated may or may not represent an actual example. Parry describes them as formidable-looking weapons, seven inches long, formed from a trade blade set with three rivets into a wood or bone handle. He notes their use, especially in scaling, and says they were never used in fighting. Later on Parry describes the use of the knife in eating: a piece of meat is taken in the mouth and then cut off close to the lips, Parry marvelling at the dexterity with which young children eat, never cutting their lips. It is possible that this example was made by Sorby in Sheffield.

1/15. Barbed lance point. The engraving shows a blade set in a barbed ivory foreshaft. The illustration is not keyed into a description, however, but it may represent the head of a lance—that is, a fixed-head spear, used to dispatch caribou. This is described as follows: "They have a spear called *ippoo* for killing deer in the water. They described it as having a light staff and a small head of iron; but they had none of these so fitted in the winter" (508).

1/16. A composite snow knife, *panna*, comprising an ivory blade fitted with a lashed whalebone or caribou-antler handle (503). Parry notes that they are exactly the same as those he saw on the west coast of Hudson Bay in 1820. Parry distinguishes between the ivory knives and the "much more serviceable kind, made of iron and called *panna*." This may or may not represent an actual example. Those that survive

are often made with ivory blades and whalebone handles, lashed together, the porous bone handle providing a better grip than would an
ivory one.

1/17. Seal breathing hole indicator (*keipkuttuk*, 510). When hunting at seal breathing holes on the winter sea ice, two artifices are used:
one is down or fluff that might be disturbed by the expulsion of air
from the emerging seal as it breaks the surface of the water at the
bottom of the breathing hole; the other (*keipkuttuk*) is a long, slender
instrument of bone that is pointed at one end and placed sticking up
above ice slush at the bottom of the hole when freezing; as the seal
comes up for air, the indicator is disturbed and the hunter knows to
strike. Parry describes the delicacy of the instruments as sometimes
like "fine wire." This seems to be an actual, unlocated example.

1/18. Seal harpoon ready for use (507–508). The engraving illustrates a fully rigged harpoon with a bone ivory foreshaft, harpoon
head, line, and bladder. Parry describes in detail the process of at-
taching the harpoon head to the foreshaft and securing the line with
what sailors call a "slippery hitch," a knot that comes apart with a tug
when the harpoon is embedded in the prey. He describes in detail,
presumably from first-hand observation, the way in which a toggle
turns sideways and secures the seal.

1/19. Bird dart (508–509). Parry describes this instrument in
detail: "The *nuguee*, or dart for birds (19), has, besides its two ivory
prongs at the end of the staff, three divergent ones in the middle of
it, with several small double barbs upon them turning inwards." He
compares its forms to those elsewhere and says that it was launched
with a throwing stick or *atlatl*. He also maintains that it is only the
bird dart which is launched with a throwing stick. However, in other
parts of the Arctic, especially Alaska, throwing sticks were used to
launch harpoon darts against sea mammals. The print was probably
engraved after a Lyon watercolour in the British Museum sketchbook.

1/20. Walrus and whaling harpoon (508). Parry says that

[the] largest weapon is that called *katteelik*, with which the walrus and
whale are killed. The staff of this is not longer, but much stouter than

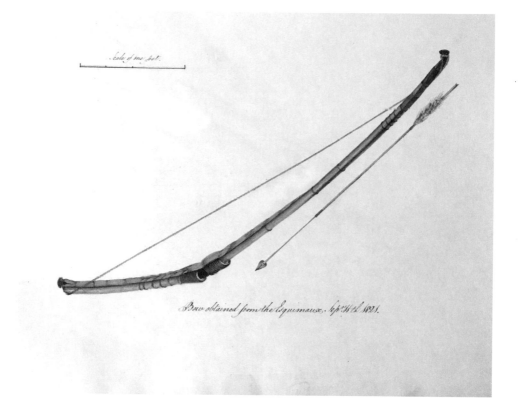

Scale of one foot.

Bow obtained from the Esquimaux. Sepr. 11th 1821.

"Bow obtained from the Esquimaux, Sepr. 11th 1821." Lyon 1824. © Trustees of the British Museum

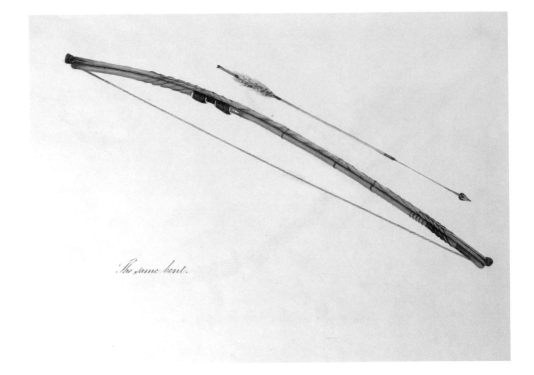

"The same bent." Lyon 1824. © Trustees of the British Museum

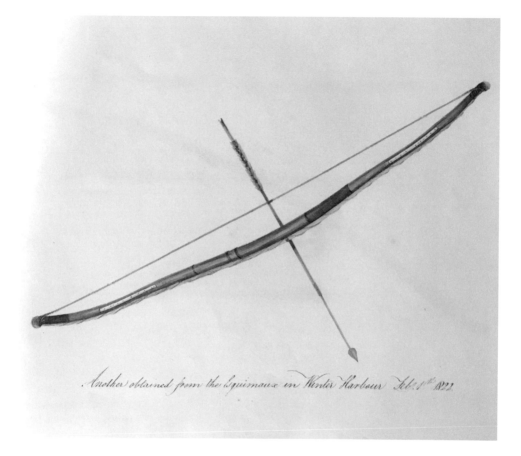

"Another obtained from the Esquimaux in Winter Harbour Feby. 1st. 1822." Lyon 1824.

"Weapons used by the Esquimaux A. Lance used in killing an Animal or large Fish after it is caught or wounded. B. For throwing at Birds. C. For catching Salmon or smaller fish in Shallow Water, by confining them to the bottom, the two side pieces of bone opening with pressure & the centre being pointed runs into them." Lyon 1824. © Trustees of the British Museum

"An Harpoon used in killing the Seal, Walrus &c when in their Canoes & which they throw with great accuracy. 3. Another but which instead of throwing is stuck into the above when they get close to it, the person using it retaining the staff in his hand but a bladder being attached to the end of the line which is about 4 or 5 fathom long, they haul him up when exhausted. 1. A spare point for 2, the one bone, the other iron. 5 a case for 4. 6. a small Hatchet the Iron of which was English manufactured with the initials of makers name, but the handle which was rather curiously cut to fit the hand was done by the natives." Lyon 1824. © Trustees of the British Museum

"Needle or Bodkin. The neatness with which they sew is extraordinary. 2&3 Shade for the eyes. These poor beings during the summer months suffer much from snow blindness, but as a preventive they wear a shade of bone or wood, as above. 4. A Comb. The hair is perfectly black, glossy, and straight, coarse, and not very clean." Lyon 1824. © Trustees of the British Museum

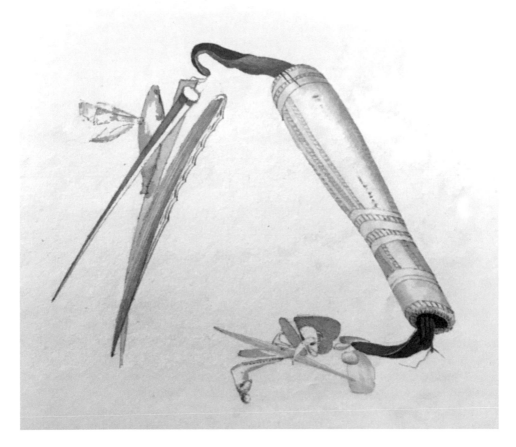

[needle case, no caption] Lyon 1824. © Trustees of the British Museum

"Nee-a-kood-loo. A Native of Southampton Island on August 27 1824." A Sallirmiut man paddling a craft made of three inflated sealskins, connected by blown intestines. His paddle is made of whale bone. The Sallirmiut are thought to have been a distinct, long-isolated Inuit group living on and around Southampton Island (Salliq). The last of the Sallirmiut, a man named Qingaq, lived out his life in the Igloolik area (Inuksuk IE-004, 1986). G.F. Lyon 1825, 55, Library and Archives Canada that of the others, especially towards the middle, where there is a small shoulder of ivory securely lashed to it for the thumb to rest against, and thus to give additional force in throwing or thrusting the spear.

1/21. Harpoon foreshaft (508). Here Parry illustrates the foreshaft for the foregoing heavy harpoon. He very neatly describes how the foreshaft disengages from the harpoon head after the moment of strike:

> The ivory point of this weapon is made to fit into a socket at the end of the staff, where it is secured by double thongs, in such a manner as steadily to retain its position when a strain is put upon it in the direction of its length, but immediately disengaging itself with a sort of spring, when any lateral strain endangers its breaking.

The engraving of the disengaged foreshaft derives from a sketch in the Lyon notebook. He also describes the full sealskin float used to slow down the walrus or whale. This is followed by a full description of walrus and whale hunting (508–509).

1/22. Bow (510–512). Parry's description of Inuit bows is detailed and comprehensive. He says that the best bows are made of one piece of fir, but that this is seldom available. Instead, two to five pieces of bone (often antler) are bound together with long lengths of sinew and with strengthening wedges at the arms and the belly. He uses nautical terms to describe the way in which the bows are constructed—"tree nail" for pegs to hold the pieces of the bow together, and "woolding" for the binding.

1/23. Bird feet bag (537). Parry describes the little bags used to hold sinew and other articles, probably including lamp wick: "which are sometimes made of the skin of birds' feet, disposed with the claws downwards in a very neat and tasteful manner." This example has probably perished. As mentioned above, Leah Otak's mother Zipporah Piungittuq Inuksuk made such a bag for the British Museum in 2000.

1/24. Bow case and arrows (511–512). The bow case, no doubt filled with arrows, is not mentioned in the text. However, Parry describes both the arrows in detail and discusses the skill with which the bow was used. Although he does not use any complimentary terms, the bald statement of the trial indicates the considerable respect in which he held Inuit marksmanship:

> We tried their skill in archery by getting them to shoot at a mark for a prize, though with bows in extremely bad order on account of the frost and their hands very cold. The mark was two of their spears stuck upright in the snow, their breadth being three inches and a half. At twenty yards they struck this every time; at thirty sent the arrows always within an inch or two of it; and at forty or forty-five yards, I should think, would generally hit a fawn if the animal stood still. These weapons are perhaps sufficient to inflict a mortal wound at something more than that distance....

1/25. Needle case (537). The engraving illustrated seems to be taken from life and has not yet been located. It was, however, included in the Lyon watercolour sketchbook. Parry describes its linear-cut decoration, which relates to that used on goggles, on combs, and in tattooing. As ever, attached to the needle case are other domestic articles, including marrow spoons, amulets, ivory fish lures, and awls.

1/26. Bowl of muskox horn (503). Parry describes this as being made out of the broad base of the horn; he does not here describe the likely process of boiling and softening the horn before opening and spreading it to form the shallow bowl. This depiction may represent the example at the British Museum.

1/27. Woman's knife or *ulu* (504). Parry says that the better sort of knife was made of iron, and that this one had the imprint of Wild and Sorby. Sorby was the family name of famous Sheffield cutlers who exported steel blades around the world.[12] The engraved example, of iron, with an antler or bone shaft and handle of muskox horn, has not been located. Parry notes that when an Inuk made an *ulu*, small slivers of iron were used (along the edge of a curved bone blade), and that the iron was likely traded through "indirect communication" from trading posts on Hudson Bay. Parry describes acquiring a knife from Togolat, and it is of course possible that this is the example here illustrated (523).

It is appropriate to finish this essay by describing something of the importance of one object: a small, dehaired, bleached sealskin water cup or bucket, listed in the appendix at 2/14. Uniquely, this item has a rim stiffener constructed of a strip from a tin can. This object symbolically acts to show how quickly Inuit incorporated new materials and techniques in their lives; that flexibility and ingenuity is all the more telling in that tin cans provided in the 1820s a new way of preserving food in Europe. On departure, supplies provided by the Admiralty included canned food made by Donkin, Hall and Gamble (later Hall and Donkin), founded in 1813 by Bryan Donkin, who had bought and developed a French patent. Canned food was tried out by Sir Joseph Banks, the Duke of Wellington, and the royal family, and then the firm acted as supplier to the Royal Navy. Obviously the finished tin cans would have provided ample trading metal for the expedition needing to acquire food and equipment. More interestingly, Inuit immediately learned to use the different materials; Parry commented on a woman mending a tin kettle with hole in it by using solder from a meat tin can. Lyon in Repulse Bay also described trading for cans:

> Captain Parry gave the women some presents, but nothing afforded so much delight as the empty tin meat cans, which they hugged and kissed with the liveliest demonstrations of joy. One of the men parted readily with his bow, arrows, and quiver ... (Parry 1824, 453; Lyon 1824, 75, 184S)[13]

Cans were, therefore, an important article of wealth, so it was noted that a young husband from Igloolik needed to be a good hunter and to own tin cans. At the end of the winter season Lyon commented on departing Inuit:

On the 13th, a party walked out to witness the departure of our winter acquaintances. Two sledges stood ready packed with skins and household furniture to a yard in height. Tin, pots, bottles, and jars, hung dangling all round the sides ...

And of course Leah's life, moving from the land to the settlement of Igloolik, demonstrates that same ability to change and learn, to adapt and incorporate, and to hybridize and develop knowledge that was shown by her forebears in the 1820s. It is impossible, of course, for non-hunting southerners to imagine the kind of fortitude and degree of intelligence required of individuals and communities to adapt to change as rapidly as that which occurred in Leah's lifetime.

APPENDICES

Inuit Collections Associated with Parry: The Official Collection

In the early 19th century, accessions into the British Museum were listed in a donations book and only occasionally itemized. During the 1820s, however, accessions were sometimes accompanied by summary lists, as was Parry's collection of 1824 and F.W. Beechey's of 1828. The 1824 list begins with Inuit materials and then continues with other items, especially birds. At the moment it is not clear in whose hand this was written. It might for instance have been written by a naval explorer, but the internal evidence suggests that it was written by a curator: one of the unique items is the baleen mattress, which has a secondary misidentification as a fishing net. This implies that the cataloguer did not have first-hand experience of the material. Practically speaking, baleen was used in fishing equipment, but this item could not have been used as a net; this suggests that the author of the list was given information about the collection second-hand as a curator, and some general details of the use of baleen, but then conflated and misidentified this artifact. Unlike earlier lists from voyages there is no systemization of the collection, and no numbering. Menzies, for instance, on the return of Vancouver's voyage in the 1790s, numbered his materials and to some extent differentiated place of collection and artifact type. The 1824 collection itself, which includes the oldest Inuit clothing from Canada, itemizes artifacts that are not necessarily important, and—in the case of the bird spear and sealing harpoon—artifacts that are incomplete. This implies that the collection was brought together rather late in the day, sometime after the return of the voyage, and with limited interest, for instance, in providing a complete set of clothing, kayak, and hunting gear. Curiously, no attempt was made to memorialize individual Inuit who had been associated with the voyage.

Collection List—1824

2/1–25. Materials presented to the British Museum, April 10, 1824. Until the middle of the 19th century collections were not catalogued as such: the accession was recorded in the donations book, and in the 1820s items would be listed in ink without numbers in folio booklets; that for the Parry collection is labelled "Catalogue of Objects Obtained on Capt. Parry's Sec. Voy: 1824."[14] The current number of the object, when identifiable, follows the 1824 description.

2/1. "Esquimaux Lamp. Igloolik." Am1824,0410.1

2/2. "-------------- breeches Winter island."

2/3. "--------------- winter mittens. Winter island."

2/4. "--------------- ancle-shoes."

2/5. "Net used for laying under the beds & for fishing." Am1824,0410.5

2/6. "Spoon of the horn of Musk ox." Am1824,0410.6

2/7 "iron knife."

2/8 "bone knife." Am1824,0410.8

2/9. "Musk ox horn cup. Winter island." Am1824,0410.9

2/10. "Bones worn as ornaments by women. Savage Island." Am1824,0410.10

2/11. "Platted sinew used for Eq. Bows. Igloolik." Am1824,0410.11

2/12. "Eye shade Winter island." Am1824,0410.12

2/13. "------------ bowl. do ----------." Am1824,0410.13

2/14. "Skin Water vessel do." Am1824,0410.14

2/15. "Seal Skin dressed by the savages Esquim[aux] of Savage island." Am1824,0410.15

2/16. "Part of Esqu bird dart Savage Island." Am1824,0410.16

2/17. "Little basket Middle Savage island." Am1824,0410.17

2/18. "Part of Equ spear Igloolik."

2/19. "Hair of the musk ox." Am1824,0410.19

2/20. "Instrument for sucking water out of the Ponds. Igloolik." Am1824,0410.20

2/21. "Potstone [unreadable crossed out] Equ cooking pot id." Am1824,0410.21

2/22. "Womans inner boots Winter Island." Am1824,0410.22

2/23. "Instr. Used for seal fishing Igloolik."

2/24. "Womans dress." Am1824,0410.24

2/25. "Hair skin blanket Winter island."

3/1–10. Materials presented to the British Museum, March 13, 1926. The collections register records: "Presented by Sir F Sidney [*sic*] Parry, KBE, CB," and "Specimens collected by Capt. (afterwards Admiral Sir) W.E. Parry, F.R.S. on his second voyage for the discovery of a North-West Passage, 1821–1823. The Eskimo specimens are from IGLOOLIK." However, only the initial items in the list are Inuit, and the collection includes a pair of Cree moccasins, a Peruvian pot, and materials from Parry's time in Australia and the Pacific. The donor, Frederick Sydney Parry (1861–1941), worked for Customs and Excise (1904–25) and may have combined materials which he had inherited from his grandfather Edward Parry with those from other sources. This is suggested by the snow goggles in the collection, which came from government offices in the 20th century. Frederick Sydney Parry's granddaughter, Ann Parry, is Edward's biographer.[15]

3/1. "Composite ivory & bone snow knife."

3/2-3. "'Ivory marrow spoon' and a second."

3/4. "Soap-stone cooking pot. One side has been mended."

3/5. "Skin model of kayak."

3/6. "Wooden Arctic spectacles. Copy of Eskimo. Found in the

Admiralty off (ice?) 1911."
3/7. "Ivory bag handle."
3/8–10. "'Bone toggle,' three dog trace fastening rings for dog
harness."

Further items are in other British Museum collections, Edinburgh,
Exeter, and Oxford:

4/1. Kayak (*qajaq*) (Am1994,Q.2). This kayak, in the British Museum collection, was identified by John MacDonald of the Igloolik
Research Centre as having been made by Charles Purfer, Captain
Lyon's carpenter on the *Hecla*. Purfer built the kayak frame following
the "best Esquimaux models." The kayak's sealskin covering was sewn
in place by Inuit women (Lyon 1824, 409). A replica of this kayak was
built by MacDonald in 2000 as a prop for Igloolik Isuma Production's
film *Atanarjuat: The Fast Runner* (2001). MacDonald used "detailed
structural drawings" made by Michael Morgan (1996), "paid for by
Morton and Estelle Sosland."[16]

4/2 and 4/3. Samples of ring and beads (Am1926,0313.39) taken
to and from the Arctic. A "cask" of rings was taken out as gifts, and
"According to attached label, this string of beads was assembled by a
young Inuit ['Esquimaux'] girl who was on board HMS Fury accompanying her sick brother during Parry's expedition 1821."[17]

4/4. Collection in Edinburgh. A list of this collection, "Parry
Material," numbering approximately fifty items, is available from the
Department of World Cultures, National Museum of Scotland. Some
of the items illustrated by Lyon are likely to be identified.

4/5. Sled and kayak in Exeter (see Pearce 1976).

4/6. Two small collections from Parry's circles were given to the
University of Oxford's Ashmolean Museum in the 1820s. Captain
George Francis Lyon (1795–1832) presented a collection of some
thirty pieces in 1824, and Lieutenant Francis Harding (lieutenant on
the *Griper* under Lyon) gave a collection of some twenty-four pieces
in 1827. These donations were recorded in the Ashmolean's manuscript
catalogue (for a transcription, see MacGregor 2000, 242, 245) and
partially recorded (Duncan 1836, 185–187). In 1886, the objects were

transferred, along with the rest of the Ashmolean's "ethnographic" holdings, to the newly founded Pitt Rivers Museum. As part of its founding collection, the latter also holds an ivory lure (1884.11.15) that was apparently collected by Lyon on the *Hecla* and acquired by General Pitt Rivers by 1874.[18]

4/7 In Edinburgh, at the National Museum of Scotland, a group of fifteen items from Parry's Second Voyage have been identified. These were recorded on November 29, 1823, at the University Museum:

> Arrived last Saturday evening a Box; addressed as follows: "Professor Jameson, Museum, Edinburgh. Admiralty Office, 12th November 1823." It was found to contain specimens of Rocks collected during the late expedition under Capt. Parry. The collection presented by Mr. Fisher, consists of the following articles: 1st Box. Specimens of the clothing worn by the Eskimaux, being chiefly of Rein Deer fur... [19]

Robert Jameson (1774–1854), geologist and natural historian at the university, would have been particularly interested in the minerals, which filled the second box from Fisher. Alexander Fisher was surgeon on the *Hecla* on Parry's first two voyages. Unfortunately the ethnographic articles were not listed, and a research project is now underway to identify surviving artifacts. Two, an ulu and bighorn sheep horn scoop, are illustrated in Briony Crozier's initial report.[20] The university collections went to the new Edinburgh museum in the 1850s.

4/8 A small number of objects collected by Parry are held in the museum of the Bath Royal Literary and Scientific Institution. They were accessioned in 1845 as a donation from Parry's brother, Dr. C. Miller Parry, and are listed under six headings. As with the Edinburgh collection, further research is required to determine provenance and affiliation.

ACKNOWLEDGMENTS

Generous assistance in the preparation of this paper came with the Toronto Dominion Fellowship at the Inuit Art Foundation, Toronto, awarded in 2015, to research early Inuit collections. The author would like particularly to thank Pat Feheley, Jimmy Manning, and Sarah Milroy at the Foundation, and especially to acknowledge Scott Mullin and the generosity of the Toronto–Dominion Bank.

BIBLIOGRAPHY

Brody, Hugh. 1987. *Living Arctic: Hunters of the Canadian North*. London: Faber and Faber.

Craciun, Adriana. 2016. *Writing Arctic Disaster*. Cambridge: Cambridge University Press.

Crozier, Briony. 1999. "From Earliest Contact: An Examination of Eskimo and Aleut Art in Scottish Museum Collections." Research paper, University of St Andrews.

Duncan, Philip Bury. 1836. *A Catalogue of the Ashmolean Museum, Descriptive of the Zoological Specimens, Antiquities, Coins, and Miscellaneous Curiosities*. Oxford: S. Collingwood.

Gagnon, Jeanne. 2011. "A Very Backward Experience." *Northern News Services*, August 22. www.nnsl.com/frames/newspapers/2011-08/aug22_11be.html.

Geoghegan, T. 2013. "The Story of How the Tin Can Nearly Wasn't." *BBC News Magazine*, April 21. www.bbc.co.uk/news/magazine-21689069.

Inuksuk, Aipilik. 1986. Interview IE-004. Igloolik Oral History Project. Igloolik.

Issenman, Betty. 2002. "Erudition and Emotion at the British Museum." *Études/Inuit/Studies* 26, no. 1: 235–238.

King, J.C.H., ed. 1989. *Living Arctic: Report and Catalogue*. London: Trustees of the British Museum and Indigenous Survival International.

King, J.C.H., and Henrietta Lidchi. 1998. *Imaging the Arctic*. London: British Museum Press, and Seattle: University of Washington Press.

Lyon, G.F. 1824. *The Private Journal of Captain G. F. Lyon, of H. M. S. Hecla, during the Recent Voyage of Discovery under Captain Parry*. London: John Murray. https://archive.org/stream/privatejournalc01lyongoog#page/n8/mode/2up.

MacDonald, John. 2014. "In Memoriam Leah Aksaajuq Umik Ivalu Otak (1950–2014)." *Études/Inuit/Studies* 38, no. 1–2: 297–300.

MacGregor, Arthur. 2000. *Manuscript Catalogues of the Early Museum Collections, 1683–1886 (Part I)*. British Archaeological Reports, International

Series 907. Oxford: Ashmolean Museum.

Parry, A. 1963. *Parry of the Arctic*. London: Chatto & Windus.

Parry, William Edward. 1824. *Journal of a Second Voyage for the Discovery of a North-west Passage from the Atlantic to the Pacific*. London: John Murray. https://archive.org/stream/cihm_42230#page/n5/mode/2up/search/540.

Pearce, Susan M. 1976. *Towards The Pole: A Catalogue of the Eskimo Collections*. Exeter Museums Publication No. 82. Exeter: City of Exeter Museums & Art Gallery.

Roskill, Stephen W. 2004. "Parry, Sir (William) Edward (1893–1972)." In *Oxford Dictionary of National Biography*, rev. ed. Oxford: Oxford University Press. www.oxforddnb.com/view/article/31530.

Shephard, Sue. 2001. *Pickled, Potted, and Canned: How the Art and Science of Food Preserving Changed the World*. New York: Simon & Schuster.

University of Edinburgh Museum. 1823. "Weekly Report Volume 2, Saturday 29." Edinburgh: National Museums Scotland.

CHAPTER 5

Inuit Oral History

Statements and Testimony in Criminal Investigations—The Case of the Killing of Robert Janes, 1920

Kenn Harper

"A word is dead when it's been said, some say.
I say it just begins to live that day."
Emily Dickinson

INTRODUCTION

WHILE INUIT ORAL HISTORY has been much collected and studied in recent years, I believe that there is a sub-genre that has been given very little attention, but which has a body of information sufficient to support its study. That sub-genre comprises statements and testimony given in coroner's inquests, preliminary hearings, police investigations, and court proceedings themselves.[1]

I have looked at one such body of work, the copious records which form the investigation of the killing of Robert Janes in 1920 and the trial of Nuqallaq (Noo-kud-lah), Aatitaaq (Ahteetah) and Ululijarnaaq

(Oorooreungnak)[2] in Pond Inlet in 1923. These records in fact serve as a major source of the information I used in researching a book I have written on this subject, which was published in 2017.

A word is necessary on my approach to, and understanding of, oral history.

The anthropologist Julie Cruikshank (1994) considers oral history to be "a more specialized term [than oral tradition] usually referring to a research method where a sound recording is made of an interview about first-hand experience occurring during the lifetime of an eye-witness" (404).

I agree to a point. I don't think that an oral history need necessarily be of a first-hand experience from an eyewitness. The second-hand re-counting of an event by a person who heard it from another (perhaps a participant or an eyewitness) may be an equally valid source—it is that narrator's oral history of a significant event. Indeed, it may be all we have for certain events.

Alessandro Portelli (1998) has noted, "Oral sources are *oral* sources. [Emphasis in original.] Scholars are willing to admit that the actual document is the recorded tape, but almost all go on to work on the transcripts, and it is only transcripts that are published." And: "The transcript turns aural objects into visual ones, which inevitably im-plies changes and interpretation" (64).

This is more in keeping with my conception of oral history. For me, oral history is oral history at the moment that it is spoken, and thereafter if it is recorded and preserved on a voice-recording device. Everything beyond that point—be it a written record taken verbatim by a third party in the original language, or a written record trans-lated verbatim into another language, or a paraphrase of the original speech—is, to me, a derivative of oral history. And all derivatives have the possibility of distortion and error. Even if written down verbatim, as the speaker provides the original speech, there is room for error in the transcription, especially as few writers can keep up with the normal pace of oral speech. Unless it is simultaneously recorded on a voice-recording device, there is no possibility to go back to an original to check the accuracy of the transcription. The possibility for error is compounded when the speech is in Inuktitut but the written record of it is in another language such as English and comes to us through an interpreter. And it is further compounded when that interpreter is untrained.

THE BACKGROUND[3]

In 1920, Nuqallaq, an Inuit leader in northern Baffin Island, shot and killed Sakirmiaq—Robert Janes, a white man and independent trader from Newfoundland—on the sea ice near Cape Crauford on the northern tip of Brodeur Peninsula, Baffin Island. Janes had been in the district since 1916, trading from his post at Patricia River, near present-day Pond Inlet. Abandoned by his backer in St. John's and denied passage south in 1919 by rival trader Henry Toke Munn (Kapitaikuluk) of the Arctic Gold Exploration Syndicate, Janes planned to return south by travelling by dogsled from Patricia River via Navy Board Inlet, Lancaster Sound, Admiralty Inlet, Igloolik and the west coast of Hudson Bay, and from there to Winnipeg and Newfoundland. While leaving the district, he camped with a group of Inuit at Cape Crauford and argued with them over debts in furs that he claimed they owed him. Nuqallaq, natural leader of the group, had had a complex relationship with Janes. Early in the trader's stay in the district, the two had quarrelled over a woman, a problem that had disappeared when Nuqallaq took another woman as his wife. Janes had also had disputes with other Inuit over furs and debts. At Cape Crauford, when Janes began to threaten to shoot the Inuit and their dogs if the men did not turn over their furs to him, the Inuit decided that Nuqallaq should kill Janes if he did not cease his threatening behaviour.

Nuqallaq was a leader of his people, an *angajuqqaaq*, a camp boss. At Cape Crauford he initially tried to avoid Janes, then to placate him, even going so far as to act as an intermediary between Janes and the other Inuit. When Janes's offensive behaviour continued, he tried to counsel the trader, informing him of the consequences of his deviant actions, as a camp leader would have done with an Inuit member of his own community. But when Janes resumed his aberrant behaviour, and when Nuqallaq and other men of the community knew with certainty that Janes was a threat to the survival of their camp, Nuqallaq knew that he must commit the act that his role as leader demanded. There was no external authority to whom they could report Janes's behaviour, no police from whom to seek help or protection. Even then Nuqallaq wavered, telling his wife that he would like to simply flee the camp in the night. But he knew that he could not. He knew that his campmates relied on him to rid them of the threat in their midst.

Father Guy Mary-Rousselière, a priest who lived in Pond Inlet for over thirty years, recognized the killing for what it was: a necessary measure to maintain social control. He wrote in 1988,

> Janes' [sic] murder might be considered as a typical example of 'execution' in a primitive society such as the traditional Eskimo community. The community felt itself endangered by unreasonable conduct, accompanied by violent threats. The question was discussed and the sentence applied. (Atagutsiaq and Mary-Rousselière 1998, 10)

The Inuit did not conceal the killing of Robert Janes. Rather, they reported it to a rival trader with an explanation of the reasons why Janes was killed. That trader, Munn of the Arctic Gold Exploration Syndicate (despite its name, a fur trading company), reported the killing to the RCMP in Ottawa by letter in the fall of 1920. A police officer was sent to Pond Inlet in 1921 to investigate. Staff Sergeant Alfred Herbert Joy sent his report to Ottawa the following summer, recommending that a trial for three accused be held the following year in Pond Inlet.

In 1923 a judge, crown prosecutor, defence attorney, and court clerk travelled to Pond Inlet aboard the C.G.S. *Arctic* for the murder trial of Nuqallaq, Aatitaaq, and Ululijarnaaq. On August 30, 1923, the jury—five members of the ship's crew plus the ship's wireless operator, all white males—returned its verdict, acquitting Aatitaaq, but convicting Nuqallaq and Ululijarnaaq of the lesser charge of manslaughter, with a recommendation for leniency for Ululijarnaaq. The judge passed sentence immediately. Ululijarnaaq was given two years imprisonment with hard labour at the police guardroom in Pond Inlet. Nuqallaq was sentenced to ten years' imprisonment in Stony Mountain

Penitentiary in Manitoba. This was the result of the first murder trial in what is today Nunavut.

Aatitaaq (left), Nuqallaq (centre), and Ululijarnaaq (right) were photographed in Pond Inlet during the investigation of the killing of Robert Janes. All three stood trial. Photo by Lachlan T. Burwash / Library and Archives Canada / PA 099050

THE INVESTIGATION: ORAL HISTORIES
Some, but probably not all, of the Inuit deponents in the investigation of the killing of Janes were literate in the Inuktitut syllabic orthography, but their statements (with one exception)[4] were given orally in Inuktitut and not reduced to writing in syllabics. An interpreter heard their statements in Inuktitut and recorded them, either in verbatim translation or in paraphrase, in English. All of the deponents in Baffin Island were Inuit with the exception of Wilfrid Caron, a French-Canadian trader. I have included his statements with the Inuit testimony because of his long-term association with the Inuit and his fluency in their language, which gave him an in-depth knowledge of the circumstances.[5]

Henry Toke Munn and the First Testimonies
Munn reached Button Point, on Bylot Island, on September 1, 1920, and learned immediately of the killing of Janes. In a letter to the authorities in Ottawa, he wrote,

> I have to report to you the killing of a Newfoundland man named
> Robert Janes in April of this year, by a native named Nuqallaq (Noo-
> kud-lah), as gathered by me from native reports on the arrival of my
> ship at Ponds [sic] Inlet on September 1st.[6]

Munn wrote that he would investigate the murder during the
course of the winter by taking evidence from the natives.

Munn was quick. By the following day he had already interrogated
Nuqallaq and Uuttukuttuk (Oo-took-ito), and reported by letter, "I
have asked Nuqallaq why he did this. He states, 'Janes has said for a
long time he was going to kill me; he has told many natives so; I was
afraid and so I shot him first.'"[7]

He continued,

> Janes had very often threatened to kill Nuqallaq…. Had Nuqallaq pre-
> meditated murder he could have shot Janes when he met him alone
> with Uuttukuttuk. Nuqallaq was frightened by Janes [sic] repeated
> statements to natives he would kill him and believed Janes would do
> this on the first opportunity.[8]

How had Munn acquired this information? By his own admission,
he spoke Inuktitut imperfectly. George Diament presumably spoke it
even less well. The only other white man there, Wilfrid Caron, spoke
Inuktitut well but English imperfectly. Nuqallaq was one of two Inuit
in the district who had a smattering of English, the other being Tom
Kunuk, whose Inuktitut name was Takijualuk, and who worked for
Munn. The rest of the Inuit spoke only a trade jargon English or none
at all. It is not surprising, then, that Munn's recounting of Nuqallaq's
reasons for killing Janes gives reasons that differ markedly from those
given by other Inuit subsequently questioned. It was a garbled version
collected by Munn quickly within his first two days back in the North.

Munn's resident trader, George Diament, left for Peterhead on
the ship in September 1920. He made a statement there briefly mentioning Janes's troubles with Nuqallaq over a woman, but went into

considerable detail on his threats to the camp at Cape Crauford, and countered the focus of Munn's statement by saying, "I gathered from the natives that they were afraid to tackle Janes (a white man) and that Nuqallaq was the only one who had the courage to shoot him."[9]

Munn also arranged to have his former trader, James Florence, who had been in the district from 1916 until 1919 and returned in 1920, make a statement. Florence's information focused on the troubles between Janes and Nuqallaq over a woman, Kalluk (Kudloo), and troubles between Janes and Umik (Oomee, Ooming), the killer's father. He remarked, "I was not astonished on learning that ... Nuqallaq had shot Janes, as Janes did everything to bring this about by his treatment of him, and Nuqallaq was in constant dread of being shot himself by Janes ..."[10]

Wilfrid Caron was not in the district at the time of the killing. He made his written statement at Pond's Inlet on September 6. In it, he states simply that "R. Janes was shot by an Eskimo named Nuqallaq, who gave as an excuse that he was afraid Janes would kill him." Caron described only the two men's problems over "an Eskimo girl" and the altercation between Janes and Umik, mentioning nothing about Janes's extortionate trading methods and threats to Inuit in general.[11]

In the summer of 1921 Munn returned to Peterhead and wrote again to Ottawa with new information. He had conducted his own "Enquiry into the Murder of R. Janes ..."[12] and had taken brief statements from Uuttukuttuk, Nuqallaq, Kunuk, Qaumauk (Kar-il-nee, Kahlnahl), and Kaukuarjuk (Quaquajuak); all of this he forwarded to Ottawa.

These statements comprise three pages of type. Although brief, they are interesting in that, with the exception of Uuttukuttuk's statement, they are in question-and-answer format, although in three of the interviews only one open-ended question was asked. (To Kunuk and to Kaukuarjuk: "What do you know about this affair?" To Qaumauk: "Were you at Cape Crawford [sic] when Janes was there?")

Munn noted in his summation, "The evidence taken above was read over to each Native by using an Interpreter and the Witness stated it was what they said. The evidence was taken through an Interpreter."[13]

The three pages of Inuit statements provided very different information than what Munn had previously provided. In these five statements, remarkably, there is no mention whatsoever of Janes's trouble with Nuqallaq over the Inuit woman, Kalluk. They focus entirely on Janes's trading methods and his threats to the Inuit, especially during his days at Cape Crauford. Munn, however, did raise the subject of the woman briefly in his summation.[14]

Ottawa had already gone into action, sending Staff Sergeant Alfred Herbert Joy to Pond's Inlet in the summer of 1921[15] to conduct an official investigation. Unfortunately he arrived a few days after Munn's departure and so was not privy to this new information, knowing only Munn's previous information emphasizing Janes's trouble with Nuqallaq over a woman. Had he had the newer information, he might have begun his investigation with a different perspective.

This ends the involvement of Captain Munn in securing Inuit testimony.

Coroner's Inquest

Joy exhumed Janes's body from its grave at Cape Crauford and returned with it to Pond Inlet on January 21, 1922. Two days later, he convened a Coroner's Inquest with a jury comprised of three white men, all traders. They were Wilfred Campbell Parsons, manager of the Hudson's Bay Company (HBC) post, whom the Inuit called Nujaqanngittuq, the bald one; Gaston Herodier, his clerk, who either then or later acquired the name Ataataluk, the poor father (he would later sire a child in the community); and Wilfrid Caron, known to the Inuit as Quvviunginnaq, the one who always had a tear in his eye.

The Crime Report that serves as a report on the Coroner's Inquest does not state who the interpreter was, but we must assume that it was the HBC interpreter, James Tooktosina (also known as Jimmie Ford), or the HBC manager, Wilfred Campbell Parsons. We do not know what facility Parsons had in Inuktitut.

The inquest lasted until February 11. Maniq (Munne) described the shooting and added that he was very afraid of Janes and happy to see him dead; he had rewarded Nuqallaq with a white fox pelt for his actions. Qaumauk and Siniqqaq (Sinnikah) gave similar testimony. Katsak (Kutchuk) testified that Nuqallaq had told him that he needed to shoot Janes before Janes killed somebody. None of these men claimed to have actually heard Janes threaten to shoot Inuit or their dogs; the only person who gave such testimony was Uuttukuttuk, Janes's dog-driver on his final journey, who stated that he had told the other Inuit about it.

The evidence given by these Inuit at the Coroner's Inquest was recorded in the first person, and it also appears as paraphrastic information in Joy's three-page report to Ottawa on February 13, 1922.[16]

The Inuit often complained about the interpreting of James Tooktosina. Tooktosina had been recruited as an HBC interpreter to assist in matters of trading, not to translate sensitive material related to a killing. In making suggestions to Ottawa for the trial that would take place in 1923, Joy asked Ottawa to arrange with HBC that Tooktosina continue to be made available. Whether this was an expression of his faith in the man's abilities as an interpreter or simply a matter of practicality is unclear; Joy was worried that Tooktosina might take furlough in 1923 and be replaced by a different Labrador interpreter less familiar with the local dialect.[17] Inuit complaints about Tooktosina's interpreting will be discussed more fully below.

PRELIMINARY INQUIRY

By mid-July 1922 Nuqallaq, Aatitaaq, and Ululijarnaaq were under open arrest at Pond Inlet. Joy then called a Preliminary Inquiry, which commenced on July 10 at Button Point and lasted until July 20. The three accused were present. In advance of the inquiry Joy had taken Statutory Declarations over the period of February to June from twelve Inuit (fourteen statements) and Wilfrid Caron, in the event that these statements might be needed as evidence at the trial.

At the inquiry Ataguttaaluk (Ahtootahloo), Siniqqaq, Ijjangiaq (Edineyah), and Maniq (Munne) (from whom statements had previously been taken), as well as Uuttukuttuk and Katsak, were deposed. The Statutory Declarations previously taken from Kaukuarjuk, Nutarariaq (Nootakgagayuk), Kunuk, and Ivalaaq (Ivahlung) were entered as evidence. This constituted the evidence for the prosecution. Nuqa-llaq questioned four of the prosecution witnesses, and Aatitaaq one of them.

Evidence for the defence was Statutory Declarations previously taken from Paniluk (Peneloo), Amarualik (Amooahlik), Qamaniq (Kama-nuk), and Manu (Munoo). The accused Nuqallaq's wife, Ataguttiaq (Ahtooteuk), was deposed, as was Wilfrid Caron. Statements were also taken from each of the three accused.

All of the statements and depositions referred to are contained in full in the records of the Preliminary Inquiry. In addition, Joy pre-pared a six-page typed Crime Report on July 22, 1922, in which he summarized the testimony of each witness. This summary, too, con-stitutes a record of oral history, although paraphrastic in nature and taken through an interpreter, then summarized by Joy.

Although the deponents' statements read as a continuous narra-tive uninterrupted by questions from the prosecution, it is obvious that such questions were asked and were standard. For example, each deponent begins his statement with information on his family and residency (Katsak: "I am a married man. I have two children. I have lived in the district of Pond Inlet a good many years." Ataguttaaluk: "I am a married man. I have no children. I have lived around Arctic Bay most of my life.")

As another example, the prosecution apparently asked about Janes's threat to shoot the Inuit or their dogs. (Katsak: "I never heard Janes say he would shoot the Eskimo or their dogs." Ataguttaaluk: "I never heard Janes say he was going to shoot the Eskimo or their dogs. I only heard this from my wife and some other people.")

The theorist Alessandro Portelli has addressed the subject of omit-ted questions in the printed record of oral history:

The final result of the interview is the product of both the narrator and the researcher. When interviews, as is often the case, are arranged for publication omitting entirely the interviewer's voice, a subtle dis-tortion takes place: the text gives the answers without the questions, giving the impression that a given narrator will always say the same things, no matter what the circumstances … When the researcher's voice is cut out, the narrator's voice is distorted. (Portelli 1998, 71)

Portelli has also pointed out that the interviewer may shape the narrator's response by the way he structures his questions. This only increases the possibility for distortion when the interviewer's questions are not reproduced as part of the written transcript. The interviewer may become a "partner in dialogue.… Instead of discovering sources, oral historians partly create them" (Portelli 1998, 72).

The fact that so many Inuit deponents were subjected to the same set of questions (although the questions themselves are generally unrecorded) allows each informant to, purposely or unknowingly, corroborate other informants' statements. Conversely, the possibility also exists for refutation. In the case of the testimony in this event, however, there is a general consistency between accounts, which leads to the assumption of veracity.

THE TRIAL

On August 25, 1923, the trial of the three accused finally got underway, with a southern judge, defence lawyer, prosecutor, and clerk of the court. William Duval, a former whaler and resident of the Arctic for over four decades, was engaged as interpreter. The six jurors were all white, and five of them, from the ship's crew, spoke only French. Bizarrely, it was decided that the Crown Prosecutor should translate for the jury.

On the first day, Inuit witnesses for the prosecution testified; they were Urulu (Oo-orloo), Katsak (known to the white men as John Brown), Ataguttaaluk, Umik, Maniq, Siniqqaq, and Uuttukuttuk. Ijjangiaq had starved to death in Admiralty Inlet that spring, but his deposition made at the Preliminary Inquiry was admitted.

The prosecution continued its case two days later with more testimony from Uuttukuttuk, followed by Kaukuarjuk, Nutarariaq, Kunuk, Ivalaaq, and Paumik (Palmee), and completed its case the following day with Iqaqsaq (Ekussah), Miqutui (Mikotooe), Iqipiriaq (Ekepireyah), Tupirngat (Toopingun), Paniluk, and additional testimony from Maniq.

The Inuit testified factually about the events of Janes's death. The trial record that exists does not contain verbatim transcripts, but rather a summary of the proceedings and the paraphrastic evidence of the Inuit. It is apparent that the Inuit respondents were all answering a standard series of questions. Their answers described the events at Cape Crauford, with very little offered about previous events during Janes's time as a trader at Patricia River.

Kunuk, an Inuk with whom Janes had argued over fox skins at Cape Crauford, offered a testimony which is representative of all the Inuit testimony. A court document summarized it thus:

> He had known Janes at Patricia River and he met him at Cape Crau-ford where he had arrived before him. Janes asked him for foxes, but he could not give him any because he had "cached" his skins and he could not find them because the place had been hidden by recent snowstorms. He then had an argument with Janes but he does not remember what was said. Nuqallaq was present at the argument and he remembers that he told him that Janes had said that he was going to shoot the dogs. He then went to his igloo with Nuqallaq and took his gun because he was frightened. He remembers Nuqallaq told him to get his gun because Janes was looking for his own. He stood then at the back of his igloo waiting for Janes who did not come back. Then he went to Nuqallaq's igloo and left his gun outside near the door. Janes was killed on the following day. He knew Janes was going to be killed because Nuqallaq told him on the afternoon of the day of the murder that he was going to kill him. He was in his igloo when he heard two shots, he then went out, saw Janes lying on the ice and went about fifteen feet from him. Ululijarnaaq and Aatitaaq were close to Janes. He saw blood on Aatitaaq's trousers and somebody drew his attention to it, adding that he got it when he pushed Janes down so that he could not get to Nuqallaq's igloo. Aatitaaq was near enough to hear this conversation but did not say a word. Janes was still alive, speaking, lying down, and he called Ululijarnaaq, saying "I am hurt!" Ululijarnaaq did not move. Nuqallaq then arrived with a gun and he saw him shoot Janes in the head. Janes was dead.[18]

Bizarrely, the defence called as its first witness the interpreter, William Duval. Nuqallaq and Aatitaaq took the stand in their own defence. Wilfrid Caron had died after falling overboard from the *C.G.S. Arctic* on its journey to Pond Inlet, but his statement from the preliminary trial was admitted. Amarualik was unable to attend the trial and had sent a letter to Joy explaining his absence; the defence requested that Amarualik's deposition at the Preliminary Inquiry be admitted as evidence, but the crown refused.

The trial ended on August 30, 1923. Nuqallaq and Ululijarnaaq were both found guilty of manslaughter, but with a recommendation for clemency for Ululijarnaaq. Aatitaaq was found not guilty.

Nuqallaq, emaciated and ill, is shown being reunited with his young wife, Ataguttiaq, at Pond Inlet, after a two-year incarceration in Stony Mountain Penitentiary in Manitoba. Photo by Richard Finnie / Library and Archives Canada / PA-202073

COMMENTARY

All the statements taken and testimony given during official proceedings were for one purpose: to present and understand the facts surrounding the killing of the trader Robert Janes by Inuit at Cape Crauford in 1920. Almost all of the statements are presented as continuous narratives uninterrupted by questions or comments from an interlocutor. But a comparison of the sequence of the information given by the various Inuit makes it apparent that the elements of the narration were given in response to questions. No list of those questions has survived; their contents can be guessed from the answers given.

The information provided for the prosecution was quite different from that provided for the defence. Statements and depositions for the prosecution were generally introduced by a brief statement of the individual's residency and marital status, and then by information relevant to the killing. These statements could be said to demonize Janes, and one wonders whether, in the case of statements taken before the trial, editing of these statements was done by the police after or during the interpreter's provision of the Inuit deponents' information. Conversely, information provided for the defence tended to dwell on matters that humanized Janes.

This genre of oral history does not provide us with detailed life histories—that was not its intent. For some of the deponents, it provides meagre biographical information. The information provided is a detailed recounting of the circumstances surrounding a particular event. In the case of the Janes killing, motive was important, and many of the unwritten questions must have asked why Nuqallaq did what he did. Beliefs are not delved into in any great detail. Nonetheless, this genre is worthy of further study.

I want to conclude this essay with a discussion of the problems surrounding the interpretation provided in the investigation and at the trial.

INTERPRETATION

All statements or oral depositions during the investigation (that is, before the trial) were given through an interpreter, with the exception of that of the only white person questioned, Wilfrid Caron. With that exception, the investigation and the various official proceedings relied entirely on interpretation between Inuktitut and English (and in some cases between French, English, and Inuktitut).

Captain Munn's hurried investigations in 1920–21 were probably facilitated by Tom Kunuk, his main Inuit assistant in his trading efforts and a man who, as noted earlier, spoke "very limited English." Munn also claimed some facility in Inuktitut, although this is probably part of his usual braggadocio.

Other than Tom Kunuk, the only other Inuk who spoke passable English was the accused, Nuqallaq.

In 1921, when the Hudson's Bay Company established its first High Arctic trading post at Pond Inlet, it hired James Tooktosina, a man from Labrador, as post interpreter. Staff Sergeant Joy of the RCMP began his investigation into the killing of Janes that same year. There is no indication in official records that the RCMP had made prior arrangements to use Tooktosina as interpreter, but it is fortunate that he was there. Joy used him as his interpreter whenever he was available. For the Coroner's Inquest, however, it is unclear whether Tooktosina was available, as the Statutory Declarations do not indicate who acted as interpreter. Parsons, who may have had some limited facility in Inuktitut, and RCMP officer Finley McInnes may also have acted as interpreters on occasion.

Joy also used Tom Kunuk as interpreter on one occasion. Wilfrid Caron acted as his interpreter on another occasion. Caron had been in the district for many years and spoke Inuktitut better than English.

The Inuit often complained about the interpreting of James Tooktosina. He was bilingual in Inuktitut and English, but his Labrador dialect differed considerably from the dialect spoken in northern Baffin Island. He arrived in Pond Inlet with the HBC in 1921 and had no previous familiarity with the dialect. Joy's dilemma was that, other than the accused Nuqallaq himself, Tooktosina and Tom Kunuk were the only Inuit in the district who spoke more than a few words of English. Tom Kunuk worked for Munn's trading enterprise and was not always at Pond Inlet, spending much time at Button Point. And therein lay Joy's dilemma. James Tooktosina spoke better English than Tom Kunuk and could therefore express better to Joy in English what he heard and understood, but the Inuit had difficulty in understanding him. Kunuk understood his fellow *Tununirmiut* better than did Tooktosina, but couldn't express himself as well in English. Joy almost always opted for Tooktosina as interpreter.

At the trial itself, a number of facts concerning the interpretation are troubling. William Duval was totally fluent in Inuktitut, yet the Inuit were not satisfied with his work. They were concerned that Duval often began to interpret before a person had finished talking, and they thought that he was confusing the listeners. At one point Kaukuar-juk, frustrated, seized the old man by the shoulder and told him his opinion of his methods, asking him to wait for the speaker to finish before he started to interpret.[19] (Another oral history account by the same narrator attributes the intervention to Nuqallaq himself.)[20] After that altercation, the Inuit felt that the interpretation improved. Portelli (1998) has noted that oral testimony is "never the same twice.... Even the same interviewer gets different versions from the same narrator at different times" (71).

Bizarrely, the defence called Duval as its first witness, and his testimony did not help the Inuit cause. The court record summarized his testimony thus:

> The natives say that a white man is "mad" when he is a little excited, swears, gets "heated up" during an argument, and that does not mean that he is threatening them. This is what he understood from the evidence given by all the witnesses in this case when they said that Janes was "mad." If Janes had threatened them, they would have said so.

He stated that the Inuit generally like white men and are not afraid of them. In the only glimpse into native customary law that this trial showed, Duval also noted that "it has been customary that when a man is murdered, the murderer is at his turn killed by a relative of the murdered."[21] Duval's comments serve to cast doubt on all the Inuit testimony and make light of the desperate situation the Inuit had found themselves in in the spring of 1920. Moreover, contrary to the implications of his statement, Janes had definitely threatened the Inuit.

Only one of the jurors, all of whom were crewmembers of the C.G.S. *Arctic*, spoke English, so they needed the court proceedings translated into French. But William Duval, despite his French surname, did not speak French. (His surname was originally Duvel and he had been born in Germany, immigrating to the U.S. at the age of two.) It was decided that the Crown Prosecutor would interpret for the jury.

Leopold Tellier, defence counsel, gave his final argument to the jury directly in French, with no interpretation, the result being that the accused could not understand their own counsel's argument on their behalf.

Joy asked that a letter written by Amarualik explaining why he could not be present at the trial be entered as an exhibit. Joy provided an official translation. Amazingly, to add to the plethora of inappropriate acts associated with this trial, the letter had been translated— rather poorly, it must be noted—by the accused, Nuqallaq, and the translation was certified correct by Tom Kunuk (Harper 2012).

Today, almost a hundred years later, the necessity for and quality of interpretation provided at criminal trials is occasionally controversial. As recently as March 14, 2016, *Nunatsiaq News* reported that a judge found the testimony of a man she had convicted of murder to be "non-credible, based, in part, on his use of court interpreters" (Rohner 2016).

The records of the trial of the killers of Robert Janes provide rich material for the Northern historian. All of the Inuit testimony contained therein began as oral history.

BIBLIOGRAPHY

Atagutsiaq [Anna] and Mary-Rousselière, Guy. 1988. "Eye-witness Account of Robert Janes's Murder." *Eskimo* (Spring–Summer): 10.

Cruikshank, Julie. 1994. "Oral Tradition and Oral History: Reviewing Some Issues." *Canadian Historical Review* 75, no. 3: 403–418.

Harper, Kenn. 2004. "The Immoral Ethic of Conquest: Inuit and Qallunaat Reactions to the High Arctic Murder Trial of 1923." In *Proceedings of the 14th Inuit Studies Conference*, compiled by Robert O. van Everdingen, 77–93. Calgary, Alberta: The Arctic Institute of North America and University of Calgary.

———. 2012. "Amarualik's Letter: A Syllabic Letter from 1923." In *Linguistic and Cultural Encounters in the Arctic: Essays in Memory of Susan Sammons*, edited by Louis-Jacques Dorais and Frédéric Laugrand, 135–142. Quebec: Les Cahiers du CIERA.

Miller, Bruce Granville. 2011. *Oral History on Trial: Recognizing Aboriginal Narratives in the Courts*. Vancouver: UBC Press.

Portelli, Alessandro. 1998. "What Makes Oral History Different." In *The Oral History Reader*, edited by Robert Perks and Alistair Thomson, 48–58. London and New York: Routledge.

Rohner, Thomas. 2016. "Experts Worry Nunavut Judge's Ruling Might Deter Others from Using Interpreters." *Nunatsiaq Online*, March 14.

CHAPTER 6

The People's Land —
The Film

Hugh Brody

I N 1973, TWO YEARS AFTER first travelling to the Arctic, I gave a
lecture at the Commonwealth Institute in London about life in the
Canadian North. It was one of the first times I had spoken in public
about my work in the settlements of Pond Inlet and the Belcher
Islands, the places that Inuit called Mittimatalik and Sanikiluaq. I was
surprised by how easy it seemed to be to share some of what I had
learned about Inuit history, culture, and, above all, the relationship
of hunting peoples to their lands. As if the freedom of being there,
in the magical intellectual and physical spaces of hunters, had given
me a freedom to speak, or an ease with the ideas that were emerging,
or a new confidence; as if the energy of the wonderful Inuit who had
been my teachers and that of the Arctic itself could flow through me.
Clarity of light, of land, of life, offering some new clarity of mind, or
at least my own ability to trust that there was a clarity that could find
its way into what I said.

And there were things that I was determined the world should hear. The men and women of Leah's generation had many stories to tell, some of which they had been reluctant to share with the outsiders, the Qallunaat. There had been many difficulties, and there was a good deal of anger; yet there were also the Inuit habits of quiet avoidance of conflict and the Qallunaat way of causing fear and silence. I understood from the elders I knew best that one of their reasons for taking so much time teaching me and making sure I heard their stories, their history, was their expectation that I would pass on what I was learning to those in the south who seemed to have so much power over what was happening in the North.

After the lecture in London, a man came up to me and introduced himself as Brian Moser. I knew the name—this was the person who had created the television series *Disappearing World*. On Wednesday evenings, on the Independent TV channel, anthropology was being given a chance to reach a huge audience. Each episode in the series was made by a marriage—between an anthropologist and a documentary director. The anthropologist could give access to a society, often in very remote places; the director and technical crew could do the filming. The anthropologist could lead the film crew to stories, histories, personalities that would usually be far beyond the reach of media. The new filmmaking technology—lightweight and sturdy sixteen-millimetre cameras and Nagra sound recorders able to create on-the-spot high-quality sync sound—meant that the filmmakers could work for long periods deep in the most inaccessible communities, and bring what they recorded to mainstream television.

Brian Moser's vision resulted in some of the very first and the very best anthropological films to be seen on British television—not least because, for the first time, the people in the films could be heard as well as just seen. *Their* ideas about the world, their storytelling, their heritage were given unprecedented recognition. Long interviews provided intelligence, narrative shape, and, above all, respect. Voices were translated into subtitles, so, for the first time, an audience could hear the sounds and cadences of these other languages, and feel that people from very far away were speaking to them across immense divides, but with clear sense. And the politics of the Indigenous world, the injustices that were being endured and the protests against injustice, could also be heard and, in a new way, with new authenticity and force, be understood. I did not like the title *Disappearing World*: the people I knew and many of those I had seen and heard in the films of the *Disappearing World* series were determined that they would not disappear. But I was in awe of what Brian and his teams had achieved: Indigenous people, societies that had almost never before been heard or understood, on mainstream, primetime TV. And, after the lecture at the Commonwealth Institute, he proposed to me that I be the anthropologist in an episode of the series. An episode about the people of Pond Inlet.

We met and talked through the possibilities. I was reluctant; I did not feel able to commit the Pond Inlet community to this kind of process and exposure. As can happen with those who have spent long periods immersed in "their people," I was full of anxious protectiveness. Part of me felt I must keep these representatives of the media out; I was uneasy about what might seem like a terrible intrusion into people's lives. And something about turning the long and intense fieldwork experience into a fifty-five-minute television program unnerved me, and then there was the problem of the series title: the people I was working with in the Arctic were very much set upon not disappearing.

When I hesitated, Brian Moser suggested that the director of this episode be Michael Grigsby, and that to appreciate the nature of his work we should have a screening of a film he had completed the previous year. This was *A Life Apart*, his film about fishermen who lived from and through the rigours of the Icelandic fishery and suffered what the film set out to show as the parallel rigours of great physical hardship and exploitation by the owners of the boats. Brian also invited two of Grigsby's collaborators to this screening: cameraman Ivan Strasburg and soundman Mike McDuffie. The film was revelatory—of its subject, because of the way it took its time and gave time to the people in it, and of filmmaking, because of the absence of narration and the way it built such careful respect for the fishermen and their lives. With this approach, this team, I was indeed happy to be part of the making of the Pond Inlet episode.

But the people of Pond Inlet must give their approval. I would go back to Pond Inlet, explain the proposal, and get a community response. In fact, all those I met with in the community were enthusiastic about the idea, especially Anaviapik and his circle of elders. But they proposed some conditions: the people of Pond Inlet should determine what parts of their lives would be included in the program, they should have some way of approving what was in it before it was completed, and, when it was completed, they must be the first in the world to see the episode. They also wanted to be given an assurance that it would be seen by "the government." Brian was happy to agree to these conditions: I would be able to pass on to the film crew what the people wanted them to film, Granada would pay for a community representative to come to London during the edit, and everyone would do what they could to set up some kind of screening for government personnel in Ottawa.

So, in June 1974, the Granada film crew arrived in Pond Inlet. After many long conversations I had been given to understand what the Inuit of Pond Inlet wanted them to film. Fishing on the spring ice, seal hunting at breathing holes, narwhal hunting at the floe edge, collecting guillemot eggs from the cliffs of Bylot Island; everyday life in the settlement; and interviews—storytelling—about the issues that were most on people's minds: the way southerners had dominated the Inuit, how the schools had been set up without respect for Inuit parents, the poor condition of the houses that had been built for the Inuit, the way the oil and gas companies seemed to claim to own the Arctic, the need for the young to spend more time hunting, the vital importance of the land, and the Inuit right to continue to regard their lands as their own. If a TV program was to be made about their lives, they wanted to be sure that their dismay about much that had happened would be understood and their claim to their lands and lives be heard.

I had been apprehensive about a film crew bursting into the homes and lives of the Inuit I knew. I had imagined that people would be uncomfortable, perhaps resentful; that they would avoid the camera, or go silent, or at least be distorted by self-consciousness. I was very unsure about how an interview could be managed; I supposed I would ask questions and Inuit would give answers. But how were these questions to be prepared? And how could the answers be kept to the point at issue, or an uneasy silence be dealt with? I was new to documentary filmmaking and full of ideas about its potential to distort reality or, indeed, prevent there being any *reality* at all.

I was wrong—about almost everything. The day the crew arrived I talked with Anaviapik about some of my worries. He said he thought it was very easy to know what to do, and he delivered a simple view of my problems: *qaujimanginguarniarpugut taimak.* "We will pretend not to know, that's it." And that's what the people did: when the camera appeared, they just went on with whatever they were doing, pretending, with immense assurance and great skill, not to know there was a film crew anywhere near them. I watched with amazement and admiration: people playing a game of checkers in their front room, a woman scraping a sealskin in front of her house, a hunter preparing his harpoon, a man managing his dog team—wherever we went, whatever we filmed, the Inuit were at ease, untroubled, unselfconscious, and, they would tell me, delighted that the film crew was there. They pretended not to know. Their pride in themselves, the assurance with which they went about daily lives, their great skills on the land—these were what I could see, as I had not seen them before, or what I could newly appreciate because, in my eyes at least, the people's confidence in themselves had not before been at any risk. The camera and the microphone, the technology for putting their lives on record, were given the most profound welcome because the technology, and the crew managing the technology, were taking the time, were working hard, to watch and to listen—and this was to pay the Inuit way of life and view of things the greatest and most valuable of compliments. Implicit in the process, built into the relationship between the film crew and the people, was respect. A respect—a watching and listening, a concern to see and to understand—that had so often been denied to people, or had been the very opposite of what the southerners tended to bring to the North.

Icing of runners. Taken on a journey from Pond Inlet to Arctic Bay, April 1972.
Photo by Hugh Brody

After two weeks of filming what people did, at home and out
on the land, in the streets of Pond Inlet and in its institutions—the
trading post, the shop, the church—the time came for us to film the
interviews, the storytelling. The Inuktitut word for this, *unikkaarlluni*,
combines the two ideas into the one concept: to tell stories and relate
history, to bring the past to life in the voice of the one who speaks,
which is oral culture.

The first of these interviews, the first *unikkaarlluni*, was to take
place in Anaviapik's house. I had asked him what he would like to talk
about first, what stories he would want to put on film. He said we must
begin by talking about the power of the Qallunaat, the way southerners had come and dominated Inuit. I asked him where he would like
to be for this first interview. At the kitchen table, he said, where people
usually sat and talked. But he did not want to be alone. He would
sit there with his wife Ulaajuk and there should be a visitor. When
visitors came—that was when people shared memories and stories
about the past. He would arrange for his friend Qanguq to visit for
this first storytelling (he invited Uutuva to be there for the next one).

They would sit at the kitchen table. But I should be there, too, he said. I explained that I would not want to be in the film. I could ask questions, but only they would be on camera. That's a good idea, he said, but I should sit with them, to one side, and then I could ask questions and interrupt if they were speaking too much or had strayed from the subject we were wanting to film.

We sat at the table. Ivan Strasburg sat to one side of the room, the camera resting on his lap, avoiding the clutter of a tripod. Mike McDuffie rigged a microphone that could hang from the end of a fishing rod that he held above the table, so it could get good sound from all at the table without having to move a boom from speaker to speaker. Everything was ready for the first shot. Mike Grigsby, who sat alongside Ivan, said we should begin. I said to Anaviapik, Ulaajuk, and Qanguq that all was ready if they were. And that the idea was that they would talk about the way southerners had been so very dominant in Inuit life. I did not ask a question—I was not given the chance. They began to speak, sharing memories and thoughts about the history of the relationship between Inuit and Qallunaat, the southerners. After ten minutes Ivan signalled to me that he had run out of film: a sixteen-millimetre magazine contained four hundred feet, just over ten minutes of film time. He had to put on a new roll. I asked the Inuit to pause. There was a delay while Ivan reloaded, and Mike tested his sound and adjusted the microphone's distance from the end of the fishing rod. The Inuit got themselves fresh cups of tea. After a few minutes the crew was ready to film again. I explained to the group alongside me at the table that the camera was now reloaded, and was wondering what question to ask to relaunch the conversation. Before I said a word, they resumed—at the exact point where they had left off. The last thought at the cut was picked up. On they went, for another ten minutes. Speaking with ease, without self-consciousness, holding to the theme, giving one another the space to tell anecdotes, chuckling at one another's humour. They spoke with precision, clarity, elegance. And reminded me that here were people for whom oral culture was their culture, for whom to be able to set out thoughts and tell stories was central to being an effective adult.

At the very start of the first of those filmed conversations, Annaviapik shared memories with Qanguq. They spoke in their usual thoughtful, calm voices:

> **Anaviapik:** Those Qadlunaat, they had all the power, and were extremely frightening.
> **Qanguq:** Yes, they were feared.
> **Anaviapik:** We always followed whatever rules they made. That's the way it was.
> **Qanguq:** Yes, even the adults were afraid of the Qadlunaat.
> **Anaviapik:** The Qadlunaat seemed to be the real bosses. Because they were the bosses. Even when Inuit were told to do things against their traditions, they would never say no. In the old days we were easily scared, of the Qadlunaat.
> **Qanguq:** I couldn't tell whether Qadlunaat were good, or whether they were rotten.
> **Anaviapik:** Yes, we were intimidated by them.

This transcription of their words, translated into subtitles, cannot do justice to the lightness of touch, the humour, and yet also the intensity of what they said. They spoke with elegant clarity, with neither haste nor hesitation, and with a wish above all to share their history as they had lived it, as they understood it. I was being given a lesson—in the nature of Inuit oral culture, but also in documentary filmmaking. Ivan and Mike had no idea what was being said, but they paid close attention, watching and listening, making sure that what they filmed and recorded was as good as it could be, and thus showing great patience and great respect. They were demonstrating to me how technicians should conduct themselves. But they were also revealing to me the way documentary film could fit with oral culture. Far from being rendered shy or evasive, the camera and microphone caused the people to be at their best. They were being seen and heard, being taken seriously, being given a chance to send out their views to the world. In the heart of colonial history, at a colonial frontier, in the eye of the new developmental politics, under the threats of the oil and gas industry, the suggestion that the Arctic somehow belonged to newcomers from the south, and against a backdrop of governmental indifference and mismanagement, they were going to speak their minds, and speak them well.

Sitting at the table in his small and crowded house in the Pond Inlet settlement, Paulussi Inukuluk, one of Anaviapik's sons, talked about moving in from a life on the land and becoming a labourer, and of how he came to realize that well-being depended on living as much as possible as a hunter. And he talked about his struggle with southerners' ideas of education.

> For two years I actually went to school, in the Adult Eduction Centre. We had a Qadlunaat teacher called "Spider." That's the only name I knew him by, "Spider." I gradually came to understand just how tiring some things are. I even began to think Qadlunaat are amazing! They do so much work that doesn't look like work at all. In fact, it's very tiring. That writing, just using that little pencil, is very hard going.

As Inukuluk spoke his voice took on the weariness of the time he was remembering, and he lit up his Inuktitut with infixes to give remarkable emphasis—indications of surprise, bewilderment, realization. Oral culture is performance. Speakers are in relationship to those who are hearing them, be it a few friends at the kitchen table, a group of children in a classroom, the family lying at the edge of sleep in a tent, or a film crew from London. What happens is not just a matter of the words. A transcript of what has been said cannot capture the storytelling, nor can a voice recording. But film can show the performance; and the performance can be given energy and richness because it is being filmed. I was learning that filming can be a rich and powerful way of honouring, showing, and sharing what Indigenous peoples, or any peoples for whom oral culture is at the centre of life, have to say and what they are.

I realized that this must become a central part of how I worked: I must learn to be a filmmaker. Thus it was that the Arctic in yet one more way changed my life, the way I would work, the kinds of experiences

I was going to have. How can one find the words to thank the Inuit who gave their time, took such care, shared their knowledge, to make sure I could be well in all ways? My one hope is that the work itself, the ways in which so many Inuit helped me to help others to see, is what they would have hoped for. But, in the end, the pride, wit, skill, and great humanity of the people in Pond Inlet speak for themselves.

Anaviapik was a close relative and special favourite of Leah's. Like Anaviapik, Leah embodied so much that has been at the core of Inuit strength and vitality, and she was also a wonderful teller of stories, a creator of oral culture. To make the film in Pond Inlet was an opportunity to follow the lead of that remarkable culture, to take the lead from men and women like Leah. To write about the film now is to be reminded that Leah and Anaviapik, and hundreds of others in the North, were determined that Inuit history be known, Inuit knowledge respected, and Inuit land—the people's land—be a continuing source of every kind of nourishment for the Inuit.

CHAPTER 7

"*Tass' Nuann'!*"

Tradition, Sports, and Friendship
at the Kayak Club Nuuk

Birgit Pauksztat

WHY WOULD PEOPLE BE INTERESTED IN TRADITION? And why
would they want to become actively involved in preserving it?
Previous research has often highlighted the political dimensions of
preserving—or revitalizing—tradition. Indeed, the example of the
Kayak Club in Nuuk, Greenland, suggests that the initiative to establish the club was partly linked to political goals. However, in order to
sustain an interest in tradition, and hence its preservation as an integral part of culture, tradition must have personal meaning for those
involved. As the case of the Kayak Club Nuuk shows, the personal
meanings attached to tradition can vary between individuals, and
they can change over time.

The essay starts with an overview of the history and the activities of
the club. I will then explore members' reasons for joining the club and
what they liked about their membership in the club. The focus will be

on two periods: the first years after the club's foundation (c. 1983–85), and the late 1990s, when the club was well-established.

The essay is based on interviews I conducted in spring 1999 with thirty-two individuals who were members of the Kayak Club Nuuk at that time, and with five men and women who had been members of the club during the 1980s. In addition, I draw on archival documents, conversations with H.C. Petersen, and conversations and observations from when I was a member of the club in 1997–98, and during later, shorter visits to Nuuk.[1]

THE KAYAK CLUB NUUK

Historical Overview

Until the early 20th century, the kayak (Grld. *qajaq*, pl. *qaannat*) was fundamental to Greenlanders' subsistence, both as a hunting tool (*piniut*) and a means of transport (Petersen 1997). In connection with the transition to commercial fishing, it was gradually replaced by other types of boats, until the kayak had almost disappeared in the 1970s (Beretninger vedrørende Grønlands Styrelse 1944; Petersen 1997).

The 1950s and 1960s were characterized by modernization and development efforts in Greenland (Dahl 1986; Sørensen 1983). In the 1970s, this gave rise to a counter-movement that led to the introduction of the Greenlandic Home Rule Government (*Namminersornerullutik Oqartussat/Hjemmestyre*) in 1979. The aim was not only greater political independence from Denmark, but also a re-appreciation of Greenlandic values and traditions, many of which were already on the verge of falling into oblivion. The kayak had always been closely associated with the traditional hunting culture, and in particular with the *piniartoq* or hunter—the epitome of the "true Greenlander" (Langgård 1998; Thomsen 1996). Therefore, it played a special role as a symbol of Greenlandic identity and Greenlanders' ability for survival.

This was the context for the initiative of a group of young Greenlanders, members of the youth organization of the Siumut party (*Siumut Inuusuttai/Siumut Ungdom*). Under the motto "Siulitta napassutaat sooq katersugaasivimmiiginnassava? Qajaq atoqqilertigu!"

("Why should that which made possible the survival of our ancestors only be in a museum? Let's use the kayak again!"), they set themselves the goal to "take the Greenlandic kayak out of the museum" and use it again, in order to prevent its disappearance. The idea was met with some skepticism, as a founding member of the club recalled. For many, the Greenlandic kayak was "a thing of the past," and it certainly did not go together with "young, long-haired Greenlanders with a cigarette in the corner of the mouth."

Undeterred by this, the kayak club *Qajaq*, later renamed *Peqatigiiffik Qajaq Nuuk* (Kayak Club Nuuk), was established on September 15, 1983, in the Greenlandic capital Nuuk. The newly established club, the first of its kind in Greenland, was a great success. It received generous support from "everyone":

> We really were overwhelmed by the success in the first years. We had not expected that so many people would join and support us. Because, when we first had started, everything was really easy. Everybody wanted to contribute, financially, and we did not have to make an effort, or organize bingo-events to raise money. The whole thing came by itself, from the municipality, from the Home Rule Government, and from private people. (interview with 1980s member)

The kayak movement spread quickly in Greenland. In 1984 there were already nine kayak clubs, in 1985 the number had risen to seventeen, and in 1986 there were twenty local clubs. In the 1990s the number of kayak clubs decreased again. Today there are about ten kayak clubs in Greenland.

In 1985, the clubs joined together to form the Greenlandic Kayak Association, *Qaannat Kattuffiat*. In 1990, the Greenlandic Kayak Association joined the Sports Confederation of Greenland (*Kalaallit Nunaanni Timersoqatigiit Kattuffiat/Grønlands Idrætsforbund*).

Qajaq, 1983

During the first years, the main activities of the club's board were the planning and organization of future activities, and the preparations for establishing the Greenlandic Kayak Association. In addition, much effort was put into collecting as much information as possible about, among other things, kayak building, the preparation of seal-skin and making of kayak clothing, different types of rolls, and the equipment used for hunting. Here, the support of H.C. Petersen, who acted as a consultant for the club, was of great importance. He had conducted extensive research about the hunting culture, especially about the kayak (e.g., Petersen 1994, 1997).

Kayak building first got off the ground after January 1985, when the Nuuk municipality made an old storehouse in the old colony harbour available to the club as a workshop. The young men[2] learned kayak building from experienced older kayak builders, from books (especially *Qaanniornermut ilitsersuut*, Petersen 1981[3]), and from studying old drawings and museum kayaks. With regard to form and construction, kayaks were built "in the traditional way," that is, "according to the last stage of development, from about 1900" (interview with 1980s member). The cover was made of canvas, an adaptation to contemporary constraints, but legitimized by historical precedent and the *Qaanniornermut ilitsersuut*.

Learning paddling and rolling first started later, with the support of some older men, after the first kayaks had been finished or bought. In 1985, plans were made for a "Kayak and Nature School" (*Sungi-usarfik qajartornermut asimiinnermullu/Qajaq- og Naturskole*). This was envisioned as a four-week summer camp where two elders from Uummannaq would teach about twenty participants paddling, rolling, and how to survive in nature by using traditional Greenlandic knowledge. Greenlandic history was on the program as well.

From this, it is apparent that in the first years, the "tradition-preserving use of the kayak" (H.C. Petersen, pers. comm., January 10, 1999), or the planning of such use, was central to the club's activities. Interestingly, the club was not only about the kayak, but more broadly about the traditional hunting culture with the kayak as a central element. However, the use of the kayak for sports was on the agenda from the beginning:

The clubhouse of the Kayak Club Nuuk in March 2015. Photo by Birgit Pauksztat

> When we started to talk about establishing the club, the cultural aspects had top priority. Although at the same time, we recognized that we would not come very far if we stuck only to the cultural essence. We had to add something popular as well. (interview with 1980s member)

This "popular" element was the use of the kayak as *timersuut* (sports equipment) and, in connection with that, the arrangement of Greenlandic kayak championships. Making the kayak attractive to a broader public, especially young people, was considered a necessary condition for the success of the club, and hence the preservation of the Greenlandic kayak. The planning of the Greenlandic kayak championships started already in 1984, based on kayak games and exercises known from the past in Greenland (cf. Petersen 1994). The first Greenlandic Kayak Championship, consisting of a race for men over a distance of three kilometres, was held in 1985 in Sisimiut in connection with the annual meeting of the Kayak Association.

Peqatigiiffik Qajaq Nuuk, 1997–99

In the late 1990s, as well as today, the annual cycle of club activities was mainly influenced by the seasons and the Greenlandic Kayak Championship. In the winter, kayak building in the clubhouse was the most important activity. The clubhouse, workshop and meeting place for the club's members, is located in the historical centre of Nuuk, the old colony harbour, a popular gathering spot for locals and a point of attraction for tourists.

In kayak building, club members no longer strictly followed the *Qaanniornermut ilitsersuut* (Petersen 1981). Instead, they sought to improve the kayak type described in the handbook, and to adapt it to their own needs and preferences. In doing so, they drew on their own experiences, but also looked to museum kayaks and (in one case) European kayak types for inspiration and technical solutions. In this way, the *kinngusaarut*, a very low kayak type for rolling, was developed in the early 1990s. Another type that was developed in the late 1990s was the *sukkaniut*, a fast kayak for racing. In addition, members experimented with new methods of construction, and some of these spread gradually within the club as well as between clubs. Examples were the fastening of the crossbeams with pegs instead of mortising, the additional use of glue, and the use of new materials, such as nylon for covering kayaks (first used in 1997).

Some members of the club paddled during the winter. In the late 1990s, training sessions organized by the club started in spring, depending on the weather, and became more frequent as the championship came closer. Starting in 1992, and throughout the 1990s, the club organized a training camp for its members at least once a year. Rolling, in particular, was taught frequently and intensively, not only for safety reasons. With a view to the championship, members practiced thirty different types of rolls, as well as some other rolls that they had invented. Rolling also was (and still is) at the centre of the kayak shows arranged on the Greenlandic National Day and for tourists.

Since 1993, the Greenlandic Kayak Championship has taken place in July, each year in a different town. Disciplines include short- and long-distance races, a cross-country race, relay races, rolling (individually and synchronously in groups of three), harpoon throwing (*saaqqutersornerit*), and rope gymnastics (*allunaariaqqattaarnerit*). Since 1996 these disciplines have been arranged for men and women, divided into different age categories.

In the late 1990s, the championship appeared mainly as a sports event. However, tradition-preserving aspects were important as well. Firstly, the disciplines were historically documented or could be traced back to historical examples. The fact that they formed part of the championship was an incentive to practise them in the clubs, or provided the opportunity to try them out at the championship. The latter was often the case for harpoon throwing (*saaqqutersornerit*), which was not usually taught in Nuuk (or in many other clubs) in the late 1990s. In 1998, the participants from Nuuk and other clubs used the time immediately before the competition to learn how to handle harpoons and throwing boards, or to brush up on what they had learned at previous competitions. Secondly, competition rules encouraged the preservation of tradition. Kayaks were built according to the competition rules. Equipment (such as harpoons) and sealskin clothing were often made especially for use during the championship (Pauksztat 2005).

WHY BECOME A MEMBER?

Over the years, the number of members and activity levels have fluctuated considerably in local kayak clubs in Greenland, largely depending on the presence of enthusiastic and committed individuals. In Nuuk, most of the founding members left the club between 1985 and 1990. Some left Nuuk after they completed their education, some passed away, and some left the club as their interest declined, or after personal conflicts and disagreements. Thus the number of members decreased; in 1990 there was only one active kayaker in the kayak club in Nuuk. The members who joined the club around 1990 therefore had to start almost from zero to build the Kayak Club Nuuk up again. What makes people interested in joining the club and investing time and effort in it?

For the founding members of the club, their desire to preserve the kayak and the traditions associated with it was an important reason for establishing the club:

Because to us, the kayak was part of the traditional Greenlandic culture, one of the driving forces in Greenlandic culture, next to the language. Because the kayak is a product of many years' work, a very beautiful development of a particular piece of equipment, we thought. And we thought it would be a shame if it would be forgotten and only be regarded as a museum piece. We wanted to highlight the kayak as evidence that the hunting culture had been at a high level of technical development. That was very important to us.

Some recalled that their search for their own identity had played a role. Strengthening one's ethnic identity and demonstrating this identity to the outside world were important concerns in the 1970s and early 1980s, and many turned to traditional Greenlandic culture to look for their ethnic roots (Sørensen 1994). This was because, together with language skills, knowledge about traditional culture was perceived as a key component of "true Greenlandicness." In addition, the past provided "a moral ideal and an invocation of Greenlandic strength" (Sørensen 1994, 109, author's translation) that could help to strengthen self-confidence. One of the club's members from the 1980s explained:

Our ancestors, they were almost gods in the view of many people. [...] That is, the ancestors, they have always been role models, and it is them one has to emulate. And that is of course not something that you are not influenced by. So they have a big place in our hearts.

In the late 1990s, the reasons mentioned for joining the club were notably different. Of those who were members in 1998, only 19 percent had joined because they wanted to help to preserve the kayak, and only one man mentioned the search for his own identity as a reason.[4]

Most of those who have become members since 1990 joined because the club promised enjoyable leisure activities. One man recalled: "[I became a member] not because I was particularly interested in kayak building, that came only later. We only wanted something to do to pass those winter nights—Nuuk is a small town, there is nothing happening here!"

Social connections were important as well. Prompting or persuasion by friends and relatives played a role for 59 percent of the members in the late 1990s. Adults, especially those over forty years old, often became members in order to support their relatives or the members of the club.

In 1991 and 1992, the club arranged teaser training sessions in order to attract more members, especially more children. Many of these children left again, but others stayed, "and then their friends came along, and even more children" (interview with 1980s member), both boys and girls. Incidentally, this contributed to a gradual change in gender connotations associated with kayaks, which in the past had been considered the domain of men. One woman recalled:

> My husband always tried to persuade me to give it a try, but I did not want to. Also because [I thought] 'well, that's something for men, and not for women.' But then I watched and I saw those girls and boys, and young girls and women, [and I thought] 'if they can do it, I can certainly try it perhaps.'

Another young woman, who became a member in the late 1990s, recalled:

> Why I wanted to become a member ... That was because my boyfriend, he built kayaks and paddled and things like that. We had just got together. And so I got a little inspired, because he said all the time, 'Come on, try it.' And I was like, 'No, I don't feel like it, that old Greenlandic stuff ...' But then I tried it, and I really loved it, and so I started paddling. And then, I think I tried it twice, and the second time, I could roll. And so I just continued.

A feeling of success when paddling the first time was decisive not only for this woman, but for *all* of the sixteen- to twenty-five-year-olds, and in total for 34 percent of the members.

WHAT DO YOU LIKE ABOUT THE CLUB?

In my interviews in 1999, I asked those who were members of the club at the time what they liked about the club and its activities. The answers showed a number of recurrent themes.

Social Interactions and Friendship

Friendship and social interactions were mentioned by almost all (29 of 32 interviewees, making this the most frequently mentioned theme. Some members told me that the cohesion among members of the kayak club in Nuuk was stronger than in other Greenlandic kayak clubs, and much stronger than in other sports clubs. "We are a big family," as one man put it.

Social relations were particularly close among the younger members. A young woman recalled: "We were almost always together, all of us, we were always together. We went to [youth] clubs and played the guitar and sang and did all kinds of things, we were almost always together."

Adult members also enjoyed being together with other club members, "that you can go down there [to the club house] on Saturdays or whenever you feel like it, and have a chat with the others."

In addition, the kayak club provided opportunities for meeting new people and making new friends. One man noted that "new friendships develop most easily when you have something in common." And a young woman explained: "It's also this about friends, and new friends, and new faces. [...] Because there you also meet new people and make new friends. I made really many new friends when I was at the championship in Paamiut last year."

Recreation: Sports and Leisure Activities

For many, building a kayak and/or being able to handle a kayak (e.g., keeping your balance, paddling in rough weather, and especially being able to roll) presented a personal challenge. Of 32 interviewees, 24 mentioned this as something they liked about the club and its activities, making this the second-most frequently mentioned theme. "That's the challenge, definitely, the technical challenge of it," a man told me with regard to kayak building. With regard to paddling and rolling, there was the additional challenge from others, an element of competition, for instance in the kayak championship. A young woman explained, "Yes, you really have to give everything. The power. And then challenging others, and they challenge me. That's fantastic, I love that, there is nothing better." This included "to show others what I can, *that* I can do it" (interview with a young woman), as well as the pride of having accomplished something: "Today I learned a roll, *kinnguffik puarlallugu nerfallaallugu* [the standard roll], I just did it for the very first time. That was fun!" (entry in the club's guestbook, September 15, 1996, by a young man)

Some highlighted that there was room for creativity—on the one hand when developing new technical solutions, or trying out new constructions, new forms, and new materials in kayak building, and on the other hand when inventing new rolls and other tricks:

And then we try to come up with new rolls, special rolls for kayak shows. […] For instance, taking a cigarette in one hand, then capsize, and then come up again, without extinguishing the cigarette. And then pushups on the kayak … for that I get out of the kayak [i.e., the cockpit], stand up and then do push-ups, and then [I go] back into the kayak again. (interview with a young man)

Relatedly, some members appreciated the opportunity to exchange experiences and tips for technical solutions with other members.

Tranquility and relaxing were important to many members. One man explained:

And it is great, it does me good, relieves the stress. […] You probably experienced that yourself, you go down there [to the club house] for three hours, and sometimes you talk a lot and sometimes you don't talk at all but you are simply there and do things, and […] it's a really nice evening off. Because your thoughts get off all these other things, you are so focused on just getting this here right, and to just shape this here nicely, and that's incredibly relaxing. That's what I like about it.

Another man noted that "it is nice to come somewhere where you talk about completely different things, where people talk about completely different things. And you really talk about many things, not just about kayaks."

Being close to nature was another important theme:

> It's because … paddling is a fantastic experience. You are not in the city, as with all the other types of sport. You are in nature, and close to the animals, and you watch them, and hunt them … I think that's the best thing with it.

Members also valued the freedom associated with paddling, which they contrasted with the many rules that govern other types of sport. Because, as one young man put it, "when paddling, you do what you want—as long as you don't make a mistake."

Other themes related to sports and leisure activities more generally, without necessarily having a connection to kayaks. Many liked the training itself, to push themselves and to exhaust themselves

Start of the men's short distance race at the Kayak Championship in Nuuk, July 2016. Photo by Birgit Pauksztat

physically. One young woman said, "It is important to me to be able to train. I feel best when I have been outside and trained."

Others mentioned travelling to other parts of Greenland in connection with the championship, to other countries to give kayak shows, or to training camps outside of Nuuk, where there was "another landscape that you can look at."

Traditional Knowledge and Greenlandic Identity

Interestingly, for many, preserving the kayak became more important *after* they became members and became actively engaged in kayak building and/or paddling. One young woman explained:

> I had never thought about that, that there had been hunters in my family. But when I started with paddling, some of my relatives said, "you are doing what your ancestors did." And I thought, "oh, that's good that I do what my ancestors did."

Indeed, when members explained what they liked about the club and its activities, many referred to the Greenlandic aspects of kayaks and kayak-related activities, in particular Greenlandic identity and traditional knowledge about kayak building and use. One of the most frequently mentioned themes (by 20 of 32 interviewees) was learning traditional knowledge and skills. Some members saw their membership in the club and participation in activities around the kayak as a way to connect with their ancestors' way of life—or, in the case of Danish members, to learn about Greenlandic culture:

> One of the reasons for why I wanted to build a kayak was also to understand a little more about Greenlanders, a little more about Greenland. [...] Because when I build a kayak, I find out how it is constructed, how they thought, you put yourself a little bit in their shoes [...] and you get an understanding for how they thought, and why they built it that way.

In most cases this theme was mentioned with regard to kayak building. Two people mentioned it more broadly with regard to the traditional hunting culture. One young man mentioned this with regard to his Greenlandic language skills, which he thought had improved after participating in the championship.

Participating in activities related to the kayak allowed members to demonstrate their Greenlandic identity to others, or to strengthen or confirm it to themselves. "Especially when you are paddling, you feel really 'Greenlandic.' You feel proud to be able to paddle," a woman told me. A man explained:

> And that's what I wanted as well, to find my identity. [...] Normally, I only deal with airplanes and motors and propellers. All the books are in English. And after a while you notice that part of you is missing, you are not yourself. And I noticed that when I became a member in the club, I could satisfy this need, fill this void. And that was indeed the case. And all the old language that is used in connection with kayak building, all these old expressions for the different things, that's our old words, which we are gradually forgetting. That's almost identity ...

Many liked being able to pass on their own knowledge and demonstrate to others what kayaks can be used for, for instance during kayak shows: "That you show it to other people, so they can see what kayaks are, *ilaa*, how you ... how skilled the Greenlanders were in the past, those who really went hunting."

For many, this transmission of knowledge was connected with pride in their own abilities (e.g., being able to build your own kayak, or being able to roll) and a sense of national pride. A young woman explained:

> It is wonderful to show others that I can do that. And to show them that this is a Greenlandic tradition, and that it is wonderful. *Tassami*, there are lots of tourists for whom you give kayak shows, and show them how wonderful it is to be Greenlander ... showing them that

'we can do that,' and then they go, 'wow, she did a roll!' That's great
fun, and I like that a lot.

Supporting the Club and Its Members

Through their membership in the club, members also appreciated
the opportunity to work towards goals that were important to them:
preserving the kayak, supporting the club (e.g., raising money, attracting more members), and supporting its members. These themes
were most frequently mentioned by older members, and by those who
wanted to support their relatives or the members of the club through
their membership. In most cases, these points were mentioned in
combination with some of the other themes discussed above (notably
"social interactions and friendship"), suggesting that the wish to preserve the kayak and/or to support the club and its members was not
the only reason for membership in the club.

CONCLUSIONS

So why would people be interested in tradition? And why would they
want to become actively involved in preserving it? Interview responses
suggested that members valued the club for various reasons. Interestingly, preserving tradition was not the main goal for everyone, and it
was usually not the main reason for joining the club. Rather, it often
emerged as a side effect, or a consequence, of individuals' involvement
in the club.

Responses showed considerable variation between individuals, as
well as noteworthy differences between the themes mentioned by club
members in the early 1980s and in the late 1990s. In 1983, club membership seemed to be strongly connected with the wish to preserve
the kayak and members' sense of identity as Greenlanders. In 1999,
identity still seemed important, but interview responses suggested a
wider range of motives for members' active involvement in the club,
including social interactions and friendship, and their interests in leisure activities and sports.

The ability to meet a variety of interests was the main strength
of the club, making it possible to attract a sufficiently large number

of members to make the club viable. As the founding members had foreseen, this provided the basis for preserving the kayak. However, the variety of interests also held the potential for conflicts. In particular, developing new kayak types, experimenting with new materials and methods of construction, or inventing new types of rolls might be considered to clash with the goal of preserving traditions (Pauksztat 2005).

For the kayak club, therefore, the challenge was (and is) to find a way to accommodate these different interests. Examining the activities of the club in the late 1990s suggests that the members had found a compromise that allowed them to balance these different interests (Pauksztat 2005). Members could participate in a range of organized activities or engage in additional activities (such as hunting trips), either individually or with others. Interview responses suggested that many activities appealed to different individuals for different reasons. The Greenlandic Kayak Championship is a good example. It provided an opportunity to meet "friends and new friends," to exchange experiences and learn from members of other clubs, and to compete in

Some of the participants posing for a group photograph at the end of the Kayak Championship. Nuuk, July 2016. Photo by Birgit Pauksztat

various disciplines. Although the sports aspect was prominent, the competitions also provided strong incentives for preserving traditions. In particular, the competition rules set standards that exerted an influence beyond the championship itself. Nevertheless, outside of the competitions, members could in principle act according to their own preferences, providing a certain degree of flexibility.

In sum, it seems that the founding members' "recipe" of combining tradition with "something popular" has been highly successful. Despite considerable fluctuations in membership, the club has remained viable by attracting both Greenlanders and non-Greenlanders for over thirty years.

BIBLIOGRAPHY

Beretninger vedrørende Grønlands Styrelse. 1944. *Sammendrag af Statistiske Oplysninger om Grønland.* Copenhagen.

Dahl, J. 1986. *Arktisk selvstyre: Historien bag og rammerne for det grønlandske hjemmestyre.* Copenhagen: Akademisk Forlag.

Langgård, K. 1998. "An Examination of Greenlandic Awareness of Ethnicity and National Self-consciousness through Texts Produced by Greenlanders 1860s–1920s." *Études/Inuit/Studies* 22: 83–107.

Pauksztat, B. 1999. "Bedeutung und Funktion des Kajakvereins in Nuuk, Grönland, für seine Mitglieder." MA thesis, University of Cologne.

———. 2005. "Kayak Clothing in Contemporary Greenlandic Kayak Clubs." In *Arctic Clothing of North America: Alaska, Canada, Greenland,* edited by J.C.H. King, B. Pauksztat, and R. Storrie, 115–120. London: British Museum Press.

———. Forthcoming. "Kontinuität und neue Entwicklungen im Kajakverein in Nuuk." In *Grönland: Kontinuitäten und Brüche im Leben der Menschen in der Arktis,* edited by F. Sowa. Leverkusen: Budrich UniPress.

Petersen, H.C. 1981. *Qaanniornermut ilitsersuut/Instruktion i kajakbygning/ Instruction in Kayak Building.* Nuuk: Atuakkiorfik.

———. 1994. *Qaannamik pinnguaatit.* Nuuk: Atuakkiorfik.

———. 1997. *Den store kajakbog.* Nuuk: Atuakkiorfik.

Sørensen, A.K. 1983. *Danmark-Grønland i det 20. århundrede: En historisk oversigt.* Copenhagen: Nyt Nordisk Forlag Arnold Busck.

Sørensen, B.W. 1994. *Magt eller afmagt? Køn, følelser og vold i Grønland*. Co-penhagen: Akademisk Forlag.

Thomsen, H. 1996. "Between Traditionalism and Modernity." In *Cultural and Social Research in Greenland/Grønlandsk kultur- og samfundsforskning 1995/6*, 265–278. Nuuk: Ilisimatusarfik/Atuakkiorfik.

CHAPTER 8

Living, Travelling, Sharing

How the Land Permeates the
Town through Stories

Claudio Aporta

I WENT TO IGLOOLIK FOR THE FIRST TIME in the summer of 1998, as a master's student of anthropology at the University of Alberta, to look at how GPS was affecting Inuit orienteering techniques. My interest, however, was not properly timed, as the technology was just being introduced and it was only being used tentatively by some hunters, mainly to deal with fog while hunting walrus in the summer. Two years later, back in Igloolik, it was my own GPS that helped me understand the significance of Inuit trails. A number of short trails mapped by the GPS while following hunters turned out to be "permanent" routes, remembered and passed down through many generations. Since then, mapping Inuit trails became a sort of personal and professional obsession—and, gradually, an interconnected mobility system emerged, starting with Igloolik and then expanding first north towards northern Baffin Island and the High Arctic, and then in all other directions: east to Clyde River, west to Kugluktuk, and south to Salluit and Kangiqsualujjuaq (George River) in Nunavik.

What first got my attention was the permanence and the interconnection of the routes, both on land and ice, and the fact that the trails from adjacent communities eventually link. Then it was their timing, as trails are not only laid out in space but also in time. Trails are quintessentially seasonal, as they are travelled in connection to precise events, such as the recurrent presence of animals and the formation or breakup of the sea ice. A final point of interest came from the realization of an obvious fact: that trails actually start and end at the travellers' doorsteps, hence connecting (then and now) domestic space with "public" space (the town, the camp) and eventually with the land. Over the years, the pursuing of these ideas through the mapping of trails has resulted in what some may view as the discovery of the obvious (that Inuit need trails to travel), but—for some reason that I do not altogether understand—the mapping has also become somewhat important to many Inuit individuals and communities. Indeed, mapping sessions in the communities are always rewarding experiences, as participants tend to see these Inuit "road maps" as important, both as a demonstration of systematic land use to the outside world and as a legacy to younger generations.

The most rewarding and revealing aspects of this research, however, preceded the mapping sessions, and they were connected with the incomparable experience of travelling the land with friends in Igloolik, as well as with discussing the trips and the stories back in town at the Igloolik Research Centre. The stories I brought from my trips were also compared (and fundamentally enriched) with the narratives of the Igloolik Oral History Project. It would not be an overstatement to say that the articulation of ideas for my doctoral thesis was the result of the discussions that followed these trips.

This essay describes, in an informal manner, the significance of mobility in Inuit lives through a description of journeys undertaken by the author, generally associated with hunting, fishing, and visiting. The narrative that follows is a composite of journal notes, memories, and interview excerpts, organized in three phases of travel: departing, journeying, and returning.

The observations based on trips came out of travelling along with a number of hunters, including George Qulaut, Theo Ikummaq, and, mainly, Maurice Arnatsiaq and his family. As mentioned above, before and after the trips there were friends in town that helped me understand my notes and interpret my experiences. Most of them were associated with the Igloolik Research Centre, and they chiefly consisted of John MacDonald, Louis Tapardjuk, and Leah Otak. This essay is a humble homage to the people in Igloolik who had the patience to host me, teach me, and guide me through many years, mainly during several trips between 2000 and 2006.

DEPARTING

Before moving to permanent settlements in the late 1950s and early 1960s, Inuit were seminomadic, adapting their residence and travel patterns to seasonal variations, availability of resources, social interaction, and eventually (in some areas) to the timing and requirements of whaling and trading. Travelling was living, as the home and the trail were not distinct realms. There were departure places and destinations, to be sure, as well as hellos and goodbyes and expectations for arrivals, but the sense of time was not attuned to fixed schedules (e.g., leaving for a trip on Thursday after work and coming back on Sunday evening). There is a sense of anxiety today when travellers expected to arrive at a certain time are "late," which points to the fact that travelling and residing have become two distinctive spheres. There were also seasonal camps, which people surely regarded as "home," but they did not exist as standalone settlements. Their very structure was fluid, and their existence was connected to the seasonal trajectories of people and, mainly, to the presence of animals.

Travelling the land today involves departing from a domestic and social environment that is often in tension with well-established practices (e.g., hunting) that need to be in tune with environmental events and phenomena. The tensions are everywhere, from the inadequacy of house kitchens and dining rooms to prepare, store, and eat country food, to conflicts regarding the timing of a trip, which must be adjusted to employment and schooling obligations, rather than (or in addition to) seasonal and weather considerations. Trips take Inuit away from the hassles of settlement life, of Gregorian time, of overcrowded houses, and of jobs and schooling. Leaving the borders of the town feels like transitioning into a different rhythm of life, as people establish ongoing relationships with the physical landscape, atmospheric events, the sky, the sea, and animals—relationships that have been forged over the course of many generations, and that are recreated not only in travelling but also in stories, and in the place-names that people use. Those relationships are crucial for Inuit life in the Arctic, as they infuse landscapes and seascapes with social dimensions that are needed to live (and thrive) in such environments.

Regardless of the changes brought by settlement life, Inuit hunters' sense of time contrasts sharply with that of most outsiders, such as myself. During my time in Igloolik I travelled many times outside of the settlement, with Inuit and with non-Inuit residents, and it was only with non-Inuit that I found reassuring timeframes that were similar to my own expectations (e.g., leaving the day after tomorrow after breakfast). Adapting to Inuit times of departure was excruciating at first, as it took me a while to figure out that "the right time" to depart was whenever everything was ready (in an hour or in a day).

It is this tension of Inuit hunters both aligning with and resisting the new timeframes and other frameworks of settlement life that makes urbanization such a complex process. Life in town and life on the trail are indeed seen as separate realms. It is remarkable that Inuit see the land as being "outside" of the settlement. Remarkable because, to an outsider, the settlement is as immersed in the land as anything could be.

The late Noah Piugaattuk reflected on the tension of life in the settlement:

Men who enjoy going out on hunting trips must know how to make an enclosure with snow. Today one cannot see any boys playing outdoors cutting snow blocks. Making pretend igloos or anything to do with making igloos. Why this is happening is that no one is encouraging them to do it because they are too much on their own. Teachers are teaching what they are supposed to teach, but if a youngster can be encouraged to work with snow, he can learn how to work with snow … We the elders are to be blamed in most part as we just let things happen especially to those who do not have the knowhow … [In the past…] when we started to go along on hunts we were not knowledgeable, we needed advice from the older people, and we were given the task of tending to the dogs, this was the starting point of our gaining knowledge. (Piugaattuk, IE-070)

"Tending the dogs" was an entry point (one of many) into the type of knowledge that could only be gained through performing. Piugaattuk (like most elders) would not consider himself as truly knowledgeable, as knowledge was not really acquired. Knowledge was discovered or generated within ongoing processes of learning, and through relationships with others. Children building pretend igloos, a common sight in the camps, was the beginning of the discovery of those relationships that were essential for survival.

As I will show below, the land and town realms are not completely separated from each other, as the town permeates the trail (or camp) and vice versa. But the perception of difference is real, both as one leaves the town physically and as is expressed in people's narratives.[1]

Departing the town on a trip is a powerful experience. While taking part in the preparations for the trip, one has the sense of being immersed in a long-established ritual that involves packing necessities, securing loads to the sled, checking and double-checking hunting and fishing gear, and, today, ensuring that the snowmobiles or boats are in proper working condition and filling the engines up with oil and fuel. As the snowmobiles wind their way through the streets and buildings of the town, rounding up corners so that the heavy sleds won't get entangled in street signs or power poles, the travellers make their way to the edge of town, where hundreds of tracks intersect, departing in a myriad of different directions. Eventually a well-trodden trail will be followed, in turn reaching the sea ice (unless travelling is within the island) and heading towards a given destination, slowly leaving behind the comforts and hassles of the settlement.

JOURNEYING

The experience of travelling has changed over time, and yet, moving in the landscape with Inuit hunters, one has the impression of taking part in an old ritual. It is not only that one is travelling in a long-established system of trails (even when most of it is invisible to the untrained eye), but also (and mainly) that such movement occurs in a timely fashion, as trails are always travelled at certain times in connection not to precise, fixed dates, but to what I like to call "events" or "encounters." Most of these events are connected to seasonal and environmental processes, and they involve some kind of encounter (with the solid sea ice, with fish, with other travellers, etc.). Some of these events are fairly precise, such as the presence of caribou in Majuqtulik in the late fall, while others are more comprehensive, such as the formation of landfast ice in a bay.

The trip from Igloolik to Majuqtulik, which will be the basis for the narrative in this section, is defined by a number of events that align

Trail to Majuqtulik.

so that people can journey safely and successfully. The first event was (at that time, alas no longer) the expected presence of caribou around the part of Baffin Island were Majuqtulik is located. The second[2] was the freezing of the rivers and lakes used for most of the trail. The third was the formation of sea ice that separates Igloolik island from the mainland (Melville Peninsula). When all these conditions were present, hunters would wait for the stabilization of the sea ice between the island of Saglaarjuk and the Baffin coast. The yearly journey to Majuqtulik was triggered not by the arrival of a precise date, but by the state of the sea ice in Fury and Hecla Strait. More precisely, preparations for the trip for most people start after an advanced party of experienced hunters have made the first crossing and reported back to the community by shortwave radio.

The trail between Igloolik and Majuqtulik has always been travelled at the same seasonal time (albeit in significantly different ways, as I will show later) in order to connect Inuit hunters with caribou.[3] While journeying, travellers experience the land not as if they are moving in abstract space, but in the form of unfolding horizons.

Well-established named places are in fact clues as to how Inuit will travel this trail. These place-names are themselves "events," as in reality they do not exist as discrete symbolic attachments to land features, but as part of a perceived (either in actual travel or in narratives) landscape. The place-names are experienced from the trail (or from memory) as part of a social and seasonal connection to the land that is manifested through the individual. They exist as perceived (or experienced) places, and as such they are not merely associated with locations but, more properly, with "encounters." The raised beach at the end of the bay (Atikittuq), the island that blocks the currents (Simik), the lake where you can find cod fish (Uugarjualik), the little bay that is sheltered from the wind (Ummiakkuvilik), the place that has plentiful berries (Paurngaqtuuq), the cliff where falcons nest (Kiggavialaaq), and the shallow waters where fish would be trapped in tidal pools at low tide (Tinujjivik)—all reveal a phenomenological approach to the land, where people and other entities (animals, winds, plants, currents) meet. The main feature that makes the names experiential, however, is not their linguistic structure, but the fact that they play a critical role as a representational technique in narratives. Places are seen, described, and experienced (in no particular order) as part of an ongoing engagement with the shapes of the land, the phenomena of the environment, and the meetings with other fellow inhabitants (humans and non-humans) of the world. In that sense, the name Tasiujaq (Hall Lake) is significant not so much for its meaning—"like a lake," or, more specifically, "a lake with connections to the sea"—but for the place it occupies in people's memories, narratives, and experiences.

Today, Inuit tend to describe the outside of their settlements as "out on the land," and they tend to describe journeying (as well as hunting, fishing, and camping) as periods of joy. It is perhaps that continuous connection to the land that people rediscover or re-enact when travelling and camping. In the past, the gathering of people was an organic phenomenon (closely related to their connections with nature), whereas today the settlements are shelters that remain outside of the cycles of the environment and the seasons. Noah Piugaattuk, for instance, remembered how telling and doing, travelling and gathering, remained inextricably linked:

> During the time when there were different camps, there would be caribou hunters that went inland, usually two men, during summer. The main purpose on these caribou hunts was so that they would get skins for clothing. Sometimes, there used to be strong winds that affected a lot of camps. Sometimes winds would be so strong that a tent could not handle it and could not stand and [was] sometimes blown away even when it was trying to be kept from blowing away. So when the winter came and people gathered, they would exchange stories about what they had done during the preceding summer. (Piugaattuk, IE-070)

Journeying (and what happens along the journey) today involves a rhythmic engagement with the world, and the re-establishment of time-honoured relationships that are often experienced as severed by life in town. This severance of people's lives from long-established rhythms and relationships with the natural world is perhaps the most important legacy of the process of semi-urbanization, but it is not total.

New technologies of travel and orienteering are indeed helping Inuit to keep up with these relationships in complex ways. Snowmobiles allow Inuit to hunt within limited timeframes, as their speed reduces the time needed to reach destinations and to return. GPS units allow for more efficient orienteering techniques in bad visibility, or the ability to reach a precise location. Improved hunting technology permits shooting from longer distances with better accuracy. At the same time, these technologies alter people's relationship to the environment in several ways, from preventing travellers from immersing themselves in the land while travelling (which was a common way of learning about the land while travelling with dogs), to decreasing the level of skill needed to orient and hunt. These technologies altered people's relations with their environment, but they also allowed for the maintenance of such relations. They are important parts of the ways in which people in Igloolik deal with the tensions of life in the settlement.

My trip to Majuqtulik, with Maurice Arnatsiaq, happened in December 2000, but I remembered it clearly for several reasons:

- It was my first "long-distance" travel in the Arctic;
- It involved enduring a significant blizzard that lasted several days (including while we were travelling to the camp);
- Most of the travelling happened in the dark, as days become short towards the end of November;
- We joined, and were joined, by many other hunters travelling to Majuqtulik for the same reasons;
- The trip included the crossing of extremely rough sea ice, which was only just becoming stable, on the Fury and Hecla Strait;
- We used orienteering techniques based exclusively on the winds (as the visibility was near zero, Maurice used the feel of the wind on his face to make the crossing and reach the camp);
- I learned why autumn is never listed among the preferred seasons for travelling in the Arctic: short days, high winds, deep and soft snow, and the sea ice still forming.

None of the many hunters I met during the week-long trip complained about any of the adverse conditions listed above. They were there to hunt caribou, which they eventually did because the caribou were, at that time, predictably, there. The fact that about fifteen hunters from Igloolik and Hall Beach had made the trip at approximately the same time, crossing the sea ice as it was just beginning to stabilize, following similar trails, reveals the time-space fluxes that characterize the social nature of the Arctic. The same trail and the same camp would be deserted at other times, as Inuit hunters' journeys are synchronized with the journeys of caribou and with the movements and behaviour of the sea ice. The trail becomes a social place because of the knowledge of such timely relations. The place-names, the hunting places, the fishing lakes, and the trails themselves are embedded in a space-time matrix in which Inuit hunters weave their lives. It is no wonder, therefore, that travelling is seen as connecting, and the settlement as disrupting such connections. But the land manages to come back to the settlement in many forms, through songs, stories, and the outcomes of the hunting and fishing trips, and through the returning travellers themselves.

RETURNING

I have described the contemporary settlements as sites of tension, and there is quite substantial evidence that shows that they are indeed places embedded with increasing social, economic, and cultural conflict. The last section of this essay will look at the settlements in a more hopeful light, as it will reflect on ways through which "the land," with all its power and its long-established connections, still manages to permeate the settlements and the people who live in them.

Many of my most memorable experiences in Igloolik were of times spent and shared in the Igloolik Research Centre, then run by the Nunavut Research Institute. Built in 1975, this unique steel and fibreglass circular structure atop a central pedestal remains an architectural oddity, jokingly referred to as a flying saucer or a mushroom. It is now operated by Nunavut's Department of Environment.

Claudio Aporta and Maurice Arnatsiaq discuss a GPS reading during a place-names survey near Igloolik. October 2000. Photo by John MacDonald

At the time of my research, life in the Research Centre was fas cinating. It was a place that many people from the community liked to visit, and where countless long and informal conversations happened—involving members of the staff (from those working in maintenance to the ones who took care of the Igloolik Oral History Project), frequent local visitors, and the occasional visiting research-ers. The building was a place for science (with its many labs, filing cabinets, equipment, and computers), but its very design was inviting to Inuit in the community. The offices and labs were distributed around the circumference of the building, with windows allowing for observa-tion of every part of town and beyond. It was naturally bright, owing not only to the numerous windows but also to a translucent Plexiglas cupola on the ceiling. Finally, it had a large and inviting common area where conversations and meetings could be easily hosted. This open public space contrasted markedly with other buildings in Igloolik, such as government offices, schools, and private houses with their compartmentalized, squared, and—relatively speaking—uninviting spaces less conducive to facilitating social interaction and sharing.

Because of its windows and its elevated position, the building offered a privileged view of all the surroundings, and one of the favourite pastimes of staff and visitors was to observe the comings and goings of travellers. They were practically endless, as all seasons (except for brief times in the spring and summer when the ice around is too unstable for snowmobiling or not open enough for boating) allow for the movements of travellers, be they by boat, snowmobile, ATV, or pickup truck. The building, unlike most other structures in the town, provided a seamless connection between the people inside and the land outside, and it became a platform for weather and sea ice observation and an open space for sharing stories. The comings and goings of travellers are characteristic of the ongoing relationship that Inuit in Arctic settlements still have with the rhythms of nature. All travellers returning from trips are of interest, as they bring with them two types of crucial items: the outcomes of the trip (fish, meat, skins, eggs, etc.), and, significantly, the stories and news that are connected to the things they bring, the land they visited, and the people they met. The land's bounty brought by the returning hunters, together with their news, are crucial in the sense that they integrate (and create) the social and economic fabric of the community, not just within the settlement but within the land.

The numerous travellers returning to the town most days and most nights enable the weaving of relationships that keep people connected with each other outside of the settlement, creating a social scape[4] in a land that most non-Inuit would perceive as "wilderness." Travellers returning to town bring the outcomes of the encounters (and also their mishaps, as, for instance, not all hunting trips are successful), and they share them. The role of sharing networks among Inuit has been described too many times to warrant a place in this essay, but in the context of my story it is important to note that nothing that happens on the trail has any innate value, or any meaning, if it is not transformed into narrative and shared. Why would anybody hunt a polar bear if the story (and the spoils of the hunt) cannot be shared? Travellers are expected to share their meat, their fish, their furs, and their news. Hunting and fishing trips not only contribute to the local economy and diet in the form of commodities, but they also physically and symbolically connect community members with the land and its resources.

I may add here that, for me, during my research, returning to town had other meanings. In my return trips with Maurice, it was not uncommon to travel to the point of exhaustion, often to meet some work or school obligation of someone in the travel party, or needing to arrive in time for church services. From the trail, and especially at night, the road back seemed exceedingly long. I recorded in my journal to have seen the settlement on the horizon as a "column" of light from as far as thirty kilometres. As we drew nearer, the airport light would be seen, and then numerous flickering lights that would gradually expand and become more distinguishable, until the town could actually be seen in full. Battered, hungry, and cold, returning for me was connected to the delights of a hot shower, an enormous hot meal, and a long and deep sleep in a soft bed. It was also about regaining my private space (which virtually disappeared during the trips) and about typing up my notes and uploading the data from my camera and GPS unit. As an ethnographer, and considering what others before me experienced in the Arctic, I was lucky, as I had many comforts that were not available to many of my predecessors. I often wished, however, to be an ethnographer of earlier times, to be able to live as Inuit used to. This logic, of course, is peppered with an ethnocentric nostalgia, so well defined by George Wenzel (1991) as "a semantic telescope that is used the wrong way round." In fact, I was part of a new and changing reality that involved us all (the hunters in the travelling parties and me). "Returning" today is filled with complexity as people struggle to bring the land to the town. The opposite is also true: the settlement permeates the land, bringing gear, stories, and commodities that, to a degree, redefine the relationships between people and nature. As much as the modern home and settlement separate people from land, their boundaries are both stern and porous, existing in a tension that is part of life.

Whatever the case, hunters eventually return home and to whatever awaits them in the settlement, good and bad. Soon enough, though, it will be time to plan for another trip. Maybe seals will be available at the floe edge, or ptarmigan beyond the hills, or the whales will arrive, or it will again be time for berries or eggs. As long as those connections are kept, urbanization will not completely prevail. As the older generations pass (especially those that were born and grew up before the establishment of the settlements), new challenges arise. How to keep their stories and knowledge alive? How to deal with both climatic and social changes? How to adapt to new economic and political realities?

CONCLUSION

There is a treasure in Igloolik that is often overlooked. Past human achievements are often measured by their visual impact (e.g., the pyramids in Egypt or the ruins of Machu Picchu), but Inuit achievements are far subtler. They include a formidable body of knowledge that has allowed people to thrive in an environment that to most other peoples is forbidden. But the concept of "body of knowledge" only scratches the surface of that complex relationship that Inuit have with their environment. As Tim Ingold (2000) has argued, it is in the unveiling of relationships that people truly learn, through a process that he calls *enskilment*. Many books have been written describing this or that aspect of Inuit knowledge, but knowledge separated from skills (and actual performance) has only partial meaning in the Inuit world. This is perhaps true of any knowledge, but in the Inuit approach to learning, knowledge, skills, and performance are fundamentally entangled, to the point that separating them is detrimental or nonsensical.

Before departing on my first long hunting trip, in October of 2000, Maurice Arnatsiaq asked me to look at how he was loading his sled, carefully threading a length of rope through every item in the load and securing it to the wooden bars of the sled. He then asked me to load my own sled and, to my surprise, never came back to check how my job was done. About an hour after our departure, and as I was following him on the sea ice, he stopped and came to check how I was doing. Laughingly, he pointed at my sled, and, to my dismay, I noticed that half of my load was gone. That was the first of many of my

"Qallunaaq-like" clumsy acts, but it was also a powerful lesson. I was supposed to pay utmost attention to his explanations if I was to travel with him. And even though we lost a good part of two hours retrieving my things and reloading the sled, he was always in good humour (and told and retold the story many times after that). I am happy to say that I never lost my sled load again, but it took such an experience to make me realize how important observation and performing were in the Inuit approach to learning. This is the reason why, for instance, teaching how to build an igloo in the context of a formal school program may be seen by some as ineffective.

Passing down knowledge in new ways, however, has become a priority for Inuit communities, as elders themselves identify the changing nature of life and of learning. Recording knowledge is, in this sense, a high priority in most communities, and new appropriate contexts (new ways of performing and developing skills) are sorely needed. The Igloolik Oral History Project is, indeed, a treasure: a repository of incredible wealth in the form of narratives carefully recorded and curated over several decades of uninterrupted work. At the time of my research, it was also the love and skill of people like Louis Tapardjuk and Leah Otak, which they dedicated to their interviews and translations, that made each one of those interviews unique. It is perhaps in the wonderful randomness of topics, within and between interviews, and in the depth of their treatment that the Igloolik Oral History Project stands as one of the treasures of the Arctic. In those narratives, many of which are still told outside of the project's archives, the land has found yet another way to bring those long-established relationships to town.

BIBLIOGRAPHY

Ingold, Tim. 2000. *The Perception of the Environment: Essays in Livelihood, Dwelling, and Skill.* London: Routledge.

Nuttall, Mark. 1992. *Arctic Homeland: Kinship, Community and Development in Northwest Greenland.* Toronto: University of Toronto Press.

Wenzel, George. 1991. *Animal Rights, Human Rights: Ecology, Economy and Ideology in the Canadian Arctic.* London: Belhaven Press.

CHAPTER 9

"Once in a Long While"

The Igloolik Oral History Project as a
Resource with Which to Understand Suicidal
Behaviour in Historic Inuit Society

Jack Hicks

INTRODUCTION

IN THIS CHAPTER, I draw on historical and cultural knowledge presented in the Igloolik Oral History Project (IOHP) to challenge contemporary theories of the origins of sharply elevated rates of mental distress and suicidal behaviour in Inuit communities. Inuit oral history narratives, such as those found in the IOHP, provide a window to the past, but they also serve as a valuable resource for communities today to help make sense of the present.

In what follows, I draw on stories from this collection, stories from Iglulingmiut Inuit elders now long gone but still recognized for their wisdom and foresight. I draw on numerous individual accounts to contest the crude simulacrum that Inuit society was and is a "high-suicide-rate" society: in other words, that the present-day high rate of suicidal behaviour is somehow sanctioned, and seen as "traditional."

THE IOHP AS A RECORD OF THE PAST AND A CULTURAL RESOURCE FOR THE FUTURE

The motivation leading to the conception of the IOHP in 1986 was a general concern, shared by Igloolik's elders, over troubling changes in their society since their move from the land into settled communities in the late 1960s and early 1970s.[1] Among the younger generations, Inuit values, skills, and knowledge deemed essential for a healthy, productive life were being eroded at an alarming rate. Most troubling for the elders was the ongoing decline of Inuktitut, the only medium through which Inuit culture could be properly transmitted. The transition from camp life to settlement life was seen as the cause of a fundamental rupture in Inuit society. It was this historic break in the transmission of Inuit knowledge and values that the IOHP sought, at least in part, to address through the systematic recording of elders' knowledge, coupled with outreach programs for the youth involving extensive "on-the-land" skills training.

One of the strengths of the IOHP is the breadth of topics addressed in the interviews. A partial list of topics covered (some in greater depth than others) includes personal and family histories; the introduction of Christianity; social change; dispute resolution; child nurturing and development; traditional medicine; spirituality and shamanism; hunting techniques; animal ecology; skin preparation and sewing; shelter construction; local geography and place-names; astronomy; weather conditions; navigation; traditional games and music; and legends and myths.[2]

The IOHP has no parallel in the Canadian Arctic in terms of its scope, ease of accessibility, the sheer number of interviews, and the range of perspectives recorded. The IOHP is seen by some as reflecting the "traditional knowledge" of Canadian Inuit generally.[3] This is problematic in that there were (and still are) significant degrees of cultural difference between Inuit groups across the Canadian Arctic. The different groups sometimes had different patterns of contact, settlement, religious conversion, and other important sociohistorical experiences. If similar interviews had been conducted during the same period with elders of the same age range—for example, in the

Pangnirtung area or the Kugluktuk area—the results would have reflected the different historical experiences of those areas. Because the IOHP is an *Igloolik area* undertaking, one needs to exercise particular care when using specific material from the IOHP interviews to make generalizations or extrapolations about Inuit culture and society across Nunavut. There are, of course, cultural and historical parallels, nuanced according to each local area. However, we should be cautious when extrapolating specific conclusions drawn from these interviews to other Inuit communities across Nunavut—and cultural claims for groups in other parts of the Inuit homelands need to be supported by information from sources other than the IOHP.

Another precaution to be observed when working with oral histories in general is the inducement to take the information or testimony of one individual to be representative of the whole group. Individual impressions or opinions about specific events or activities are, of course, in themselves important and valid, but do not necessarily give a full reflection of the way the event was experienced by all in the community. The IOHP sought to address this difficulty by conducting interviews on key topics with many different elders. Moreover, individual elders were typically interviewed numerous times on the same topic, each interview building on the previous one. In this way, a level of consensus and understanding could be achieved around the community's experience of various historical processes (for instance, the introduction of Christianity, or the move from the land into the settlement). This same approach was used successfully to understand how, in traditional times, Iglulingmiut structured and maintained social control.[4]

The IOHP records the perspectives of Igloolik elders who lived during a specific time period. Many of the elders interviewed had lived experience of the period before Christianity and the period of conversion to Christianity. Rosie Iqallijuq, for instance, recalls seeing the Inuit Christian proselytizer Umik in the 1920s during his visit to the Igloolik area:

They say it was Umik who started it off, directed by a minister called Uqammaq,[5] who had shown some Inuit how to go about converting people to Christianity. As Umik was from this region the minister sent him here to convert the people.

Umik soon became mentally imbalanced. He was trying hard to convert the people to Christianity while, at the same time, his son Nuqallaq, who because he had murdered the trader Robert Janes, was taken away to a penitentiary.[6] It was so pitiful to see Umik in this state. He would hurt himself and he just kept on talking and talking, he was trying to keep his self-harm to himself, being very careful that he did not hurt others.

He talked so much when he was in that state. I remembered the time he shook the hands of my in-laws Ukangut and Itturiligaq when he arrived at Ugliarjjuk.[7] We were the only people there at that time. Umik [and his travelling companions] had passed through [our camp] on their way back from their journey to Mittimatalik [Pond Inlet]. It was around this time Umik's son was arrested and taken away. As Umik shook hands with my father-in-law, he said: "*Gutip irninga qallunaat nunaannut angiraujaungmat, paliicillu kanaitallu piungittumik piqujijunniirtualungmatta.*" ["The son of God has been taken home to the land of the Qallunaat (the white man); the police and the Canadians have discouraged anyone from doing wrongful acts."][8] This was the first time I ever heard mention of Canadians. As I was young at that time I would not forget what I had just heard. (Iqallijuq 1991, IE-204)

Noah Piugaattuk adds to Iqallijuq's account of Inuit knowledge relating to the killing of Robert Janes. It is noteworthy that Piugaattuk's perspective was that Nuqallaq was arrested not only for having killed Janes—an action, it is said, that one individual was called upon to do after the entire group had concluded that Janes posed a danger to them all—but also for having mistreated his first wife to the point that she killed herself:

Q. So [Janes' killers] were never told that they were liable to get arrested?
A. Yes. They were asked questions to get their version of the story.
That summer a ship [from the south] left for Pond Inlet to deal with
the matter, taking along a white man[9] who made his home in [south-
ern Baffin Island] but had lived previously in the Arctic Bay area. He
was fluent in Inuktitut.

Nuqallaq was known for his abusive behaviour toward his wife. His
first wife got so tired of him that she took her own life. When Nuqallaq
and his wife were out hunting alone it was said that when they returned
his wife had lost a lot of weight. Nuqallaq's abuse of his wife was also a
factor when they arrested him for the killing of the white man, Robert
Janes. One must understand that under the circumstances, there was
little else the Inuit could have done but to kill Janes.... That was the
main reason for Nuqallaq's arrest, but his conviction also took into
consideration that he was an abusive man. (Piugaattuk 1991, IE-041)

Many elders recorded their reflections on how Inuit live today, in
towns with "too many people."[10] There are numerous poignant observations on how dramatically social relations have changed since the
move from the land into the settlement. Michel Kupaaq noted:

Relatives or in-laws were not allowed to own private things. If they
were related to each other then everything was owned in common....
In the old days, they would pool all their property, allowing everybody to have equal access to it. Nowadays the difference is that you
have to pay in order to use an item even if it is owned by one of your
relatives. That is what people do today, but in the past all the things
that were in the camp were accessible to anyone without any thought
of having to pay. Today people have to pay in order to use something
they want to use... that is the difference. (Kupaaq 1987, IE-021)

If interviews with Igloolik elders had been conducted twenty years
earlier, the range of life experiences would have been different. If the
interview process started today, there would be less direct knowledge
of life in the camps. In this sense, the timing of the IOHP interviews

was fortuitous—one might even say optimal—in that it captured the perspectives of Inuit who had lived through decades of remarkable and profound transition and change.

One key aspect of the IOHP is the frankness with which the elders discussed behaviours deemed immoral by Christian missionaries. The topic of "wife exchange," for example, was discussed by Hubert Amarualik with admirable matter-of-factness:

> Q. Was this part of the custom when one man was barren, so in order for the couples to have a child they would exchange wives?
> A. Yes. That was the main reason, in order to help the other couple. In addition, it was a sign of friendship.... It was not meant to be used to hurt the other, but when it did it was treated with disdain.
> Q. It is also said that they used to borrow one's wife (*nuliijautigiik*).
> A. This was practised in a situation where the man was planning a lengthy trip, perhaps to spend the summer inland, or on any other extended hunting trip. The man would leave his wife behind if they had too many children and take, in her stead, a woman who did not have so many children to care for.
> Q. Did they practise that because the man needed someone to sew for him?
> A. Yes. The man would need someone to sew for him, but, being a man, he would also have a man's desires. That was the way it was.
> Q. It is not that they saw it as a sin?
> A. They did not even consider it to be immoral. They enjoyed it and did not think it immoral. This was part of their custom. (Amarualik 1993, IE-275)

Interviewees discussed suicidal behaviour with the same forth-rightness.

CAUSES AND FREQUENCY OF SUICIDE

In the following interview, George Aqiaq Kappianaq repeats the phrase "once in a long while" to describe the frequency with which Inuit took their own lives:

Q. What about suicide, has that been practised from time immemorial?
A. Yes, once in a long while. The first suicide I ever heard about was [name withheld]'s ... indeed I saw his remains, at least part of his remains. I have since believed that suicide did occur, from the two brothers, [name withheld] and [name withheld], along with [name withheld] and [name withheld], from whom I got the information about [name withheld]'s suicide, who was the husband of [name withheld], and father of the late [name withheld].

There were also suicides by hanging. This was usually the case when a person got so tired of his illness that he was driven to commit suicide by hanging. First a hole punched through the ceiling of an igloo, a line is run through it, and a crossbar placed outside [the igloo] to secure the line. Then with a thong rope he would hang himself. The hole [in the igloo ceiling through which the line is secured] is above the floor, not above the bed platform. The noose is then placed around his neck ... and he hangs himself, clear of the bed platform, so his feet cannot touch its surface. That was the way they used to hang themselves.
Q. Was this practice condoned?
A. No, it was discouraged. But there were cases where persons were ill for so long that they became tired of living and so they would commit suicide. This has been going on since time immemorial, but it is now more frequent. From what I have heard, in the past [suicides] occurred far apart, once in a long while. (Kappianaq 2000b, IE-456)

Kappianaq also gave a frank account of [name withheld]'s death:

Q. Did [name withheld] shoot himself intentionally?
A. Yes, he shot himself. I was but a child then, but I knew that he had shot himself. He had committed suicide.
Q. What was the cause of this suicide?
A. It was said that [name withheld] was the cause of this suicide. Apparently he was the boyfriend of [name withheld's] wife. [Name withheld] was a young man, a bachelor.... This happened at Amittuq.[11] [Name withheld]'s grave is there, not secured except for few rocks elongated in form.

Q. Was it because he committed suicide that the grave was fixed in this manner, or was that the way they buried their people?

A. That was the way they buried their people in those days. [Amittuq] is like this area where everything is gravel, and there are not many stones. [Name withheld]'s remains were positioned below a raised beach, parallel to the contour of the beach. A few stones were placed around the corpse. I suppose the body was [soon] eaten by animals as there was nothing left except for the skull. We saw the skull in the spring ... the skin was still attached, complete with hair, since it was fresh, in fact it was still not a year old. (Kappianaq 2000a, IE-455)

Piugaattuk used the expression "every now and then," but clearly in reference to assisted suicide:

Q. Were there suicides in the past?

A. This is known to have had happened every now and then. There were cases when a person would take his own life unknown to others. This happened when this person had done something that he was not supposed to have done. I have never seen this personally but I've heard about it at the time when Inuit had very little to work with.

Q. Was suicide acceptable or was it unaccepted?

A. In those days it always caused conflict among people, suicide is never acceptable.... It causes animosity between the family of the person who is killed and the family of the one who did the killing. It is bad and should be discouraged.

Q. You mean [helping someone] to commit suicide?

A. Yes. This has always happened. That is why the police will arrest the one who killed a person.

Q. Was it a bad thing to help a person who wants to die?

A. It was not acceptable because of the reluctance of the person being asked to help. That is why it is bad. It was not accepted in any way.

Q. But was it practised?

A. It might have been done, but I personally have not witnessed it. Indeed, I have not heard of a case.[12] But I have seen the people of Nattiling where there was a man who committed suicide by shooting himself. He did not die immediately, making a mess of himself and looking extremely pitiful. It was clear that he was only going to be in agony so he was shot dead. That is the only case that I have seen.

If it was known that person might want to commit suicide, they used to take away anything he could use to kill himself with.... You can tell if a person is thinking about committing suicide, as Inuit we are always alert about the behavior of certain persons. Some will be discovered by the words that they might have said. (Piugaattuk 1986b, IE-011)

By speaking frankly about something that was condemned by the missionaries, Piugaattuk encouraged young people to talk openly about things that many people don't want to have discussed.

Piugaattuk was insistent that there was no "youth suicide" in the past:[13]

Q. As you know today, young people commit suicide, perhaps because they have too much on their minds. Did this happen in the past among young people?
A. No, there were no such suicides in the past. This problem is a recent one, beginning when people moved into the settlements. Now [suicides occur] when [young people] have too much on their minds and do not make any attempts to resolve their problem by bringing it out. If they [talked about it] then this wouldn't happen. If they keep things to themselves, without seeking help, suicide is usually the consequence. This phenomenon is as modern as the people.... [Suicide results] when a person makes no attempt to come out with his problems, this is known to destroy an individual's morale. (Piugaattuk 1987, IE-030)

Kupaaq suggested that suicide was almost unknown in the past because Inuit were taught to take care of each other, to watch out for each other, and to share their thoughts with each other:

Q. Young adults had to help their fellow human beings in those days.... In what way were [they] taught ... I mean ... in what way were they to act to help other people?

A. Our parents used to teach us to help other people—that is before the arrival of the Qallunaat. Nowadays people are not taught or made aware of this because the Qallunaat and Inuit are living together. If the person had been counselled, then he or she wouldn't act in such a manner, but sometimes they commit suicide.

Q. What is the reason that people are not being taught today anymore?

A. Our younger generation know more about the ways of living today than the older generation. That is the reason why they are not taught because they know more about the ways of living nowadays. The older Inuit do not fully understand the ways of living today and because of that lack of knowledge they are staying quiet. [Young people] who are now living between two different cultures seem to take their own lives before their time of death arrives … They are in a limbo between two cultures so they take their own lives.

Q. In the old days, when people apparently were not, or less, confused, did suicide occur?

A. No … I have never seen anyone commit suicide in those days.

Q. Not with old people that felt that they were becoming a burden?

A. No … I have never witnessed anyone committing suicide in this region or the fact that they felt worthless to others. It is only now I hear of people hanging themselves. (Kupaaq 1987, IE-021)

Some of the interviews give specific reasons why suicide occurred in the past. Rosie Iqallijuq identified one specific risk factor for suicidal behaviour: spousal violence.

Q. When a couple were having a problem, could they solve their problem by talking it out or was beating always involved?

A. They could solve their problem just by talking. When a woman got tired of being beaten she would just commit suicide and people used to be scared of that happening. (Iqallijuq 1987b, IE-027)

There is no way of knowing whether she was referring solely to the suicide of Ullatitaq (Nuqallaq's wife) in 1916—a death that would have been known to all Inuit in the North Baffin area—or whether

Ullatitaq's self-inflicted death was one of several or many by women trapped in abusive relationships.

Inuki Kunuk noted that the unexpected loss of loved ones could result in what we today term a "traumatic grief response" and /or "survivor guilt":

Q. What advice was given to those who had lost partners in hunting or travelling accidents?
A. … There were occasions when persons who lost a partner while hunting became so overwhelmed by the loss that they would just leave themselves to the same fate. However, I have not heard of anyone who has actually done that. My personal opinion is that if the person who loses a [hunting] partner happened to be an orphan, while the victim had plenty of relatives, the survivor might be so devastated that he would feel no need to live while the other died. Because of that [I knew how] I was going to feel had my partner drowned, so I did not have in mind to die [even though this] outcome would have made me so apprehensive. [Besides] I could probably give an account of the circumstances of the loss to anyone who might have suffered from the loss of a partner to accidental death. One may feel so sorry that they survived an accident while the other did not, but they must never think about killing themselves. (Kunuk 1990, IE-116)

Kunuk's interview also sheds light on the vulnerability of orphans in such situations.

Rosie Iqallijuq told of an elder who was left behind on a hunting trip:

Q. I have another question which is probably sad. In the past when an elder thought himself as a burden, they would request to be left behind. This is what happened in other regions, and sometimes they would commit suicide. Was it like this in this area?
A. No, it didn't happen like that. But there is a story from away back about Uttugi. The person he was named after was old and he used [to] travel by boat and by kayak. One day his son—his real son—decided

to leave him on an island. His son said to his father, "Uttugialuu, I am going to leave you on this island."

The old man answered very slowly, "Yes."

So the son got him off the boat and left, not intending [on] going back to get him. Someone else picked him up. He still had life in him and was taken home. (Iqallijuq 1987a, IE-026)

She elaborated:

Q. When the Inuit felt that the elder was a burden, did they just leave them?

A. It is said that, that this used to happen. Some would be left behind in isolated places to die. I used to hear a story about someone who always kept remembering the way his grandmother looked, staring at them, when they left her.... When they were preparing to leave her behind in an igloo, the grandson would keep going back to the igloo [but the boy's] father or the mother would grab him and take him to the sled. He didn't want to leave because of his love for his grandmother. That happened, but it was very rare. (Iqallijuq 1987a, IE-026)

The fact that these two stories by Rosie Iqallijuq are the *only* stories of someone being left behind on a hunting trip in the entire IOHP is a significant comment on how infrequently such desperate measures occurred.[14]

Far from discussing suicide as something that was common in the past, these elders speak of it as something that was *uncommon*. It happened, from time to time, but not as a matter of routine. Rather than commenting on how frequently suicide occurred in the past, these Igloolik elders express great sorrow over the rate of suicide in recent decades.

SUICIDE AND THE AFTERLIFE

The pioneering Greenlandic/Danish polar explorer and anthropologist Knud Rasmussen famously wrote, after the Fifth Thule Expedition conducted research in northern Foxe Basin in the early 1920s, that

Iglulingmiut did not fear death: "People in danger can often hear him calling out: 'Come, come to me! It is not painful to die. It is only a brief moment of dizziness. It does not hurt to kill yourself'" (Rasmussen 1929, 74). Kappianaq stated that even those who had been murdered could look forward to a "jubilant" afterlife, which is particularly interesting in that his explanation was redolent of Rasmussen's phrasing:

> ... people that had been killed by someone would go to a place in the heavens in the same sphere as the moon. It is said that people who have been killed will feel pain only momentarily, [and] once they have felt the [wounds] that caused their death they will no longer feel pain ever again. They will live in a place where they will forever be happy and jubilant. So it was said that the only thing to fear when someone is killed is the pain that killed them which might be a stab or an arrow, after that there is nothing to be apprehensive about. When we were informed about death we were told that there is nothing to fear should someone kill us. This was said possibly so that we would not fear death of someone else's making. We were constantly assured that death was nothing to fear and the place where one would end up after death, a particular place in the heavens, was a jubilant place to be in. (Kappianaq 1990, IE-155)

The fact that suicide sometimes did occur is evidenced by the references to the fate of those who died by their own hand.

Sarah Haulli stated:

> Q. Is it true that when shamans made a journey to the place of the dead that they would see some of the people who had committed suicide?
>
> A. It is said so. What I have heard is that those who committed suicide continued to be in the position they were when they killed themselves. (Haulli 1990, IE-099)

François Quassa elaborated on this point:

Q. Going back to the earlier discussion about the souls of the dead, did they have to get killed in order to go to heaven?
A. No, others would go to heaven as well, there was a special mention of the ones that were murdered as they wanted to assure their living relatives that they were happy and not to worry about them. They would want them to know that the only thing that they suffered was a brief pain. It has been said of the ones who committed suicide that they were pitiable to look at. They will always and forever try to kill themselves. For instance those who had hanged themselves, it is said they will continue to try and kill themselves in this manner for eternity. The state they are in makes one feel deeply sympathetic towards them. It is said those who are the victims of murder, and those who die of natural causes, are always very happy. No one has ever just vanished on dying; they always have gone to [a particular] place of after death. (Quassa 1990, IE-156)

And Nathan Qamaniq commented:

I used to have a recording of Amiimiarjjuk. I really wish that people could listen to it, but I have lost the tape. It deals, in part, with shamanism. In the recording Amiimiarjjuk mentions that people who tried to commit suicide are with Kannaaluk [the great one at the bottom of the sea, sometimes called Sedna] where, it is said, that [Kannaaluk] badgers or torments them, frequently. [Amiimiarjjuk's] words make [the act of suicide] extremely disagreeable.
Q. So Kannaaluk badgers them badly?
A. Yes, it is said so, that Kannaaluk badgers them, and still [the suicides] try and try to kill themselves. Yet these are the very same that have been dead for a long time … yet they continue to do things to kill themselves by any means, including suicide. They are in a place that is extremely tiresome and extremely disagreeable. (Qamaniq 2001, IE-493)

The highly disagreeable fate of those who die by suicide would have been a serious deterrent to those contemplating suicide for anything other than the most compelling of reasons. The dire eternal consequences of committing suicide points *a priori* to the existence of suicide in historic Inuit society, albeit it was likely uncommon. If suicide did not exist, why the need for the warning?

MENTAL DISTRESS

One important belief expressed by many interviewees was the danger of keeping troubling thoughts to oneself, and the risk of not confiding in others so that they might assist you with them.

Piugaattuk stated:

> [Worrying] is not good for your health.
> Q. Does worrying deteriorate the mind?
> A. Absolutely … worrying deteriorates the mind. We shouldn't have negative thoughts about other people but instead you should try to have positive thoughts towards others. (Piugaattuk 1986a, IE-008)

Amarualik, when asked if people should confess all their wrong-doings, explained:

> Definitely. We must confess [our wrongdoings]. The world is not going to change, at least according to our old beliefs … the behaviour of a person is going to continue on, no matter. When you engage in something that you are not supposed to do and keep it a secret because it's very embarrassing, the longer you keep the secret, the more difficult it will be to disclose it. They say that if you confess your wrong-doing to someone you trust he will keep it to himself. It is important that this person is not the type who will tell others about your wrong-doing. This still applies today. You may be embarrassed if you discover that your confidant tells others. This was fearful and no doubt still is today.
>
> We are humans and will remain so despite the fact that our ways of doing things have changed from the past. When we are engaged in

something that we are not supposed to be doing and keep it a secret because it is embarrassing, this will have an effect on our lives ... confession will make you happier. If [you disclose] your wrong-doing to a confidant who makes you welcome and encourages you to confess, then you can mingle again among your peers in their daily activities without hiding yourself.

If you are guilt-ridden but cannot confide in anyone [your guilt] will keep building up inside you. It is best that you rid yourself of that guilt. You may be a young person or you may be an elder, it does not matter what age you are. Once you are rid of your guilt you have nothing to be remorseful about. If we confess our action to anyone that we are comfortable with, then it will make you much better. (Amarualik 1993, IE-275)

Amarualik responds to a question about the possibility of unresolved guilt and remorse leading to suicide when a person can find no one to confide in:

That is right, [these circumstances] can lead to people taking their own lives when they cannot find someone to talk to. They become withdrawn from others in public places. Money is now a contributing factor no matter where you go, even the community hall where it costs money for you to get snacks. These are the things that add to misery. I personally have lost a grandchild to suicide, and there are other things that happen that one would rather not experience. These are the things that contribute to one's misery. It is desirable that you try and rid yourself of all the things that keep you in misery. It is dreadful when, too late to do anything about it, you suddenly realize that someone has a problem. But when harm has already been done, when you finally get to hear about the source of the problem it is a very difficult thing to accept. It is best that you confess your wrong-doing to a person who will make you feel welcome and will listen to your problem—then you are going to feel much better.

Anyone, including myself, who notices there's something amiss in a person's behaviour, should step in and try to help that person.

You can tell very easily by observing [a person's] behaviour. If the [personality] changes then there is something wrong. If the person wishes to talk then he must be made welcome. The numbers of elders are not many but they are silent, they do not share what they have heard about the virtue of life so this makes it much more difficult. (Amarualik 1993, E-275)

There are numerous other detailed discussions of mental distress, what causes it, how to prevent it from occurring, and how Inuit dealt with it when it did occur.[15]

Not only do interviews conducted for the IOHP stress the importance of not keeping troubling thoughts to one's self, it is also clear that both individuals and groups did—and should—intervene when they sensed worrying behaviour on someone's part.

THE SIGNIFICANCE OF THE KNOWLEDGE RECORDED IN THE IOHP INTERVIEWS

In Nunavut today one hears a wide range of beliefs expressed, by both Inuit and non-Inuit, about the rate and nature of suicidal behaviour in historic Inuit society—everything from "Inuit never died by suicide before the white man came" to "suicide was commonplace, especially among elders." This question is of more than academic interest: young Inuit who believe that suicide was "part of our culture" may interpret that belief as a form of "social licence" sanctioning suicide as a way out of crises in their own lives.

In an earlier publication (Hicks 2017c) I examined several different sources in pursuit of clarity on this question. The first are records of explorers and early anthropologists: Captain William Edward Parry (1824) and his crew, Captain Charles Frances Hall (1865), Franz Boas (1888), and Knud Rasmussen (1929, 1931). While their records contain fascinating details, they are insufficient to allow us to understand the rate and nature of suicidal behaviour prior to the Inuit transition to life in settled communities.

My two other sources present data from the first half of the 20th century.

My second source is twenty-eight records of death by suicide[16] in the Northwest Territories between 1920 and 1945 contained in Royal Canadian Mounted Police (RCMP) reports found in the National Archives. Of these twenty-eight, one was by a non-Inuk (an RCMP officer) and another was by a "Siberian Eskimo" employed by the Hudson's Bay Company.[17] While there was a wide range of causal factors among the twenty-six cases of suicide among Inuit from the Canadian Arctic, untreated physical illness (including blindness) and mental illness was the most common. There were also cases of mental distress (including traumatic grief) and relationship problems (including adultery, spousal violence, and the inability to find a marriage partner). The only youth in the cohort was a seventeen-year-old boy; unfortunately the report on his death is an outlier in that it does not provide sufficient detail to allow us to come to a clear understanding of what his reasons may have been.

The overall tone of the RCMP reports was not unlike police reports on cases of suicide today. Each case was carefully investigated and written up as the individual tragedy that it was. There is no indication that RCMP officers or supervisors viewed suicide as a commonplace "custom" among Inuit. On the basis of those twenty-six RCMP cases, using data from the 1931 census, I calculated a rate of death by suicide by Inuit in the Northwest Territories of about 20 per 100,000 population for the period 1920 to 1945. This is higher than the rate of 3.0 per 100,000 population calculated for Greenland for the period 1900 to 1930 by the pioneering medical officer Dr. Alfred Berthelsen,[18] which may reflect the more difficult living conditions and absence of formal medical care in most of the Inuit regions of the Northwest Territories.

My third source is the field notes of anthropologist Asen Balikci, who conducted research among the Arviligjuarmiut at Pelly Bay during the winter of 1959–60. Balikci recorded stories quite different in character (i.e., often bizarre and/or dramatic) than those that the RCMP recorded, among which were "one ten year old boy [and] 5 young adults 15 to 20 years old."[19] Balikci calculated a fantastically high suicide rate—"a frequency of 575 Arvilingjuarmiut suicide per 100,000 living for one year."[20] My analysis of Balikci's field notes[21] disputes his claims, which contrast sharply with the perspectives of the Oblate missionary Franz Van de Velde, who served at Pelly Bay from 1937 until 1965.[22]

Van de Velde's observations for Pelly Bay were paralleled by those of his fellow Oblate missionary Jean-Marie Trébaol, stationed at Igloolik, just before the transition to life in a settled community. Trébaol (1958) compiled a list of all souls—both Catholic and Anglican—living in the Igloolik area in the late 1950s, with personal and family observations on a great number of Inuit.[23] He noted just one suicide, but quite a number of murders[24]—a ratio consistent with the early RCMP files in the National Archives.[25]

CONCLUSION

The significance of the Igloolik Oral History Project is that it presents the carefully documented knowledge of Inuit elders in the community of Igloolik about both the things they saw and experienced during their lives, and the societal beliefs they were taught as they were growing up. The interviews collected, preserved, and made available in the IOHP are of tremendous significance to our understanding of the rate and nature of suicidal behaviour in historic Inuit society.

Through their interviews for the IOHP, now-deceased Igloolik elders purposefully and skilfully drew on their life experiences to teach future generations how to explain and address mental distress—something which, kept hidden, unnoticed and unchallenged, could result in suicide behaviour. However, they also tell us that actual suicidal behaviour was *not* common in the past. Their comments on suicidal behaviour by Inuit during the first half of the 20th century are very different in tone than what Balikci's famous writings[26] on the subject might lead one to expect. They are, in fact, closer in tone to that of RCMP reports from the period 1920 to 1945. If we could go back in time to 1930 or 1940 and interview a senior RCMP official with responsibility for the Arctic, he might describe suicide behaviour by Inuit as occurring "once in a long while" or "every now and then"—as Piugaattuk and Kappianaq did when they were interviewed as part of the IOHP.

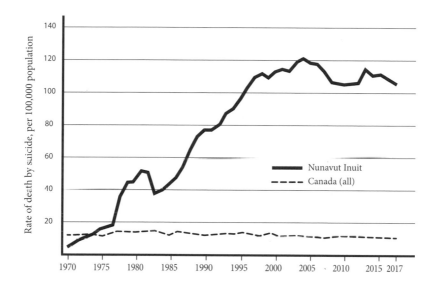

Source: Hicks (2015), with data added for 2015, 2016, and 2017.[27]

Many Igloolik elders recorded their reflections on how Inuit live today, in towns with "too many people," how the move from camp life to life in settled communities occurred, and what the impacts of the transition have been. Among the most significant impacts have been the demise of the traditional ways in which Iglulingmiut structured and maintained social control, and the effects this has had on the socio-emotional well-being of children and youth.[27]

Piugaattuk, Kappianaq, and many others of their generation lived long enough to observe and reflect deeply on the meaning of one of the most devastating "suicide transitions" in all of human history—one by which they and their immediate families, in Igloolik and beyond, were profoundly affected. The graph below starkly reveals the immensity of this Nunavut-wide tragedy but not, of course, the pain and suffering behind the many young, individual Inuit deaths comprising the graph's tragic trend.

People trying to understand the root causes of the sharp increase in the rate of suicidal behaviour in Inuit society in recent decades should focus on the colonial disruptions to Inuit lifeways,[28] their enduring intergenerational consequences[29] (including elevated rates of mental distress[30]), high rates of early childhood adversity[31] and their epigenetic impacts,[32] and the failure of public health authorities to address them,[33] rather than on supposed characteristics of historical Inuit culture or "Indigenous exceptionalist" perspectives on suicide behaviour.[34]

Piugaattuk's observation that "this phenomenon [of sharply elevated rates of suicidal behaviour] is as modern as the people" is penetratingly insightful. It is more than social commentary; it is an admonishment of contemporary social realities.

BIBLIOGRAPHY

Amarualik, Hubert. 1993. Interview IE-275. Igloolik Oral History Project. Igloolik.

Balikci, Asen. 1960a. "Suicidal Behaviour among the Netsilik Eskimos." Paper presented at the Annual meeting of the Canadian Political Science Association, Kingston.

———. 1960b. *Suicidal Behaviour among the Netsilik Eskimos*. Report prepared for the federal Department of Northern Affairs and Natural Resources.

———. 1961. "Suicidal Behaviour among the Netsilik Eskimos." In *Canadian Society in Perspective: Sociological Perspectives*, edited by Bernard R. Blishen et al., 575–588. Toronto: The Macmillan Company of Canada Ltd.

———. 1970. *The Netsilik Eskimo*. Garden City, N.Y.: The Natural History Press.

Berthelsen, Alfred. 1935. "Grønlandsk medicinsk statistik og nosografi I: Grønlands befolknings-statistik 1901–30." *Meddelelser om Grønland* 117, no. 1: 1–83.

Boas, Franz. 1888. *The Central Eskimo. 6th Annual Report of the Bureau of American Ethnology for the Years 1884–1885*. Washington, D.C.: Smithsonian Institution.

Bockstoce, John. 1986. *Whales, Ice, & Men: The History of Whaling in the Western Arctic*. Seattle: University of Washington Press.

Chachamovich, Eduardo, et al. 2015. "Suicide among Inuit: Results from a Large, Epidemiologically Representative Follow-back Study in Nunavut." *Canadian Journal of Psychiatry* 60, no. 6: 268–275.

Crawford, Allison. 2015. "A National Suicide Prevention Strategy for Canadians: From Research to Policy and Practice." *Canadian Journal of Psychiatry* 60, no. 6: 239–241.

Crawford, Allison, and Jack Hicks. 2018. "Early Childhood Adversity as a Key Mechanism by which Colonialism is Mediated into Suicide Behaviour." *Northern Public Affairs* 5:3.

Fossett, Renée. 2001. *In Order to Live Untroubled: Inuit of the Central Arctic, 1550 to 1940.* Winnipeg: University of Manitoba Press.

Government of Nunavut; Nunavut Tunngavik Inc.; Royal Canadian Mounted Police; and, the Embrace Life Council. 2010. *Nunavut Suicide Prevention Strategy.* Iqaluit: Nunavut Tunngavik Inc. www.tunngavik.com/files /2010/10/2010-10-26-nunavut-suicide-prevention-strategy-english1.pdf

———. 2017. *Inuusivut Anninaqtuq Action Plan 2017–2022.* Iqaluit: Nunavut Tunngavik Inc. Iqaluit. inuusiq.com/wp-content/uploads/2017/06 /Inuusivut_Anninaqtuq_English.pdf

Grant, Shelagh D. 2002. *Arctic Justice: On Trial for Murder, Pond Inlet, 1923.* Montreal and Kingston: McGill-Queen's University Press.

Hall, Charles F. 1865. *Arctic Researches and Life among the Esquimaux: Being the Narrative of an Expedition in Search of Sir John Franklin, in the Years 1860, 1861 and 1982.* New York: Harper & Brothers.

Harper, Kenn. 1985. "William Duval (1858–1931)." *Arctic* 38, no. 1: 74–75.

———. 2017. *Thou Shalt Do No Murder: Inuit, Injustice, and the Canadian Arctic.* Iqaluit: Nunavut Arctic College Media.

Haulli, Sarah. 1990. Interview IE-199. Igloolik Oral History Project. Igloolik.

Hicks, Jack. 2009. "Toward More Effective, Evidence-Based Suicide Prevention in Nunavut." In *Northern Exposure: Peoples, Powers and Prospects in Canada's North*, edited by Frances Abele et al., 467–495. Montreal: Institute for Research on Public Policy.

———. 2015. *Statistical Data on Death by Suicide by Nunavut Inuit, 1920 to 2014.* Report prepared for Nunavut Tunngavik Inc. www.tunngavik.com /blog/2015/09/15/pdf-statistical-data-on-death-by-suicide-by-nunavut -inuit-1920-to-2014/

———. 2017a. "Suicide Prevention as a Social Justice Issue: The Political Epidemiology of Canada's Failure to Address Elevated Rates of Suicide Behaviour in Indigenous Communities." Paper presented at the Alternate Routes conference "Social Justice and Social Inequality," Holgúin, Cuba.

———. 2018a. "A Critical Analysis of Myth-Perpetuating Research on Suicide Prevention." *Northern Public Affairs* 5:3.

———. 2018b. "Nunavut: Conceived in Austerity." In *Canadian Provincial and Territorial Paradoxes: Public Finances, Services and Employment in an Era of Austerity*, edited by Carlo Fanelli and Bryan Evans. Montreal and Kingston: McGill-Queens University Press.

———. 2018c. *Suicidal Behaviour by Inuit in the Eastern and Central Arctic during the 19th and the First Half of the 20th Century*. Self-published, Kindle Direct Publishing.

Hicks, Jack, and Graham White. 2015. *Made in Nunavut: An Experiment in Decentralized Government*. Vancouver: UBC Press.

Inuit Tapiriit Kanatami. 2016. *National Inuit Suicide Prevention Strategy*. Ottawa: Inuit Tapiriit Kanatami. https://www.itk.ca/wp-content/uploads/2016/07/ITK-National-Inuit-Suicide-Prevention-Strategy-2016.pdf

Iqallijuq, Rosie. 1987a. Interview IE-026. Igloolik Oral History Project. Igloolik.

———. 1987b. Interview IE-027. Igloolik Oral History Project. Igloolik.

———. 1991. Interview IE-204. Igloolik Oral History Project. Igloolik.

Kappianaq, George Aqiaq. 1990. Interview IE-155. Igloolik Oral History Project. Igloolik.

———. 2000a. Interview IE-455. Igloolik Oral History Project. Igloolik.

———. 2000b. Interview IE-456. Igloolik Oral History Project. Igloolik.

Kunuk, Inuki. 1990. Interview IE-116. Igloolik Oral History Project. Igloolik.

Kupaaq, Michel. 1987. Interview IE-021. Igloolik Oral History Project. Igloolik.

Labonté, Benoit, Adel Farah, and Gustavo Turecki. 2015. "Early-life adversity and epigenetic changes: Implications for understanding suicide." In *Revisioning Psychiatry: Cultural Phenomenology, Critical Neuroscience, and Global Mental Health*, edited by Laurence J. Kirmayer et al., 206–235. Cambridge: Cambridge University Press.

MacDonald, John. 2001. "The Igloolik Oral History Project." *Meridian* Fall/Winter: 1–3.

———. 2008. "Inuit Qaujimajatuqangit versus IQ: Musings on an Arctic Acronym." In *Northern Imaginary 3rd Part*, edited by Patrick Huse, 88–92. Oslo: Delta Press.

Parry, William Edward. 1824. *Journal of A Second Voyage for the Discovery of a North-West Passage from the Atlantic to the Pacific; Performed in the*

Years 1821-22-23, In His Majesty's Ships Fury and Hecla, Under the Orders of Captain William Edward Parry, R.N., F.R.S., and Commander of the Expedition. London: John Murray.

Piugaattuk, Noah. 1986a. Interview IE-007. Igloolik Oral History Project. Igloolik.

———. 1986b. Interview IE-008. Igloolik Oral History Project. Igloolik.

———. 1986c. Interview IE-011. Igloolik Oral History Project. Igloolik.

———. 1987. Interview IE-030. Igloolik Oral History Project. Igloolik.

———. 1991. Interview IE-041. Igloolik Oral History Project. Igloolik.

Qamaniq, Nathan. 2001. Interview IE-493. Igloolik Oral History Project. Igloolik.

Qikiqtani Truth Commission. 2010. *QTC Final Report: Achieving Saimaqatigiingniq.* Iqaluit: Qikiqtani Inuit Association. qtcommission.ca/sites/default/files/public/thematic_reports/thematic_reports_english_final_report.pdf

Quassa, François. 1990. Interview IE-156. Igloolik Oral History Project. Igloolik.

Rasing, Willem. 1993. "The Case of Kolitalik on the Encounter of Iglulingmiut Culture and Canadian Justice." In *Continuity and Discontinuity in Arctic Cultures,* edited by Cunera Buijs, 91–107. Leiden: CNWS.

———. 1994. *"Too Many People": Order and Nonconformity in Iglulingmiut Social Process.* Nijmegen: Faculteit der Rechtsgeleerdheid, Katholieke Universiteit.

———. 2017. *Too Many People: Contact, Disorder, Change in an Inuit Society, 1822–2015.* Iqaluit: Nunavut Arctic College Media.

Rasmussen, Knud. 1929. *Intellectual Culture of the Iglulik Eskimos. Report of the Fifth Thule Expedition 1921–24,* Vol. VII, no. 1. Copenhagen: Gyldendal.

———. 1931. *The Netsilik Eskimos: Social Life and Spiritual Culture. Report of the Fifth Thule Expedition 1921–24,* Vol. VIII, no. 1/2. Copenhagen: Gyldendal.

Trébaol, Jean-Marie (compiler). 1958. *Liber Animorum* of St. Etienne Mission, Igloolik. [Translated from the French by Georgia, 1983.]

Turecki, Gustavo. 2018. "Early-life adversity and suicide risk: The role of epigenetics." In *Phenomenology of Suicide: Unlocking the Suicidal Mind,* edited by Maurizio Pompili, 39–49. Cham, Switzerland: Springer International Publishing.

Van de Velde, Franz, Trinette S. Constandse-Westermann, Cornelius H.W. Remie, and Raymond R. Newell. 1993. "One Hundred Fifteen years of Arviligjuarmiut Demography, Central Canadian Arctic." *Arctic Anthropology* 30, no. 2: 1–4.

CHAPTER 10

A Marriage in Nunavik

Louis-Jacques Dorais

M ANY YEARS AGO, I made three short visits to Igloolik (in 1975, 1986, and 1991) to conduct linguistic and anthropological fieldwork there—once with Leah Otak as a much-appreciated collaborator. However, I cannot consider myself cognizant in Iglulingmiut language and culture.[1] My only relevant publication dates back to 1978; it consists of an introductory description of the North Baffin dialect of Inuktitut as spoken in Igloolik (Dorais 1978). This ignorance explains why my contribution to this book rather deals with a region (Nunavik) and a community (Quaqtaq) that witnessed my first as well as my latest sojourns in Inuit Nunangat, the land of the Inuit. The topic of my essay, the description and discussion of a wedding celebrated in Quaqtaq, should, nonetheless, sound familiar to the Iglulingmiut.[2]

TRADITIONAL MARRIAGE

In pre-contact Inuit society (*Qallunaaqalauqtinnagu*, "when there were no Qallunaat"), marrying was a simple affair without ceremonial formalities. When a boy and a girl from two acquainted families had reached puberty and acquired the knowledge and skills necessary to

perform the life-sustaining activities expected from adults, and possessed the basic implements to do so—ideally, a few dogs, a kayak,
a harpoon, bow and arrows, and a knife for men; a lamp, a cooking
pot, an *ulu*, a needle, and some thread for women—their parents told
them that they now were husband and wife. Generally speaking, the
girl went to live with the boy's family, although it often happened that
the bridegroom stayed with his new in-laws for about two years before the couple moved to the camp of the boy's parents. These unions
could easily dissolve during their first months of existence, but as
soon as a viable baby was born, they usually lasted for good.

In the Eastern Canadian Arctic at least, such informal marriages
remained customary until the 1960s, except that in later years the
consent of the future spouses was generally taken into consideration.
One young Qallunaaq woman I knew, who in 1965 had been sent to
do fieldwork in a small Nunavik village, in a very short time became
extremely skilled at sewing, cooking seal meat, and making bannock.
During an evening visit to a local family, the lady of the house told her,
"Tonight, you don't need to go back to your place. You will share my
son's bed and become his wife." The young woman, who had already
learned enough Inuktitut to make herself understood, explained that
she was soon to return down south to her parents and could not agree
with her host's proposal. Her explanation was accepted without problem.

The introduction of Christianity to the Canadian Arctic, which
started in the last quarter of the 19th century[3]—by 1920–30, most
Inuit had been baptized—brought some changes. In all Christian
denominations, marriage must be sanctioned by a religious ceremony (*katititaugiaq* or *katititauniq*, "the fact of being put together"),
whereby a church minister unites the bride and groom before God. In
many parts of Inuit Nunangat, however, missionaries were very few
in number and formal weddings could only be conducted if one of
them was available. This occurred when a missionary happened to
visit a camp that was home to one or more couples who had not been
religiously married yet, or when such couples went to trade at a post
where a mission had been established. Marriage thus often took place,
if at all, after several years of common life and, eventually, the birth

of children. This distinction between customary unions—the couple is considered by the community as being *aippariik* ("the two halves of a pair," i.e., married)—and officially sanctioned marriages has remained the habit among Inuit. Up to now, couples may wait until they have children to decide if they will organize a formal wedding or not.

Before the last three or four decades, religious weddings were very simple. The few Anglican ones I attended in Nunavik during the 1960s consisted of a short service presided by a minister (*ajuqiqtuiji*). The bride and groom wore fine (albeit far from fancy) clothes, while most participants were in their everyday garb. After the church ceremony, a lunch—or bannock and tea—may have been served to family and friends, but on a very modest scale. As time went by, however, the social and economic conditions of the Inuit changed. Through school, the media, and travel outside Inuit Nunangat, Inuit grew familiar with Qallunaat ways pertaining to marriage. Many among the younger generations thus became increasingly eager to organize Qallunaat-style weddings. This is why, as we shall now see, contemporary Northern marriages often look very much like their southern Canadian middle-class equivalents, although they preserve a uniquely Inuit atmosphere.

SOME EXTRACTS FROM A TRAVEL DIARY

With 410 residents in mid-2015, Quaqtaq is one of the smallest Canadian Inuit communities. Lying at the northwestern entrance to Ungava Bay, in northern Nunavik, it is known for its abundance of wildlife, although over the last few years caribou appear to have been on the decline. The Quaqtamiut remain grounded in Inuit culture—Inuktitut is their default language and hunting, fishing, and camping activities (*maqainniq*) have preserved their importance—but at the same time, the village functions as a modern, well-organized community, due in good part to the presence of dynamic local leaders (see Dorais 1997).

During my career as a student and teacher of anthropology, I have had several opportunities to conduct research in Quaqtaq. I had long planned to conclude this career by making a short visit there in 2015. I wished to celebrate with the Quaqtamiut the 50th anniversary of my first summer of fieldwork in that community (and in the North), from mid-May to early September 1965, by sharing with them my souvenirs and the pictures I had taken at that time. This is why, on a Friday in August 2015, I boarded in my hometown of Quebec City an Air Inuit flight bound for Kuujjuaq and beyond. The first part of the flight, to Schefferville and Kuujjuaq, went well. On arrival in the administrative centre of Nunavik, however, passengers were told that the next scheduled stop, Kangirsuk, was presently closed due to foul weather, and that the flight would be delayed a bit. Finally, after some four hours of waiting, Air Inuit decided to skip Kangirsuk and fly directly to Quaqtaq, Kangirsujuaq, and Salluit, the end of the line.

In the Kuujjuaq terminal, I had noticed the presence of a Quaqtamiuq woman I knew, who had just arrived from Montreal carrying two large sacks displaying the name of a tuxedo-renting store. She told me these suits were to be worn at a marriage that would be celebrated in Quaqtaq the following day. As I re-boarded the airplane, I immediately felt the atmosphere was special. The lady was chatting with three or four passengers from Kuujjuaq, also headed for the wedding, and everybody joked and laughed a lot. I learned that the groom was Taniali, the eldest son of a prominent Quaqtaq family involved in municipal, school, and church-related activities—and nephew of the tuxedo-carrying lady. He was to be united to a young woman originally from Kangirsuk. The couple already had two small children.

Alas! When the plane tried to land in Quaqtaq, fog and violent winds prevented the pilot from completing his landing. Just before touching ground, he had to boost the engines and the aircraft rapidly regained a cruising altitude, heading towards the next scheduled stop, Kangirsujuaq, while some passengers seated in the back were shouting ironically, "Bye-bye Quaqtaq!" A few minutes later, however, when the pilot told us it was impossible to land in Kangirsujuaq, retaliatory cries of "Bye-bye Kangirsujuaq!" were heard from the Quaqtaq passengers and their Kuujjuaq friends. The plane finally landed in Salluit, where I had to spend a very expensive night at the local Co-op Hotel, although I was fortunate enough to benefit from the presence of an Inuk educator and interpreter from Kangirsujuaq, also stranded there. Before departing from Kuujjuaq, he had had the prudence to buy some food that he generously shared with me.

On the next day, Saturday morning, the airplane resumed its flight back to Kuujjuaq. We overflew Kangirsujuaq, still shrouded in fog, but this time we were able to make a landing in Quaqtaq around noon. My sister (*najaapiga*), the daughter of my now-deceased adoptive parents, the couple who had welcomed me into their family in 1965 and every time I had returned back to Quaqtaq since, was waiting at the airport. I learned from her that the wedding ceremony, originally scheduled for 1:30 p.m., had been postponed until 4 p.m. in order to accommodate outside visitors and, I suspect, to ensure that the tuxedos had arrived. She drove me to her home, where I was to stay, explaining that everyone was welcome to attend the marriage and reassuring me that I could attend too, even if I had not taken any formal attire with me.

THE CHURCH CEREMONY

The wedding ceremony was held at Quaqtaq's Full Gospel Christian Church under the leadership of Reverend Eva Deer, the local *tasiuqti* ("arm- or hand-holder," i.e., [religious] guide, church minister; see Deer 2015), who had donned for the circumstance an *amauti*-like robe. When I entered the church a little before 4 p.m. it was almost empty. The attendants were rehearsing hymns, waiting for people to arrive. The ceremony actually started around 4:30 p.m., when the *tasiuqti* judged that participants were numerous enough. Some more persons joined afterwards, so that by the time the last latecomers had arrived, the relatively large church was about three-quarters full. Except for myself and five other Qallunaat—two teachers and three spouses of local residents—all bystanders and attendants were Inuit.

After having welcomed the audience and given a few instructions—notably to remain seated without taking photos during the religious part of the ceremony—the *tasiuqti* invited the bridegroom, his three best men (among whom were his brother and one of his cousins), and his parents to proceed to the front in order to take pictures. The four young men were wearing the tuxedos brought from

Downtown Quaqtaq, August 2015. Photo by Louis-Jacques Dorais

Montreal. The *tasiuqti* then asked the audience to stand up in order to salute the bridal procession. The bride entered at the back of the church, arm-in-arm with her father and preceded by her three maids of honour. She wore white wedding garb, while each maid wore a blue full-length dress and carried a bouquet of artificial flowers of the same colour. During the procession, Richard Wagner's "Bridal Chorus" was played on the church's electric keyboard.

The best men and the maids of honour sat down on the front stage, and the *tasiuqti* said an opening prayer. The bride's father then formally "gave away" his daughter (*aittuutigilugu*, "having her as a gift"). The spouses promised to remain faithful to one another and exchanged their wedding rings, after these had been blessed by the *tasiuqti*, who said the rings were a symbol of loyalty. The bride and groom then kneeled before the *tasiuqti*, who blessed them by laying her hands on their heads before proclaiming them husband and wife, explaining in English to the Qallunaat guests that if "a change occurred in their life-style," they should always give precedence to the interests of their family. The newlyweds kissed each other—the bride showing some reluctance to do so in public—and took a seat on the stage.

This was followed by a short sermon during which the *tasiuqti* explained that marriage is the most important event in one's life, because it constitutes the very basis of the family institution. Two hymns were then sung, and the *tasiuqti* declared that the ceremony was now finished. She invited the newlyweds and their witnesses to sign the official church and governmental records while people in the audience chatted and progressively left the room. The whole event had lasted some fifty minutes.

THE BANQUET

The wedding banquet was scheduled at 6:30 p.m. in the school gym. Everybody was welcome, but once again, the hall was almost empty as I entered it, although it filled up during the next half-hour. A high table for the newlyweds, the best men, and the maids of honour, who sat facing the audience, had been set at one end of the gym. Another table at the opposite end displayed a buffet of Inuit- and Qallunaat-style foods brought in by the guests. No alcohol was served (water and fruit juice were available, though), but a few persons came with their own beer or spirits. The audience, including the newlyweds' families, sat where they wanted, a number of six-seat tables having been laid out in the middle of the room. Each table had a small bell that people rang when they wished the bride and groom to kiss. The hall was adorned with banderoles and balloons.

People helped themselves to food, going to the buffet table and bringing their plates back to their seats. When nearly everyone had taken their places, the groom's father said a few words of welcome in Inuktitut and English—the latter for the four or five Qallunaat present at the banquet. After guests had stopped eating, two or three relatives of the newlyweds made very short speeches in Inuktitut. The bride's father declined an invitation to speak, but her mother entertained the audience by imitating the sound of an airplane engine. The newlyweds then left their seats and walked to a small table displaying a rather big wedding cake. They cut it and exchanged a piece that they ate, before the cake was shared by all children present in the room.

Many guests had brought gifts that were stacked on the floor at one end of the high table. After the cake episode, the bride and groom sat in front of the table. A maid of honour and a best man took these gifts one by one, announcing the nature of the gift, the name of the donor(s), and, should there be one, reading the attached card—most generally written in English—before handing the gift to one of the newlyweds, who opened it. These wedding presents included money (never less than a hundred dollars), kitchen and other home utensils, fishing gear, and so on.

Around 10 p.m., the banquet part of the evening was finished. While a quartet of musicians started tuning their instruments (guitars, drums, and cymbals), the chairs and tables were pulled along the walls. After some fireworks had been shot outside the front door of the school, it was time for dancing. For several hours, disco music alternated with reels. Many people left the gym when they felt tired, but a number of guests continued to celebrate late into the night.

SOMETHING UNIQUELY INUIT

At first glance, the description above could probably apply to a majority of middle-class weddings celebrated in Ottawa or Montreal. Like a large part of the modern Inuit way of life, the marriage I attended in Quaqtaq borrowed many of its surface characteristics from the mainstream cultural baggage common to 21st-century urban North Americans. However, as is the case with contemporary Inuit culture as a whole, Taniali's wedding remains different from any Qallunaat event of the same type. Most differences have to do with its general atmosphere rather than with specific recognizable traits, although it is possible to identify some uniquely Inuit specificities.

The setting of the marriage, a small Nunavik village, gave it a special colour. Everybody was invited to attend, but as a counterpart, community members were expected to contribute food to the banquet. No fancy attire was required from the guests. Except for those directly involved in the event, people wore ordinary, but clean clothing. Schedules were less compelling than they might have been elsewhere. The religious ceremony was delayed to accommodate outside visitors and, together with the banquet, it started somewhat later than forecast. Finally, despite the instructions of the *tasiuqti*, church discipline was not really respected. People took pictures during the ceremony and kids ran everywhere. The latter included the children of the newlyweds, who joined their parents on the stage two or three times.

The principal trait that contributed to the Inuit atmosphere was the prevalent use of Inuktitut. The entire church ceremony was conducted in that language, except for explanations that the *tasiuqti* gave in English from time to time, to accommodate the half-dozen Qallunaat attending the wedding. The same linguistic pattern was observed at the banquet. Inuktitut was the only language heard (with the exception of two or three tables with at least one Qallunaaq guest), but the bridegroom's father said a few welcoming words in English, and most wedding cards read aloud after the banquet were written in the language of the Qallunaat.

Entering deeper into Inuit culture, it is possible to identify some other specificities, although their actual relevance remains hypothetical. For instance, in contrast with what happens quite often in southern Canada, the wedding ceremony was organized in the groom's home community—where the couple was residing—rather than in the bride's hometown of Kangirsuk. Could this be a reminiscence of traditional marriage, where the girl usually went to live with her in-laws? In a similar way, as happens with most, if not all Inuit couples, Taniali and his wife waited till they had children to get formally married. Is this a continuation of the old pattern whereby formal marriages were generally celebrated after several years of common-law matrimony? Or does it simply reflect a popular trend among younger Canadians (my own son and his wife waited till they had two children before they got married)? And finally, could the bride's apparent shyness in church stem from traditional Inuit modesty, which prohibited the public expression of intimate sentiments? Maybe.

We probably stand on firmer cultural ground, though, when it comes to gift-giving. The Inuit have always been recognized for their generosity in sharing goods and services, and this appeared obvious on the occasion of the Quaqtaq wedding. The presents offered to the newlyweds were numerous and relatively costly, even if the donors were not always affluent. Publicly announcing the names of the givers ensured that their social reputation—so important in a small community where everyone knows each other—was recognized by all.

A last point might be characteristically Inuit: the importance given to family life in what the *tasiuqti* had to say during the wedding ceremony. This became particularly manifest when, as already mentioned, she stated that marriage is the most important event in one's life, because it constitutes the very basis of the family. Inuit and Christian values surely concord here, but in the context of Full Gospel evangelical Christianity—as practised in southern Canada at least—I would expect that the most important event a person could experience should be spiritual rebirth followed by adult baptism.[4] The fact that, in the *tasiuqti*'s discourse, founding a family through marriage appeared as almost equally momentous as being born again might be a manifestation of the primary importance family ties have for the Inuit.

This importance also became visible in the *tasiuqti*'s assertion that if a change occurred in the lifestyle of the new couple, they should always give precedence to the interests of their family. This "change in the lifestyle" may be interpreted as the realistic recognition that if, someday, the husband and wife choose to bring an end to their marriage, the family ties and the responsibilities uniting each of them to their children and, eventually, grandchildren would remain the same and should be preserved by all means.

The marriage I attended in Quaqtaq in August 2015 might not be typical of all Inuit weddings. The groom's family was rather well off and informed on southern Canadian customs and manners—hence the quite elaborate, Qallunaat middle-class style of this celebration, a style that could be absent from many other matrimonial events organized in Quaqtaq or elsewhere in Inuit Nunangat. However, despite its outwardly mainstream North American look, this wedding remained uniquely Inuit, both in its subtle references to traditional culture and in the importance it laid on family links. On top of that, it provided local residents with an occasion to reinforce community life through the enactment of a village-wide event that allowed everyone to rejoice in common and to show their solidarity with their fellow Quaqtamiut.

BIBLIOGRAPHY

Deer, Eva. 2015. *Eva Deer: An Inuit Leader and Educator/Une leader et éduca-trice inuit/Sivulirti amma ilisaiji.* Quebec City: Université Laval, CIERA.

Dorais, Louis-Jacques. 1978. *Iglulingmiut uqausingit: The Inuit Language of Igloolik N.W.T./La langue inuit d'Igloolik T.N.O.* Quebec City: Association Inuksiutiit Katimajiit.

———. 1997. *Quaqtaq. Modernity and Identity in an Inuit Community.* Toronto: University of Toronto Press.

CHAPTER 11

Reclaiming the Past and Reimagining the Future

The Igloolik Oral History Project, Education, and Community Development

Sheena Kennedy Dalseg

I MET LEAH OTAK IN THE SPRING OF 2009. Like many southern-based researchers, I first travelled to Igloolik as a master's student.[1] And, also like many southern researchers, I arrived in late April—Nunavut research licence in hand, along with a rather long list of tasks and objectives for my stay in the community. Although my graduate research was focused on the Northern social economy, my primary reason for being in Igloolik was to work on a project I became involved with through my supervisor, which was initiated by Paul Quassa and Brian Fleming, then mayor and senior administrative officer of Igloolik, respectively. The Hamlet Council wished to carry out a community socio-economic baseline study to gather their own information about Igloolik and its residents so that the community could be better positioned to negotiate potential impact benefit agreements, and to measure changes taking place in the community once the Baffinland Mary River iron ore project[2] got underway.

Through all stages of the Igloolik Socio-economic Baseline Study project, which spanned much of the next eighteen months, I worked closely with a small team of co-researchers and Hamlet staff.[3] This project served as my introduction to Northern community research. Among a great many lessons, both personal and professional, these first Northern research experiences instilled in me a deep appreciation for the value of research that responds directly to community informational needs and priorities. They also laid the foundation for the subsequent work I've been involved with in Igloolik, including my own dissertation research, which focuses on the historical and ongoing relationship between formal schooling, community development, and social change. In the first part of this short chapter, I reflect on my research experiences in Igloolik, and on the influence that the Igloolik Oral History Project (IOHP) has had on my work as a source of methodological and analytical inspiration. In the second part of the chapter, I share some preliminary observations from my research about the relationship between the imposed system of education and the development of local institutions like the IOHP and the important role they played in Igloolik's history as a community and in the larger movement towards Inuit self-determination. Leah's own educational experiences and her educational work are very much at the centre of both.

MY INTRODUCTION TO IGLOOLIK AND THE ORAL HISTORY PROJECT

As part of the preliminary community research for the aforementioned baseline study, I spent most of my time during that first spring 2009 trip introducing myself to people around town and chatting informally about the baseline study to try to get a sense of what topics and indicators should be included in the surveys we would eventually design. Before I arrived, I had dedicated much of the previous six months to reading everything I could find about Igloolik and the surrounding North Baffin region (and in doing so encountered the work of many of the authors featured in this book!). As such, I knew about the Oral History Project, and I was keen to explore the collection while I was in town. On my first visit to the IOHP office, I arrived to find Leah and John MacDonald listening to recordings of elders singing traditional *aja-ja* songs. It was the first time I'd ever heard an *aja-ja* song and I will never forget it. John then gave me the official tour of the space, providing me with a brief historical overview of the project and explaining how to use the collection's interviews. I spent a short time looking through the electronically indexed files that day, and then returned multiple times during my stay in the community for longer and more focused research stints. Over the next two years or so I returned to the community about half a dozen times, for several weeks each time, to carry out various phases of the baseline project.

During one of these trips, I stopped into the blue building[4] to see Leah, and we ended up talking about education. I learned that Leah had been among a small cohort of young Inuit who, having been identified by their teachers as being particularly bright or "promising," were selected to attend public school in Ottawa and other southern cities, where they were billeted with Qallunaat families. The government referred to this initiative as the "Eskimo Experiment."[5] While we did not get into too much detail at this time, Leah did explain how the "Ottawa Experiment" (as she called it) worked, and suggested that the introduction and expansion of institutionalized education through formal schooling had had a profound effect not only on her as an individual but on her whole family.

I cringe somewhat looking back at this conversation because I am ashamed to admit that I think it was really the first time that I truly realized how recently these events had taken place in the North—what "in living memory" really meant. People like Leah, who were at least fifteen years younger than my own grandparents, had lived through what I had been reading about in books and government reports that seemed rather detached and dated. I mention this here because it highlights how important it is to learn—to the greatest extent possi-ble—from the people who lived through a particular period or set of events; to hear what their experiences were, and to try to understand how they perceive(d) what happened to them or their community in their own words. Oral history projects like the one in Igloolik make this possible and for that they are invaluable to both community members and others. I am grateful to Leah for taking the time to share a small part of her story with me that day.

After the completion of the Igloolik Socio-economic Baseline Study in early 2011,[6] other opportunities arose that allowed me to remain involved with projects based in Igloolik, including the Dig-ital Indigenous Democracy project led by Zacharias Kunuk and his team.[7] When I decided to pursue doctoral studies in public policy at Carleton, I returned to Igloolik to meet with community members to discuss my ideas for a potential project related to school-community relations. The idea for this project arose in large part out of the inter-views and informal conversations I had with Iglulingmiut (including that particularly memorable one I mentioned with Leah Otak at the Oral History Project office) while working on the baseline study. It was clear to those of us conducting interviews and focus groups for the baseline study that many people in Igloolik—parents, grand-parents, students, educators, and others—had deep concerns about the education system and about the historic and ongoing nature of the relationship between the school and the community. These con-cerns and reservations are not surprising given the colonial history of Northern development and the role of formal schooling as an instrument in the Canadian state's project of imposed social change; however, it was striking how many community members spoke of the school as a foreign institution, despite its fifty-plus years of existence in Igloolik and the many important and positive changes that have taken place in recent decades with respect to staffing, curriculum, and parental/community involvement in the education system.

During this initial trip in May 2013, I met with Francis Piugattuk—then chair and long-time member of the District Education Authority[8]—and had a long discussion that set the direction for my doctoral research.

Francis and I worked together on the baseline study and we are both keenly interested in education. We discussed a wide range of issues related to education and schooling in Nunavut more generally, as well as issues and challenges specific to Igloolik. Francis explained to me the role and priorities of the Igloolik District Education Authority at the time and we talked about how my ideas for a research project might align with some of the priorities of the DEA and community. Parental engagement was (and remains) a significant concern not just in Igloolik but across Inuit Nunangat. Indeed, it appears as a top priority in the 2011 National Strategy for Inuit Education, and recently the government of Nunavut also identified it as a priority issue (National Committee on Inuit Education 2011; Government of Nunavut 2014). Parental engagement is intimately tied to community-school relations as well as attendance, literacy, and graduation rates—other areas of concern both in Igloolik and across Nunavut as a whole. Francis and I also discussed the legacies of an imposed education system and their connections to these contemporary challenges.

It was clear that my dissertation research needed to take a historical approach, not least because it is still possible to speak to the people who experienced the introduction of formal schooling in Igloolik, both the generation who were young parents at the time and the former students themselves. Using both archival and interview research, my dissertation, which is still in progress, traces the evolution of local responses to imposed changes to social life in Igloolik beginning in the late 1950s.[9] I decided to focus on the relationship between the community and the school—an institution that has touched the lives of nearly everyone in Igloolik in some form or another.

In designing this project, I drew inspiration from the IOHP. As readers of this volume will have gleaned from other chapters, the Igloolik Oral History Project was established in 1986 following a meeting of Igloolik elders, during which the group decided that documenting and recording local history and traditional knowledge was necessary.[10] The staff of the Igloolik Research Centre (IRC)—then a federal agency, and later an arm of Nunavut Arctic College—coordinated the project on behalf of the elders. The small but dedicated IRC staff assisted with fundraising and financial management; they conducted, transcribed, and translated interviews along with the elders and visiting researchers; and they also provided organization and archiving services to ensure that the collection of interviews would be easily accessible to community members, educators, researchers, and others who were interested in learning from the elders. Interviews covered a wide variety of topics and were frequently enriched by the detailed responses made to informed questions asked by visiting researchers.

The Igloolik Laboratory, framed by "sun dogs" (parhelia). These are called *tuglirutit* in Igloolik, after the traditional "hair sticks" worn by Iglulingmiut women. In Inuit cosmology, the sun was invariably personified as feminine. Igloolik, March 2018. Photo by Sean Guistini

The IOHP has served as one way for Iglulingmiut to document family histories, knowledge, and experiences before moving into the permanent settlement now known as Igloolik. In total, more than six hundred interviews were conducted over twenty-five years. All interviews are available in three formats: the original Inuktitut audio recordings, Inuktitut transcriptions, and English translations.

By the time the IOHP was established in the mid-1980s, outside researchers, like me, had been coming to Igloolik to learn about and from Inuit in the North Baffin region for decades. The historical relationship between southern researchers and Inuit communities was at best asymmetrical, and at worst exploitative. Research and researchers were—and in many ways still are—implicated in the larger colonial project of Northern "development." Some of the enduring concerns about Northern research practices have been that research is often not relevant to Northern communities; that it does not reflect the informational needs or priorities of Northerners; and that it is often conducted without adequate and meaningful consultation with and involvement of communities. Important steps to counteract this, such as the creation of the research licensing system, as well as research guidelines for both researchers and communities,[11] have certainly gone some way towards altering the Northern research paradigm; however, community-driven projects like the IOHP remain the exception rather than the rule.

The IOHP has laid an important foundation for research in and about the community of Igloolik. As a local library and archive, the IOHP can offer both resident and non-resident researchers an opportunity to learn more about the community, managed by a community member with experience conducting research and working with researchers; and it is a place where researchers can, if they are so inclined, strive to make a contribution through sharing their own work with the project. In my case, the IOHP served as a critical resource for the knowledge and analysis it holds from the elders who participated in the project, and for its methodological insights and lessons as well.

The majority of the existing oral history interviews in the project's collection focus on aspects of life before the move into permanent settlements, because this was the main objective of the project when it began. Several of the interviews, however, touch on early interactions between Qallunaat and Inuit in the region, offering some glimpses into the early days of the settlement and the relationship between government officials and Inuit residents, as well as some commentary on the newly established school and community council, for example. These oral histories are invaluable as an educational resource for Igluling-miut, Nunavummiut, and visitors alike, and it seemed to me that there was an opportunity to continue the story of "what happened here" by recording oral history interviews with present-day elders who have seen the evolution of the community from its inception.

Working closely with Francis Piugattuk, who acted as a trusted advisor and interpreter, we began to conduct oral history interviews with people in Igloolik who represented different generations of the community, beginning with those who were the young parents (now elders) of the first cohort of students to attend the federal day school in Igloolik after it opened in 1961. The purpose of these oral history interviews was to document the different perceptions and experiences people in Igloolik had with formal schooling; whether and how these have changed over time; and to what extent these have shaped the relationship between the school and the community.

By taking a comprehensive and in-depth view of the community over a relatively long period of time, and by speaking directly with community members who have witnessed the development of the community since the settlement was established, it has been possible to identify a number of key periods in Igloolik's history and to situate these within the broader context of northern political and social development. One particularly important period in Igloolik's history came in the years leading up to and including the founding of the IOHP.

ORAL HISTORY, EDUCATION, AND COMMUNITY DEVELOPMENT

Earlier I described briefly the specific origins of the IOHP, but the political economic context within which the project was created is also important to consider—especially its ties to the formal education system and its relationship to locally driven community development in Igloolik.[12] It seems to be no coincidence that many of the younger generation of Iglulingmiut who were involved in the IOHP as interviewers or managers in the early days were among the first cohorts of students to experience the newly developing federal school system—

both residential and day schools—in the late 1950s and 1960s. Nor is it likely a coincidence that they have all gone on to leadership positions in Igloolik and beyond.

These individuals, like Leah, were part of a generation of Iglulingmiut who were, for the most part, born outside the boundaries of the emerging settlement of Igloolik. They spent their early years immersed in their respective extended families, developing the skills, values, and characteristics needed to become healthy, knowledgeable, productive members of society, just as generations of their ancestors had before them. This well-functioning system of teaching and learning was interrupted when the parents and grandparents of these young people were informed by either church or government officials that it was time for their children to begin formal schooling, either at the residential school in Chesterfield Inlet or at the federal day school in Igloolik, built in 1960. The recently released Truth and Reconciliation Commission reports, and the critically important work done by the Qikiqtani Truth Commission between 2007 and 2013, reveal in no uncertain terms what the immediate and enduring effects of this imposed education system have been for Indigenous individuals, families, and communities across Canada, including Igloolik (Truth and Reconciliation Commission of Canada 2015; Qikiqtani Truth Commission 2010; Qikiqtani Inuit Association 2010).

Through my own conversations with former residential and federal day school students from Igloolik and elsewhere in the North Baffin region, I have learned that many responded to their "deprogramming" (Watt-Cloutier 2000, 115) educational experiences in the church and state-run school system by actively seeking out the guidance of elders, parents, and older siblings in an effort to reclaim the language, knowledge, and experiences they lost or missed while they were in school. The Oral History Project was, and is, an extension of this process of reclaiming these central aspects of individual and collective identity, belonging, and community membership. Louis Tapardjuk, one of the original interviewers with the IOHP, writes explicitly about his motivation to participate in the IOHP in his book *Fighting for Our Rights: The Life Story of Louis Tapardjuk*:

We [that is, my generation] were caught in the middle. That is why there are so many problems with the former residential school students, including myself. But rather than feeling sorry for myself, I decided to look into my own culture. I started researching my own culture after my Chesterfield Inlet experience. That is why I took such an interest in the Igloolik Oral History Project. I needed to learn what I had missed out on. (Tapardjuk 2015, 43)

At about the same time as the IOHP was forming, another reclamation project was becoming increasingly formalized. In 1982, the NWT Legislative Special Committee on Education tabled its final report, *Learning: Tradition and Change in the Northwest Territories*. The Special Committee on Education (SCOE) was established to examine all aspects of the developing education system in the Northwest Territories. The SCOE visited thirty-five communities across the Northwest Territories, meeting with parents, educators, and other community members to hear their concerns and dreams for the education system in the territory. One of the key recommendations from the committee's final report was that the government of the Northwest Territories provide resources and support to advance one of the central tenets of the NWT education system: the principle of local control over education, which was seen as the antidote to the previous colonial school system (Legislative Assembly of the NWT 1982). In this vein, the committee recommended that the Northwest Territories make funds available for regional bodies to be established that would serve as boards of education across the territory. The first regional education board created was the Baffin Divisional Board of Education (BDBE) in 1985. Several of the key players in the early days of the BDBE were from Igloolik, also former students of the federal school system. The BDBE comprised representatives from all the Baffin community education societies. It had its own budget and a small staff. The board took its work very seriously, and right away began to take on the enormous task of developing a renewed vision for education in the Baffin region, which included creating Inuit-language classroom materials and teacher resources, training existing staff, and meeting directly with parents and communities, among other things. The BDBE had two main objectives: to provide the opportunity for deliberate and meaningful family and community involvement in education, and to develop a bilingual and bicultural education system for students in the region.[13]

It is well known that this period of time was critically important for Inuit self-determination across Inuit Nunangat, and education was one of the first areas over which Inuit sought to regain control.[14] Through the reclamation of the education system, which began in the 1970s and became more entrenched following the implementation of the SCOE's recommendations in the early 1980s, important strides with respect to Inuit self-determination were made not just at the national level, as is often argued, but also (and importantly) at the community level, as can be seen in Igloolik's case. The link between education and community development at the local level meant that by thinking through how the school system needed to change and what sorts of skills, characteristics, and values Inuit youth educated in the Eastern Arctic at the time would need to become healthy, knowledgeable, and productive members of society, Iglulingmiut were, in effect, reimagining and developing a vision for the future of their community. Developments in the area of education also coincided with the proliferation of other local institutions and initiatives, such as community newspapers and radio stations, adult education, cooperatives, elders and youth committees, women's sewing groups, and Inuit-owned businesses. The locally driven community development of this period served to infuse more meaning into life within the boundaries of a permanent settlement.

In a much larger place, that these developments and innovations in the content and structure of education took shape at virtually the same time as the creation of local institutions like the IOHP and others could be construed as a coincidence. In the North Baffin region, taken together, this constituted a movement of sorts: a movement towards local self-determination by the people of Igloolik. Much attention is often paid to the activities of those who were active in the Inuit rights movement at the national level, and for good reason; however, there were important and meaningful initiatives taking shape at the local level as well during this period, which are sometimes overlooked. Oral histories like the ones housed in the IOHP help to illuminate the diversity and complexity of societal responses to social and political change.

Since its inception, the IOHP has been at the centre of the ever-evolving relationship between education and community development. Local teachers and others have consulted materials from the project's rich collection for various educational purposes, such as school curricula, radio programs, and community events and celebrations. In Igloolik the local movement towards self-determination is intimately bound up with the IOHP, and through her work Leah actively participated in this movement by connecting the IOHP elders with the schools, advising teachers and educators in the community, and working patiently with visiting researchers to ensure that research in Igloolik was carried out respectfully and in accordance with cultural protocols.

I was at the IOHP office when I learned of Leah's death on March 7, 2014. I knew, of course, that Leah had been very ill, but it was still a shock. Leah was deeply loved and very well respected—a champion of education and language, of intergenerational and cross-cultural transmission and exchange of knowledge. She dedicated her professional life to the Oral History Project. It is impossible for me to know or fully understand the value of Leah's work to the people of Igloolik, but it is clear that the Oral History Project would not be what it has been and is without her passion and deep commitment over thirty-plus years. I am sure many will agree that perhaps the greatest gap in the Igloolik Oral History Project is the absence of Leah's own voice and knowledge from the collection of recorded interviews. This absence reminds us of two critical aspects of oral history projects like Igloolik's: first, that each person carries with them important knowledge that is both unique to the individual and constitutive of the collective heritage of a group or society; and second, as the elders who originally conceived of the project in the 1980s keenly understood, time is of the essence. Each generation has its own set of challenges and opportunities to navigate, which it does by drawing on the experiences of its predecessors. Even though the Oral History Project began as a means to document knowledge and language about aspects of life that are, perhaps, no longer materially familiar or common, it has the potential to be a "living" archive. That is, a place where the people of Igloolik, along with those of us who are fortunate to work with the community and the people who call it home, can continue to document different elements of social and cultural life over time—and, equally important, a place from which to draw ongoing strength and inspiration for many years to come.

BIBLIOGRAPHY

Abele, Frances. 1987. "Canadian Contradictions: Forty Years of Northern Political Development." *Arctic* 40, no. 4: 310–320.

———. 2009. "Northern Development: Past, Present and Future." In *Northern Exposure: Peoples, Powers and Prospects in Canada's North*, edited by Frances Abele, Thomas J. Courchene, F. Leslie Seidle, and France St-Hilaire, 19–65. Montreal: Institute for Research on Public Policy.

Amagoalik, John. 2007. *Changing the Face of Canada*. Edited by Louis McComber. Iqaluit: Nunavut Arctic College.

Amarualik, Julia. 2014. Igloolik Oral History Project Interview: Archives of the Igloolik Research Centre. Igloolik, Nunavut.

Ammaq, Michelline. 2014. Igloolik Oral History Project Interview: Archives of the Igloolik Research Centre. Igloolik, Nunavut.

Arvaluk, James. 2007. *That's My Vision: The Life Story of James Arvaluk*. Edited by Noel McDermott. Iqaluit: Nunavut Arctic College.

Attagutaluk, Joe. 2014. Igloolik Oral History Project Interview: Archives of the Igloolik Research Centre. Igloolik, Nunavut.

Avinga, Susan. 2014. Igloolik Oral History Project Interview: Archives of the Igloolik Research Centre. Igloolik, Nunavut.

Brody, Hugh. 1975. *The People's Land: Inuit, Whites and the Eastern Arctic*. Hammondsworth, United Kingdom: Penguin Books.

Cohn, Norman, and Zacharias Kunuk. 2012. "Our Baffinland: Digital Indigenous Democracy." *Northern Public Affairs* 1, no. 1 (Spring): 50–52.

Damas, David. 2002. *Arctic Migrants/Arctic Villagers: The Transformation of Inuit Settlement in the Central Arctic*. Montreal and Kingston: McGill-Queen's University Press.

Digital Indigenous Democracy. 2012. "NIRB Baffinland Decision Recommends Digital Indigenous Democracy." Press Release, September 25. www.isuma .tv/en/DID/nirb-baffinland-decision-recommends-digital-indigenous -democracy-press-release.

Government of Nunavut. 2014. *Sivimut Abluqta: Stepping Forward Together 2014–2018*. Iqaluit: Government of Nunavut.

Greenwald, Barry, dir. 2009. *The Experimental Eskimos.* Whitepine Pictures and Paunna Productions.

Hicks, Jack, and Graham White. 2015. *Made in Nunavut: An Experiment in Decentralized Government*. Vancouver: UBC Press.

Ikummaq, Theo. 2014. Igloolik Oral History Project Interview: Archives of the Igloolik Research Centre. Igloolik, Nunavut.

Inuit Tapiriit Kanatami and Nunavut Research Institute. 2007. *Negotiating Research Relationships with Inuit Communities: A Guide for Researchers*. Edited by Scot Nickels, Jamal Shirley, and Gita Laidler. Ottawa and Iqaluit: Inuit Tapiriit Kanatami and Nunavut Research Institute.

Isherwood, Geoffrey B., et al. 1986. "Educational Development in the North: Preparing Inuit Leaders for School Board Control." *Education Canada* 26, no. 3: 9–15.

Kadlutsiak, Josiah. 2014. Igloolik Oral History Project Interview: Archives of the Igloolik Research Centre. Igloolik, Nunavut.

Kennedy, Sheena, and Frances Abele. 2011. *2009–2010 Igloolik Socio-economic Baseline Study*. Report Prepared for the Hamlet of Igloolik. Ottawa and Igloolik: Carleton Centre for Community Innovation.

Kennedy Dalseg, Sheena. 2015. "Creating Citizens, Building Societies? Adult Education in the Eastern Arctic as if Community Mattered." *Historical Studies in Education Special Issue North of 60* 27, no. 1 (Spring): 99–119.

———. 2016. "Keeping the Future in Focus: A Case Study of Illiniariuqsarvik Igloolik Head Start." In *Care, Cooperation, and Activism in Canada's Northern Social Economy*, edited by Frances Abele and Chris Southcott, 101–112. Edmonton: Polynya Press.

Kennedy Dalseg, Sheena, and Frances Abele. 2015. "Language, Distance, and Democracy: Development Decision Making and Northern Communications." *The Northern Review* 41: 207–240.

Kunuk, Vivi. 2014. Igloolik Oral History Project Interview: Archives of the Igloolik Research Centre. Igloolik, Nunavut.

Kunuk, Zacharias. 2014. Igloolik Oral History Project Interview: Archives of the Igloolik Research Centre. Igloolik, Nunavut.

Legislative Assembly of the Northwest Territories, Special Committee on Education. 1982. *Learning: Tradition and Change.* Yellowknife: Legislative Assembly of the NWT.

McComber, Louis, and Shannon Partridge. 2010. *Arnait Nipingit: Inuit Women in Leadership and Governance.* Iqaluit: Nunavut Arctic College.

McGregor, Heather. 2010. *Inuit Education and Schools in the Eastern Arctic.* Vancouver: UBC Press.

National Committee on Inuit Education. 2011. *First Canadians, Canadians First: National Strategy on Inuit Education 2011.* Ottawa: Inuit Tapiriit Kanatami.

Okpik, Abraham. 2005. *We Call It Survival: Life Stories of Northern Leaders.* Edited by Louis McComber. Iqaluit: Nunavut Arctic College.

Qattalik, Daniel. 2014. Igloolik Oral History Project Interview: Archives of the Igloolik Research Centre. Igloolik, Nunavut.

Qikiqtani Inuit Association. 2010. *Qikiqtani Truth Commission: Thematic Reports and Special Studies 1950–1975.* Iqaluit: Qikiqtani Inuit Association.

Qikiqtani Truth Commission. 2010. *Achieving Saimaqatingiiniq: Peace with Past Opponents.* Iqaluit: Qikiqtani Inuit Association.

Quassa, P. Aarulaaq. 2008. *We Have to Know Who We Are: The Life Story of Paul Quassa.* Edited by Louis McComber. Iqaluit: Nunavut Arctic College.

Qulaut, George. 2014. Igloolik Oral History Project Interview: Archives of the Igloolik Research Centre. Igloolik, Nunavut.

Rasing, Willem. 2017. *Too Many People: Contact, Disorder, Change in an Inuit Society, 1822–2015.* Iqaluit: Nunavut Arctic College Media.

Scott, James C. 1998. *Seeing Like a State: How Certain Schemes to Improve the Human Condition Have Failed.* New Haven: Yale University Press.

Tapardjuk, Louis. 2015. *Fighting for Our Rights: The Life Story of Louis*

Tapardjuk. Edited by Jaypeetee Arnakak, Frederic Laugrand, and Louis McComber. Iqaluit: Nunavut Arctic College.

Tester, Frank, and Peter Kulchyski. 1994. *Tammarniit (Mistakes): Inuit Relocation in the Eastern Arctic 1939–1963.* Vancouver: UBC Press.

Truth and Reconciliation Commission of Canada. 2015. *The Final Report of the Truth and Reconciliation Commission of Canada Volumes 1–2.* Ottawa: Truth and Reconciliation Commission of Canada.

Ulayaruluk, Abraham. 2014. Igloolik Oral History Project Interview: Archives of the Igloolik Research Centre. Igloolik, Nunavut.

Uttak, Louis. 2014a. Igloolik Oral History Project Interview: Archives of the Igloolik Research Centre. Igloolik, Nunavut.

———. 2014b. Igloolik Oral History Project Interview: Archives of the Igloolik Research Centre. Igloolik, Nunavut.

Uyarak, Hannah. 2014. Igloolik Oral History Project Interview: Archives of the Igloolik Research Centre. Igloolik, Nunavut.

Watt-Cloutier, Sheila. 2000. "Honouring Our Past, Creating Our Future: Education in Northern and Remote Communities." In *Aboriginal Education: Fulfilling the Promise,* edited by Marlene Brant Castellano, Lynne Davis, and Louise Lahache, 114–128. Vancouver: UBC Press.

———. 2015. *The Right to Be Cold: One Woman's Story of Protecting Her Culture, the Arctic and the Whole Planet.* Toronto: Allen Lane Canada.

CHAPTER 12

Leah Aksaajuq Otak

A Life in Language[1]

John MacDonald

L EAH AKSAAJUQ OTAK, whose life and work this volume com-
memorates, was part of a generation of Inuit who lived through
perhaps the most momentous period in Canadian Inuit history: the
move from the land to the settlement. Much more than mere physical
relocation, the move marked a watershed between two antithetical
ways of living and being. This transition, in Leah's view—one shared
by most of her contemporaries—heralded a rapid loss of Inuit autonomy followed by a corresponding decline in the integrity and primacy
of Inuit culture, values, and particularly language. In an interview
with Sonia Gunderson in March 2006, Leah's own words aptly capture
the essence of the move as something irretrievably left behind, with
little gained in its place: "We left everything at the camps and moved
forward [in time], [but we were] not more advanced."[2]

For Leah's generation, the most significant social consequence of
settlement dwelling was the loss of independence. Life on the land,
living in seasonal camps, had by comparison been free, relatively secure,

and, in Leah's words, "much more simple." On the land, they lived at a manageable distance from the government agencies that, following the move into settlements, would increasingly encroach on their daily lives. Leah attributes the loss of autonomy to the dominant role in decision-making casually assumed by the government's settlement administrators, at the expense of traditional leadership: "When we moved into the settlement, we suddenly had wrong leaders, people who were not experienced. That's where we took a sharp turn. Suddenly you didn't have elders running things. You had organizations running things ..." Leah deeply felt the consequences of this abrupt transition and understood its effect on the elders. When young Inuit, who knew only the physical comforts of settlement living, suggested to her that life on the land without modern amenities must have been a struggle, she wryly pointed out that they "didn't have to worry about bills," adding emphatically that "for the elders it wasn't a struggle at all, not like they are struggling today."[3] Testifying before the Qikiqtani Truth Commission in 2008, she stated, with reference to families from the camps crowding into the settlement: "They became confused and dishevelled. It seemed to be a very backward experience for our parents."[4]

The move from the land and its consequences would come to define and determine important aspects of Leah's life. She reluctantly accepted the finality of the move, fully aware that there was no going back, no practical way of emulating, in a semi-urban setting, what had been left on the land. And so, as a young adult, she worked in various capacities, usually as a translator and interpreter, for government agencies, initiating change among her people. Far from contradictory, this work, she believed, helped to make transition to the inevitable easier, particularly for the elders. Nevertheless, she remained acutely aware of what had been lost in terms of traditional knowledge, skills, and, above all, the weakening of her language, Inuktitut, which she passionately regarded as the essence of Inuit being.

Leah was born in a sod house—a *qarmaaq*—at Iglurjuat,[5] on Baffin Island, in March 1950. From birth, she carried and honoured three ancestral names: Aksaajuq, Umik, and Ivalu. She spent her early years in hunting locations throughout this area, some 150 kilometres northeast of Igloolik. By her own account, she enjoyed a halcyon childhood, secure in the affections of her parents, Aipilik and Zipporah Piungittuq Inuksuk, and her grandfather, Aaraaq, of whom she was a particular favourite. She also was especially welcomed in other camps around Iglurjuat because of the kin relationships conferred through her many namesakes.

Like most Inuit children of her generation in this part of the Eastern Arctic, Leah travelled with her family on their annual rounds of seasonal hunting camps, moving in response to the migrations of the animals on which they depended. She learned by observation and example, taking on increasingly complex tasks commensurate with her developing skills. Her intellectual life was enhanced through the rich storytelling of her elders, especially her grandfather. Her mother taught her to write in Inuktitut syllabics.

In the early 1960s Leah started her formal education at the recently constructed day school in Igloolik, run by the then federal Department of Northern Affairs. For the first few years she was a boarder living in the school's hostel until her family moved to Igloolik in the mid-1960s, a move resisted by her grandfather, who was mistrustful of the government's "in-gathering" or settlement policy.[6] Leah showed a ready aptitude for Qallunaat-style learning and was "hand-picked" for education in the south, enrolling in Ottawa's Algonquin College in 1968.[7] Further educational pursuits took her to Inuvik and Fort Smith, where she studied nursing and social work.

Leah's working career was characterized by variety and productiveness. Her early employment centred around medical interpretation, social work, and community administration, positions which made good use of her training and language skills, enabling her to hone her role as a "cultural broker" between the old and new realities of Inuit life. For a period in the early 1980s she worked for CBC Northern Service in Montreal, hosting a morning show in Inuktitut, and she became a well-known radio voice throughout the Eastern Arctic, noted for her nuanced, accurate Inuktitut. Between her more permanent assignments she had stints as a First Air ticket agent, a freelance translator, and a heavy-equipment operator working on the expansion of Igloolik's freshwater reservoir.

It was, however, her employment with the Igloolik Research Centre and her participation in the centre's oral history work during the final decades of her life that best suited her interests. Leah was now able to give full energy and scope to her passion for preserving Inuit cultural heritage. She joined the centre in 1996 as operations manager in charge of coordinating fieldwork support for visiting researchers. In this capacity she became closely involved with the centre's Oral History Project, then beginning its second decade. Leah quickly made her mark on the work by extending the project's goals and scope. For the next twenty-five years, through her language and administrative skills, she contributed immeasurably to the consistency, continuity, and overall success of the project.

Leah also brought a much-needed feminine perspective to the project through her interviews with female elders on topics such as childbirth, childrearing, sewing, and skin preparation.[8] Her underlying approach to oral history documentation matched that of the Inuit elders whom she interviewed: the emphasis, she insisted, should always be on the proper use of language. In this way, the information gathered in the interview was, to some extent, secondary to the quality and sophistication of the language used to convey the information. In Leah's words:

> Preserving oral histories is so important for future generations, because our language is changing fast. It's beginning to be like English [in] structure. Instead of saying a long word, we say it broken up with English ... "English-Inuktitut" is taking over.... There's a big difference between the way Inuit spoke in the past and the way they speak today. It's getting so shallow.... But if people get interested, they can use the oral histories to learn—not just words, but how [elders] would express themselves.[9]

Leah often remarked on the dignified demeanour of the many elders she interviewed; there was a certainty about them, a gentle sense of purpose. They knew who they were. They were comfortable in their roles, and they spoke elegantly and confidently about their life on the land, and the skills, knowledge, and philosophies needed to successfully shelter, feed, clothe, and nurture their families. In Leah's view these qualities were the mark of not only comfortable self-esteem, but also community identity—qualities she rarely saw in the younger generation of Inuit raised and schooled in the settlement. The identity confusion experienced by many of Igloolik's youth, concomitant with widespread social malaise, she believed was a direct result of the rapid cultural upheaval following the move from the land. Settlement life with all its demands and distractions had deprived Inuit youth of the essential conditions that had given Leah her own strong sense of identity and purpose: a secure upbringing on the land, deeply immersed in Inuit language, values, and customs. As she states:

> When we were growing up, we had certain laws we had to follow to live a peaceful life. Now everybody's getting so confused. People are hungry for something, and they don't know what it is. It's their culture.... Even having a little knowledge of that helps you to know where you come from.[10]

When interviewing, Leah always encouraged elders to use traditional Inuktitut expressions, terms, and constructions, fast falling out of use since moving into the settlement. "There's not many words I don't know, so I would challenge elders to use words I didn't understand. I would write [them] down [and the elders] would explain [their meanings] to me."[11]

Leah's near-obsession for word-collecting extended far beyond her work with the elders' project. Wherever she was, at home, visiting, or camping on the land, she was constantly on the alert for new words and expressions, which she would hastily write down on any scrap of paper at hand, later to enter in a vocabulary list she was compiling. She was intending one day to bring out a dictionary. Poignantly, for months after her death, co-workers and family members regularly came across these little scraps of paper—sometimes "sticky notes"—

scattered around Leah's home or office, inevitably bearing some obscure Inuktitut word, rendered in her beautifully distinctive syllabic
handwriting.

Skin sewing and preparation were Leah's principal avocations. Here she is shown
working on the twelfth and final stage of the lengthy process of preparing a caribou
skin for clothing. This stage is known as *tasijuktuq* (stretching), after which the skin
was designated *iniqsimajuq*—completed. Photo by John MacDonald

In addition to Leah's committed involvement with oral history
work, her long association with the Igloolik Research Centre placed
her in a pivotal role of establishing and maintaining productive links
between visiting southern researchers and the people of Igloolik.
Respected by all parties, she handled, often behind the scenes, these
sometimes sensitive negotiations with tact and adroitness. Leah's
grasp of the complexities of conducting scientific research in Arctic
communities was fittingly recognized through her appointment to
the Canadian Polar Commission, on which she served for a two-year
term.[12] As amply demonstrated through the contributions to this

volume, researchers working at the centre, regardless of their disciplines, were in one way or another indebted to Leah. Her ability
to bring researchers and community elders together in an interview
setting, to coherently frame researchers' questions in Inuktitut, and
to translate and elucidate, in English, the elders' answers, served to
enhance the resultant discourse significantly. During her time at the
centre, numerous academic papers, theses, and several monographs,
many based on Igloolik elders' interviews, were published in Canada
and abroad, acknowledging Leah's crucial assistance.[13] Shortly before
her death in 2014, Leah undertook her own project, co-editing and
introducing the book *Inuit Kinship and Naming Customs,* drawn
from Igloolik elders' interviews on traditional naming practices—
tuqłurausiit.[14] Sadly, she did not live to see this book in print.

Over the years, Leah worked closely with southern museums,
including the National Museum of the American Indian in Washington, advising how best to display and represent Inuit cultural objects.
Notably, she played a guiding role in the British Museum's acclaimed
2001 exhibition on Inuit clothing—*Annuraaq*—and, at a conference
in London relating to this exhibition, she presented a paper titled "Iniqsimajuq," detailing the complex stages of caribou-skin preparation
for use in clothing. Her paper was later published in a volume issued
by the British Museum on the conference's proceedings (King et al.
2005). Her work with museums helped to modify some of the misgivings she had about their institutional motives. While in London, she
assisted British Museum curators and conservators in further documenting Igloolik materials long held in the stores, marvelling at the
efforts made to preserve Inuit clothing, thrilled to be handling items
made in Igloolik almost two hundred years ago: "I was amazed how
well-preserved most of the clothing was, especially the older pieces ...
the skin was still soft, and the sinew stitches almost as tight as when
they were first made" (MacDonald 2001).

Locally, Leah's service in the community was driven by the same
interests and enthusiasms so evident in her work at the research centre.
Her expertise in Inuktitut made her the "go-to" person on language
matters for Igloolik's young Inuit teachers. While always supportive of

Inuktitut teachers, she could be critical of the government's approach to teaching Inuktitut, finding it self-serving:

> In teacher training, no one monitors how Inuktitut is taught. No one is monitoring how well the teachers are speaking. The government solution comforts themselves—but it's not Inuktitut.... Kids love to learn their language ... but we're not providing them with good quality education.[15]

Never one to idly complain, she would seek opportunities to enhance the use of Inuktitut. She thus became the driving force behind Igloolik's "Language Week," a six-day, activity-packed event designed to celebrate and promote Inuktitut throughout the community. Louis Tapardjuk, during his time as minister of Nunavut's Department of Culture, Language, Elders and Youth, adopted Leah's "Language Week" concept, making it a territory-wide annual event. Tapardjuk, who for many years worked closely with Leah on the Oral History Project, unstintingly acknowledges her role in promoting Inuktitut:

> She was most adamant about proper Inuktitut pronunciation; proper Inuktitut being spoken. That was her passion. She was aware of the changes coming to language with the young children in school and that's why, with her encouragement, we started the "Language Week."[16]

Moving beyond language and always the energetic volunteer, she often took the lead in organizing numerous community events aimed at preserving aspects of Iglulingmiut heritage. Among these were courses on traditional sewing and skin preparation, local radio shows on language preservation, and Igloolik's annual re-enactment of festivities traditionally observed on the "return of the Sun" each January—*Siqinnaarut*. She also volunteered on community committees dealing with health, education, and culture.

Leah's personal life was marked by an extraordinary degree of tragedy and loss, which she bore, characteristically, with quiet, dignified fortitude, countering the heartbreak with the joy and satisfaction

Essential tools used by Leah's mother for caribou skin preparation. They include *tasiuktirut* (stretchers), variously made of metal, stone, and bone; a metal *saakut* (scraper); an *ulu*; and a sharpening tool. Photo by John MacDonald

of nurturing her large, extended family, of whom she was immensely proud and supportive. Leah will be remembered for many things: for her long advocacy of Inuit heritage, particularly Inuktitut; for her volunteer community work in Igloolik; for her accomplishments as an interpreter and translator; and for her knowledge and skills as a seamstress. Those who knew her well will especially remember her, as she would have wished, as a caring and compassionate mother, grandmother, aunt, sister, and friend.

ACKNOWLEDGMENTS

Sonia Gunderson kindly gave access to the interview transcript of her recorded conversation with Leah Otak in March 2006. Rhoda Innuksuk, Leah's sister, and Rebecca Awa, both from Igloolik, provided information on Leah's younger years and education, and Louis Tapardjuk, interviewed by John MacDonald in September 2015, thoughtfully shared his views on Leah's contribution to Inuktitut preservation.

BIBLIOGRAPHY

Damas, David. 2002. *Arctic Migrants/Arctic Villagers: The Transformation of Inuit Settlement in the Central Arctic*. Montreal and Kingston: McGill-Queen's University Press.

Engelstad, Bernadette Driscoll. 2013. "Review of *Caribou Skin Clothing of the Igloolik Inuit* by Sylvie Pharand." *Études/Inuit/Studies* 37, no. 2: 203–206. www.britishmuseum.org/research/news/research_visit_to_igloolik.aspx

King, J.C.H., B. Pauksztat, R. Storrie, eds. 2005. *Arctic Clothing*. London: British Museum Press.

MacDonald, John. 2000. *The Arctic Sky: Inuit Astronomy, Star Lore, and Legend*. Toronto: Nunavut Research Centre/Royal Ontario Museum.

———. 2001. "Igloolik Clothing on Display at New British Museum Exhibit." *Nunatsiaq News*, March 2. nunatsiaq.com/stories/article/igloolik _clothing_on_display_at_new_british_museum_exhibit/

Otak, Leah, and Peesee Pitsiulak-Stevens, eds. 2014. *Inuit Kinship and Naming Customs*. Iqaluit: Nunavut Arctic College.

Pharand, Sylvie. 2012. *Caribou Skin Clothing of the Igloolik Inuit*. Iqaluit: Inhabit Media.

CHAPTER 13

Encounters

Reflections on Anthropology and Cultural Brokers

Willem C. E. Rasing

PERSONAL ENCOUNTER

A CCORDING TO MY DIARY, I visited Mark and Thérèse Ijjangiaq in their tent near Iqsivataujuq, on Igloolik Island, in the afternoon of Monday, July 24, 1989. My small shelter tent was pitched beside the canvas tent of Victor Aqatsiaq and his wife Suzanne Niviattian at some distance, closer to Igloolik Point. As I approached the camp, I saw Ijjangiaq sitting outside his tent on the raised beaches that one finds on that part of the island. In a soft drizzling rain he was busy flinching a sealskin on a piece of wood. The scene struck me. I could not resist the temptation of taking a picture, as I had not seen an Inuk man clean a sealskin before. I briefly stood there watching, reflecting on the possibility of Ijjangiaq having only female namesakes and that this would allow the performance of female chores for an adult male. Determined to look into this more closely in the weeks to come, I went over to greet him. He looked up from his work and smiled. He nodded, indicating that I should go inside to have some tea. My diary (originally in Dutch) proceeds as follows:

> Inside the tent there were two young and partly dressed children (perhaps grandchildren?), besides Thérèse (Qillaq) on the mattress which covered half the floor of the tent, and—to my surprise—Leah Otak … daughter of Siporah [Zipporah] and Aipillik [Apilik]. Unmistakably a sister of Rhoda … similar appearance, similar smile…. Being not able to converse much with the unilingual Thérèse, and the two children being busy with each other, I was happy Leah was there to talk in English. My Inuktitut is still poor. Leah proudly started telling me right away about the sealskin boots, the anorak, and wind-pants she had made. I have to admit that I was certainly dealing with a good seamstress; no wonder, with such an excellent mother as teacher. Leah told me she was not in Igloolik in 1986–87 but in Arctic Bay at the time. I asked her about the Inummariit in Arctic Bay, the Legal Elders Committee. According to her, the organization had lost much of its efficiency after some leading elders had died. After tea

Mark Ijjangiaq working on a sealskin. Igloolik Point, July 1989. Photo by Willem Rasing and bannock, I went outside with Leah, thanking Thérèse, who was busy tending the *qulliq*, with the brightest smile I could produce. We said goodbye to Ijjangiaq who had not entered the tent. We walked into the direction of Aqatsiaq's tent but then Leah went back to Igloolik. I decided to go for a stroll. I walked towards the qarmait in the direction of Neerlonakto, and then followed the coast along Igloolik Point. I walked more than two hours. (Rasing 1989, 96)

Little did or could I know, when our ways parted that afternoon, that our lives would become intertwined in later years.

PROFESSIONAL ENCOUNTER: ANTHROPOLOGY

As a trained anthropologist I am interested in culture, in particular Inuit culture. Trying to learn about culture is trying to understand the people who "are" or "possess" that culture, and who together constitute "society." Culture is produced by human beings. It is mediated by the people who embody it, whose lives "reveal" it, whose acts maintain or change it. Although all members of society contribute to it, each one does so, and experiences and views it, in a different way. Culture, therefore, does not exist in a neutral, unequivocal way but presents itself in various voices. It is always and at all times a matter of interpretation.

But anthropology that seeks to understand the culture of "the Other" is also a human endeavour. The *facts* that anthropologists look for in a study of the Other, *cultural facts*, are constructs or interpretations "made" by the people whom they study. *Facts*, as such, do not exist. They are constructed, created, interpreted, by people. The Latin base of the word *factum* ("made") should remind us of this, but this fact is often forgotten. What we consider as "facts" are the experiences lived, and mediated, by "the Other." But if culture is interpretation for those who embody, experience, and mediate it, the anthropologist trying to understand the culture of "the Other" is likewise forced to interpret. As much as *cultural facts* are mediated or interpreted by the people under study, the anthropologist—again—mediates or interprets these cultural facts, constructing them into *anthropological facts*.

Interestingly, this occurs in a *process shared* by the anthropologist and "the Other": anthropological facts are constructed in the very process in which they are acquired. This process is called "life" by "the Other"; the anthropologist, who intrudes into the life of the Other, calls it "research." It is worthwhile to look a bit closer into the specific nature of this research process, as Leah and I came to share one.

HUMAN ENCOUNTER: PARTICIPANT OBSERVATION

The anthropological endeavour has never been phrased more succinctly and more aptly than by Hortense Powdermaker (1966): "The anthropologist is a human instrument studying other human beings and their societies" (19). The trademark of the anthropologist, the time-honoured method of participant observation, means full immersion into a foreign culture. It is trying to think, see, feel, and sometimes act as a member of that other culture—but, at the same time, to think, see, feel, and act as a trained anthropologist from another culture. It implies finding a balance between *involvement*, needed for understanding how culture is mediated/interpreted by those who are the subject of study, and *detachment*, required for a valid mediation of cultural facts into anthropology. However, participant observation requires involvement and detachment also from the people with whom the anthropologist shares the experience of fieldwork.

In a context of observation and interaction, the anthropologist in fact asks "the Other," at times literally, to self-consciously reflect upon the cultural facts and explain them in such a way that the anthropologist is able to make anthropological facts of them. When asked about particular events or aspects, that person must find (new) ways of mediating his or her interpretations to the outsider-anthropologist (who often does not understand even the most obvious things). In this sense, "the Other" is *detached* from his or her culture, but *involved* in the anthropologist's project. The more intimate the sharing of experiences, the more detachment from one's own culture—and involvement in the research project—is required; utmost detachment and involvement is demanded from *(key) informants/research assistants*, by whom the anthropologist is informed continuously. They mediate between their own culture and that of the anthropologist, acting as translators—sometimes literally—between two different cultural worlds or different sets of experiences (translating emic into etic concepts). They are *intimately involved* in the fine art of the anthropological endeavour. They are *cultural brokers* who *share* with the anthropologist the experience of crossing cultural boundaries. They both live in culturally mediated worlds, caught up in webs of meaning they have spun themselves, and of which *both are conscious*. If the anthropologist is an "involved outsider" in the research, the cultural brokers are "detached insiders." In my view, their contribution to anthropology is underestimated. This essay seeks to reflect upon their role and pay tribute to them. I was lucky enough to have been able to work with several excellent cultural brokers/research assistants. Leah was one of them.

SHARED ENCOUNTER: CULTURAL BROKERS

The cultural broker/research assistant gives external form to his or her own experiences by presenting them in ways that meet the anthropologist's queries in an interaction process, and in a language they both understand. This is the shared experience, the common ground, of the interpretative science called anthropology. When the anthropologist is not fluent in the local language, which is often the case at the start of field research, the mediation qualities of the research assistant are crucial. This certainly was the case for me.

When my anthropological endeavour in Igloolik began in 1986, finding a good interpreter was of the essence. There were two qualified and certified interpreters; one of them was too busy, and things did not work out with the other one on a more personal basis. While trying to get started and get acquainted with the community of some nine hundred souls, I could only conduct a few formal interviews with Igloolik elders thanks to George Qulaut interpreting. But, as he was engaged by the Research Centre, I could not continue to make use of his services (although he became involved in the project in many other ways: introducing me to people, organizing and taking me on hunting trips, sharing his house with me, providing me with an Inuktitut

name, being a trusted friend). Just as I began to get desperate after
three weeks without an interpreter, things turned for the better when
I met Paul Irngaut. He had just returned to Igloolik after years in Ottawa and was prepared to engage himself in the project. Paul provided
assistance in every imaginable way and became a stronghold of the research. He had great interest in the research theme, and he displayed
real sensitivity to issues of language and translation; we often had long
discussions on the precise meaning of words, concepts, or expressions
used by those who gave us their "facts"; indeed, conveying meaning
from one language into another is not just a matter of translation but
requires—yet again!—*interpretation*. Paul had an almost natural sense
of the demands and pitfalls of anthropological data-gathering (that
he had been married to an anthropologist may have played a role).
He was also instrumental in selecting individuals who were knowledgeable on specific topics. It did not take me long to actually *realize*
what it means that knowledge, as part of culture, does not exist in an
unequivocal way but is presented in multiple voices. The effect of this
is particularly felt in a traditionally oral culture such as that of the
Inuit. Indeed, Inuit knowledge was above all individualistic in nature,
learned and passed on more within families than in society at large.
Inuit are well aware of this, including the cultural brokers on whom
I relied in this respect. All this came to the fore particularly during
the series of taped interviews with Igloolik elders during my 1986–87
field research, which Paul facilitated and which became part of the
Igloolik Oral History Project (MacDonald 2000). We developed our
own method of interviewing, and I learned as much from Paul as he
might have learned from me. "Interview" may perhaps even be an
improper word for a session in which but a few questions were asked
and interviewees usually gave lengthy answers in a narrative form. Before each session, we discussed the nature of the topics I suggested to
reflect upon and whom we should approach; Paul then contacted that
person. During the sessions, I asked questions in English, which Paul
translated into Inuktitut. Paul summarized the answers—usually only
highlighting the lengthy exposé—after which I posed a new question.
But after a few sessions, Paul began to add (additional) questions by

himself. This enriched the interviews, and contributed to the depth and quality of the information gathered. Like me, the interviewed elders noticed Paul's interest and involvement in the subjects we discussed. All interviews were then meticulously translated into English. Paul listened to the tape-recorded original version and translated it piece by piece on paper first. I then read the written transcript, and we discussed anything that was not clear to me or to him. Paul then recorded the final translated text by reading it aloud onto a tape. Copies of all the Inuktitut and English versions of the interviews were stored in Igloolik (and were later digitized).

In the summer of 1989, in a second term of research, Louis Tapardjuk took over Paul's role as facilitator/interpreter and informant. He too displayed exceptional qualities with respect to anthropological enquiries in general and to the nuances of translating meanings or concepts from one language to another in particular. Based on my experiences with Paul, I developed a similar constructive way of interviewing Inuit elders with Louis. It was gratifying to see that Louis also displayed a sincere interest in gathering information about his own culture and that he too began to ask (additional) questions during the interviews. Without Paul and Louis, my study of Iglulingmiut ways of maintaining order and dealing with nonconformity would have had to rely on far fewer, and less rich, ethnographical "facts."

LANGUAGE ENCOUNTER: NARRATIVE

Besides the mediation of those who "live" their culture, and the anthropologist's mediation of constructing anthropological facts from cultural ones, there is yet another layer of mediation or interpretation: making a narrative story by *constructing connections* between the cultural, and the anthropological, "facts." If "facts" are—as reminded above—"made" in an etymological sense, the Greek word *poièsis*, "making," reminds us of the *poet* as being a "maker." The stuff from which an anthropological story is made is not just "facts"; far more significant is abstracting relations between these facts. The anthropologist's writing is putting flesh to the bone, is attributing meaning to facts, is making sense of people's actions, is revealing the symbolism of, or in, their behaviour, is tracing how changes, and the effects of changes, are followed through over time. In narrative writing, the anthropologist—out of necessity—constructs an abstract reality (which does not even have to be "real" to the people studied) by portraying a network of social relations. In modern narratives, the anthropologist also reflects upon his or her own role and presence in the lives of "the Others." In all narratives, something is lost.[1] In my narrative, I tried to portray a network of social relations with a focus on its basic structuring rules and following through how these functioned over an extended period of time. Making a narrative requires detachment from those who are portrayed but also involvement in the cultural "facts" mediated into anthropological ones in a language for mutual understanding shared by the cultural broker and the anthropologist. In that sense, my narrative (Rasing 1994) is nearly as much the work of Paul Irngaut and Louis Tapardjuk as it is mine.

Following from my narrative's long-term perspective, I decided to conduct a follow-up study to assess what had changed and what had remained after the initial terms of field research. So, I returned to Igloolik, and I stayed there from early August to late November 2005. Much had indeed changed, not so much in the physical layout of the settlement or in the daily lives of most people, but in its social composition. I felt I was drowning in the sea of young people: nearly 50 percent of the almost 1,400 souls were under twenty years of age, and 80 percent were under forty. It was like intruding into a new community once more. Only a small group of middle-aged and elderly people recognized me, and most of the elders that I knew had passed away. Nevertheless, I intended to interview a number of the remaining elders on the issue of change. How pleased and reassured I was when Leah Otak agreed to be my facilitator, interpreter, and informant. Like her predecessors, Leah was good in selecting and approaching interviewees. We agreed upon whom to interview on what topics, and we conducted the interviews not in the office space of the Research Centre (meanwhile moved to the "blue building"), but in the cookhouse of the Research Centre. Leah was great in comforting the interviewees as well as in facilitating the interviews, and she was really marvellous in matters of language and translation. She was very sensitive to Iglulingmiut culture and the use and meaning of specific Inuktitut words. She was sadly aware of the great language loss that the shift to sedentary life and other aspects of cultural change had caused. She loved the older Inuktitut used in the days of the nomadic hunting camps. Just like Paul and Louis, Leah too would sometimes summarize a lengthy answer and add in her soft-spoken voice, "I think he is ready to tell more about this…. maybe we should ask him?" Invariably, this produced additional information which I would not have gotten by myself.

I certainly would never have gotten any information on changes in the use of materials acquired through hunting. For that reason, she (and I was there too) interviewed her mother Zipporah. I will never forget how the two of them—actually, the three of us—got carried away in talking about the use of walrus skin and sealskin as the covers of tents, kayaks, and *umiaks*, how they should be prepared, how they were to be stitched together, what kind of needle and thread to use for what purpose, and so on. The sun, just above the horizon, turned to orange as it shone through the kitchen window of Zipporah's house, illuminating both their faces that were close together. There was tea and cookies, there were subdued voices, giggles now and then, small talk also. We discussed matters that at first glance were little and futile, but in fact were of crucial importance for survival. Is there anything more significant than that? I cherish the memory of such moments; they brighten field research. Indeed, anthropology is a human endeavour that at times has its highlights.

ENCOUNTERS WITH THE SELF

With the same dedication as Leah had when facilitating the interviews, she also worked as caretaker of the Igloolik Oral History Project files. During one of the conversations we had in her office in 2009, when I visited the community again, she recalled the interview with her mother. She said her mother had enjoyed so much the opportunity to explain and show us things from the past. Leah, being knowledgeable about and interested in Inuit skin clothing herself, added that she too had learned things that afternoon that she would otherwise never have gotten to know. In particular, she had learned some knowledge regarding preparing skins for an *umiak* (that, indeed, had surprised me as well, as this type of traditional Inuit boat had long since gone from northern Foxe Basin). Acting as a cultural broker made Leah even more conscious of her own culture than she already was. The same holds, I think, for Paul and Louis. Our communal endeavour ignited the spark of interest in their own culture that they already had. Both continued to pursue their interest by interviewing elders on their own after I had left the community in 1987 and in 1989. In this way, they contributed largely to expanding the amount of data collected in the Oral History Project.

All engaged in the anthropological endeavour learn something about the others and themselves. Every human being understands more of himself or herself by meeting and trying to understand others, and the shared experiences of those involved in anthropological field research only enlarge this. This is also the case for those who provide information. Noah Piugaattuk, who was interviewed dozens of times, often thanked us for the questions that made him reflect upon his own (past) life. I always felt a bit awkward about interviewing him time and again; I realize now that he was grateful because he too learned. The cultural brokers not only gained more knowledge about their own culture and history but also learned more about themselves. Interestingly, George, Paul, and Louis all got involved in politics. After his work for the Qikiqtani Inuit Association, George Qulaut was elected MLA and became the Speaker of the House. Louis Tapardjuk was twice elected as MLA and was minister of several departments of the Nunavut government. Paul Irngaut also ran for election, although he was not elected. There is some parallel between a cultural broker and a politician: both speak out on behalf of others.

I too learned more about myself as a person and as an academic. In all the time I had to maintain a balance between involvement and detachment during the fieldwork, I was very aware of who I was, what I was doing, what role I was to play. This is the anthropologist's *impression management* (Berreman 1962). In interactions with "the Other," an anthropologist must be self-conscious and careful at the same time:

ethics are involved. I had to learn to find the right ways of acting and managing the impression I made upon others. So, I consciously spent the same amount of time with Anglicans and Catholics, attended both churches, shopped alternately in the Hudson's Bay store and the Co-op, did not attach myself too closely to any family, and so on. Whether this was really necessary is not relevant: *I* felt I had to participate in this manner. I think I matured as a person during the fieldwork. I was uncomfortable at first with the Inuktitut name that I was given: "The Questioner" (Paqulluk). My uneasiness came from my awareness that asking questions was traditionally not a proper thing in Inuit culture, and from one of my professors, who had always emphasized that field-work should consist in note-taking from participation, observation, and informal conversations, not in asking (direct) questions. As time wore on, however, I began to use my Inuktitut name as an honorary nickname and considered it a token of being accepted. Despite the advice of my professor (whose fieldwork concerned the genesis of the Mafia in a Sicilian village), I kept asking questions, and so lived up to my Inuktitut name.

ANTHROPOLOGY: ENCOUNTERS IN TIME AND SPACE

There is a mutual dependence between the anthropologist and cul-tural broker/research assistant. Although both depend on each other, both share the same process, and both may get something out of it, this does not mean that the relationship is an equal one. Power is an element of all human relations, including those between anthropol-ogist and broker. Traditionally, their balance of power was uneven, as anthropology was intimately linked to a colonial setting. The In-uit in Arctic Canada were no exception; their experiences with the southerners intruding into their lives in the course of the 20th century were profoundly colonial in nature. Although many aspects of this "internal" colonial situation were still prevalent in 1986, the relation-ships between Inuit and non-Inuit had begun to change. The context of my 1986 fieldwork differed considerably from that of Van den Steenhoven, my predecessor and mentor, who studied Inuit law in the 1950s, though we both worked for the same federal authority. Van den Steenhoven simply travelled north, pitched his tent, and began collecting data—no further questions asked. But I had to acquire a "research permit" from the Science Institute of the Northwest Territories and permission from the Hamlet Council of Igloolik. Such procedural requirements were indicative of the changed conditions, and a less uneven balance of power between Inuit and researchers (Rasing 2008). It reveals that the conditions for research, the context within which the anthropologist has to operate, cannot be ignored or be left out of the picture. Traditionally, anthropologists tended to mask the (colonial) context of their research in their writings. They often portrayed the society studied as an isolated entity (as not being related to a wider setting), as being static (as if society does not change over time), and by leaving themselves out of the narrative. But no anthropological endeavour occurs in a void. No matter where it takes place, any community that is studied is connected in one way or the other—or in many-stranded ways—to the outside world. This has to be taken into consideration and must be accounted for. Likewise, ongoing changes in culture and society must be addressed. That the anthropologist's presence as an intruder into the world of "the Other" affects that world also cannot be ignored anymore. That cultural brokers are important in an anthropological narrative must be credited as well. I have tried to pay heed to all these aspects in my narrative efforts.

This leaves us, finally, with the *purpose* of the anthropological endeavour. It is never easy to know why research is conducted or whose interests will be served in the end, as Brody (2001, xii) remarks. Indeed, the purposes of anthropological research may be diverse, and do entail the risk of being used in a detrimental manner. Procedural requirements and other restrictive regulations that demand that the purpose of the research is made explicit may, to a certain extent, counter such misuse. Although valuable, however, these checks are no guarantee; neither can the anthropologist's good intentions prevent misuse of the findings. Ultimately, it is the integrity of "the instrument studying other human beings and societies" that is at stake. Anthropological research, conducted for whatever purpose, always entails a *personal relevance*. What it is that makes up this personal reason is equally difficult to know. I came north to study Inuit culture and try to understand Inuit. Why, I don't know. I was just curious to learn how Inuit society succeeded to survive, in a relatively peaceful way, in a demanding environment without a state organization, formal leadership, (fixed) laws, legal procedures, or specialized functionaries. This was my leading question and my driving force; why that question intrigued me, I don't know. Whatever the value of my answer is, that is up to others to decide, but the process of trying to find and come up with this answer was definitely worth the experience. If this is also true for those with whom I worked so closely together, and upon whose contribution I reflected in this essay written in memory of one of them, then my anthropology endeavour has at least been profitable to me and them.

Emile Imaruittuq's tent near Igloolik Point. July 1995. Photo by Willem Rasing

BIBLIOGRAPHY

Berreman, Gerald R. 1962. *Behind Many Masks. Ethnography and Impression Management in a Himalaya Village.* Ithaca: Society for Applied Anthropology, Cornell University.

Brody, Hugh. 2001. *The Other Side of Eden: Hunter-Gatherers, Farmers and the Shaping of the World.* London: Faber and Faber.

MacDonald, John. 2000. "The Igloolik Oral History Project." *Meridian* (Fall/Winter): 1–3.

Powdermaker, Hortense. 1966. *Stranger and Friend: The Way of an Anthropologist.* New York: Norton & Co.

Rasing, Willem C.E. 1989. *Diary, June–August 1989.* Unpublished document.

———. 1994. *"Too Many People": Order and Nonconformity in Iglulingmiut Social Process.* Nijmegen: Faculteit der Rechtsgeleerdheid. Reeks Recht & Samenleving Nr. 8.

———. 2008. "Law, Politics and Anthropology: Political, Scientific and Ethical Aspects of Legal-Anthropological Research in Arctic Canada & Nunavut (1978–2005)." In *"Inuit Canada": Reflexive Approaches to Native Anthropological Research,* edited by Pascale Visart de Bocarmé and Pierre Petit, 59–89. Brussels: Peter Lang.

CHAPTER 14

Ujakkat

Iglulingmiut Geology

Susan Rowley

This article was co-authored by the following elders, who shared their knowledge and are no longer with us, and by Leah Otak, without whom this project would not have been possible:

Hubert Amarualik, Ben Arnajuak, Mark Ijjangiaq, Thérèse Ijjangiaq, Aipilik Inuksuk, Zipporah Piungittuq Inuksuk, Isaac Irngaut, Annie Kappianaq, George Aqiaq Kappianaq, Martha Nasuk, Leah Otak, Michel Kupaaq Piugaattuk, Noah Piugaattuk, François Quassa, Tausaruapik, Rachel Ujarasuk.

While this research remains incomplete, it is presented here as a tribute to the remarkable work of Leah Otak.

INUIT WAYS OF KNOWING THE LAND are complex and multi-layered. Home is the places and spaces lived in by ancestors with the requisite knowledge transmitted from generation to generation through words and deeds. In this essay, I present a few case studies on Inuit geology— each looking at slightly different questions surrounding knowledge. The introduction describes the genesis of the project and the methods used. This is followed by descriptions of the different rocks.

INTRODUCTION

The idea to conduct this research arose from the Igloolik Archaeology Field School. This field school, started in 1987 and organized by Carolyn MacDonald and Susan Rowley, sought to demonstrate linkages in knowledge across cultures, to demonstrate respect for these knowledges, to instil pride in identity, and to demonstrate practical applications of the abstract concepts youth were learning through the formal education system. As part of their work in the field school, the students created an exhibit for the community. The youth selected the pieces, spoke to family and elders about them, wrote the labels, and were present during the exhibit in the school. During our excavations we uncovered many stone tools. In addition, we found numerous stones that appeared to have been imported from locations other than Igloolik Island. What were these stones, how were they used, and why had they been brought back to the island?

Leah Otak and I started a small research project in 1993, taking a few of the materials excavated to elders and asking the names of the materials as well as their uses and sources. This work continued in 1994 and 1995. We received additional support from the Polar Continental Shelf Program, which enabled us to take elders out to the source locations. Our methods were very low-tech—we visited people with some of the stone tools and rocks from the field school excavations, a few paper maps, and a tape recorder. The tapes made during this project are all part of the Igloolik Oral History Project. When an interview is referenced in this essay, the name of the speaker as well as the tape number are provided. Leah Otak conducted all interviews in Inuktitut. They were later translated and transcribed by Louis Tapardjuk.

The elders interviewed had all been interviewed many times, both as part of the groundbreaking Igloolik Oral History Project and for many different research projects. They also knew me both as someone who flew in and flew out to run the field school and as the daughter of Makkuktunnaaq (Graham Rowley), who had spent time with their families in the late 1930s. Our initial interviews were very tentative— we knew little about the rocks except for some of their Inuktitut names. As the interviews progressed we not only learned tremendous amounts but also realized that we might have misunderstood knowledge shared in earlier interviews. This led to several follow-up visits with people.

From 1993 to 1995 we were able to survey for archaeological sites and visit raw material source locations with elders via helicopter. Having the elders on-site was a remarkable experience as we watched memories resurface of places they had not visited in years. In terms of our project we were able to learn much more than in the interviews in town. While at the quarry sites we would collect samples of the rock and ask the elder to verify our identifications. Through this method we were able to ascertain the qualities that made a particular rock high or low quality. Having the elders with us was also critical to locating the quarries. While people pinpointed locations on our paper maps, the sources proved so localized that in most instances we would have missed them by ourselves.

Quarry sites in this region can be elusive. This is because we expect these locations to have large quantities of material and for evidence of human activity to be readily visible. In this region, that is not the case. Generally, the quarry locations are places where, if you search carefully, you can find the rock in question. In most locations it is rarely available in abundance. At one site, three of us searched for over an hour and only managed to find one specimen. In the few instances where the material is abundant, there tend to only be a few pockets of high-quality material.

"I do not know the place. The people that made their home in that vicinity should know about it" (Marc Ijjangiaq 1993, IE279). Ijjangiaq here is reminding us that people know their homelands, the places they live on, that they walk over, and whose resources they depend on throughout life. This important teaching reminds us that when someone doesn't know, it doesn't mean the knowledge no longer exists, simply that we need to seek out others whose homes are in different areas. Therefore, what is presented here is part of the knowledge shared by elders whose home territories encompassed the area of northern Foxe Basin, from Agu Bay in the west, north to Ikpiarjuk (Arctic Bay), east to Piling, and south to Saniraijak (Hall Beach).

GEOLOGY

Inuit employ multiple senses to identify stones. In our interviews clear indicators were given that particular stones can be recognized by sight, sound, touch, or taste cues. Indications of each are provided in the descriptions of the different stones as relevant.

Uluksarnaq (material for making *ulu*; slate). Scattered across the surface of Igloolik Island are reminders of previous generations and earlier occupants—ancient homes and tent rings, jumping stones, caches, traps, and *inuksuit*, along with their belongings of stone, bone, antler, and ivory. Due to the rapid isostatic rebound in this region of Nunavut, Igloolik Island continues to grow. Indeed, when Graham Rowley met an elderly woman named Ulluriaq in 1939, he was told, "She is indeed old. Even the land has grown up since she was a girl" (Rowley 1996, 217). This rebound provides a relative dating method for ancient occupations. At sites located at an elevation of approximately twenty to twenty-three metres above sea level, a greenish *uluksarnaq* suddenly appears in abundance in the form of ground harpoon end blades, and even snow knives.

> Q. Did your mother or grandmother talk about *ulu* before the metal?
> A. There is a stone called *uluksarnnak*, these were used for *ulu*, or at least a cutting tool. The blade was ground to thinness, as a matter of fact as you file away the stone you would look up the blade to see if the light is coming through, when that happens it is thin enough, that is the stone *uluksarnnak* which was used as a cutting tool. (Rachel Ujarasuk 1994, IE-298)

> Those particular stones were used as blades on *ulu* including knives. Those types of stones are really sharp. *Uluksarnnait* are hard when they are black. There are two different types, one being black and the

other green. They were used as blades, they would be in small pieces mortised into a tenon on a walrus tusk and the pieces would be placed one after the other. (François Quassa 1993, IE-284)

The greenish *uluksarnaq* continues to be found in sites at lower elevations above sea level on Igloolik Island, but in nowhere near the same abundance as at the sites in the twenty- to twenty-three-metre level. Later sites have a greater usage of black *uluksarnaq*. Why does this shift occur? The elevation and other changes in material culture is indicative of a transition referred to by archaeologists as the transition from late pre-Dorset to early Dorset culture. Was this greenish *uluksarnaq* traded into the region? Or, as was hypothesized by Meldgaard (1962), was it the result of new peoples or new ideas entering the region (94)?

Elders immediately recognized this stone as *uluksarnaq* from the place called Uluksarnnat—located twenty-seven kilometres northwest of Igloolik Island: "This is the place where you can find nice green *uluksarnnak* on the beach" (François Quassa, 1993, IE-284).

> This would have been from Uluksarnnat.
> Q. What were these used for?
> A. Sometimes they were used for knives, *ulu*, and *sakuuti* (scrapers). This type of stone can only be found in that place for the people that resided in the Amittuq region. That was the only place that they were able to get those type of stone as they are the only hard stones that [are] available in this region. (Hubert Amarualik 1993, IE-280)

Later, Leah and I were able to visit Uluksarnnat with François Quassa. There we located sheets of greenish slate identical to the tools and flakes we had encountered in the archaeological sites. Taking elevations at the site, it soon became apparent that this particular source of *uluksarnaq* only appears at elevations of twenty-three metres above sea level or less. The knowledge shared by François Quassa, Hubert Amarualik, and others has transformed our questions about the past. Now we can see, for this material, in this region, that a new resource presented itself to the occupants and they were eagerly using it, exploring its uses and learning its limitations. After a short period they now understood this material and its use shifted to the functions for which it is most suitable.

Kangilirjjuaq (stone for grinding; silt stone). Grinding is one of the most important techniques Inuit used prior to European contact for manufacturing tools and ornaments. Stones, some with hard inclusions, are used as whetstones. Similar to sandpapers of different grit, Inuit seek out stones for the different stages of manufacture, from shaping to smoothing and polishing.

In describing the process of making a tool from *uluksarnaq* (slate) François Quassa notes:

> You would take a small piece … and grind it with a *kangilirjjuaq*, you would keep check[ing] on it, when the light starts to go through the stone then that was the indication that it was now sharp.
>
> Q. Would you wet the stone as you grind it?
>
> A. Yes, you would wet the *kangilirjjuaq* as you use it to grind the other stone, that way it seems to be more effective in whetting.
>
> Q. Was there a difference between red and black *kangilirjjuaq*?
>
> A. The black ones are much better for whetting, the red ones are not as good for they are softer than the black ones.
>
> Q. Before they started to have metal needles while they still used bone for needles, were the *kangilirjjuat* used to sharpen them?
>
> A. Most likely, they would have used them to make a fine point on the needle, the black ones are quite effective on bones as well.
>
> Q. Sometimes we find harpoon heads that are polished, do you know if they would have been polished?
>
> A. Most likely, they would use bedrock for that purpose, the whiter bedrocks are also very sharp while the black bedrocks are not as sharp. They would have used the whiter bedrock to polish.
>
> Q. There would be just a big boulder to finish these off?
>
> A. Yes, they would use the whiter type to polish, if the surface is smooth. (François Quassa 1993, IE-284)

A caribou skin drying atop a rock collection gathered by Piungittuq Inuksuk. She was an avid and knowledgeable collector of geological specimens from the Igloolik area and beyond. Photo by John MacDonald

Later we were able to travel with Zipporah Piungittuq Inuksuk in search of *kangilirjjuaq*. Sitting on a white bedrock boulder, she demonstrated how the finishing polish would be put on a harpoon head by rubbing it against the rock. This knowledge led us to identify a boulder at Arnaquakksat, an ancient camp we were excavating, as a boulder used in the same way.

We had also been told that you could judge the quality of each stone by licking it. However, until we actually participated in selecting materials with our tongues, gaining a sense for how *kangilirjjuaq* stuck to our tongues, we were still unclear how to judge a specimen. Licking the rock allows you to feel the texture of the stone and determine its grit and therefore its suitability as a grinding stone.

In the vicinity of Isurttuq, there are stones that were used for grinding (*kiinautiksait*). They used to choose the type they wanted by licking on the stone to test the texture. Some were thinner than others. So when they licked the stone they could tell which was better and which was not....

Q. How can you tell the difference in stones by licking?

A. You would lick the stone and find that they are different. I am not certain how you can tell the difference. They would do the same as they would with an *uluksarnnat*. They used to get some stones for grinding in that area. Yes, they used to lick the stone when they were looking for grinding stone. It is said that their tongues used to wear out ... because they were looking for the right stone. (Martha Nasuk 1993, IE-281)

Kangilirjjuaq can be classified into a family—not only are there different types, but they have different names.

I know where there are *kangilirjjuat*, it is at a place that is called Kangilirjjualik. However, you cannot find them at a glance, you have to look for them. They are close to this lake on this side towards the island Nuvuk&irpaaq. There are different types, there are reddish ones and there are greenish colours and they are not completely black. The darker ones can get sharper than the other ones. The reddish ones are not as strong.

Q. Are there different names for them?

A. The black ones are called *angusirgnait* while the reddish ones are called *arningaq*. (François Quassa 1993, IE-284)

Zipporah Inuksuk: This *arningaq* is [a] good one, they used to check the texture with their tongue when they were looking for the right type of stone that would be used for grinding stone, they would check the surface. They would check it with their tongue, the ones that were smooth and slippery they were said to be *amiraaktarnartut* and could not sharpen knives very well. The one when you check with your tongue were coarse were not *amiraaktarnartut*, they would make a good grinding stone.

Q. Would that be applicable to both *arningaq* and *angusirngaq*?

Aipilik Inuksuk: That is right, they would be the same.

Q. Are there other varieties of *kangilirjjuaq*?

Aipilik Inuksuk: I believe there are no other types, however, *arningait* come in different colours, sometimes they have a nice green colour to them, almost yellowish.

(Aipilik and Siporah Inuksuk 1993, IE-285)

Q. While we are talking about *kangilirjjuat*, are there different types of *kangilirjjuat*, for instance there are *angusirngaq*, so are there more?

A. Yes. *Angusirgnait* are like this which is black, not completely black … here on the island right at the end … there you can find *arningait* of the *kangilirjjuat*…. It has the colour of a moulted skin. Those types are really good for sharpening stone.

Q. Do they make knives sharper than using *angusirngaq*?

A. Yes, they have a good grinding, that is the type with a moulting skin colour, and there appears to be grains in them. You can find them sticking out of the ground in the places where there is *ijjuq* (sod) and *maraq* (mud). (George Kappianaq 1993, IE-283)

There are three varieties of *kangilirjjuaq*: *angusinarq* ("the male," generally dark grey to black in colour and harder), *arnirnaq* ("the female," usually red and softer), and *makkuttuq* ("the immature one," generally pale-ish green with reddish splotches). *Makkuttuq* was rarely used. It was considered by some to be part of the *kangilirjjuaq* family but was too soft, "immature," to be of much use. *Arnirnaq* is coarser than *angusinarq* and would be used to shape a tool during the preliminary grinding stages, while for the final grinding *angusinarq* would be used.

In 1994 we visited a small source location for *kangilirjjuaq* with Ben Arnajuak and Tausaruapik, two elders from Saniraijak. In the middle of a swampy area there is a small outcrop marked by three *inuksuit*. The grinding stones are pushed to the surface through the active frost heaving in this area. Arnajuak and Tausaruapik noted that people still prefer these stones to the whetstones available in the store.

Ukkusiksaq (material to make a pot; soapstone). The definition of soapstone in Western geology is a soft metamorphic rock consisting primarily of talc. However, in common usage the term is used to stand for the material of Inuit carvings, no matter how inaccurate this is. For the elders we worked with, *ukkusiksaq* maintains its strict definition—this is the material from which pots can be made. They used the term *sananguagaksaq* (material to carve) to cover a wider range of materials. "This piece here is an *ukkusiksaq*, there are all kinds of *ukkusiksait*, there are the types that have sparkles in them, and there are those that do not appear to have any grains" (François Quassa 1993, IE-284).

The types of *ukkusiksaq* influenced the ways the *qulliit* (lamps) made from them functioned, because each type had very different properties when it came to absorbing seal fat and giving off heat. Human factors were also at play as the expertise of the carver to form the wick edge determined the wick's efficiency in drawing fuel.

> Q. What name would they give this stone?
> A. This is part of a pot. Some of the *ukkusiksait* have shiny spots, which were called *turqiktugalaat*, so when they look at that soapstone and see those shiny spots they would say that it has *turqituqaurtuq*.
> Q. So they call it *turqituq* because they are bunched together?
> A. Yes. I believe that they do not get dirty as easily when they are used for pots. This piece here is a piece of an *ukkusik* (pot), because it is thin. There are different types of *ukkusiksait*, there are this type with spots of shiny particles and there are those which are air tight. Then there are those that have a streak in them. Then there are those that have hard particles embedded in them like sand and these cannot get nice and smooth. (George Kappianaq 1993, IE-283)

> Q. They are all called *ukkusiksait*, could you make a *qulliq* or an *ukkusik*?
> Aipilik Inuksuk: They can be made into an *ukkusik* if the stone is soft enough. There are all types of *ukkusiksait*, there are some that are softer than the others.
> Siporah Inuksuk: These two are different but both are *ukkusiksaq*. That one is greenish and some of them are much greener while some are black. In those days they had all kinds of *qulliit* from different

stones, there were some that had a nice black *qulliq* and some that had ordinary *ukkusiksaq* and some had real *ukkusiksaq* which are the type that do not have any sparkling stones mixed into them, these were called *ukkusiksakkarik*. The type with sparkling stones mixed into them were used for *qulliq*. They were all different some were nice black ones. Q. Are the different *ukkusiksait* different when you use them for *qulliq*, did they differ in using up fuel?

Aipilik Inuksuk: It is said so. The harder ones are better but the edge where the flames are lit gets *ujaravvik* so that it burns out the wicks much quicker. The soft ones do not get *ujaravvik* as quickly therefore do not use as much wick as the harder one.....

They were all different. Some *qulliit* used to use up more fuel when the back was not high. When the back is high the stone does not get as hot. It is also said the *ingniq* on the *qulliq* (lip of the *qulliq*) is the cause for fuel efficiency. It used to be said when the lip is *ukpikaattuq* it uses up fuel much faster. That is when the lip does not have a full edge. When the lip has sharp edges and the back is not too low then the *qulliq* can have lower fuel consumption. That was the way it was, the *ingniit* differ.

Siporah Inuksuk: I used to hear about the *qulliit* that tend to get hot. It was said that some *qulliit* tend to get hotter than others depending on the type of *ukkusiksaq* they are made of. (Siporah and Aipilik Inuksuk, IE-285)

While most *qulliit* were made from *ukkusiksaq*, other materials were also used. Some were used out of expediency, such as natural hollows in rocks that could be used when people were travelling in the interior, Melville Peninsula, or Baffin Island. Others were selected by preference. For example, Martha Nasuk had a lamp made from *qakurtanguat*, a soft, white-yellow limestone found in only one location.

Yes, something that they could make *qulliq* with. At Nirliviktuuq I know of a place on the fore shores where there are white soft stones, these type of stones were also made to a *qulliq*. When the tide went out there were some of these white soft stones, which were thin.

These types of stone when made to a *qulliq* give off more heat than *ukkusiksaq*, possibly because they have been in salt water. Aakuvaapik and I each had a *qulliq*, mine was the white one. We started to cook meat at the same time with our *qulliq*. My *qulliq* was much faster in cooking the meat because it gave off more heat. The flames tend to burn out of control (*isiula*), perhaps the stone is salty so they tend to get hotter.... They are yellowish....
Q. Did they use fuel faster?
A. Yes, because the fuel gets warmer.
(Martha Nasuk 1993, IE-281)

The type that my *avaannuk* had which are yellowish stones are known as *qakurtanguat* are taken from Nirlivittuuq. I have a piece outside that I am using as a *nuqartuutit* (anchor) for my tent, that is the type my *avaannuk* had for her *qulliq*. That was the stone I got from Kipsigaq that I was going get a *qulliq* from.

Ordinary stones are never called *qakurtanguat*. If there was stone of the same colour then they would be called *qakutajaq* [limestone].
(Siporah and Aipilik Inuksuk 1993, IE-285)

We visited a number of sites where contemporary carvers quarry *sananguagaksaq*. These were mostly *ukkusiksaq*; however, we only visisted one source that matched the *ukkusiksaq* found in our excavations. In 1995 Hubert Amarualik took us to the source of the stone used by his family when replacing lamps they had gifted to others:

My mother had relatives in that area [Tununirusiq] so when we got there her relatives liked her *qulliq* so they took it. They did not trade for it nor did they pay anything for it. I have seen this happen more than once. (Hubert Amarualik 1993, IE-280)

The source location was simply two boulders of *ukkusiksaq* on the tundra that are gradually shrinking as people extract more of the stone. When we arrived Hubert at first thought he had mistaken the location because the boulder was so much smaller. He remembered from his childhood that the larger boulder had steps carved into it so that people could climb on top. The second, smaller boulder was where people would carve their names as they passed by on their way into the interior to hunt caribou. Apparently there used to be a soft, green *ukkusiksaq* in the area between the two boulders; however, the surficial stone is all gone. But Hubert remarked that one could still retrieve larger pieces of very soft stone by digging into the ground.

Uqsuriak (from *ursuq*, meaning blubber; a white talc). This is another stone that was occasionally used for making lamps, but only small ones. It is a very soft, white stone sometimes used for carving (Aipilik Inuksuk, IE-278). Some examples from the 1970s are coloured with pen ink, which bleeds into the surface of the stone, leaving a purplish colour. The elders we interviewed did not consider it to be an *ukkusiksaq*. They also noted that *uqsuriak* is the word used by people from the Kivalliq region for an entirely different rock—quartz.

> Siporah Inuksuk: Yes, one time someone found an old *qulliq* made from that type of a stone. It would have been a small *qulliq* but it was made of an *uqsuriak*.
>
> Aipilik Inuksuk: Anything that was easy to work with [was] kept in the past.
>
> Q. A while ago you mentioned that *uqsuriat* were used to remove fat?
>
> Aipilik Inuksuk: Yes. The type that have a trace of *mirqusaat* are good as cleaning powder. My father use[d] to file some of that stone using a rasp file.... With that he would make powder that would be used to clean fat off fox pelts and other fur bearing animals. They used to become so clean even without being washed. (Siporah and Aipilik Inuksuk 1993, IE-285)

François Quassa describes the sound of *uqsuriak*: "They are white and very soft. Sometimes there are some around. When you bang it against a stone, they sound as if they were padded with something soft. They do not have any harsh banging sound" (François Quassa 1993, IE-284).

Uqsuriak is a rock whose use increased with fur trading, specifically for use when treating fox pelts.

The *uqsuriak* is a soft stone. These types of stones were used to clean fox pelt fur as they are good in removing fat.

Q. How do they use it, do they use a small piece to rub it against the fur?

A. No, they grind it into powder and then spread it on the fur when they are going to remove the fat.

Q. So then you would just spread it on the fur and remove it afterwards?

A. Yes, they would beat the skin with a beater when removing the powder. It is the same principle as using flour to rid the fat from the fur.

Q. Was this used by only a few people or was it widely used?

A. For those that lived in a place where there were those types of rocks, they would have used them. (Martha Nasuk 1993, IE-281)

Mirqusaaq (from *mirquq*, meaning animal fur; asbestos). We asked people if rocks belonged to the same family in the case of materials that were found in close proximity to one another or where elders indicated that different materials could be used to create the same item. At one point Leah and I were trying to understand the relationship between different rocks used for lamps and pots.

> Some *ukkusiksait* have a mixture of *mirqusaaq* in them so these types of stone made good *ukkusik* (pot) as they do not break easily. As for *mirqusaat* they do not make good *ukkusik* as they have too much grain therefore they tend to split. (Siporah and Aipilik Inuksuk, IE-285)

> … *mirqusaat* are really soft and shave very nicely with plenty of grains. When I saw one at Maniittuq I thought of them as a rope and have a look of a piece of wood that have been on the ground for a long time. (François Quassa 1993, IE-284)

In discussions of *taqqutit* (lamp trimmers), *mirqusaaq* was frequently mentioned, as in this excerpt from Aipilik and Siporah Inuksuk:

Q. Were the *mirqusaat* used for anything?

Aipilik Inuksuk: They were used to light a fire.

Siporah Inuksuk: They were also used as *taqquti,* in those days they use[d] to have wooden *taqquti* as well as *urpigak* to light a fire with. In the places where there were no *aqqiruat* then they would use wooden *taqquti* which they could use to light a fire as well as *urpigaq.* It is said that those types of stones did not burn out quickly and when you are using it to trim fire they do not catch on fire. On the other hand they could be lighted up to get a fire.

Aipilik Inuksuk: They were not meant for that particular task but they could be used to trim flames. Any other type of stones cannot be lighted up, but those type of stones could light up if you add a little bit of fuel to it, indeed I have seen some used. (Siporah and Aipilik Inuksuk 1993, IE-285)

Augiujaq (from *auk*, meaning blood, and *augiaq,* meaning blood clot; red ochre). In Late Dorset period sites in the Igloolik region many small lamps are coated, on the interior, with red ochre. More recently Inuit children played with red ochre, either crushing it into a powder or using it to draw pictures on other rocks, while adults used *augiujaq* to write messages.

We used to play with *augiujaq* by pounding them into powder and they do look really good when they are crushed, so these are *augiujaq.*
Q. What did you use them for once you crushed them?
A. For anything, you can pretend them to be flour or tea or anything of your imagination.... They make good markers on bed rocks because they come out very well, in addition we used to use red *kangil-irjjuat* to write with. (François Quassa 1993, IE-284)

In those days we did not have any pencils to write with, so we would use these stones to write on a white stone. (Michel Kupaaq 1993, IE-282)

Annie Kappianaq noted that:

It is said that in those days when someone was going to make a trip into another community the woman would request something from that other community, perhaps it might be an Arctic cotton that the woman wanted so she would draw something on a piece of skin. She would use that stone *augiangujaq* to write with. These would have been used to write with. (Annie and George Kappianaq 1993, IE-283)

Qilliqiaq (from *qilla*, meaning brilliant; mica). Igloolik Island is a limestone outcrop and so many rocks, located on the nearby Canadian Shield, are only present if imported by people. One of these is *qilliqiaq* or mica. In some regions, especially around Igluligaarjuk (Chesterfield Inlet) and Kimmirut (Lake Harbour), mica is found in large sheets (Tyrrell and Biodiversity Heritage Library 1897, 245; Hamilton 1994, 80–81). However, in our excavations we only find small fragments. Many of the elders remember collecting and playing with *qilliqiaq* as children because of its transparency and the ability to peel off layers. No one recalled any functional uses for *qilliqiaq*: We really liked them because they make good toys to play with. We used to get them just to play with them" (Martha Nasuk 1993, IE-281).

Marc Ijjangiaq: I have never heard of anyone asking for these types of particular stones. We used to collect them only to play with them. Some of them are really easy to shave.
Q. Where can you find these types of stones?
    …
    Marc Ijjangiaq: You can find these in places where there are rocky landscape[s]. You cannot find them in fragmented limestone areas (tuapajaak), well at least they are harder to find in them. You can find them [in] bedrock.
Q. When they found some of that, possibly by children to play with, would they have taken them with them?
    Thérèse Ijjangiaq: They used to take them back with them. When they played with them they would shave them off and use them to play because you can see through them and you would peek through them. (Marc and Thérèse Ijjangiaq 1993, IE-279)

It wasn't only children who collected this rock.

Q. As children did you collect them?
A. Very much, they were really nice to have, you got a joy out of finding them.
Q. Were they also collected by the adults?
A. Yes. They would refer to them as *qilliqiaq*. They would go out for a short walk, perhaps they would go up to a rise to look around for game animal[s] so when they returned they would have that type in their hand that they had come across as they walked. (Annie and George Kappianaq, IE-283)

Aqirruaq and *Kuniaq* (something that can be shaped; Argillite). This rock is a grey stone with brownish streaks that is found around Ikpiarjuk (Arctic Bay). Many carvings from there use this stone (Michel Kupaaq Piugaattuk, pers. comm). This is the preferred material for *taqqutit* (lamp trimmers)—while it can be carved, it is harder than *ukkusiksaq* and is heat resistant. *Kuniaq* is noted as being the same type of rock, but darker and coming from a different source (Siporah and Aipilik Inuksuk 1993, IE-285).

Q. We heard people use many different materials to make *taqquti*, if you had a choice what would be your preference?

Aipilik Inuksuk: I would prefer the greenish *aqqirruaq*. *Uluksarnnait* also make good *taqquti* but they have a grain length-wise so they tend to break off at the tip. *Aqirruat* do not have any grain so they do not break off easily.

...

Siporah Inuksuk: While we were at *qarmat*, people were making *taqquti* from a *kangilirjjuaq*, they were reddish, but when they were used as trimmer to the flames they tend to crack and break off. That is because they have been in the salt. (Siporah and Aipilik Inuksuk 1993, IE-285).

Here again sound is used in the identification process:

If you were to go to a place where there were *kuniaq* and these were on top of the ground. If you step on the stones you would notice that they had a metallic sound. Then you would know that they are indeed *kuniaq*, they do not have the sound of an ordinary stone, they make a ringing sound like metal. That goes for *uluksarnnait* as well. (François Quassa 1993, IE-284)

Aligut (quartz crystals). Quartz crystals, including amethyst, can be found in small pockets. Functionally they were used as drills:

These were called *puttutaut* (making holes with), they are hard so they could be used to bore holes with them. They would use them when they are making harpoons or any other tools. In those days it was necessary to bore holes in the tools. (Siporah and Aipilik Inuksuk 1993, IE-278).

Several elders identified *aligut* as being alive (Amarualik; Z. Inuksuk; Kappianaq, pers. comm.). George Kappianaq mentioned that crystals are like clams: you need to get them in the bright sun. If you shade them they'll disappear.

Tunujak (from *tunu*, caribou back fat; quartz). This rock can be found in many places and was used primarily as a strike-a-light when iron files became common. While other uses are given by ethnographers, the elders we spoke with had not heard of these uses.

Kukiksaq or *Angmaaq* (chert). During the pre-Dorset and Dorset periods, *angmaaq* was the material of choice for most stone tools. Elders told us that their ancestors also used *kukiksaq* for tools on occasion while preferentially using *uluksarnaq*. Finding *kukiksaq* sources was one of our hoped-for outcomes. While the elders knew of the use of chert for blades, they themselves had only used it for strike-a-lights. Any beach *kukiksaq* can be used for this purpose. This type of low-quality *kukiksaq* is found throughout the region. Hubert Amarualik, in looking at our archaeological finds, identified one source of high-quality chert, however; as it was outside the study range we were unable to visit. This does, however, point to the existence of extensive trade networks over time.

> Thérèse Ijjangiaq: In this area we call them *kukiksaq* but people who reside (*avanirmmiut*) over there. That is Tununirmmiut call them *angmaat*.
>
> Marc Ijjangiaq: We in this area call them *kukiksaq* while they call it *angmaat*. These were used as blades ... they could be used for harpoon heads. They had multi-purposes.
>
> Thérèse Ijjangiaq: They could also be used as a cutting tool because the blade does not break as fast and they would also be sharp.
>
> Marc Ijjangiaq: That is right, they do not get easily dull because they are hard. (Marc and Thérèse Ijjangiaq 1993, IE-279)

Ingniq (unknown—possibly iron pyrites or magnesium rocks). In the case of *ingniq* we were unable to determine the type of rock through description, and despite visiting the source locale twice we were unable to find any samples. *Ingniq* is most frequently translated as chert or flint. However, it is apparent that this is an inaccurate translation for the Igloolik area. Prior to the introduction of iron Iglulingmiut could start a fire by using a fire drill or creating a spark by rubbing two pieces of *ingniit* together. People quickly learned to start a fire by striking a piece of *angmaaq* (chert) or *tunujak* (quartz) against the edge of a file when iron became available. This method was much easier than using *ingniq*. *Ingniq* was only available in one relatively remote location in northeastern Foxe Basin (Noah Piugaattuk 1993, IE-277) In contrast, *angmaaq* and *tunujaq*, of a quality suitable to be used as strike-a-lights, are available throughout the region.

> Q. Are *angmaat* and *ingniit* different?
>
> A. They are very different from each other. The *ingniit*, when you tap them they will chip off, while *angmaat* are much harder. (Siporah and Aipilik Inuksuk 1993, IE-278)

Ingniit are black [rocks] used to make a fire with. With two black
ingniit he would strike them together, once he starts to strike against
each other, below them would be *kaniruq* and the spark would start
to fall. That one where the sparks are to land is a material that can
smolder. You cannot see the smolder but in the dark you can see
small sparks. When you strike the two together the one below starts
to smolder. (Noah Piugattuuk 1993, IE-277)

With *ingniit* all you have to do is bang into them to produce sparks
which fall down. Those were the stones that were widely used to start
a fire. (Annie and George Kappianaq 1993, IE-283)

I have seen them tried and seen the results, I have not used them....
We caught up to the time when these were in the possession of the
people.... We of the older generations have seen these while they
were used, but there was no longer a need for them so we no longer
used them. We have heard about them being used but we did not use
them. (Hubert Amarualik 1993, IE-280)

In 1993 an unsuccessful attempt was made to locate the source
of *ingniit*. We originally felt this would be a relatively simple task as
the source location, Ingnittaqvik, is marked on topographic maps. In
addition, everyone we talked with knew what *ingniit* looked like, how
it tasted, and where it could be found: "They are black but more red
than black. When you lick them you will find the taste very sweet.... It
is not sweet like sugar but when you lick it you still get the sweet taste
and sour" (Michel Kupaaq 1993, IE-282).

We attempted to locate the source again in 1994 with elder Isaac
Irngaut. We brought samples of every rock in the vicinity that even
vaguely matched elders' descriptions back to Igloolik. Noah Piugaattuk dismissed them immediately. Noah told us that when he was
young people no longer used *ingniit*, having already transitioned to
using chert and iron files. However, his family made certain that he
knew of this technology should he need it in the future. His family always stopped at Ingnittaqvik on the way into the interior to go caribou

hunting. Despite his parents already having an iron file and a small collection of matches, they always collected *ingniit*. In fact, "they would gather more than they need so that there would be enough for the people that had no one to get them for them" (Noah Piugaattuk 1993, IE-277).

Through talking with elders we learned that Noah Piugaattuk was the only person then alive who had collected *ingniit*. Noah accompanied us to Ingnittaqvik in 1995, but we remained unsuccessful in locating *ingniit*. His memories serve to illustrate how *ingniit* fell out of use and provide a model for how knowledge is maintained and transmitted across generations. When Noah was a young boy in the early 1900s his family lived in eastern Foxe Basin. At this time his family used an iron file and *angmaaq* to start fires. However, his family still collected *ingniit* and showed the young boy where to go. This ensured transmission of both the location and use to the next generation. It was always possible that iron files and matches might not be available in the future and therefore youth needed to know where to find this valuable and rare resource. Among families that did not visit this location, the name, use, and physical description was transmitted. As a result, in the early 1990s, almost a century after it fell out of common use, many people still knew about *ingniit*.

This preliminary work on Iglulingmiut geology demonstrates the in-depth knowledge the people have of their lands. Rocks are classified primarily based on function; *ukkusiksaq* is stone for making pots, and *uluksarnaq* is stone for *ulus*. To identify stones at the source, the senses of sight, taste, sound, and touch are used. Knowledge about rocks and their functions is transmitted across generations even when alternative technologies are available. This research also affirms the importance of Marc Ijjangiaq's words—"The people that made their home in that vicinity should know about it" (Marc and Thérèse Ijjangiaq 1993, IE-279)—for future research.

BIBLIOGRAPHY

Hamilton, John David. 1994. *Arctic Revolution: Social Change in the North-west Territories, 1935–1994*. Toronto: Dundurn Press.

Meldgaard, Jorgen. 1962. "On the Formative Period of the Dorset Culture." In *Prehistoric Relations between the Arctic and Temperate Zones of North America*, edited by J. Campbell. Montreal: Arctic Institute of North America, Technical Paper 11.

Rowley, Graham. 1996. *Cold Comfort: My Love Affair with the Arctic*, 1st ed., vol. 13. Montreal and Kingston: McGill-Queen's University Press.

Tyrrell, James Williams, and Biodiversity Heritage Library. 1897. *Across the Sub-arctic of Canada, a Journey of 3,200 Miles by Canoe and Snowshoe through the Barren Lands*. Toronto: W. Briggs.

CHAPTER 15

Reflections on a Flag

John MacDonald

Igloolik, April 1, 1999. A brilliant, chilly day. I stood on the snow-covered sea ice in front of the town along with most of the community's residents to witness something exceptional: the unveiling of Nunavut's flag, marking the creation of Canada's newest territory. Beside me, sharing in the excitement—and pondering what the flag might look like—was Aimie Panimera, then the mayor of Igloolik. Moments before the flag unfurled from its temporary pole on the ice, Aimie murmured, "I'll be fine with anything ... as long as it doesn't have an inuksuk!"[1] In turn, I hoped my hunch of the flag sporting some stylized version of the North Star would prove groundless.... Of course, it didn't; nor did Aimie's hopes for something other than an inuksuk.

IN THIS ESSAY—INFORMED MAINLY by the Igloolik Oral History Project interviews—I muse on various cultural and figurative aspects of the symbols adorning Nunavut's flag: the inuksuk and the North Star. I suggest that these symbols are perhaps less than ideal icons for Nunavut, and paradoxically serve to reinforce southern Canadian stereotypes most commonly thought to convey the idea of

North, especially its Arctic regions.[2] A major part of my discussion involves tracing the extraordinarily rapid rise, romancing, and appropriation of the inuksuk as a universal Canadian symbol, almost as familiar as the maple leaf on our national flag.[3]

At the outset, I wish to stress that my comments on Nunavut's flag are not intended as a gratuitous criticism of those involved in the flag's conception, design, and endorsement. On every front, they were bound by the quaint procedural rules of the Canadian Heraldic Authority governing the creation of official flags and coats of arms, a process ultimately requiring the approval of Canada's Governor General and the Queen.[4] Nevertheless, in the years since the flag's unveiling in 1999, it has become a source of pride, celebrated by Nunavummiut.

Flags and emblems, regardless of their underlying symbology, have a way of achieving their intended purpose of fixing and affirming group identity and cohesion. With specific reference to Inuit symbology, Nelson Graburn posits that the aim of symbols is to "maximally express difference and "otherness" in situations where ethnic recognition is of prime importance."[5] Nunavut's flag, regardless of the debatable provenance of its symbols, quickly achieved this goal, proudly taking its place among the pantheon of Canada's provincial and territorial flags.[6] This accepted, there are nevertheless several important observations to be made on the flag's derived symbols in terms of their wider cultural history and significance within Nunavut. These considerations will offer some context to the flag's symbology, as yet unavailable through official sources, and begin to address the often inadequate and confusing statements—particularly on inuksuit—made through the popular media.

The flag of Nunavut is remarkable on several fronts, not least in that both of its graphic elements—the inuksuk and the North Star— represent "guidance." The official website of Nunavut's Legislative Assembly tells us that the "inuksuk ... symbolizes stone monuments which guide people on the land," while the North Star is "the traditional guide for navigation."[7] The central role of guidance attributed to both these symbols is taken for granted, facilely leaving the impression that across Nunavut Inuit traditionally travelled throughout their lands using inuksuit and the North Star as their principal guides. Such a view, I shall argue, is problematic in that it conceals the remarkable, multifaceted complexity and genius of traditional Inuit wayfinding—a skill that enabled countless generations of Nunavummiut to access their land and its life-giving resources under virtually any conditions of weather, without star or inuksuk.

THE NORTH STAR

The lesser of the flag's symbols—the North Star, also known as Polaris—can be covered briefly here. Suffice it to say that there are several better astral choices more universally suited to Nunavut in terms of Inuit traditions, mythology, and navigational usage. In Nunavut's more northerly communities, including Igloolik, Arctic Bay, Pond Inlet, and Resolute Bay, the North Star, while obviously seen, is barely noticed and little used in navigation.[8]

One elder, Eli Amak, while generally knowledgeable about his astronomical traditions, had heard about Nuuttuittuq (as the North Star is called in Inuktitut) but could not point it out: he "had no knowledge of that star."[9] Another, Zacharias Panikpakuttuk, first learned about the North Star's existence from the archaeologist Graham Rowley in the late 1930s.[10] For Abraham Ulajuruluk, Nuuttuittuq was a mere curiosity:

> I positioned a harpoon pointing directly at this star.... In the morning I checked it and discovered that [while other stars had changed their position] the harpoon still pointed at the star.... I had discovered the stationary star *Nuuttuittuq*![11]

The North Star's iconic reputation as the quintessential guiding star in the more temperate latitudes of the northern hemisphere dwindles appreciably in the higher latitudes because, as Theo Ikummaq of Igloolik notes, "it's almost directly overhead ... it won't tell you where you are going, so that star is not ... reliable."[12]

Nuuttuittuq did have its adherents among some of the elders interviewed, notably those whose formative years were spent in areas well south of Igloolik, where the lower altitude of the North Star would have increased its usefulness in wayfinding.[13] George Kappianaq, for instance, who grew up in the Ukkusiksalik (Wager Bay) area, mentions how useful Nuuttuittuq could be as a directional aid for hunters stranded on moving sea ice.[14]

However, for Iglulingmiut generally, Nuuttuittuq was not considered a primary guiding star.[15] Stars used by Iglulingmiut for orientation usually tended to have qualities the North Star lacked: lower maximum altitudes above the horizon, usefulness as markers of diurnal and seasonal time, and a role in Inuit mythology, the latter being important for star recognition. "Stars," as Noah Piugaattuk tells us, "have legends behind them to pinpoint their exact location."[16] Inuit celestial mythology does indeed map large swaths of the visible sky, assigning memorable roles to stars and constellations, graphically defining their spatial relationship to each other, but in Nunavut, apparently no celestial mythologies involve the North Star.

From a traditional perspective, the two stars comprising the Inuit constellation Aagjuuk, recognised and celebrated across the Inuit world, may have better served the flag's iconography. For communities above the Arctic Circle, the sighting of Aagjuuk marked a period of transition and heralded the sun's return to the horizon after winter's darkness.[17] Aagjuuk's annual appearance in the midwinter sky variously signified hope and renewal, and for Iglulingmiut triggered a festival whose main purpose was to "strengthen the land" (*nunagiksaqtut*). What better symbology for the new territory?[18]

INUKSUK: THE MAKING OF A MODERN ICON

The *Canadian Encyclopedia* correctly notes that the inuksuk as a symbol is "often intertwined with representations of Canada and the North."[19] Elena Rivera MacGregor, who designed the logo for the 2010 Winter Olympic Games, describes the inuksuk as representing the "heart of Canada."[20] Driven by the North's enduring appeal to the notions and fancies of southern Canadians, this widespread, effusive appropriation of the inuksuk as a national icon, saturated with meaning and significance far removed from its cultural origins, is surely unique in the annals of our national iconography.[21]

The rise of the stylized, human-shaped, "anthropoidal" inuksuk as a pervasive Canadian symbol had its likely beginnings in the early 1960s, with the installation of three impressive inuksuit brought, stone by stone, from Cape Dorset and reassembled at Toronto's Pearson Airport in 1963.[22] Since then, the inuksuk's popularity across Canada has grown rapidly: witness the miniature and large-scale representations of inuksuit seen outside public buildings, along Canada's highways and byways, on lakeside cottages, and suburban lawns. Schomberg, Ontario, boasts the "world's largest" inuksuk—11 metres high and weighing in at 82,000 kilograms.[23] The structure's proliferation in national and provincial parks is considered by park managers as a menace akin to invasive plants, its littering of highways condemned as "Inukshukification."[24] Abroad, awareness of inuksuit is promulgated through their gracing of Canadian embassies in several countries, including the United States and Japan. Googling "inukshuk" (the common popular spelling of "inuksuk") garners over a million results, including a dizzying excess of photographs and graphic representations of its anthropoidal form.[25]

Today's universal popularity of the inuksuk, as both a symbol and an ornamental structure, is plausibly sustained by three singular events: first, the creation and introduction of Nunavut's territorial flag in 1999; second, in the following year, the publication of Norman Hallendy's beautifully photographed, evocative book *Inuksuit: Silent Messengers of the Arctic*, of which, astonishingly, over thirty thousand copies were sold; and third, the (still controversial) choice to use a pastiche inuksuk for the official logo of Vancouver's 2010 Winter Olympic Games.[26] The exposure resulting from this latter decision was to give the inuksuk global recognition as a symbol indelibly associated with Canadian identity. It also underscored, if any underscoring was needed, the inuksuk's "proper" anthropomorphic form—legs (one or two), torso, arms, and head—as the structure's genuine representation.[27] Any other form was simply an aberration—certainly in the South but increasingly in the North as well, a point memorably illustrated by events in Igloolik leading up to the community's celebration of the millennium.

THE IGLOOLIK CASE

In September 1999, the Igloolik Hamlet Council took the decision to erect an impressive inuksuk high on the limestone bluff above the community. It would be built from massive slabs of local limestone, a sturdy-legged, Colossus-like anthropoid with arms outstretched, compliant with the received orthodoxy of proper form. Such an inuksuk, it was thought, would boost Igloolik's fledgling tourism industry—after all, was this not exactly the kind of edifice tourists from the South expected as part of their genuine Arctic experience? Besides, many other Arctic communities boasted such structures. But there was a problem from the start. Some of Igloolik's elders demurred, pointing out that *this* kind of inuksuk was not *their* kind of inuksuk. Respecting the elders' wishes, it was agreed that the municipality would construct its Colossus, but it would be flanked on each side by inuksuit (or *inuksugait*, as they are properly called in Igloolik) representative of the relatively nondescript, slightly tapering stone cairns traditionally built by Iglulingmiut.

Although not originally conceived as a marker of the impending new millennium, the project, by obvious default, became such.[28] And so the millennium—as with all New Years in Igloolik—was duly announced by the clanging of the little Anglican church's bell, the incongruous singing of an Inuktitut hymn to the tune of "Auld Lang Syne," fireworks crackling above the sea ice, and the local contingent of the Canadian Rangers firing off their rifles. Imposingly, on the bluff above the town, stood the massive floodlit inuksuk, legs astride, its outstretched arms supporting a large sign studded with electric lights tracing out the number 2000.[29]

Seen against the Igloolik skyline, the image of the large, "non-conforming" anthropoidal inuksuk, flanked by a couple of modest "traditional" cairns, stood as a stark allegory for the tension in the community between modernity and tradition, past and present, loss and change.

Children sliding on the steep slope below Igloolik's "millennium" inuksuk. The stone cairns flanking the central inuksuk represent the inuksugait commonly found in the Igloolik area—they were erected at the request of the community elders to clearly distinguish these structures from the invasive human-like inuksuk. Igloolik, 2006. Photo by John MacDonald

    The "millennium" inuksuk dominated the community for several years, until there were calls by some community members to have it taken down. It transpired that traditionally, an inuksuk built in human form could mark a place where murder had been committed. This troubling association led some to attribute several tragedies befalling the community since 1999 to the inuksuk's malign influences. In response, the Igloolik Hamlet Council decided to render the structure less anthropoidal, as well as safer, because children were climbing on it. The subsequent amputation sanctioned by the Council left the inuksuk bereft of its head, arms, and most of its torso. It now stands ingloriously above the town, forlornly Ozymandias-like.

    Perhaps aware of the Igloolik case, Inuit cultural activist Peter Irniq has for years engaged in a personal, ongoing campaign to discourage the building of human-like inuksuit, calling them "fakes," and pointing out that Inuit "rarely stacked rocks to resemble people" and that when they did, such structures could mark spots associated with murder and suicide.[30]

INUKSUIT AND NAVIGATION: GUIDING YOU HOME

If the ubiquity of the Vancouver Olympics logo entrenched the orthodoxy of the inuksuk's idealized humanlike form, the promotion of its
romance and mystique was left mainly to Norman Hallendy's hugely
popular book. Through the spectacular, sometimes illusionary, visual
power of Hallendy's photography—along with the deferential tones of
his text—the ordinary becomes extraordinary. Virtually every cairn
or inuksuk-like structure, no matter how prosaic or uncertain its
origin or function, is somehow imbued with weighty significance.[31]
To be clear, inuksuit were, and remain, extremely culturally important for Inuit, serving numerous temporary and lasting purposes both
idiosyncratic and collective.[32] Importantly, however, the extent of the
structure's regard and use varied from region to region, from north
to south, throughout the Arctic, a point often obscured by Hallendy's
influential work. Unintentionally, his perspectives on inuksuit have
effectively become the orthodoxy, increasingly embellished, appro-
priated, and conscripted to support various causes and commercial
enterprises.

Untethered from its cultural origins, the iconic inuksuk has taken
on a life of its own, extending far beyond its mere physical proliferation on landscapes near and far. Nowhere is this more evident than in
the mythology fashioned around its role in guidance, which deems the
inuksuk pre-eminent, an impression bolstered by its prominent representation on Nunavut's flag. The pervasiveness of this idea is seen, for
example, in the wide use of the inuksuk symbol by businesses wishing
to promote their products and services. Implicitly or explicitly, the
unfailing ability of the inuksuk to "put you in the right direction" is
invariably suggested. For example, a Toronto-based investment firm
going by the name Inukshuk Capital Management pledges to help its
clients "navigate the world of investing and guide them towards reaching their financial goals."[33] Similarly, a realty brokerage company in the
same city, whose trademarked logo is an inuksuk, happily espouses
what it calls the "Inukshuk philosophy" to affirm the organization's core
mission "to guide you safely and comfortably through the sale and/or
purchase of your cherished asset, your home."[34]

The popular assumption that inuksuit in themselves formed the basis of Inuit navigation, or that purpose-built "directional" inuksuit constituted widespread navigational systems, unfortunately detracts from our appreciation of the scope and intricacies of Inuit wayfinding practices. This is not to say that inuksuit played no part in navigation. Emphatically they did, but their role was fractional, not paramount. This was certainly the case among the Iglulingmiut and, I suggest, more generally across Nunavut.

Traditional Inuit navigation (and therefore survival) depended on extensive, culturally framed, experiential knowledge of the land and its resources in all conditions of weather, both summer and winter. Attention was brought to bear on every environmental sign and circumstance—distinctive landmarks, wind directions, the set of snowdrifts, the "lay of the land," the orientation of lakes, rivers, raised beaches, and the panoramic unfolding of horizons.[35] Vegetation, sea currents, clouds, and the position of stars and the sun were also part of the mix. Clues could be derived from the behaviour of birds, sled dogs, and other animals. Generally, the winter routes travelled by Inuit were those used by countless generations of their ancestors, routes chosen over terrain best suited to accommodate dog teams pulling ice-shod sleds.[36]

Distinctive locations along these long-established routes were given place-names, typically descriptive of some unique topographical or ecological feature of the spot, or referencing an associated personal, communal, or legendary event. In this way, the land was defined through an intimate, multi-layered knowledge of its physical, ecological, and cultural geography. This knowledge, passed down from generation to generation, was renewed and enriched over time by each generation's experiences and histories. The extent to which individuals were able to absorb and apply this knowledge determined, among other qualities, their skills in navigation.

Nathan Qamaniq uses the Inuktitut terms *aangaittuq* and *aangajuq* to differentiate navigational skills. One who is *aangajuq* "will lose his bearings as soon as he gets out of the community because he is not observant ... he will travel blindly." By contrast, the *aangaittuq* person is observant, actively aware of the surrounding environment: "he knows where his destination is, no matter what his location."[37] In this sense, *aangaittuq* is akin to the concept of "situational awareness"—a highly informed engagement with one's environment in all its dimensions and dynamic variables, including the ability to act appropriately under changing circumstances. Qamaniq's concept of *aangaittuq* ideally expresses the confident, productive relationship Inuit have with their environment at many levels. Orientation skills are a part of this complex.[38] In this context, the notion that Inuit navigated primarily by progressing along a trail from one inuksuk to another—from signpost to signpost, as it were—is to impose an unwarranted mechanistic approach on Inuit wayfinding.

INUKSUIT: MORE CONVENIENCE THAN NECESSITY

To travel is to leave signs, ephemeral, subtle, or substantial. The time-honoured overland routes of Inuit are thus tangibly marked by evidence of previous human passage and occupation. Accrued over many years, such signs comprise a telling assortment of stone structures built over generations for various purposes. They might include, in various stages of integrity or dilapidation, caribou drive cairns, hunting blinds, long-abandoned sod houses, caches, tent rings, windbreaks, fox traps, rope stretchers, kayak stands, telescope-resting platforms, markers for lake or riverside fishing locations, and, not infrequently, human-augmented post-glacial erratic boulders, made distinct by a topping of rocks or even caribou antlers.

Along these routes, promontories and distinctive elevated points used as observation locations were typically graced by a marker of sorts, elaborate or minimalist, usually the latter. Probably some, more than we care to acknowledge, would have been built for recreational purposes—or, as Rachel Ujarasuk puts it, "to kill time."[39] Expanding on this point, Theo Ikummaq explains that inuksuit could be built

just … where somebody had camped, and then decided to make an inuksuk … not necessarily to mark a trail, but maybe out of boredom … a lot of times it is out of boredom that they build these things.[40]

Whatever their original purpose, remembered and recognized, these structures were incorporated into the cultural landscape and could on occasion, as we shall see, aid in wayfinding. They were also useful in narrating details of travel, spatially positioning a journey's events by referencing commonly known, human-built structures to relevant topographical information and place-names. After the fact, such structures, though obviously not part of any intended "system," cumulatively came to define these trails, their inferred alignments and linkages, making it appear that they were built and placed as intentional route markers.[41] Therkel Mathiassen, an archaeologist with Rasmussen's Fifth Thule Expedition, may well be exemplifying this point when he describes "much frequented" routes, especially part of the "main road" between Naujaat and Igloolik, being marked by cairns.[42] Constructed randomly over time, these assorted structures demarcated long-established routes merely by dint of their existence. Nowadays, abandoned sleds, snowmobiles, aircraft wreckage, oil drums, hunting shacks, radio towers, and so on join their ancient stone-built counterparts in defining the landscape, and thus becoming route markers in their own right.[43]

Added to the assortment of these "supplementary" landmarks are, of course, inuksuit built specifically to aid navigation. Typically, these are found marking important turnoff points along routes, the mouths of rivers, crossing points on isthmuses, entrances to bays, or where trails transition from the sea ice to the land. In addition, these locations often served as predetermined meeting points, inevitably involving much lingering while awaiting arrivals—hence the frequent and helpful proliferation of inuksuit around such places, built to occupy time. Effective use of all landmarks in wayfinding, whether human-made or topographical, depended on the navigator having thorough, often idiosyncratic, empirical knowledge of the structures' defining characteristics—in other words, the practical application of the aforementioned sense of *aangaittuq*. In this way, visible and recognized inuksuit, along with other natural landmarks, served as familiar waypoints marking progress on journeys.

A close reading of the Igloolik oral history interviews covering navigation and inuksuit clearly demonstrates that inuksuit were not generally a significant factor in Iglulingmiut wayfinding. When mentioned at all, it was usually as an afterthought. Inuksuit may have been convenient, on occasion most helpful, but ultimately hardly essential for regular travel. This finding should not surprise us. Besides the fact that significant swaths of terrain (including sea ice) used by Iglulingmiut are not differentiated by inuksuit, should navigation around Igloolik significantly rely on such markers, travel throughout the area would necessarily be severely restricted to periods of good visibility. Besides darkness and low light levels, the Arctic's notorious recurrent fog, whiteouts, mist, snow, ground drift, and full-blown blizzards would frequently obscure the inuksuit, making long-distance travel difficult, dangerous, or impossible. This clearly was not the case. Iglulingmiut in fact possessed the necessary combination of skills and knowledge needed to travel confidently throughout their lands, if need be in virtually any kind of weather: their very survival depended on this ability.

ON BEING GROUNDED

For Iglulingmiut, wayfinding was firmly based, as Aipilik Inuksuk says, "on being aware of the ground," meaning topography generally and, in winter, especially snowdrifts.[44] Snowdrifts formed by the prevailing wind, *uangnaq*, were by far the preferred guide, especially in bad weather.[45] These rock-hard, enduring drifts—called *uqalurait* due to their "tongue-like" shape—are formed (in the Igloolik area) along an axis bearing approximately northwest/southeast, the "tongue" pointing northwards.[46] For Emile Imaruittuq they were "the most reliable source for establishing bearings."[47]

Abraham Ulajuruluk refers to *uqalurait* as "your only available aid" when the visibility is obscured through darkness or bad weather—"they have a use that we surely cannot do without."[48] In the interviews, other phenomena, including winds, stars, the sun, ocean currents, and the "water sky"—the bluish colouration above the horizon indicating the direction of the floe edge—were all mentioned in a navigational context ahead of inuksuit. Moreover, Iglulingmiut elders describing travel to destinations distant from Igloolik invariably invoked routes not as predetermined progressions along trails marked by inuksuit, but as dynamic "memoryscapes," interlacing memory of place, belonging, and story with the minutiae of horizons, shores, raised beaches, lakes, river valleys, hills, and promontories. Relevant details of place-names, seasonal snow conditions, drift formation and wind bearings, and so forth completed the picture.[49]

In the following extract from an interview with Theo Ikummaq, we glimpse the essential role of memory in retaining complex interrelated details of landforms, as well as the conceptual power of Inuktitut employed to describe to others the salient features of landscape. On his way from Repulse Bay (now Naujaat) to Igloolik, Theo and his companions strayed off the trail and became "temporarily misplaced." Needing assistance, they called Theo's uncle on their shortwave radio. Theo continues:

> [My] uncle asked, "If you are facing downwind, what do you see?" So you describe what you see … a couple of hills, a couple of large hills. "Facing toward the wind, what do you see?" … Some rocky outcrops. And then "to your left (that means towards Naujaat) what do you see? Look to your left, what do you see?" I see a narrow rocky outcrop, but it ends, and then it starts again a little further on and then it continues…. And then [my uncle] just goes ahead and says: "That's the trail to take … go between that and then you will find the main trail." And such was the case. [My uncle] wasn't there. But he could determine where I was from what I described.[50]

In this era of GPS satellite navigation, productive exchanges of topographical and directional information such as this are becoming rare. Loss of specific terminologies essential for expressing subtle details of topography and spatial positioning, along with the shifting observational powers of those raised within Igloolik's semi-urban setting, has for years been taking its toll on traditional wayfinding. Noah Piugaattuk, frustrated about the demise of such skills, recalled censuring young hunters who became disoriented on a trip from Pond Inlet to Igloolik: "I lectured them ... because they were ignorant.... They could see the sun and the ground [and they still got lost]. They were old enough but were not trying to know these things."[51]

Unmistakably identifying the unique structural characteristics of any inuksuk used for orientation is a crucial but often overlooked aspect of "inuksuit navigation." The popular idea that inuksuit everywhere are envoys imbued with esoteric meaning—"silent messengers of the Arctic," as Hallendy terms them—warrants some consideration, not least in a navigational context.[52] Obviously, all inuksuit and inuksuk-like structures were purpose-built, no matter how lofty, practical, or banal the reason. The original function of many structures is often discernible through their form and context—caribou drifts and blinds, "beehive" fox traps, and meat cache markers, for instance—but with many others, less so or not at all. With such structures, in the absence of any specific local knowledge or oral history about their origins and purposes, anything we can conclude about them is pure speculation. Navigationally, at least, they carry no intrinsic meaning. In a blizzard, a disoriented traveller happening upon an inuksuk never seen before is offered no guidance at all. Logically, to use a so-called "directional inuksuk" effectively, at least two conditions are necessary: positive recognition of the inuksuk, and knowing where it points. Without such specific knowledge, using inuksuit or indeed any topographical features to make navigational decisions is downright dangerous.[53] And so, along with Rachel Ujarasuk, all we can say with certainty about any inuksuk encountered in a place not previously visited, is a doubtless comforting: "*Inuqalauqsimajuviniq aasin*"—"Indeed ... people have been here before."[54] This supports nicely William Fitzhugh's point that inuksuit everywhere, whatever their purpose, at an elemental level served to humanize landscape.[55]

THE ACCIDENTAL INUKSUK

Over some sixty years of intermittent journeying with Inuit—initially by dog team, latterly by snowmobile—in several parts of Nunavut and Nunavik, I recall only one (accidental, yet fortuitous) instance of witnessing an inuksuk being used for orientation. This was in the late 1980s, in the early spring, returning to Igloolik from a fishing trip at Ugarjualik.[56] My companion was Leah Otak's father, Aipilik Inuksuk. Crossing the narrow icebound strait between Avvajja and Igloolik Island, the brisk wind suddenly increased to gale force, engulfing us in a full blizzard. Being at this point only seven or eight kilometres from home, we proceeded in zero visibility, confident that we would run into something recognizable. We eventually did: an inuksuk. This was puzzling. We had rather expected to encounter some of the cabins on the island's shore, or failing that, the town's outlying buildings. Getting off our snowmobiles, we examined the structure carefully. The inuksuk looked vaguely familiar to me. Aipilik, however, recognized it immediately as one of the many fairly recently erected inuksuit on "Cemetery Hill," a prominent bluff to the north of the community. With our position thus established and doubly confirmed by a limestone outcrop—also recognized by Aipilik—we reoriented ourselves accordingly and drove safely home, following one of the island's ancient raised beaches known to Aipilik since his youth.

Nicely illustrating the fortuity of being redirected by an inuksuk not specifically built as a navigational aid, this incident again reinforces a core point about Inuit wayfinding: detailed knowledge of the land's topography at both the macro and micro levels is indispensable. It also demonstrates something of the role of culturally conditioned observational powers. In good weather over many years, I had skied past this same inuksuk numerous times. I had seen it, of course, but not in the way Aipilik had.[57]

RESTORING ICONS

Scott Heyes correctly observes that inuksuit "are one of the few remaining tangible fabrics of Inuit society that continue to function within an original setting."[58] He writes passionately about the need to protect the structures' authenticity and integrity within the Arctic milieu. His concerns, however, are mainly for the physical preservation of inuksuit endangered by mining and industrial development. Parallel considerations are needed to safeguard the diverse, intangible

The international reach of the anthropoidal inuksuk. Leah Otak standing beside an inuksuk gracing a garden in Sturminster Newton, Dorset, England, 2000. Photo by John MacDonald

cultural associations and uses of the inuksuk, now under immense threat owing in large part to its universal appropriation, reinvention, and incessant mythologizing.

As previously noted, orthodoxies about the inuksuk's form, function, and symbology, emanating from the south, are now increasingly espoused in communities throughout the Canadian Arctic. The proliferation of human-shaped representations of inuksuit, driven largely by tourism and the Inuit art market, serve to further validate southern stereotypes and expectations.[59] Perceptions of the "ideal" inuksuk have become entrenched to the point where surely few schoolchildren in Nunavut invited to draw one would depict anything other than the ubiquitous anthropoid.

Stereotypes are notoriously difficult to challenge, far less eradicate, and attempts to do so at best usually result in some form of accommodation. As we have seen, the elders of Igloolik, resisting the construction of their community's massive, anthropoidal millennium inuksuk, agreed to let the project proceed on the condition that it be balanced by placing, on each side of the inuksuk, two unadorned cairns, representative of the traditional *inuksugait* commonly found throughout the Igloolik area. A bronze plaque attached to a concrete block near one of the cairns spells out, in Inuktitut and English, the point the elders wished to make.[60]

Correctly resituating both the inuksuk and the North Star within their proper and varied cultural context will require significant effort, promotion, and public education. Leading by example, the government of Nunavut might start by augmenting the meagre information currently given on its Legislative Assembly's website relating to the graphic symbols displayed on the territory's flag.[61] Informed by oral histories covering astronomy, navigation, and inuksuit use, representative of all Nunavut's regions—north and south—the remedial process might include profiling something of the intricacy and ingenuity embodied in traditional Inuit wayfinding practices. Importantly, the inuksuk's role in Inuit navigation needs to be understood in its proper context, not as a basis for wayfinding, but simply as one part—albeit an evocative one—of that complex set of multiple aptitudes, skills, and their applications that have enabled generations of Inuit to travel confidently and productively throughout their lands.

BIBLIOGRAPHY

Aporta, Claudio. 2004. "Routes, Trails and Tracks: Trail Breaking among the Inuit of Igloolik." *Études/Inuit/Studies* 28, no. 2: 9–38.

———. 2016. "Markers in Space and Time: Reflections on the Nature of Place Names as Events in the Inuit Approach to the Territory." In *Marking the Land: Hunter-Gatherer Creation of Meaning within their Surroundings*, edited by Robert Whallon and William Lovis, 67–88. New York: Routledge.

Aporta, Claudio, and John MacDonald. 2005. "Navigation, Indigenous." In *Encylopedia of the Arctic* (vol. 2), edited by Mark Nuttall, 1410–1413. New York: Routledge.

Bennett, John, and Susan Rowley, eds. 2004. *Uqalurait: An Oral History of Nunavut*. Montreal and Kingston: McGill-Queen's University Press.

Briggs, Jean. 1997. "From Trait to Emblem and Back: Living and Representing Culture in Everyday Inuit Life." *Arctic Anthropology* 34, no. 1: 227–235.

Canadian Encyclopedia. 2013. "Inuksuk (Inukshuk)." *The Canadian Encyclopedia*. Last modified September 15, 2015.

CBC News. 2017. "Inukshuk Art at Toronto's Pearson Airport Angers Some Inuit in Nunavut." *CBC News*, September 27.

Davidson, Peter. 2016. *The Idea of North*. London: Reakrion Books.

Dube, Rebecca. 2007. "Enough with the inukshuks already." *Globe and Mail*, August 15.

Fitzhugh, William. 2017. "Mongolian Deer Stones, European Menhirs, and Canadian Arctic Inuksuit: Collective Memory and the Function of Northern Monument Traditions." *Journal of Archaeological Method and Theory* 24, no. 1: 149–187.

Fortescue, Michael. 1988. "Eskimo Orientation Systems." In *Meddelelser om Grønland*, Man and Society, 11.

Governor General of Canada. n.d. "Creation of the Coat of Arms and Flag of Nunavut." Heraldry. Accessed March 5, 2018. archive.gg.ca/heraldry/emb /02/index_e.asp.

Graburn, Nelson. 2004. "Inuksuk: Icon of the Inuit of Nunavut." *Études/Inuit/ Studies* 28, no. 1.

Grace, Sherrill. 2002. *Canada and the Idea of North.* Montreal and Kingston: McGill-Queen's University Press.

Hallendy, Norman. 2000. *Inuksuit: Silent Messengers of the Arctic.* Vancouver: Douglas and McIntyre.

———. 2009. *Tukiliit: The Stone People Who Live in the Wind*. Vancouver: Douglas and McIntyre.

Heyes, Scott. 2002. "Protecting the Authenticity and Integrity of Inuksuit within the Arctic Milieu." *Études/Inuit/Studies* 26, no. 2: 133–156.

Ikummaq, Theo. 2000a. Interview IE-466. Igloolik Oral History Project. Igloolik.

———. 2000b. Interview IE-478. Igloolik Oral History Project. Igloolik.

Inuksuk, Aipilik. 1988. Interview IE-039. Igloolik Oral History Project. Igloolik.

Inukshuk Capital Management, Inc. n.d. Inukshuk Capital Management. Accessed January 29, 2018. inukshukcapital.com.

Jelen, Jenny. 2010. "The Inukshukification of Highway 69." *Sudbury.com*, September 22.

Julie Kinnear Team. n.d. "About Inukshuk Philosophy." About. Accessed January 29, 2018. juliekinnear.com/about/inukshuk-philosophy.

Kappianaq, George. 1986. Interview IE-071. Igloolik Oral History Project. Igloolik.

———. 1990. Interview IE-167. Igloolik Oral History Project. Igloolik.

Kaste, Martin. 2010. "Vancouver Olympic Logo: A Smiling Marker of Death?" *All Things Considered, National Public Radio*, February 18.

Kunuk, Pauli. 1990, Interview IE-087. Igloolik Oral History Project. Igloolik

———. 1991, Interview IE-171. Igloolik Oral History Project. Igloolik.

Legislative Assembly of Nunavut. n.d. "The Flag of Nunavut." About the Assembly. Accessed February 1, 2018.

MacDonald, John. 2000. *The Arctic Sky: Inuit Astronomy, Star Lore, and Legend.* Toronto: Royal Ontario Museum/Iqaluit: Nunavut Research Institute.

MacGregor, Elena Rivera. 2010. "Why the Inukshuk Represents the Heart of Canada." *Sustainability Television*, February 2010.

Marshall, Tim. 2017. *Worth Dying For: The Power and Politics of Flags.* New York: Scribner.

Mathiassen, Therkel. 1928. "Knowledge of Topography." In *Report of the Fifth Thule Exhibition 1921–1924* 6, no. 11: 97–100. Copenhangen: Gyldendalske Boghandel.

McGhee, Robert. 2001. *The Arctic Voyages of Martin Frobisher: An Elizabethan Adventure.* Washington: University of Washington Press/London: British Museum Press.

National Geographic. 2010. "Vancouver 2010: Olympic Logo No 'Friend' to Some." *National Geographic*, February 13.

Pelly, David. 1991. "How Inuit Find Their Way in the Trackless Arctic." *Canadian Geographic* (August).

Piugaattuk, Noah. 1988. Interview IE-040. Igloolik Oral History Project. Igloolik.

Qamaniq, Nathan. 2002. Interview IE-496. Igloolik Oral History Project. Igloolik.

Rasing, Willem. 2017. *Too Many People: Contact, Disorder, Change in an Inuit Society, 1822–2015.* Iqaluit: Nunavut Arctic College Media.

RoadsideAmerica.com. 2016. "Schomberg, Ontario, Canada: World's Largest Inukshuk." Tips. July 22. www.roadsideamerica.com/tip/53759.

Siakuluk, Noah. 1996. Interview IE-384. Igloolik Oral History Project. Igloolik.

Skorondeski, Laura. 2014. "Appropriation (?) of the Month: 'Ilanaaq'—Logo for the 2010 Vancouver Olympic Games," *IPinCH* (blog), October 29.

Ujarasuk, Rachael. 2002. Interview IE-498. Igloolik Oral History Project. Igloolik.

Vallee, Mickey. 2014. "Glenn Gould's The Idea of North: The Cultural Politics of Benevolent Domination." *TOPIA* 32: 1–21.

CHAPTER 16

Our Old Sod House

Sylvie LeBlanc

We had an old sod house in Ikpikitturjuaq. This is where I lived when I was little girl. The entrance had a low ceiling and there were doors on both sides between the ice dome and our living quarters. My grandfather's bed was on one side, he had a table for his qulliq. *There was my grandfather, my uncle Qamaniq, his wife Kattuuraannuk, and two small boys, Kuuttiq and Pakak. Then at the far end were my parents, our oldest sister Kigutikkaarjuk, Qannguq, my brother Nataaq, myself, and Rhoda.*

Our tent was just below the hill, right at the end of the lake. They used to hunt. They hunted in the sea, catching seals, bearded seals, sea mammals which they cached, until the fall when the caribou herd arrives; they grazed along both sides of the hill. All the animals there taste better ... bearded seal intestines are wider and crunchier in taste, the skins are much softer, and the texture is finer, even before the skin is dried. I am falling asleep now.

THIS IS HOW LEAH AND I WOULD fall asleep every night in our tent. She would first tell a bedtime story to her daughter Makpa, then turn around and tell me a story.

Leah and I came to work together in the context of a SSHRC Partnership Development Grant, *The Inuksuit Project: Ancient and Traditional Inuit Navigational Systems on Northern Baffin Island*. The project was developed within the framework of a formal partnership between the Nunavut Research Institute, the Igloolik Hunters and Trappers Organization, the Hamlet of Igloolik, and the Department of Sociology and Anthropology at Carleton University. The project set out to document ancient and traditional Inuit navigational systems and associated navigational/directional markers (*inuksuit*)[1] in the Ikpikitturjuaq area and document wayfinding practices of Inuit and their predecessors on the land. Inuit hunters have erected route markers known as *inuksuit* to direct travellers and draw attention to the places they deemed significant. These route markers created massive navigational systems that persist as part of the Arctic landscape.

In 2012, we set out on an extraordinary journey, returning to Leah's family homeland in Ikpikitturjuaq. By boat, foot, and helicopter we travelled to individual *inuksuit*, caribou drive lanes, and navigational systems, engaging in discussions about their ancestry and meaning. It was a strong bonding experience for all the people involved and together we lived exceptional and emotional moments returning to a land that is so deeply rooted in these families' identities. We navigated for days through a terrible storm, were attacked by bears—but most of all we were able to enjoy caribou, seal, rabbits, geese, and char from this generous land: *Ikpikitturjuaq—tamainnik piksaqtali* (Ikpikitturjuaq—the land of plenty).

This was not an easy project to get off the ground, but together with the local partners not only did we live a powerful human experience, we also managed to collect an impressive set of data and produced a series of videos. Six of these videos (*Qaiqsut, Everything Tastes Better Here, Our Old Sod House, Keep an Eye for the Wolves, Inuksuksiuqti—Norman Hallendy,* and *Inuksuit*) can currently be viewed on the local television channel and the IsumaTV website.[2]

The analysis of the material is still ongoing, but early in the project it became evident that:

1. Although *inuksuit* are still used or were traditionally used up until recently in relation to hunting activities (e.g., cache markers, fishing and caribou hunting locations, camps or special places), their use for navigational purposes is an ancient practice that appears to go beyond oral memory, and possibly beyond the limits of the ethnographic and historical record. The hunters and elders interviewed had heard about their use as navigational aids, but all agreed that it was beyond their time and that this knowledge has been lost over time. Elders seventy years and older remembered hearing their parents and grandparents talking about them, but most also mentioned that, as in traditional Inuit customs, children were not allowed to listen in on adult conversations and thus paid little attention to those about *inuksuit* when they were young.

2. Caution has to be exercised with regards to any historical projections regarding the longevity of travel routes. There is a current view that Inuit have been using the same travel routes for centuries or even millennia. Modern modes of transportation—mainly snowmobiles—have contributed significantly in a shift of the exploitation range of a given territory. If, on the one hand, snowmobiles allow for faster and farther access to certain portions of the territory, they also—by intrinsic mechanical virtues—restrict access to rough and difficult terrain. This was not the case when people were living on the land, travelling by foot or dog team. With regards to an ancient wolf-hunting territory, an elder remarks that "the land is too rough, hills and mountains are too steep for ski-doo … people before us, our ancestors, created these traps [referring to wolf traps]."

I have to wonder if Leah and I ever had a real working relationship, as life and work soon became intertwined. In reviewing some of the material we had collected, Leah couldn't believe we had gathered so much information, as work was always done with a light touch, joy, and grace, with Makpa often playing among us.

Leah is now Nuna—part of the land, part of everything—standing tall on the cemetery promontory, watching over all of us. I have kept my promise to her and took my turn putting Makpa to bed.

Every Friday evening my mom would make a big pot of soup for dinner. She would begin by making a rich broth from chicken bones. She would then chop some onions, carrots, celery, turnip, potatoes. My brothers and sister did not really like onions; she had to hide them from us.

I am falling asleep now … goodnight Makpa.

Leah Aksaajuq Otak, Joanna Qamaniq, and Eunice Palluq in the remains of their sod house in Ikpikitturjuak. 2012. LeBlanc, Inuksuit Project

Sunrise, Stories, and Snowhouses

A Conversation with Leah Otak[1]

Noah Richler

T HE FESTIVAL OF THE RETURN OF THE SUN took place, as planned, on the Saturday night and a few days before modern astronomy predicted the sun would rise, as the calendar of the Inuit is now governed by electric light and requires a Saturday, a Sunday, and a working week.

Outside the perimeter of the Arctic settlement, an igloo-building contest was being held on the northwest edge of town on clear land near the new Nunavut government offices. The air was crisp, the snow compact and hard—good snow, this. Inuit construct igloos by carving blocks out from the snow around where they stand, so that the dome of their traditional winter dwelling rises as the floor beneath the builder drops. The finished igloo sits slightly beneath surface level and is protected in this way from the worst ravages of the wind.

A group of younger Iglulingmiut were building igloos in an area beyond the dozen or so adult participants, and it was clear just how much speedier and more dexterous were the elder participants, including the only woman taking part in the competition. I watched her steady progress and listened to the tearing sound of the large serrated bread knife she was using to cut blocks of snow.

Igloo building by moonlight in preparation for celebrating the sun's return. Igloolik, January 2004. Photo by Noah Richler

How long would these skills endure, I wondered? Now snowmobiles take Inuit to where the caribou are and the distances their engines will take you make winter camps less necessary. The camps are not yet unnecessary, as Iglulingmiut need to roam farther and farther to find the caribou learning to travel in a wide arc around the humans' fixed settlements, yet, more often than not, the hunters return by evening to their insulated homes, where the creation myths and cautionary tales that once kept order in the community have been subverted by the new Qallunaat canon and its subversive instruments. No need to visit when you can use the telephone. No need to weave into the knit of a story the things to be remembered—the valley where a catch is effortlessly made, a couple of tricks to snare your intended prey—when the new technology means your message and your bearings can be conveyed immediately.

"All the hunters take these radios with them when they go hunting," said Louis Tapardjuk, who, with Leah Otak, was one of mainstays of the IOHP—the Igloolik Oral History Project.[2] "Everybody is constantly informed as to what's happening and there's no good stories coming back from the land anymore. Memory is so different now."

Tapardjuk exuded melancholy. "It's a problem," he said. "In our schools we teach our language but not the culture."

"And if you had a story to tell, Louis, would you tell it to your grandchild sitting on your knee, or would you write the story down?"

"I would write it down," Tapardjuk replied.

A few of the contestants and their families had started to regroup by their vehicles, idling all the while so their engines would stay warm. Some piled onto the backs of trucks, others onto snowmobiles. Leah Otak was gathered with her family, the lot of them resplendent in their furs and beautiful against the snow. Leah, I knew, had a winter cabin out on Ham Bay, on the west side of the island. Her cabin was popular with many parents who sent their children to be with her and hear the old stories.

"When you are there, you feel as if you are alone on Earth," said Leah after some coaxing. Leah picked her words carefully, one at a time and as if out of a box. So much, in the North, is about haste not being made, about critical energy not being wasted.

"Are there any legends you know that explain the Qallunaat?" I asked.

Leah—like so many Inuit, recalcitrant until she has the measure of you—smiled a little mischievously. "There's the story of Sedna, the woman who wouldn't take a husband and married a dog and gave birth to non-Inuit," she said.

"Don't worry," I joked. "I won't take it personally."

We shared an interest in stories and their effect, so I asked her about the IOHP that had started as a project on Inuit social history and expanded from there.

"We listened to the tapes and there was so much to learn," said Leah, "so we spoke to elders [about doing a project] and went from there."

"In your mind," I asked, "what are the stories about?"

"They're about everything," said Leah. "They're about language, they're about history. When we do the interviews we encourage elders to use traditional words."

"Is anything unfamiliar to you?"

"Yes," said Leah. "In particular, I've been learning about shaman-ism. We didn't practise shamanism when I was young."

"Tell me about the Festival of the Return of the Sun."

"This month is *Siqinnaarut*," said Leah. "It's the month following the darkest time of the year, when people were spending a lot of time [in their igloos] waiting for the sun. They had many activities includ-ing string games to pass the time when the sun was not above the horizon, and when the sun came back they cut the strings."

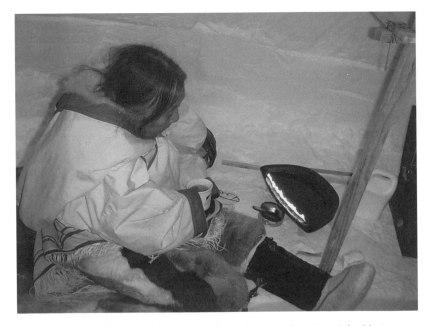

Thérèse Qillaq tends her oil lamp during the sun's return festivities. Igloolik, January 2002. Photo by Noah Richler

"It's also a time of storytelling, isn't it?"

"Oh yes. The dark months are a time for telling stories and legends."

"Is it still that?"

"Not so much," said Leah.

I asked about the school's "Language Week," another cultural initiative of which she'd been an impassioned proponent, in which the stories and legends are told in Inuktitut.

"Before moving back here," said Leah, "I was living in Arctic Bay where they don't speak as much English so I had the chance to relearn Inuktitut and be fluent again. When I came back to Igloolik I realized everybody was using two languages at the same time and at first when I was talking about Language Week on the radio everyone would call up and say, 'But I want my children to speak English.' And I would say, 'Me too, I teach my children to speak English, but I want them to be able to separate the two languages so that they learn to speak better English and better Inuktitut.' It's helped a lot of people. Of course, not everybody does it but those who do take part in a project like that tell you how much better their children speak."

"Do you encourage the children to write stories at all?"

"I try to encourage children to do anything—to write a story, a legend, or whatever they know."

"Do you think writing is affecting the way the stories are told?

"Yes. Before my time, nobody wrote anything and nobody read anything. All the legends were told from generation to generation and they had the same wordings because they were not allowed to alter anything in the story. But nowadays we have so much to read and so much to write that we are not telling the legends anymore and it is as if we have to squeeze them to provide balance. But I think there are a few children who will learn the legends now."

"So you're worried about the Inuktitut skills and language being lost. Is that because the life is changing? I know your cabin is dear to you because people go out on the land for less and less time."

"Oh yes," said Leah, "children whose parents are working all the time don't have a chance to get out before spring. They don't have the chance to experience the land and so for that reason we have a little cabin hidden away from the lights. It's more than walking distance but the children that come along with us want to come back every time."

"And you have to entertain the children by giving them stories?"

"Yes. A woman came to me one time and said, 'Thank you so much.' I asked for what and she said, 'Last night my daughter wanted me to tell her legends but I don't know how.' I don't tell the legends as they were because there would be a language barrier for a child, so I change the words a little and talk about what I saw when I was a child. I'll tell them about the setup of a sod house or how we would go on a dog team, just to use the words for telling the stories."

"Why do you think stories were invented?"

"A lot of the legends have to do with abusing animals or people who are not well. They help you to compare your life and to learn what happens if you are not being kind. They also help you find your way about the land and provide knowledge to children by doing that—our conditions have changed but people want to be a part of it. When you give them a chance to learn something they are all for it."

"I believe that some sort of course in Indigenous studies or language should be a compulsory requirement for all Canadians wanting to graduate from high school. Does that strike you as a silly plan?"

"No," said Otak, "I don't think so. That's what I'm doing in Language Week. And I discovered young people *want* to be fluent in Inuktitut."

"What are the skills of a storyteller?" I asked.

"To have the knowledge and be interesting so you give people the chance to listen."

"Do you think Inuit will be writing these stories soon?"

"Yes. But some stories are only possible in English. It's hard to tell stories with modern technology, for example, because we do not have the words."

"Can you imagine a wonderful storyteller telling a story of our current age twenty years from now?"

"I hope so. The legends were created because of incidents that happened and what they taught us. I'd say it's about time we started to create legends for today."

A half-smile indicated she wanted to go, and I watched as snow-mobilers buzzed a noisy path around the igloos of the remaining contestants. Other Iglulingmiut revved their engines and chatted, lifting their vehicles' hoods like piston heads anywhere. Quiet would have to wait until evening.

The finished igloos looked like bubbles on the snow. They melded into the blue-white plain as if they had always been there. Their domes belonged to the landscape and were organic in a way that the landed, humming buildings of the Qallunaat—the A-frames and bunkhouses found all over the Canadian Arctic, and the churches and huge sports centres complete with hockey rinks and curling facilities—were not. Later that evening I returned to the site on my own and crept inside the opening of one of the abandoned igloos. The light of the moon illuminated spots in the igloo's canopy of snow and the joins between its component blocks. The dome was an analogy of the heavens, complete with constellations and northern lights. Cold after a few minutes, I moved off the raised platform that would have been layered with furs in an earlier time, and around which Inuit would have told stories until their eyes started to droop, warding off hunger and worry and hoping for the sun's imminent return and its heralding of the calendar's easier months. I shuffled out through the igloo's tunnel exit on my belly and tried to imagine the fears, excitements, anxieties, and aspirations an Inuit hunter would have had as he did so. Evening was approaching and the field of empty igloos appeared like the pieces of some ephemeral art installation. Within days, the snowhouses would crumble and be gone. Within years, Leah's work notwithstanding, the skill of building may well be esoteric.

Contributors

Eva Aariak, currently President of the Inuit Heritage Trust and a Commissioner with the Inuit Circumpolar Council's Pikialasorsuaq (North Water polynya) Commission, has worked for many years in public service, including a term as Premier of Nunavut between 2008 and 2013. She was appointed Nunavut's first Languages Commissioner in 1999, an office she held for five years, and is a tireless promoter of Inuit culture and language. She owns and manages the Malikkaat Boutique in Iqaluit, selling Inuit arts and crafts, handmade jewellery, and books by Inuit authors.

Claudio Aporta conducted ethnographic research in Igloolik at several times between 1998 and 2006. In Igloolik he travelled thousands of kilometres with Maurice Arnatsiaq and worked on the oral history collection and place-names projects with Leah Otak, Louis Tapardjuk, and John MacDonald. Aporta has published extensively on topics related to Inuit environmental knowledge, and his ongoing research includes mapping Inuit traditional routes across the Canadian Arctic. He is currently an associate professor and the director of the Marine Affairs Program, Dalhousie University.

Hugh Brody, anthropologist and filmmaker, holds the Canada Research Chair in Aboriginal Studies at the University of the Fraser

Valley in British Columbia, Canada. He holds honorary academic positions at the University of Cambridge and the University of Kent in Canterbury. His work has always been at the crossroads of social science, writing and film. In the 1970s and '80s he lived and worked with hunting peoples in the Canadian North. From 1996 to 2012 he contributed to the ‡Khomani San land claim in the northern Cape of South Africa and made a set of sixteen films about the claim (available as the DVD *Tracks Across Sand*). Brody's books include *Inishkillane*, *The People's Land*, *Maps And Dreams*, *Living Arctic*, *Means of Escape*, and *The Other Side of Eden*. His films include *The Meaning of Life* and the feature *Nineteen Nineteen*, starring Paul Scofield and Maria Schell. He worked closely with Leah Otak on the selection of objects for the British Museum's 2001 Inuit clothing exhibition *Annuraaq: Arctic Clothing from Igloolik*.

Sheena Kennedy Dalseg is a Ph.D. candidate in the School of Public Policy and Administration at Carleton University and Managing Editor of *Northern Public Affairs* magazine. Her doctoral research, based in Igloolik, traces the evolution of local responses to social and institutional change in the community beginning in the post-war period, focusing particularly on the historical and contemporary role that formal schooling has played therein. Kennedy Dalseg first met Leah Otak in 2009, when she was working with the Hamlet on the Igloolik Socio-Economic Baseline Study. These early interactions with Leah and the Oral History Project have greatly influenced Kennedy Dalseg's approach to her work as a researcher and editor.

Louis-Jacques Dorais has researched Inuit culture, language, and society since 1965. From 1972 to 2011, he taught anthropology at Université Laval in Quebec City, and is now Professor Emeritus. In 1991, he and Leah Otak conducted interviews on knowledge and identity in Igloolik for a project on the social role of Inuit teachers. Among other titles, Dorais has published a linguistic description of Inuktitut as it is spoken in Igloolik (*Iglulingmiut Uqausingit: The Inuit Language of Igloolik NWT*, 1978), as well as a general introduction to the Inuit language (*The Language of the Inuit: Syntax, Semantics, and Society in the Arctic*, 2010).

Bernadette Driscoll Engelstad is a Research Collaborator with the Arctic Studies Center, Smithsonian Institution. She completed graduate studies at the Institute of Canadian Studies, Carleton University, Ottawa, and in the Program for the History of Art and Anthropology, Johns Hopkins University. As a curator and independent scholar, she has carried out research, organized exhibitions, and published extensively on Inuit clothing design, as well as the sculpture and graphic art of contemporary Inuit artists.

Kenn Harper is a historian, writer, and linguist who lived in the Arctic for fifty years. He lived in the communities of Qikiqtarjuaq, Padloping (Paallarvik), Pangnirtung, Arctic Bay, Iqaluit, and Qaanaaq (Greenland). He speaks Inuktitut and is a former member of the Historic Sites and Monuments Board of Canada. Kenn served as Honourary Danish Consul for Nunavut for twelve years until 2017. He is the author of *Minik, the New York Eskimo* (formerly published as *Give Me My Father's Body: The Life of Minik, the New York Eskimo*) and *Thou Shalt Do No Murder: Inuit, Injustice, and the Canadian Arctic*.

Jack Hicks served as Director of Research for the Nunavut Implementation Commission (NIC) and then as the Government of Nunavut's first Director of Evaluation and Statistics. He was Project Manager of *Qaujivallianiq Inuusirijauvalauqtunik* ("Learning from lives that have been lived"), a Nunavut suicide follow-back study. He served as the Government of Nunavut's Suicide Prevention Advisor during development of the Nunavut Suicide Prevention Strategy. Currently he is Adjunct Professor of Community Health and Epidemiology at the University of Saskatchewan, and Suicide Prevention Advisor to the Federation of Sovereign Indian Nations. He is co-author, with Graham White, of *Made in Nunavut: An Experiment in Decentralized Government*.

J.C.H. King is Von Hügel Research Fellow at the Museum of Archaeology and Anthropology, University of Cambridge. He began visiting Igloolik in 1986 for the *Living Arctic* exhibition at the Museum of Mankind, London, organized with George Qulaut, Rebecca Pappaq, Victor Aqatsiaq, Helen Oolalak, Hugh Brody, and John MacDonald. Later, with Leah Otak and Birgit Paukzstat, he worked on the *Arctic Clothing* (British Museum Publications, 2005) project. In 2016 King published an account of Indigenous people across the continent: *Blood and Land: The Story of Native North America* (London: Allen Lane).

Sylvie LeBlanc is an anthropologist and archaeologist specializing in Arctic archaeology. She is currently the Territorial Archaeologist for the Government of Nunavut and holding an Adjunct Research Professor position with the Department of Sociology and Anthropology at Carleton University. Over the past twenty years, she has been directing research projects in Nunavut, Newfoundland, and Saint-Pierre and Miquelon. She has authored several scholarly publications and has produced a series of documentaries in partnership with Leah Otak (Nunavut Research Institute) under The Inuksuit Project (available on the IsumaTV website).

John MacDonald spent most of his working life in the Canadian Arctic, including twenty-five years as coordinator of the Igloolik Research Centre. During this time he worked closely with Leah Otak, Louis Tapardjuk, and George Qulaut, documenting the oral history and traditional knowledge of the Inuit of the Igloolik area. MacDonald is author of *The Arctic Sky: Inuit Astronomy, Star Lore, and Legend*, a book stemming primarily from his collaborative work with Igloolik Inuit elders.

Birgit Pauksztat is a Senior Lecturer in the Department of Business Studies at Uppsala University's Campus Gotland in Visby, Sweden. Her interest in Greenland and the Arctic goes back to 1997, when she began studying Greenlandic history and language at the Ilisimatusarfik/University of Greenland in Nuuk. Since then, she has returned for several shorter visits to different parts of Greenland. As Thaw Special Assistant at the British Museum, she worked closely with J.C.H. King and Leah Otak on the exhibition *Annuraaq: Arctic Clothing from Igloolik* and on the associated conference and the subsequent publication, *Arctic Clothing of North America: Alaska, Canada, Greenland.*

George Quviq Qulaut is a skilled hunter, fisherman, and Nunavut politician. He was MLA for the Amittuq riding and Speaker of the Legislative Assembly of Nunavut from 2013 to 2017. He has served on numerous boards and agencies, including the Qikitaaluk Inuit Association, the Qikitaaluk Corporation, the Government of Nunavut's Inuit Qaujiimajatuqangit Katimajiingit Board, and the Historic Sites and Monuments Board of Canada. He was a founder of the Igloolik Oral History Project, and in his capacity as operations manager of the Igloolik Research Centre, he worked closely with Leah Otak for many years.

Willem Rasing is an anthropologist and historian. He teaches philosophy and is also an associated researcher with the Faculty of Philosophy, Theology, and Religious Studies at the Radboud University Nijmegen, The Netherlands. In 1985, he began his long-term anthropological study of Iglulingmiut contacts with the outside world, recently published as *Too Many People: Contact, Disorder, Change in an Inuit Society, 1822–2015.* During his fieldwork relating to this publication, he worked closely with Leah Otak in 2005 and in 2009.

Noah Richler, a frequent traveller to the Arctic, is an award-winning Canadian author, essayist, and broadcaster. He first visited Igloolik while researching *This Is My Country, What's Yours? A Literary Atlas of Canada* (McClelland & Stewart, 2006), at which time he participated in the community's Return of the Sun festivities. His other publications include *What We Talk About When We Talk About War* (Goose Lane Editions, 2012) and *The Candidate: Fear and Loathing on the Campaign Trail* (Doublebay Canada, 2016).

Susan Rowley is an associate professor in the Department of Anthropology and a curator at the Museum of Anthropology at the University of British Columbia. She worked closely with Leah Otak on numerous projects, including Inuit oral history relating to archaeological investigations in the Igloolik area, and in the organization of a summer archaeology course offered to Igloolik high school students for almost a decade, beginning in the mid-1980s. With John Bennett, she co-edited *Uqalurait: An Oral History of Nunavut* (McGill-Queen's University Press, 2005).

Nancy Wachowich is a Lecturer in Social Anthropology at the University of Aberdeen, Scotland. Her collaborative work, *Saqiyuq: Stories from the Lives of Three Inuit Women*, written with Apphia Agalakti Awa, Rhoda Kaukjak Katsak, and Sandra Pikujak Katsak, was awarded the 1999 Canadian Historical Association's Clio Award for the North and the 2000 Oral History Association (USA) Award for Best Project. Nancy Wachowich's friendship with Leah Aksaajuq Otak began in 1997, when she was living in Igloolik and conducting doctoral research. Leah's insights into Arctic colonial histories and women's skin sewing traditions have been an ongoing source of inspiration since that time. Nancy is co-founder, with Sheila Katsak, of the Mittimatalik Arnait Miqsuqtuit Collective, a women's collective that is creating a digital archive of skin sewing skills and promoting the sustainability of the art form.

Acknowledgments

The editors wish to thank those who penned essays for this collection; together, their varied contributions offer a most fitting tribute to the work of Leah Otak and her crucial role in advancing scholarly research in Igloolik and elsewhere in the Arctic.

The volume has benefited greatly from the help and advice of Leah's close family and friends. Rhoda Innuksuk and Becky Awa offered information on Leah's early life, while Louis Tapardjuk, George Qulaut, and Elizabeth Qulaut gave valuable insights on the initial endeavours to record Igloolik's oral history.

Sonia Gunderson's 2006 interview with Leah enhanced our understanding of Leah's highly informed views on the current challenges facing Inuit culture, language, and society. Photographs for several of the essays were graciously provided by Bryan and Cherry Alexander.

Mary Ellen Thomas, Nunavut Research Institute, and Sean Guistini, Nunavut Arctic College Media, provided enthusiastic support and encouragement throughout the project.

Finally, thanks are due to Jessie Hale of Inhabit Education, Iqaluit, who plied her first-rate copyediting skills to a collection of essays disparate in style and topic and made them better.

Notes

Leah Aksaajuq Otak: The Measure of a Stitch
and the Art of Translation

1. The Igloolik Oral History Project (IOHP) was a local initiative that began in the 1980s to document the stories and teachings of a generation of elders who had spent their early years practicing a land-based hunting lifestyle, travelling between seasonal family camps and trading posts. Contributors Aariak, Aporta, Qulaut, Hicks, MacDonald, Kennedy Dalseg, and Rasing all describe working with the IOHP, a resource that Leah Aksaajuq Otak administered during the last twenty years of her life.

2. For anthropological analyses of the association between narrative and agency, see also Cruikshank (1998) and Jackson (2002). For a discussion of storytelling and wayfinding among northern Indigenous hunters, see Ingold (2000) and Kwon (1998).

3. For published oral histories, see, for example, Rhoda Kaujak Katsak's autobiographical stories in *Saqiyuq: Stories from the Lives of Three Inuit Women* (Wachowich in collaboration with Awa et al. 1999) and those of the Nunavut Artic College Inuit Leaders Series. Public testimonies of social impacts of residential and federal day schooling are found in commission reports by the Qikiqtani Inuit Association (2010) and the Reconciliation Commission of Canada (2010). Scholarly accounts include MacGregor's detailed work on education policy in the eastern Arctic (2010).

4. Rasing reports four camps extant in 1986–87, comprising four families totalling thirty-nine persons (Rasing 2017, 213).

5. See also Aariak, this volume.
6. See, for example, Idlout and Otak (1995), Otak (2005), Otak et al. (2014). Some collaborations, such as those just cited, were seen through to the final stages by Leah, thus designating her as author. However, in far more Arctic scholarship than could be cited here, Leah Otak's collaborative contribution was in determining the parameters of the documentation rather than the writing up. Her placement as a key figure in Arctic scholarship and her influence on the field can thus be partially determined by reading the acknowledgment sections of theses, dissertations, and published works.
7. Law and Lin address similar instances of productive tension in collaborative post-colonial social science research, a process that they term "cultivating disconcertment" (2010).
8. Piugattuk's motivation resonated with that of Simon Anaviapik and a group of elders in Pond Inlet who expressed to Hugh Brody (Chapter 6) their reasons for participating in a documentary film project: "They also wanted to be given an assurance that it would be seen by 'the government'" (158).
9. In the context of anthropology's imperial past, see, for example, works by Kathleen Gough (1968) and Talal Asad (1974).
10. See, for example, Nicholas Thomas (1994) and Laura Ann Stoler (2009).
11. For an autobiographical account of such experiences, see Rhoda Kaukjak Katsak's account "This Group of Scientists" in Wachowich et al. (1999).
12. In my Ph.D. dissertation I address how Igloolik became known as a hub of tradition (Wachowich 2001).
13. See, for example, Engelstad (Chapter 3), but also Pharand (2013) and Wachowich (2014).

CHAPTER 1
Capturing Souls: Beginnings of Oral History Work in Igloolik

1. Transcribed from an interview with George Qulaut and John MacDonald, October 25, 2015.
2. Robert Petersen, now retired, was the first rector of the University of Greenland (Ilisimatusarfik). He served on the (Canadian) Inuit Language Commission's Standing Advisory Committee from 1973 to 1976. Jørgen Meldgaard, the Danish archaeologist, excavated early Dorset sites around Igloolik in 1954, 1957, and 1965.

3. Andy Rode was appointed scientist-in-charge of the Research Centre when it opened in 1975. Rode, a physiologist, studied the health and fitness of Igloolik Inuit over several decades.

4. Father Fournier had started the Inummariit Society in 1969. For details on this initiative, see John MacDonald in this volume (Chapter 2).

5. Thomas Kublu later acknowledged the importance of preserving traditional knowledge. The final years of his life were spent working on oral history programs for the government of Nunavut.

6. Walter Slipchenko, a career public servant, worked principally on Canada's circumpolar relations. He died in 2016.

7. By the time of his death in 1995, Piugaattuk had contributed more interviews to the project than any other participant. These interviews will form the basis of a book, in progress, to be published by Nunavut Arctic College Media.

8. Emile Imaruittuq became a major participant in the Igloolik Oral History Project. In addition he compiled an annotated listing of Amitturmiut place-names, which became the primary source for all subsequent toponomy work in the Igloolik area. Imaruittuq also assembled a dictionary of the Amitturmiut dialect under the auspices of the (now disbanded) Inuit Cultural Institute.

9. See Willem Rasing's chapter in this volume (Chapter 13).

10. *Tuqłurausiit*: terms of address and relationship based on shared naming. Inuit custom requires that, in some forms of *tuqłurausiit,* individuals bound by this relationship should not speak to each other out of respect.

11. Administered by the Canadian Polar Commission, the award is presented annually to an individual or a group that has made a significant contribution to meritorious knowledge and understanding of the Canadian North.

CHAPTER 2

Stories and Representation: Two Centuries of Narrating Amitturmiut History

1. Amitturmiut is the name by which the Inuit of present-day Igloolik and Hall Beach call themselves. In the anthropological literature, they would be included under the Iglulingmiut, as defined by Rasmussen and Mathiassen (see Mary-Rousselière 1984, 431). Rasmussen (1929) mentions the "Amijormiut," explaining that "they are part of the Iglulik tribe in the wider sense of the word" (9).

2. The term "narrative" here encompasses both written and oral records along with photographs, drawings, and paintings depicting Amitturmiut life. Beyond the scope of this essay is the emergence of other "narratives" of self-representation, particularly in political and artistic realms, in place by the 1980s. These include, for instance, land claims negotiations, the blossoming of the Inuit commercial art market, local and regional Inuktitut radio broadcasts, and the television and film output of the Inuit Broadcasting Corporation, especially from Igloolik's Isuma Productions (established in 1990). The advent of the Internet, and with it the Amitturmiut's enthusiastic embracing of social media, has created unprecedented opportunities for self-representation and discourse on cultural identity. The mundane chatter of postings is frequently punctuated with poignant reminiscences of family and community, many of them touchingly illustrated with old photographs.

3. This essay itself is, of course, of this genre.

4. Parry's "Second Voyage for the Discovery of a North-West Passage." Parry's ships were the *Fury* and the *Hecla*, the latter commanded by George Francis Lyon. (See Parry 1824.)

5. The first winter in the area (1821–22) was passed near the small island of Niuviligjuaq (duly dubbed "Winter Island" by Parry), near Maluksittan (Lyon Inlet). Here, in February 1822, he first made contact with the Amitturmiut. In 1822–23 Parry's expedition overwintered at Ikpiardjuk (Turton Bay), Igloolik Island.

6. Publishers to the Admiralty and Board of Longitude, John Murray's firm, published all of the Parry voyages, as well as Lyon's "Private Journal." See Cavell 2008 for details on the reception and sale of Arctic exploration narratives.

7. An additional account of Parry's 1821–23 expedition is found in the unpublished journal of William Harvey Hooper. Hooper's journal (currently being transcribed, edited, and annotated by John MacDonald and Willem Rasing) significantly complements the material gathered by Parry and Lyon on Amitturmiut society.

8. Lyon's skill as a portrait artist was confirmed by the Inuit themselves. Forty-five years after Lyon's visit, Charles Francis Hall showed copies of Lyon's Inuit portraits to the Amitturmiut. Hall records in his diary that these depictions of Inuit, many of them long dead, moved surviving relatives and friends to tears, so closely were the likenesses captured by Lyon.

9. One of the better-known derivatives of the expedition's journals is a children's book titled *A Peep at the Esquimaux* (1825), written in verse and illustrated with grossly distorted drawings of Inuit, based on Lyon's depictions of Amitturmiut. The book's raw racial epithets give a demeaning impression of Inuit, quite in keeping with the 19th century's view of native peoples in general. (See MacDonald 2012, 143–151.)

10. Franz Boas, in his seminal work, *The Central Eskimo* (1888), cites Parry and Lyon frequently as "authorities."

11. In February and March 1867, and again in March 1868 (Cooke and Holland 1978, 223–224).

12. See Nourse (1879, 111–113); Parry (1824, 410–412); MacDonald (2012, 142–151).

13. Many of Hall's detailed accounts of Inuit, including his travels and interactions with the Amitturmiut, are contained in his copious notebooks preserved in the archives of the Smithsonian Institution, Washington.

14. For an overview of Bernier's Arctic involvement, see Saint-Pierre (2009).

15. Tremblay 1921, 232–233; Rasmussen 1927, 16–17; Ukkumaaluk 2009, 110–111. For a well-documented, accessible account of this tragedy, see Harper (2013, 156–162).

16. Members of the expedition included: Therkel Mathiassen, Kaj Birket-Smith, Peter Freuchen, Helge Bangsted, Jacob Olsen, Aarqioq and Arnannguaq, Nasaitordluarssuk, Aqatsaq, Arnarulunnguaq, Ajako, Qavigarssuaq, and Leo Hansen.

17. An early account of Bazin's tribulations is found in Morice (1943, 207–233).

18. *Cold Comfort: My Love Affair with the Arctic* (Rowley 2007); Appendix D of Rowley's book lists publications by members of the British Canadian Arctic Expedition. For an overview of Rowley's life and career, see MacDonald (2004, 223–224).

19. Only in recent years have Amitturmiut had access to this literature, often received with mixed reviews.

20. The Amitturmiut, through trade with other Inuit groups in sporadic contact with British whalers, possessed at the time of Parry's visit a few implements made of metal. They were, however, "untouched" by direct contact with the outside world. Parry makes a point of favourably contrasting the unaffected virtues of the Amitturmiut with what he regarded as the corrupted, degraded Inuit spoiled by European contact, met with in Hudson Strait during the expedition's voyage north (Parry 1824). Exemplified in the writings of Parry, Lyon, and many subsequent

chroniclers of the Amitturmiut is Hugh Brody's point that "information" gathered by Europeans about native peoples is never neutral, but "deeply comparative. We look at 'them' with reference to 'us' … in order to note relative superiority" (Brody 1987, xiii).

21. Even Rasmussen could not escape this shortcoming. Kirsten Thisted (2010, 74) puts it well:

> With his double cultural background Rasmussen was able to give voice to the Inuit—but even when he claims to be merely a translator, it is not always easy to see where his own voice is taking over…. The cultural translator grants himself great privileges in terms of the power to represent and define, just as Rasmussen's own character and his role as a cultural translator have a tendency to command attention, to a certain degree at the cost of the material he travelled to collect.

22. Commenting on "narrative framing," Hastrup (2016, 111–133) notes that "We all do it, in some sense; our ethnographic moments are imbued with narrative framing from the start."

23. In addition, Rasmussen in his *Intellectual Culture of the Iglulik Eskimos* (1929) makes no use of Parry's or Lyon's observations on Amitturmiut culture and society, even where this would have been enlightening for comparative purposes. Not so for Therkel Mathiassen, who cites and cross-references Parry and Lyon frequently in his *Material Culture of the Iglulik Eskimos* (1928), as well as touching on Christianity and syllabic writing.

24. Rasmussen, in his summary of the Fifth Thule Expedition, *Across Arctic America* (1927), does speculate gloomily on the consequences of modernity: "There can be no step back from the Stone Age for any people that has once had contact with the white man" (303).

25. For an accessible example of Rasmussen's rendering of the Inuit "voice," see Tagurnaaq's telling of the Ataguttaaluk starvation story in Harper (2013, 156–160).

26. Lyon's meticulous drawings, published as engravings in Parry's journal, were used by the Igloolik Oral History Project to elicit information from the elders on tools and hunting implements long fallen out of use.

27. A graphic example of this tit-for-tat is the Inuit drawing of Parry: "An Igloolik Eskimo drew Parry; Lyon drew Eskimos" (see Brody 1975, opposite 120; see also Carpenter 1997, 88).

28. Parry's arrival was foretold in a song in which the singer hears the sound, carried on the wind, of ice banging against the hulls of wooden ships

making their way north (Noah Piugaattuk 1986, IE-064; 1993, IE-248). The widespread legend of Uinigumasuittuq ("she who never wants a husband") is one of the foundational narratives of Inuit in the Canadian Eastern Arctic. The legend accounts for the creation of both the white and First Nations peoples. See Kappianaq in MacDonald (2000, 237–238); MacDonald (2012, 149); Eber (2008, 19–21).

29. "It is said that [Tremblay] had a pistol so with it he shot the Island of Igloolik as he walked around the shoreline. [Afterwards] he said that Igloolik was dead and that a ship will now be able to get to the Island" (Iqallijuq 1991, IE-204).

30. According to Piugaattuk, "[Tremblay] became mentally unstable so therefore people thought if he was provoked he would be capable of murdering someone—so for that reason he never came this way again." (1994, IE-303).

31. Mathiassen (1928, 232–233) mentions that "pencils and pocketbooks ... were in great demand" for writing letters in syllabics.

32. See Rowley (2007). Establishment of the HBC at Igloolik was made largely on the advice of John Ell (Aullanaq)—an Aivilingmiuk—employed at the company's post on Southampton Island (Copeland 1985, 71). The post at Igloolik closed between 1943 and 1947 due to "unfavourable ice conditions" (Usher 1971, 132).

33. Umik, a shaman from the Tunnuniq area (Pond Inlet), introduced a form of syncretic Christianity to Igloolik, c. 1920. (See Laugrand and Oosten 2010, 49–52.)

34. The Hudson's Bay Company Archives are part of the Manitoba Archives, Winnipeg; Records of the Roman Catholic Oblate Mission are held with the Roman Catholic Diocese of Churchill–Baie d'Hudson, Churchill, Manitoba, and at La Maison Notre Dame, Richelieu, Quebec. Anglican Mission records are held at the Archives of the General Synod of the Anglican Church of Canada, Toronto, and RCMP reports at the National Archives in Ottawa. Church Missions in many Arctic locations often hold records of local significance.

35. The original of the "Liber Animorum" in French is held at St. Étienne's Roman Catholic Mission, Igloolik, Nunavut. In 1983, an English translation was made of the document.

36. Mary-Rousselière served as a priest at the RC Missions in Pond Inlet and Igloolik (Gordon 1994, 318). For details on Mary-Rousselière's life, and an extensive bibliography of his writings, including those in *Eskimo* magazine (1947–93), see Choque (1998).

37. Mary-Rousselière recorded interviews across Nunavut between the 1940s and the early 1970s. See Chapter 2 in Laugrand and Oosten (2009) for the transcript of recordings made of William Ukkumaaluk from Igloolik.

38. The bibliography of Crowe's *A Cultural Geography of Northern Foxe Basin* (1969) provides an extensive listing of significant works, published and unpublished, relating to the Amitturmiut area up until 1968.

39. See Meldgaard (1960); Rowley and Rowley (1997); Appelt et al. (2007).

40. Harrington's work was used by George Qulaut in the 1990s as a pictorial *aide memoir* when interviewing elders participating in the Igloolik Oral History Project (see King and Lidchi 1998, 19–23). Harrington's photographs are held at Library and Archives Canada in Ottawa. Malaurie's work is published in his book *Call of the North* (2001). In the summer of 1954, Richard Emerick, an archaeologist assisting Jørgen Meldgaard with his excavations on Igloolik Island (Rowley and Rowley 1997), made a short documentary film of Amitturmiut open-water hunting methods for walrus and polar bear. Available at http://nordligeverdener.natmus .dk/en/the-carpenter-meldgaard-endowment/videos-and-photos/films -from-igloolik-1954.

41. Review of *Call of the North* from Amazon.com.

42. By the 1980s, these structures had become so much a part of the Amittuq landscape that their radar towers were used as landmarks for Inuit hunters around Hall Beach. Plans to demolish these towers were strongly resisted by the Hall Beach Community Council (Picco 1993, 252; Mac-Donald 2000, 191).

43. See Mowat's *People of the Deer* (1952) and *The Desperate People* (1959).

44. For various perspectives on this policy, including confusion in government circles, see Damas (2004). Inuit transition from land to settlement informed the novel *Arctic* by Finn Schultz-Lorentzen (1976), who was, for a period in the 1970s, a government administrator in Igloolik.

45. Significantly, in the Amittuq area as late as 1985, there were still half a dozen families living on the land, but by 2005 the last of these had moved into the settlement. Some of the families tenaciously opting to remain on the land are evocatively represented in the photographs of Bryan and Cherry Alexander (see Alexander and Alexander 1996, 2011). See also Robert Semeniuk's *Among the Inuit* (2007), which visually and vividly contrasts Amitturmiut culture change at two points in recent time: the mid-1970s and late 1990s. Hugh Brody's remarkable foreword to this book elucidates the strengths and limitations of a photographic representation.

46. Amitturmiut were fortunate in that the settlements of Igloolik and Hall Beach are close to several polynyas, traditional hunting areas for seal and

especially walrus. In many other settlements, however, access to hunting grounds was more distant, thereby incurring the hunter considerable inconvenience and cost.

47. In this context, "traditional culture" is taken to mean the relatively independent, land based way of life enjoyed by the Amitturmiut prior to their move into the settlements.

48. Hugh Brody, pers. comm., August 13, 2017. The ILUOP materials go well beyond those included in the three-volume report. Currently underway is a long-term project to digitize the ILUOP's archival data with the principal intention of making it accessible to the Arctic communities whence the original material derived. Directed by Bill Kemp—one of the ILUOP's original field researchers—the project is supported by the Qikiqtani Inuit Association in cooperation with Library and Archives Canada. (See Aporta 2016).

49. Inuit priorities appear less concerned with material objects than they are with the intangible aspects of culture. The curious compulsion of Qallunaat to revere "old things" typically baffled and amused Inuit. When Inuk drum dancer Mathew Nuqingaq visited Norway in 2005, he was entertained in several rural Norwegian homes proudly displaying antique furniture, ancient cast-iron stoves, and assorted, obsolete farm implements hanging from the walls. Nuqingaq was moved to ask his host, "Why is it that Norwegians like to live in museums?" However, as Inuit become acquainted with collections of their material culture held in southern museums, they view the objects with pride and reverence and admire them for the skill and resourcefulness with which they were made by their ancestors. Increasingly museums are appreciated by Inuit as beneficial agents of cultural preservation. At the British Museum in 2001, Leah Otak delighted in seeing and handling well-preserved skin clothing collected by Parry in Igloolik 179 years earlier. Inuit appreciation of the curatorial role of museums is also demonstrated in the film *Inuit Piqutingit—What Belongs to Inuit* (2006), directed by Bernadette Dean and Zacharias Kunuk.

50. It is important to stress that here I refer only to "formal" community-wide cultural projects. In Igloolik there is a significant number of individuals and families who value highly the practice of tradition through language, storytelling, and teaching land-based life skills. However, such individuals and families are increasingly the exception, not the norm.

51. Father Fournier was "really, really pushing the parents to send their kids to the residential school" (Elizabeth Qulaut, interview, January 21, 2016).

52. Louis Tapardjuk, interview, January 20, 2016. At that time (1969), knowledge of widespread abuse of Inuit children at the residential school in Chesterfield Inlet had not come to light.

53. Elizabeth Qulaut, interview, January 21, 2016. Louis Tapardjuk (interview, January 20, 2016) recalls that some interviews were made as part of the project:

> Joe Atagutaaluk, Eugene Amarualik and Emile Imaruittuq they were running the Inummariit committee and did some of the interviews after Father Fournier started it. One of the objectives was to gather stories [legends] like *Papik* and *Kiviuq* ... other topics covered included hunting skills and ice conditions etc.

The project was a community-wide endeavour, and Lucy Tapardjuk, along with Elizabeth Qulaut, worked on the publications, transcribing and translating.

54. It is not clear if a complete run of the Inummariit Series still exists. What remains of the collection in Igloolik is kept in the archives of the Oral History Project. Unfortunately, most of the original writings and cassette tape recordings of the Inummariit interviews have long ago disappeared.

55. See Rasing (2017, 483 n187, 197); (Wachowich 2006, 127–129).

56. Microfilm copies of *The Midnight Sun—Nipisuila* (1969–74) are held at Library and Archives Canada, Ottawa. Ref: NJ.FM.1184 – AN7501509.

57. Joseph Iqqipiriaq, then an employee of the NWT government, and Keith Wilkinson, a schoolteacher, were respectively the paper's Inuktitut and English editors.

58. See Gedalof (1980, 48–49). François Tamnaruluk was also known as François Quassa.

59. In this instance, for example, an understanding of "self-parodying" form in drum-dance performance, knowledge of the personality and social status of the performer, and finally some awareness of Inuit sentiments at the time vis-à-vis the Crown. Those who knew Tamnaruluk and were present at the event, including Tamnaruluk's son-in-law, Louis Tapardjuk, characterize the glossing of the song as absurd (Tapardjuk, pers. comm., January 31, 2017). John Robert Colombo, in his anthology of Inuit poetry, makes the general point that in some Inuit songs the "singer is inclined to belittle himself and his efforts" (Colombo 1981, 15).

60. See George Qulaut in this volume (Chapter 14). In 1985 the Igloolik Research Centre, then known as the Eastern Arctic Scientific Resource Centre, was run by the federal government's Department of Indian Affairs

and Northern Development. In the late 1980s management of the centre devolved to the Science Institute of the Northwest Territories. Responsibility for the centre transferred to the government of Nunavut in 1999.

61. The Igloolik Adult Education Centre, reflecting similar concerns, brought out a resource publication in 1985 titled *Iliniaruminaqtuiit* (meaning, roughly, "things desirous of being learned"). Edited by Emile Imaruittuq, then an instructor at the centre, the book was copiously illustrated by Igloolik artists and contained information on local bird life, plants, traditional clothing, implements, hunting and butchering techniques, igloo building, and land and ice formations. This project, coordinated by adult educator Hugh Lloyd, involved several Igloolik elders as cultural consultants, including Martha Ungalak, Noah Piugaattuk, and Michel Kopak. In addition, Arctic zoologist Tom Manning advised on ornithology, and wildlife artist Brenda Carter tutored local illustrators, including Julia Imaruittuq, Madeline Ivalu, Thoretta Iyerak, Celina Iyyerak, Elizabeth Qulaut, Rhoda Ungalak, Mary Apak, Elizabeth Ikeperiar, François Quassa, and Pierre Quassa.

62. A few years after the start of the Oral History Project, the elders involved formed the Inullariit Society, which, in cooperation with the centre, organized frequent cultural enrichment "outreach programs," including ones focused on land-based skills, hunting and fishing, traditional sewing and skin preparation, storytelling, drum dancing, and "*aja-ja*" singing. In the late 1990s the centre came under the auspices of the Nunavut Research Institute, which, in turn, became part of Nunavut Arctic College (c. 2004).

63. George Qulaut's work in the mid-1980s was key to starting the project. Along with Paul Irngaut, he conducted and translated the early interviews. (See Qulaut in this volume, Chapter 1.)

64. Louis Tapardjuk, interview, September 5, 2015.

65. The work of the International Biological Programme Human Adaptability Project (IBPHAP) in Igloolik involved extensive medical testing of Amitturmiut by visiting medical researchers (see Wachowich 2001). Their studies produced many volumes of data, including photographs and interviews with Inuit participants. The Joan de Peña fonds, held at the Archives of University of Manitoba, contains many of the Project's reports. In recent years, some of the IBPHAP's work in Igloolik has become controversial because of questionable procedures around informed consent.

66. Frequently, enduring friendships extending well beyond the fieldwork phase were formed between the researcher and associate. Pacome Qulaut

named his firstborn son George in recognition of his close association
with the archaeologist Jørgen Meldgaard (Qulaut 1997, 9). Inuki Kunuk's
friendship with Keith Crowe, who conducted a cultural geography study
of the Northern Foxe Basin in 1965–66 (Crowe 1969), endured until the
latter's death in 2010.

67. Malaurie (2001, 190) conducted a socio-economic study of the Igloolik
    area in 1961–62.

68. See George Qulaut in this volume (Chapter 1). Qulaut, however, who
    worked for many years at the Igloolik Research Centre, saw clear bene-
    fits for the Amitturmiut working in cooperation with visiting researchers
    and, along with his colleagues Leah Otak and Louis Tapardjuk, skilfully
    negotiated relationships between researchers, elders, and the community
    at large.

69. See MacDonald (2000, 18).

70. Researchers, particularly social scientists, receiving field support from
    the Igloolik Research Centre (Nunavut Research Institute—NRI) are
    asked to deposit audio/digital copies of their interviews at the centre,
    where they are accessioned into the project's archives. Most researchers
    happily comply. NRI, in issuing research permits, encourages research-
    ers to include Inuit Qaujimajatuqangit ("things long known by Inuit") in
    their studies.

71. Examples of this collaboration are seen in Rasing (2017); Wachowich
    (2014); Pharand (2012); Laugrand and Oosten (2010); Bennett and Row-
    ley (2004); Aporta (2004); Mallory and Aiken (2004); Anand-Wheeler
    (2002); Richard (2001); MacDonald (2000); Saladin d'Anglure (1990);
    and Brody (1987).

72. An excellent overview of some of the issues relating to use of oral history
    is given by Julie Cruikshank (1994, 403–418). The role of translation in
    Inuit oral history also needs epistemological scrutiny. Oral Inuktitut in-
    terviews rendered in English are inevitably shifted from their original
    source. The extent to which translations succeed, or not, is based wholly on
    the skills, knowledge, and experience of the translator. Moreover, there
    are areas of Inuit knowledge difficult to express adequately in English,
    including, for instance, kinship classifications, environmental relation-
    ships, and cosmology.

73. See also Stern and Stevenson (2006).

74. Another concept is "traditional Inuit culture." Do we refer to some vague,
    idealized time in Inuit society, prior to European contact, or perhaps to

the more recent past, just before Inuit moved from the land into the settlements? Emphatically, Amitturmiut elders opt for the latter definition. For them, life on the land before the move remains the very embodiment of traditional Inuit culture.

75. For an apt example of adaptation and transformation of Christian rites, see Louis-Jacques Dorais in this volume (Chapter 10) describing a wedding ceremony in Nunavik.

76. Talking recently of the effect of the transition to settlement life on Noah Piugaattuk, one of the Amitturmiut's most prominent leaders at the time of the move, Louis Uttak poignantly recalls,

> He was no longer a leader … he just followed the wishes of the white people, easily intimidated. That is the way we Inuit were, easily manipulated and intimidated. It was only proper that we listened to the wishes of the white people, that was the way it was to be in a settlement like this. It appeared to us that we had to always listen to white people. (Louis Uttak, interviewed by Louis Tapardjuk, August 8, 2016)

77. See Nunavut Department of Education (2016); Nunavut Early Childhood Education/Kindergarten curriculum; *Anijaarniq: Introductory Inuit Land skills and Wayfinding*, CD Rom, Nunavut Research Institute, Iqaluit (2006); units on *Stars; Fish and Fishing; Boats and Ships*, Nunavut Department of Education, Iqaluit (in progress). See also: www.gov.nu.ca/sites /default/files/grade_7.pdf and http://www.umanitoba.ca/outreach /crystal/nunavut.html.

78. Two well-received British Museum exhibitions involved close cooperation with the Igloolik community. The first, *Living Arctic* (1987), presented Canada's Indigenous Arctic and Subarctic peoples as a thriving contemporary population; Rebecca Maliki, Victor Aqatsiaq, and George Qulaut, all from Igloolik, advised the museum curators (see Brody 1987). In 2001, the exhibition *Annuraaq: Arctic Clothing from Igloolik*, for which Leah Otak was the principal consultant, coincided with a major British Museum conference on Arctic clothing (see MacDonald 2001; King et al. 2005; Otak 2005).

79. Paul Apak Angilirq, for instance, used several versions of the *Atanarjuaq* legend to draft the initial treatment for the eponymous film by Igloolik Isuma Productions (2001). See www.isuma.tv.

CHAPTER 3
Restoring an Ancestral Legacy: Museum Collections, Inuit Clothing, and Communities

1. This essay develops ideas initially discussed in the article "Curators, Collections and Inuit Communities: Case Studies in the Arctic," the result of a seminar held at the Rijksmuseum voor Volkenkunde, Leiden, in 2007 (Engelstad 2010). I am most grateful to J.C.H. King and William Fitzhugh for their suggestions in reviewing this essay.

2. Charles 2005; Dayo 2005; Dewar 2005; Harachak 2005; Karetak 2005; Kleinschmidt 2005; McIntyre 2005; Maulding 2005; Otak 2005.

3. In addition to the monographs cited, see Buijs (2004); Buijs and Oosten (1997); Chaussonnet (1988); Chaussonnet and Driscoll (1994); Driscoll (1983, 1984, 1987a, 1987b); Engelstad (2005); Meade (1990); and Oosten (1997).

4. This article focuses on databases of Arctic museum collections available for public access.

5. Available at www.britishmuseum.org/about_us/the_museums_story /general_history.aspx.

6. Available at www.amnh.org/our-research/anthropology/collections.

7. For further discussion of the ethnographic work of James Mutch and George Comer, see Boas (1901, 1907); Calabretta (1984, 2008a, 2008b); Eber (1989); Harper (2008, 2016); Ross (1975, 1984a, 1984b); Saladin d'Anglure (1984). For reports and discussion of the Jesup Expedition, see Bogoras (1904–09, 1913); Jochelson (1908); Kendall and Krupnik (2003); Krupnik and Fitzhugh (2001).

8. Available at www.khm.uio.no/english/research/collections/gjoahaven.

9. Available at skinddragter.natmus.dk.

10. A smaller portion of the Gustav Holm collection, including clothing, was exchanged with the Smithsonian Institution in the 1890s and remains in Washington, D.C.

11. In 1985 the *Amautik* exhibit was presented at the Zonnehof Museum in Amersfoort, The Netherlands; the Museum of Contemporary Art (Stedlijk Museum voor Actuel Kunst) in Ghent, Belgium; and the Musée du Costume et de la Dentelle in Mons, Belgium. Charlotte St. John and Selma Karetak Eccles attended the opening at the Zonnehof Museum with Her Royal Highness, Princess Margriet of The Netherlands.

12. Under the direction of Julia Harrison, the curatorial committee for *The Spirit Sings* exhibition included Ted Brasser (Plains); Bernadette Driscoll

(Arctic); Ruth Phillips (Great Lakes); Judy Thompson (Subarctic); Martine Reid (Northwest Coast); and Ruth Whitehead (Maritimes).

13. I am grateful to J.C.H. King for his comments in linking the two exhibitions (pers. comm., March 2016).

14. For a comprehensive discussion, analysis and references, see Phillips (2011, 48–70).

15. Available at www.mnh.si.edu/arctic.

16. Available at www.anthropology.si.edu/archives_collectons.html.

17. Available at www.alaska.si.edu.

18. Available at www.alaska.si.edu.

19. The online exhibit site can be accessed at naturalhistory.si.edu/Arctic /features/yupik/index.html.

20. Available at naturalhistory.si.edu/Arctic/html/yupikwebsite/Yupik.html.

21. Available at www.inuvialuitlivinghistory.ca.

22. Available at www.isuma.tv/isuma-productions/inuit-piqutingit.

23. In a highly controversial project, design motifs derived from the shaman's garments were incorporated in the production of a fashion sweater by the British design firm KTZ. In response to family objections to the appropriation of the garment's design, the sweater was eventually withdrawn from commercial sale (Zerehi 2015).

CHAPTER 4

Inuit Lives and Arctic Legacies: Leah Otak, Edward Parry, and Igloolik

1. Many people helped with this paper, for which I am most grateful. At the British Museum: Jago Cooper, Amber Lincoln, and Cynthia McGowan. At the National Museum of Scotland: Henrietta Lidchi and Antje Denner. At the Royal Albert Memorial Museum: Tony Eccles and Malika Kraamer. At the Bath Royal Literary and Scientific Institution: Robb Randall and Matt Williams. Many thanks to you all.

2. Gagnon 2011; MacDonald 2014.

3. Brody 1987; King 1989. In Igloolik I was unstintingly assisted by John MacDonald, George Qulaut, and the late Helen Oolalak, with the Science Institute of the Northwest Territories' Inullariit Elders Society.

4. Available at www.britishmuseum.org/research/collection_online/collection _object_details.aspx?objectId=516260&partId=1&people=38693&peoA =38693-2-46&page=1.

5. King and Lidchi 1998. Both the photography and clothing conferences, as well as their publications, were generously funded by the Eugene V. and Clare E. Thaw Trust, Santa Fe, New Mexico.

6. "Given annually to a publication judged to be the best book in the field of ethnic textile studies, the award consists of a cash prize funded by an endowment established by R.L. Shep in 2000. The purpose of this award is to encourage the study and understanding of textile traditions by recognizing and rewarding exceptional scholarship." Available at textilesociety ofamerica.org/programs/awards-scholarships/shep.

7. Available at www.britishmuseum.org/research/news/research_visit_to _igloolik.aspx.

8. There were other "William Parrys" in this period: William Parry (1754–1819), Congregationalist minister and tutor, and William Parry (1773–1859), shipwright and memorialist, who took part in the Greek War of Independence and published *Last Days of Lord Byron* (1825) with a frontispiece of Byron with his second Newfoundland dog.

9. The interaction of knowledge, exploration, and publication, of drawing, tattooing, and commemoration, is eloquently explored in Craciun 2016.

10. Engravings are from Parry (1824, 548–550).

11. The page numbers referenced in this section refer to artifacts shown in Parry (1824).

12. See www.robert-sorby.co.uk.

13. See also Shephard (2001, 233–240); Geoghegan (2013); www.lindahall.org /bryan-donkin/.

14. Archives of the Department of Africa, Oceania and the Americas, British Museum.

15. A. Parry 1963; Roskill 2004.

16. See www.isuma.tv/atanarjuat/qajaq.

17. Available at www.britishmuseum.org/research/collection_online/col-lection_object_details.aspx?objectId=3543998&partId=1&searchText=beads+esquimaux&page=1.

18. The museum's records for all these objects can be accessed at www.prm.ox.ac.uk/databases.

19. University of Edinburgh Museum 1823, 83.

20. Crozier 1999, 8–9.

CHAPTER 5

Inuit Oral History: Statements and Testimony in Criminal Investigations—The Case of the Killing of Robert Janes, 1920

1. Indeed, the same statement could be made for First Nations as well as Inuit. Miller (2011) deals almost exclusively with oral testimony in native land claims cases.

2. Wherever possible, I have given Inuit personal names in the modern Roman orthography ratified by Inuit Tapirisat of Canada in 1976. On the first mention of a person, I have given at least one of that person's names from the historical record. The reader who wants to go to original sources must be aware that there is seldom consistency in the spelling of these historical names; often there are many variants. Once a character is introduced, I have used the modern spelling subsequently, which has necessitated changing the spelling of the name in direct quotes from the historical record.

3. This background section is modified from Harper (2004).

4. The exception was an undated letter written by Amarualik (Amooahlik), sent to Staff Sergeant Joy and entered as Exhibit 1 at the trial. Its author wrote it in syllabics, and it therefore does not constitute an example of oral history. See LAC, RG13-A2, Vol. 279. See also Harper (2012).

5. Two other statements were taken from two of Munn's former traders (George William Southey Diament and James Florence) in Peterhead, Scotland. These statements were not used at the trial.

6. LAC, "To the Minister, Ottawa, Canada," Munn, letter September 2, 1920, RG18-F2, Vol. 3280, File HQ-681-G4, Part 1.

7. Ibid.

8. Ibid.

9. LAC, Declaration of George William Southey Diament, October 26, 1920, Peterhead; LAC, RG18-F2, Volume 3280, File HQ-681-G4, Part 1.

10. LAC, declaration of James Florence, November 3, 1920, Peterhead; LAC, RG18-F2, Vol. 3280, File HQ-681-G4, Part 1.

11. LAC, RG18-F2, Vol. 3280, File HQ-681-G4, Pt. 1.

12. LAC, RG18-F2, Vol. 3280, File HQ-681-G4, Pt. 1.

13. LAC, Munn: "Enquiry into the Murder of R. Janes…" RG18-F2, Vol. 3280, File HQ-681-G4, Part 1, page 4.

14. All statements and Munn's letter are in LAC, RG18-F2, Vol. 3280, File HQ-681-G4, Part 1.

15. He travelled on the Hudson's Bay Company (HBC) ship *Baychimo*. The HBC established a post at Pond Inlet in 1921.
16. LAC, RG18-F2, Vol. 3280, File HQ-681-G4, Pt. 1.
17. LAC, July 24, 1922, Joy to headquarters, LAC, crime report, RG18-F2, Vol. 3280, File HQ-681-G4, Part 2.
18. LAC, RG13-A2, Vol. 279, pages 16–17.
19. Qaurinniq (Martha Akumalik) in Pond Inlet Oral History Project, March 4, 1994.
20. Qaurinniq (Martha Akumalik) in Pond Inlet Oral History Project, March 18, 1994. Although the narrator is the same, and the time between interviews only two weeks, the perpetrator of the action is different. In this instance, Qaurinniq says, "That Qiugaarjuk [Nuqallaq] grabbed this interpreter and told him, 'Look, look, you are giving out contradictory information and you're confusing the people, wait until that person has finished speaking, before you start interpreting what he had said.'"
21. LAC, RG13-A2, Vol. 2797.

CHAPTER 7

"Tass' Nuann'!": Tradition, Sports, and Friendship at the Kayak Club Nuuk

1. Large parts of this essay are translated from my M.A. thesis (Pauksztat 1999). Some of the information on kayak clothing that I collected in connection with my M.A. thesis, and for a research project supported by the British Museum in 2001, was presented at the *Arctic Clothing* conference at the British Museum in 2001, and published in the edited volume derived from that conference (Pauksztat 2005). Some of this essay touches on the tensions between preserving tradition and using kayaks for sports; this is discussed in more detail in Pauksztat (2005) and Pauksztat (forthcoming).
2. Women did not participate in kayak building during the club's first years, with the exception of a few older women who helped with the covers. In Nuuk, the first women started to build kayaks in the 1990s; the first kayak built by a woman was finished in 1996.
3. *Qaanniornermut ilitsersuut* (Petersen 1981), a handbook for building Greenlandic kayaks, was one of the most important sources of information for kayak building in the Kayak Club Nuuk and in other kayak clubs in Greenland. The instructions are based on Greenlandic kayak building traditions, but they are "not quite correct ethnographically" (H.C. Petersen,

pers. comm., January 10, 1999). They combine the characteristic forms and ways of construction of different Greenlandic kayak types. The aim was not to provide instructions for a precise historical reconstruction, but for a kayak that was as robust as possible and that could be easily built by everybody.

4. Among the interviewees who had been club members in the 1980s, the percentages were 80 percent and 40 percent, respectively.

CHAPTER 8

Living, Travelling, Sharing: How the Land Permeates the Town through Stories

1. The town is frequently considered the "white man's realm"—*qallunaani*.
2. These events are not necessarily chronological, as they can be simultaneous.
3. Inuit from northern Baffin Island have traditionally used this camp as well. A well-known seasonal camp (Aggu) was also located not far from Majuqtulik, and some people in Igloolik were born and grew up in that area.
4. A dimension, perhaps, of what Mark Nuttall called "memoryscape" (1992).

CHAPTER 9

"Once in a Long While": The Igloolik Oral History Project as a Resource with Which to Understand Suicidal Behaviour in Historic Inuit Society

1. For a detailed history of the IOHP, see the chapter by John MacDonald in this volume.
2. MacDonald 2001, 2.
3. Over the years IOHP interviews have been used extensively in the development of cultural material for school curricula used throughout Nunavut's Qikiqtani Region and beyond. This has led to anecdotal complaints voiced by some parents that the curriculum does not reflect local culture and dialect. In addition, the late Ollie Ittinuar of Rankin Inlet, who in 1987 as president of the Inuit Cultural Institute visited the British Museum's *Living Arctic* exhibition (organized in close cooperation with the elders of the IOHP), observed that the Inuit cultural materials exhibited were almost entirely from Igloolik and did not represent Inuit cultural diversity across Nunavut (MacDonald 2016).

4. See Rasing (2017). A limited edition of Willem Rasing's Ph.D. dissertation was published in his native Holland in 1994, but for more than twenty years, what I consider to be one of the most significant anthropological studies conducted in the Eastern Arctic in recent decades was essentially unavailable in Canada. It is therefore significant and wonderful that a revised and updated version has been published by Nunavut Arctic College Media.

5. Edmund Peck, an Anglican missionary who ran a mission on Blacklead Island, Cumberland Sound, between 1894 and 1905. His Inuktitut name, Uqammaq, means "[he who] speaks [Inuktitut] well." It is not clear from other sources whether Uqammaq can be said to have "directed" Umik.

6. Nuqallaq, also known as Qiugaarjuk, killed the Newfoundland trader Robert Janes in 1920. See Grant (2002) and Harper (2017).

7. Ugliarjjuk is a small islet off the western shore of Igloolik Island.

8. Implicitly meaning that Umik thought of himself as God and his son, Nuqallaq, as Jesus.

9. William Duval. For a profile of Duval, see Harper (1985).

10. This quote, which is the title of Willem Rasing's book on contact, disorder, and change in Iglulingmiut society between 1822 and 2015, comes from an interview he conducted with Emile Imaruittuq in 1986. The full paragraph reads:

> In the old days we were small groups and we hardly had any problems then. But now there's too many people here. There are different groups here.... There are too many different groups nowadays that live together in one place. There are many problems today.... In the past, the elders could deal with the problems, but now ... even the police cannot stop them. (Rasing 2017, 7)

11. A peninsula south of Hall Beach.

12. This statement is problematic, given that Piugaattuk's sibling was one of those convicted in a case of assisted suicide. This brings another factor into the assessment of oral history testament: the extent to which interviewees have their own agendas, consciously or unconsciously editing their responses. Depending on the topic, some patently do, others not so much, and there are some who appear to use the interview process as an opportunity for confession (MacDonald 2016).

13. There is a problem in the way the interviewer framed the question—it was clearly a "leading question." Piugaattuk's response is literal in that the putative conditions associated with "town suicides" among the youth did

not obtain in the old days. It's something of a tautology, but a logical answer to a literal question. On the other hand, Piugattuk could have been engaged in a bit of self-editing to reinforce the point that suicide is "unacceptable" under any circumstances, invoking the "idealism" of pre-settlement Inuit society, where youth suicide was supposedly non-existent, to underscore his point (MacDonald 2016).

14. Renée Fossett has written about similar situations in the Kivalliq region:

> The Inuit practice of "leaving people to die" has been misunderstood by being taken out of context. At least one government official noted that in times of community stress, elderly people sometimes "*voluntarily* elect to be left to starve, or die of cold." An observer in Labrador in the 1880s, while not disagreeing that voluntary election sometimes took place, had a more profound understanding. "At this time [of severe food shortage] the old and those weakened by starvation and unable to move from place to place were left to their fate, though should a party be so successful as to capture more food than would supply their immediate wants that returned at once with food to those they had left behind. My own discussions with Leo Ussak at Rankin Inlet in the 1960s led me to believe that in times of crisis, when speed of travel is essential to the survival of the community, the strongest individuals often made the difficult decision to leave those who slow them down, in order to make all possible speed to a place of relief. Among the many instances described in the documents of the Hudson's Bay Company or other observers, the stronger travellers invariably sent assistance, or returned themselves, as soon as they could, to rescue the weaker members. Sometimes, the return was too late to save all those who had been left, as happened just north of Churchill in 1844. In that instance a father and son arrived at the post, having left companions who were too weak to travel at about two days' journey to the north. When they returned with food and blankets, they found at least one member of their family dead, and another died within a few days of a rescue that came too late. Occurrences of this nature were tragically frequent, but they are not gerontocide, abandonment, neglect, or in any way uncaring or abusive behaviour. (Fossett 2001, 228)

15. Examples include Hubert Amarualik in interview IE-250; Therese Ijjangiaq in IE-196; Noah Piugaattuk in IE-011, IE-030B, IE-047, IE-048, IE-051, and IE-090; and Lucien Ukaliannuk in IE-490.

16. There were also thirteen cases of attempted suicide and/or "insanity"—a term in common usage at the time.

17. It is noteworthy that this is the only one of the twenty-eight cases in which substance abuse and child sexual abuse played a role. The man involved appears to have travelled east from Siberia via Herschel Island, which was then a bustling whaling centre—and the site of considerable depravity. John Bockstoce notes re the whalers:

> A few captains also carried their mistresses aboard ship. On their way to the island [Herschel Island] they often picked up women or young girls at villages on the Alaska coast. Captain E.W. Newth of the brig Jeanette was notorious as the "kindergarten captain" because of his penchant for native girls eleven to fifteen years old. He usually carried five aboard his ship, having more or less rented them from their parents in Alaska with trade goods and alcohol. The police at Herschel, who also frequently kept native mistresses, were unable to press charges against Newth because he had signed the girls on the ship's articles. (Bockstoce 1986, 277)

18. Berthelsen (1935) noted that the few suicides occurring in Greenland during that period were the result of serious mental illness.

19. Balikci 1960a, 4.

20. A calculation cited in Balikci's 1960a, 1960b, and 1961 publications, but—interestingly—not in his later works.

21. Unpublished document in the author's possession.

22. See, for example, Van de Velde et al. (1993).

23. It is also noteworthy that a search of Trébaol's *Liber Animorum* for the word "white" reveals the extent of Qallunaat parentage of Inuit children, even at that point in time.

24. One is of particular interest:

> K'immerpikuluk, mother of Kassungiak, was killed by a rifle shot through her upper lip, shot by Merkoalak son of Kuvianartoliak and Kiugak. It was around 1930 in the Netchilik Lake (Baffin Island) area. Merkoalak also killed his own parents. He was thrown in the water (after being tied I think) probably in Netchilik Lake when there was ice. (Trébaol 1958)

An execution, it would seem. I found no references to this event in the records preserved in the National Archives.

25. Kenn Harper has documented how RCMP concern over the rate of murder in the Arctic resulted, in 1925, in the printing of a bilingual poster

"to be displayed prominently at trading and police posts that Inuit might visit" informing Inuit of the legal prohibition on murder. "One can only wonder what impression this text made on the Inuit reading it. Aside from its white ethnocentrism, it stated boldly and incorrectly that it was the role of the police to seize and kill any Inuit murderers" (Harper 2017, 318, 330–331).

26. See Balikci (1960a, 1960b, 1961, 1970).

27. It is noteworthy that over the first fifteen years after the creation of Nunavut in 1999 there was a 6.8-fold difference in the suicide rate among the Inuit populations of Nunavut's twenty-five communities. Igloolik's rate of 83.3 Inuit deaths by suicide per 100,000 population over the period 1999 to 2014 was somewhat higher than the rates for the predominantly Catholic communities of the Kivalliq and eastern Kitikmeot regions, but substantially lower than the rates of the predominantly Anglican communities in the Qikiqtani region—Arctic Bay, Cape Dorset, Clyde River, Hall Beach, Iqaluit, Pangnirtung, Pond Inlet, and Qikiqtarjuaq (Hicks 2015).

28. As documented by the Qikiqtani Truth Commission (QTC) in its final report, *Achieving Saimaqatigiingniq* (2010). This document is available on the QTC's website, www.qtcommission.com, along with "Community Histories" and "Thematic Reports" prepared by the QTC.

29. The *Nunavut Suicide Prevention Strategy* presents a compelling hypothesis regarding the roots of the level of social suffering seen in Nunavut communities today. Shortly after the Second World War, federal government policies resulted in the coerced relocation of Inuit from seasonal camps into settled communities controlled by non-Inuit administrators. The rules that had governed historical Inuit society were replaced by the rules of a non-Inuit colonial government—with respect to education, justice, housing, and other domains:

> The cumulative effects of this massive disruption of Inuit society produced dramatic results. The first and all subsequent generations of children who have grown up in the communities embody a fundamental transition in Inuit society, away from a traditional Inuit lifestyle and towards a mix of Inuit and southern values. The generations of Inuit who have been raised in communities since have struggled with the delicate balancing act of living concurrently in two very different cultures …

> The trauma experienced first-hand by Inuit in the settlement transitional period has had an immense impact on all following

generations, as many Inuit who were negatively affected in this period did not ever heal. This unresolved trauma compromised their ability to cope with stress in a healthy manner. Negative behaviour often followed in the form of alcohol abuse, sexual, physical, and emotional abuse, child neglect, and violent crime. It is important to note that elevated suicide rates emerged within the first generation of Inuit youth who grew up in the communities. In the absence of an adequate healing process, a continuous cycle of trauma has been created, which has been passed from generation to generation. This is referred to as the intergenerational transmission of historical trauma. (Government of Nunavut et al. 2010, 6)

The same understanding informs the *National Inuit Suicide Prevention Strategy* (Inuit Tapiriit Kanatami 2016).

30. Chachamovich (2015) presents the data from the first large-scale, controlled, epidemiologically representative study of deaths by suicide in an Indigenous population, which investigates risk factors for suicide among all 120 Inuit across Nunavut who died by suicide during the four-year period from 2003 to 2006. Community-matched control subjects, who were matched by sex and age, were also included.

Psychiatrist Allison Crawford notes:

The study reveals that completed suicide is associated with higher rates of [Major Depressive Disorder], alcohol dependence, and cannabis dependence, in the 6 months prior to the act of suicide, and these individuals were more likely to meet criteria for a cluster B personality disorder, and to have increased impulsivity and aggression. They also tended to have a higher loading of familial risk, including MDD, alcohol and drug use disorders, and suicide completion. This higher burden of psychiatric illness signifies the importance of clinical risk factors that are relevant to suicide globally. In other words, the high rates of suicide in Nunavut can be understood in terms of general models of suicidal behaviour.... This is a contribution to the debate around whether suicide in Indigenous contexts is qualitatively different than suicide in non-Indigenous populations, with implications for the consequent role of mental health interventions.

Chachamovich and team limit their investigation to individual risk factors for suicide, yet one of the most striking aspects of their findings are the high rates of risk factors in the control group. Among control subjects, 22.4% had a previous suicide attempt, and both groups had similar rates of attempts among family members (27.3% of subjects and 24.6% of control subjects). This is consistent with results from the recent [Inuit Health Survey], in which lifetime suicidal ideation was 48%, with 29% of respondents reporting a prior suicide attempt.

Childhood adversity was also highly prevalent among the group of people who died by suicide, and strongly suggestive of the importance of early developmental impacts, particularly child abuse. Among people who died by suicide, 47.5% experienced childhood abuse, including sexual abuse in 15.8% (compared with 27.5% and 6.6% in control subjects). (Crawford 2015, 240)

31. See Crawford and Hicks (2018).
32. See Labonté et al. (2015) and Turecki (2018).
33. See Hicks (2009, 2017a, 2018b; Hicks and White 2015, 18–19). The situation improved significantly in June 2017, when the Nunavut Suicide Prevention Strategy Partners (Government of Nunavut, Nunavut Tunngavik Inc., Royal Canadian Mounted Police, and the Embrace Life Council) finally released a comprehensive—*and funded*—implementation plan for the *Nunavut Suicide Prevention Strategy*, which had been released in 2010 (Government of Nunavut et al. 2017).
34. See Hicks (2018a).

CHAPTER 10
A Marriage in Nunavik

1. All three visits were funded through research grants from the Social Sciences and Humanities Research Council of Canada (SSHRC).
2. To quote John MacDonald (pers. comm., September 3, 2015), "[contemporary] *katititauniq* ceremonies adopt and adapt much of the trappings and forms of the Qallunaat rite and yet retain something uniquely Inuit," and this is the case in Quaqtaq as well as in Igloolik and other Canadian Arctic communities.
3. A hundred years earlier in Labrador.

4. Even if I am reasonably informed about Christian teachings and values, I do not belong to an Evangelical church. Thus, what I suggest here is a personal opinion that may be mistaken, and may differ from what a practising Evangelical Christian would have to say.

CHAPTER 11

Reclaiming the Past and Reimagining the Future: The Igloolik Oral History Project, Education, and Community Development

1. Between 2007 and 2009, I was working towards a master's in public administration through the School of Public Policy and Administration at Carleton University. After I completed my M.A., I continued to work as an independent researcher for the Hamlet of Igloolik to finish the baseline study.

2. The Baffinland Mary River iron ore project is a large-scale mining development project located on northern Baffin Island in an area called Steensby Inlet. The project was approved in 2012 and has been in operation for several years now.

3. The 2009–10 Igloolik Socio-economic Baseline Study included several components: a community-wide household survey; in-depth interviews with two hundred working-age adults; focus groups with elders, youths, and women; and a survey of local employers, by sector. We produced an executive summary report, a full-length report, and a series of presentations for different audiences. These documents are available through the Hamlet of Igloolik (Kennedy and Abele 2011).

4. The nickname given the Nunavut government office building in Igloolik, on account of its blue siding. Officially known as the Tumivut ("our footprints") Building, it was built to accommodate the Nunavut government's decentralization policy. (See Hicks and White 2015.)

5. For more information about this policy and its effects, see Barry Greenwald's 2009 documentary film *The Experimental Eskimos*, produced by Whitepine Pictures and Paunna Productions. Sheila Watt-Cloutier (2015) also writes about this policy in her book *The Right to be Cold*.

6. Abele (2011).

7. For information about Digital Indigenous Democracy, see Cohn and Kunuk (2012). See also Kennedy Dalseg and Abele (2015).

8. Each community in Nunavut has a District Education Authority. DEAs are creatures of the Nunavut Education Act and comprise community

representatives—typically parents and/or grandparents of school-aged children and youth. The DEAs are responsible for making decisions about the delivery of education in their community, including the language of instruction, staffing, and scheduling. For more information about DEAs, see www.gov.nu.ca/education/information/district-education-authority.

9. I recognize that significant changes began to take shape well before the 1950s. I have chosen the 1950s, as others have, because this is when the federal government began a more coherent "high modernist" project of social change, which included the introduction of a housing program and formal schooling, among others. See Tester and Kulchyski (1994); Abele (1987, 2009); Damas (2002); McGregor (2010); Brody (1975).

10. In this section I draw heavily from John MacDonald's 2014 presentation at the Finnish Oral History Society meeting in Helsinki, Finland, on November 28, 2014. For more information about the history and development of the IOHP, see Chapter 12 of this volume.

11. See, for example, Inuit Tapiriit Kanatami and Nunavut Research Institute (2007).

12. For more information about the history of Northern development in the Eastern Arctic and Igloolik, see Rasing (2017); Damas (2002); Hicks and White (2015).

13. For more information about the Baffin Divisional Board of Education, see Isherwood et al. (1986, 9–15). See also McGregor (2010). Special thanks to Cathy McGregor and Joe Enook for helping me to understand the origins, activities, and importance of the BDBE for educational development and Inuit self-determination.

14. See, for example, Amagoalik (2007, 155). See also McGregor (2010, 118).

CHAPTER 12

Leah Aksaajuq Otak: A Life in Language

1. Parts of this article draw on Leah's obituary, "Leah Aksaajuq Umik Ivalu Otak (1950–2014)," published in 2014 in *Étude/Inuit/Studies* 38, no. 1–2: 297–305.

2. Sonia Gunderson, interview, March 14, 2006. Sonia Gunderson spent time in Igloolik in 2005 and 2006, researching the community's cultural preservation initiatives for articles published in the *Inuit Art Quarterly* and *Above & Beyond*. In 2007–08, she lived in Igloolik and continued her research with the help of a Fulbright grant.

3. Sonia Gunderson, interview, March 14, 2006.

4. The Qikiqtani Truth Commission (QTC) was mandated to research and take statements from Inuit in the Baffin Island area for the period of 1950–75 to better understand how government policies, programs, and decisions affected and irreversibly altered their way of life.

5. Cape Thalbitzer.

6. See Damas (2002) for a detailed description of the so-called "in-gathering" policy.

7. See Sheena Kennedy Dalseg's chapter in this volume (Chapter 11) for more on this aspect of Leah's schooling.

8. For details on the Igloolik Oral History Project see chapters in this volume by George Qulaut (Chapter 1) and John MacDonald (Chapter 2).

9. Sonia Gunderson, interview, March 14, 2006.

10. Sonia Gunderson, interview, March 14, 2006.

11. Sonia Gunderson, interview, March 14, 2006.

12. The Canadian Polar Commission, an agency of Aboriginal Affairs and Northern Development Canada, was established in 1991 with a mandate that included working "with Canadian and international institutions to determine scientific and other priorities ... and [encouraging] cooperation and collaboration in polar knowledge." See www.polarcom.gc.ca /eng/cpc.

13. As a translator, she was a key contributor to John MacDonald's book *The Arctic Sky* (1998, 2000), which includes a chapter comprising her expert transcriptions, in standard Inuktitut Roman orthography, of numerous Iglulingmiut legends relating to stars and the Inuit cosmos. Sylvie Pharand's 2012 publication *Caribou Skin Clothing of the Igloolik Inuit*—a topic dear to Leah's heart—benefited in several ways from her advice and enthusiasm.

14. See Bernadette Driscoll Engelstad's (2013) excellent review of this work in *Études/Inuit/Studies*.

15. Sonia Gunderson, interview, March 14, 2006.

16. Louis Tapardjuk, interview with John MacDonald, September 5, 2015. Nunavut's Department of Culture, Language, Elders and Youth is now the Department of Culture and Heritage.

CHAPTER 13
Encounters: Reflections on Anthropology and Cultural Brokers

1. My experience accords with that of Hugh Brody:

> For all that I had written about hunter-gatherer societies, I was left with a deep conviction that I had yet to write about that which is most important. Something lay there that eluded not just me, but many who have experienced another way of life. We write about some facets of it, some surfaces, that we make our business. But the gold we find is transformed by the reverse alchemy of our journey, from there to here, into lead. Not into nothing, not into worthlessness, but into a substance that has more weight than light, more utility than beauty, is malleable rather than of great value. What is this reality that gets left behind? (Brody 2001, 4).

May it be "poetry" that is left behind and evades us in writing our narratives?

CHAPTER 14
Ujakkat: Iglulingmiut Geology

1. A small cluster of quartzite islands to the north of Igloolik Island are known as *Uqsuriattiangujaat*. Along with other local places named in the Kivallirmiut dialect—*Nalukajarvik* (Mogg Bay), for instance—they indicate an earlier occupation of the Igloolik area by people from the Kivalliq dating back to at least the time of Edward Parry's visit in 1822 (see MacDonald in this volume).

CHAPTER 15
Reflections on a Flag

1. Inuksuk (pl. inuksuit) is a now-generalized Inuktitut term for stone cairn(s) built by Inuit, often popularly spelled inukshuk/inukshuit. In Igloolik the proper term for cairn is *inusugaq* (pl. *inuksugait*).
2. The complex, often fraught connotations attached to the concept "North" in the Euro-Canadian imagination (which are not shared by those indigenous to the North) were explored by the musician Glenn Gould in his celebrated 1967 CBC broadcast *The Idea of North*. There are many

views of what Gould's work tells us about southern Canada's attitude to the North. At one extreme, Peter Davidson (2016) characterizes Gould's broadcast as "an unconscious testimony to Canadian progressiveness and liberalism ... their attitudes to both the ecology and to the indigenous peoples ... respectful and positive"; on the other, Mickey Vallee (2014) argues that the broadcast is reflective of a new benevolent racism that made "assimilationist ideology, a requisite for post-World War II Northern resource development." In her book *Canada and the Idea of North*, Sherrill Grace (2002) offers a more integrated view through a fascinating analysis of Indigenous and non-Indigenous literature, art, and media pertaining to the North.

3. Nelson Graburn's discerning paper "Inuksuk: Icon of the Inuit of Nunavut" (2004) addresses a number of these points, but from quite a different perspective. Moreover, at the time he was writing, the morbid connotations attached to "human-like" inuksuit were not so widely known.

4. See Governor General of Canada (n.d.).

5. Graburn 2004, 78.

6. For an overview of flags and their function, see Marshall (2017).

7. Legislative Assembly of Nunavut n.d.

8. The Canadian Heraldic Authority records that

> the group working on developing the symbols visited municipal leaders, elders, schools and artist cooperatives in Rankin Inlet, Baker Lake, Cape Dorset, Iqaluit and Pangnirtung early in the process. This allowed the Chief Herald of Canada to learn about art resources and traditional ways of life and also introduced the communities to the project. (Governor General of Canada n.d.)

Note that the communities visited are all well below the Arctic Circle, where the North Star is significantly more useful as a navigational aid.

9. MacDonald 2000, 169.

10. MacDonald 2000, 170.

11. MacDonald 2000, 61.

12. Ikummaq 2000b. The altitude above the horizon of the North Star is virtually equal to the northerly latitude of the observer. Around 70° the North Star appears to be almost overhead. As such, its use as a "guiding star" is neither accurate nor practicable.

13. The farther south one goes in the Inuit world, the more useful Polaris becomes as a "guiding" star. For example, in parts of northern Quebec, approximately in latitude 60° North, Polaris is referred to as *Turaagaq*—"something to aim at" (MacDonald 2000, 61).

14. Kappianaq 1986.

15. Preferred "navigational" stars used by Iglulingmiut are in the constellations of Ursa Major (*Tukturjuit*), Gemini/Auriga (*Quturjuuk*), and Orion (*Ullaktut*) (MacDonald 2000, 168).

16. Piugaattuk 1988.

17. In European nomenclature, Aagjuuk comprises the stars Altair and Tarazed in the constellation Aquila. Traditionally for Iglulingmiut, the annual appearance of Aagjuuk was an occasion for a midwinter festival known as *tivajut* or *qaggiq* (a reference to the large, specially built igloo in which the people gathered). The *qaggiq* was socially important and symbolically complex. Aagjuuk invokes a rich and ancient symbolism associated with social, terrestrial, and ecological renewal and, above all, ensuring the land's life-giving bounty. See MacDonald (2000, 4–51).

18. Kappianaq 1990. Another astral symbol more appropriate than the North Star might have been Tukturjuk ("caribou")—in English, the Big Dipper—the most noticeable circumpolar constellation in the northern hemisphere (MacDonald 2000, 79–83). Given the enormous significance of caribou in Inuit life and culture, what better imagery than this? Tukturjuk's stars, adorning the flag with, in vexillological terms, a stellar caribou "rampant," would have aptly resonated with the standing caribou featured so prominently on Nunavut's official Coat of Arms.

19. Canadian Encyclopedia 2013.

20. MacGregor 2010.

21. Several papers have reflected on Inuit cultural symbols, including inuksuit, including Jean Briggs in her 1997 article "From Trait to Emblem and Back: Living and Representing Culture in Everyday Inuit Life" and Nelson Graburn's "Inuksuk: Icon of the Inuit of Nunavut" (2004).

22. CBC News 2017.

23. Built in 2007, this claim is endorsed by Guinness World Records. See also RoadsideAmerica.com 2016.

24. Dube 2007; Jelen 2010.

25. Intriguingly, archaeologist Robert McGhee suggests that the anthropoidal inuksuk may have evolved from the cruciform stone structures made by Martin Frobisher's crews around southern Baffin Island in the late 16th century. In this context, McGhee quotes Frobisher's chronicler, George Best, in the original Elizabethan English, as having set up "manye Crosses of stone, in token of Christians had bin there." McGhee (2001) further points out that

as we know from Frobisher and later accounts, the Inuit inhabiting these coasts were eager to attract Europeans ashore in order to trade for metal; those whom Frobisher encountered showed themselves atop hills, waving flags, and shouting in order to bring themselves to the attention of passing ships. The piled-stone figures standing along the coasts may have had a similar function, as permanent markers informing visitors of the presence of potential trading partners. If so, the knowledge that Englishmen assigned significance to boulders piled in a cruciform structure may have led to the development of what has become an iconic Arctic figure.

According to Patricia Sutherland, cruciform or anthropoidal inuksuit are not found in the Central and Western Arctic, nor are they known from the High Arctic (personal communication). This adds weight to the notion that these forms may have had European origins (McGhee 2001).

26. Hallendy 2000. For some of the controversy surrounding the choice of the inuksuk emblem for the Vancouver 2010 Olympics, see: Skorondeski (2014); Kaste (2010); National Geographic (2010).

27. Strikingly, Norman Hallendy's books on inuksuit (2000, 2009) give few examples of the now "orthodox" inuksuk (two legs, arms, torso, and head), which he refers to as *innunguaq* (a general term translating as "a model or representation of a human," not specific to stone structures). The innunguaq he features tend to be of the "one-legged" variety stylized on Nunavut's flag (see Hallendy 2009, 28–39).

28. The original idea was proposed by a municipal employee to mark his twenty-five years of service to the community. The project was subsequently endorsed by the Igloolik Hamlet Council and the community's economic development officer.

29. This association is confirmed in an interview given by Noah Siakuluk of Hall Beach (1996) and is quoted as follows (Bennett and Rowley 2004, 260):

> two men killed some people, and afterwards they built an inuksuk ... it is said that the [inuksuk] was shaped as a human facing in the direction the two men headed.... When you see this [inuksuk] it really does resemble a human figure ... with its arms spread out.

See Rasing (2017, 433–434).

30. See, for example, CBC News (2017); Kaste (2010).

31. Igloolik Island offers fine examples of the "built-while-waiting" inuksuit. The road from the town out to Igloolik Point is defined by numerous imaginative inuksuit of all shapes and sizes built by people waiting for broken-down vehicles to be repaired. Nelson Graburn also addresses this point:

> Many times, Inuit while stopping for tea or some other reason on the trail, may gather stones and pile up an inuksuk, just as "Something to do," as a record that "I was here" just as people in the south sometimes scrawl "Kilroy was here." In one trip along the shore of the Hudson Bay, we waited while a pair of mating dogs in our team became unstuck so we built an inuksuk near the shore to pass time. (Graburn 2004, 70)

32. Some examples of inuksuit purpose and function are given in Bennett and Rowley (2004, 255–261), and in Hallendy (2000, 61–62).
33. Inukshuk Capital Management Inc. n.d.
34. Julie Kinnear Team n.d.
35. The cultural/experiential framework underpinning Inuit navigation is elegantly explored by Claudio Aporta in his article "Markers in Space and Time: Reflections on the Nature of Place Names as Events in the Inuit Approach to the Territory" (Aporta 2016). David Pelly (2001) makes the point that Inuit navigators conceptualize the topography of the Barren grounds as linear landscapes "full of lines—rivers, eskers, and caribou paths—all running with some regularity in linear patterns across the tundra."
36. Before Inuit had access to steel sled runners, they "mudded" wood runners with a thick paste made from peaty material, which was smoothed down and coated with a thin layer of ice. This technique enabled the sled to efficiently travel over snow. Ice-and-mud runners were fragile and easily chipped, so whenever possible, routes were chosen to avoid rocks and boulders. See MacDonald (2000, 188–189).
37. Qamaniq 2002. Also Aporta and MacDonald (2005, 1410–1413). Qamaniq adds that some dogs possess the quality of *aangaittuq*: "If the lead dog is *aangaittuq*, even if the master loses his bearing, his lead dog will get him home."
38. For more on Inuit navigation and environmental interactions, see Aporta (2004); Aporta (2016, 67–88); and Collignon (2006). More generally, concepts of human-environmental interactions are found in Ingold (2000).

39. "In those days ... when we travel by dog team ... we never had one place we lived in. In places where we had our camps inuksuit were erected. That was the way it used to be, to kill time" (Ujarasuk 2002).

40. Ikummaq 2000b.

41. An often overlooked point about Inuit stone structures, including inuksuit, is that they were almost invariably built during periods when the ground was thawed sufficiently to release the "frozen in" rocks. The structures were generally indicative of locations occupied or used by Inuit during the relatively short period between late spring and early fall. Hence, for instance, the preponderance of stone structures such as blinds and drift fences associated with fall caribou hunting in the Igloolik area and elsewhere.

42. Mathiassen 1928.

43. See Aporta (2016).

44. Inuksuk 1988.

45. Uangnaq's approximate bearing is northwest.

46. The term *uqalurait* derives from the Inuktitut word for tongue, *uqaq*. For the important role of uqalurait in Iglulingmiut navigation, see MacDonald (2000, 173–182).

47. Inuktitut wind direction terminology varies across the Arctic. See Fortescue (1988).

48. See MacDonald (2000, 173–180).

49. See Aporta (2004).

50. Ikumaaq 2000a.

51. Piugaattuk 1988.

52. "Silent Messengers of the Arctic" is the subtitle of his first book (Hallendy 2000). Hallendy's second volume on inuksuit, *Tukiliit: the Stone People Who Live in the Wind* (2009), reinforces the "messenger" associations: *Tukiliit* translates as "those having meaning."

53. The same caveat applies to stars. An instructive legend from Igloolik tells of a hunter getting fatally lost because he took directions from the star Singuuriq (Sirius), mistaking it for Kingullialuk (Vega) (Kunuk 1990, 1991).

54. Ujarasuk 2002.

55. Fitzhugh 2017.

56. Ujarjualik is a small lake known, as its name implies, for codfish, about eighty kilometres northwest of Igloolik.

57. In a testimony to Inuit powers of observation, Theo Ikummaq talks of memorizing "thousands" of inuksuit on Igloolik's nearby land mass, the

Melville Peninsula: "If you travel enough ... each one is different. And how [do] you remember those inuksuks? I don't know [but] we do! If you have seen one, and then you sort of remember what it looks like" (Ikummaq 2000b).

58. Heyes 2002.

59. For example, see the Inuksuit carvings by Cape Dorset artists offered for sale through the online site Inuitartzone.com. www.inuitartzone.com /collections/inukshuk.

60. Unfortunately, over the years the text on this plaque has been rendered almost illegible due to graffiti and defacement.

61. In revising the website's statement, equivalency between the English and Inuktitut versions should be considered. For instance, with reference to the North Star, only the English version states that this star is "symbolic of the leadership of the elders in the community," a symbolic association perhaps more akin to European sentiments (Legislative Assembly of Nunavut n.d.).

CHAPTER 16
Our Old Sod House

1. For previous generations of Amitturmiut (people from the northern Foxe Basin, including Igloolik), *inuksuit* were commonly referred to as *inuksugait* (singular *inusugaq*).

2. See www.isuma.tv/the-inuksuit-project.

AFTERWORD
Sunrise, Stories, and Snowhouses: A Conversation with Leah Otak

1. Portions of this encounter appeared in Noah Richler's *This Is My Country, What's Yours? A Literary Atlas of Canada* (McClelland & Stewart, 2006) and are reproduced with kind permission of McClelland & Stewart.

2. See data.nwtresearch.com/Scientific/11036.

Index